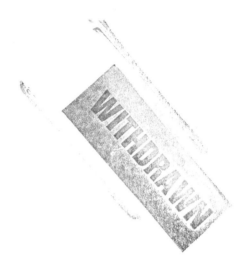

VARIORUM COLLECTED STUDIES SERIES

Naturalists and Society

David Elliston Allen

David Elliston Allen

Naturalists and Society

The Culture of Natural History
in Britain, 1700–1900

VARIORUM

Aldershot · Burlington USA · Singapore · Sydney

Published in the Variorum Collected Studies Series by

Ashgate Publishing Limited
Gower House, Croft Road,
Aldershot, Hampshire GU11 3HR
Great Britain

Ashgate Publishing Company
131 Main Street
Burlington, Vermont 05401–5600
USA

Ashgate website: http://www.ashgate.com

ISBN 0–86078–863–6

British Library Cataloguing-in-Publication Data
Allen, David Elliston, 1932–
    Naturalists and Society: The Culture of Natural History
    in Britain, 1700–1900. – (Variorum Collected Studies
    Series: CS724).
    1. Naturalists–Great Britain. 2. Natural History–Great
    Britain–History.
    I. Title.
    508. 4' 1

US Library of Congress Cataloging-in-Publication Data
Naturalists and Society: The Culture of Natural History in Britain,
    1700–1900 / David Elliston Allen.
    p. cm. – (Variorum Collected Studies Series: CS724).
    Reprints of articles originally published in various journals
    from 1956–2000. Includes bibliographical references. (alk. paper).
    1. Natural History–Great Britain–History. 2. Naturalists–
    Great Britain–History. I. Allen, David Elliston. II. Collected
    Studies: CS724.
    QH137. N28 2001
    508. 41' 09–dc21   2001022813

The paper used in this publication meets the minimum requirements of the
    American National Standard for Information Sciences – Permanence of
    Paper for Printed Library Materials, ANSI Z39.48–1984. ∞ ™

Printed by St Edmundsbury Press, Bury St Edmunds, Suffolk

VARIORUM COLLECTED STUDIES SERIES CS724

CONTENTS

BIOGRAPHY

This volume contains xiv + 298 pages

PUBLISHER'S NOTE

The articles in this volume, as in all others in the Variorum Collected Studies Series, have not been given a new, continuous pagination. In order to avoid confusion, and to facilitate their use where these same studies have been referred to elsewhere, the original pagination has been maintained wherever possible.

Each article has been given a Roman number in order of appearance, as listed in the Contents. This number is repeated on each page and is quoted in the index entries.

Corrections noted in the Addenda and Corrigenda have been marked by an asterisk in the margin corresponding to the relevant text to be amended.

PREFACE

The essays in this volume owe their existence to an interest in natural history dating from boyhood but more especially to a sudden urge that took hold halfway through my time as an undergraduate, to find out more about the different categories of people who have engaged in this group of studies in the past and to try to piece together how the subject has been shaped by changes in society as a whole. I had no training in science and up till then scant acquaintance with history either: my lightning conversion was an early result of an accidental immersion in social anthropology and of the acquisition of the novel mode of thinking that that had produced.

With the towering exception of Canon C.E. Raven, at that time producing his majestic works on the English naturalists of the early modern period, and a handful of scholars who were laying the foundations of what would grow into the substantial Darwin 'industry' of today, there seemed little interest in the history of the life sciences that was other than bibliographical or geared to the needs of taxonomy. Geology, that most essentially historical of all areas of investigation, was faring somewhat better, with a number of practitioners to whom researching into the past of the discipline itself was virtually second nature. But on the whole the history of science meant the history of physics, chemistry and mathematics. Natural history was not merely neglected, but deemed scarcely even worthy of attention, being questionably science at all as the philosophers chose to define that word. During my student days I heard only a single lecture that could be classed as history of science, and it was to be another twenty years before I encountered anyone who was specialising in that subject professionally.

It was consequently effectively in isolation that I tackled the task that I had optimistically undertaken. There were no models, so far as I could discover, for the kind of approach that seemed necessary for delineating a field like natural history that consists so largely of long-enduring practices and is concerned but relatively slightly with theoretical debates. Nor did there seem at first sight to be a sufficiency of major turning-points – with one or two obvious exceptions – that could provide a narrative with a well-defined structure. Worse still, little or no primary research had been done on many of the topics that would have to be covered. All I had a realistic prospect of constructing, within a reasonable span of years, was some rather rough-and-ready scaffolding, as a preliminary to the solid brickwork that would hopefully be laid later by other hands.

Competing interests and the pressures of a career in unrelated directions caused that project to be largely set aside for several years, and it was only after well over two decades had elapsed that it finally achieved embodiment in a book. *The Naturalist in Britain: A Social History*, published by Allen Lane in 1976, chanced to be lucky in its timing, however. For by then many historians of science were discontented with the traditional preoccupation with tracing the ebbs and flows of scientific thought and turning to explore as well how science has developed as a social entity and been subject to influences externally. There was also a growing awareness that natural history had been too long disregarded and that it constituted a kind of unknown Oriental land in its intriguing degree of strangeness. Thanks to these two trends, to my no small surprise what I had expected to be of interest to fellow naturalists more or less exclusively attracted attention and comment from numbers of academic historians as well. As a result, very belatedly, I made many contacts at last in the history of science community, contacts which have multiplied in the years since and for which I have abundant reason to be grateful. Even so, naturalists of one stripe or another have continued to be my principal audience, and almost all the pieces selected for inclusion in this volume were addressed at least primarily to those with little if any grounding in the approaches and debates familiar to history of science professionals.

In the years since *The Naturalist in Britain* appeared, conscious of its many inadequacies I have used the opportunities of conferences on relevant topics to deepen and widen, to reinterpret and document more fully several of the areas superficially excavated in that book. Eight of the essays in the following pages (I, II, IX, X, XI, XII, XIII, XV) came about in this way, whereas two others (VI and XVI) were *pièces d'occasion* purely and simply and betray that character in opening and closing remarks.

A rather special interest dating from my social science days has been the phenomena variously termed crazes, fashions or fads. Knowing of this, a leading authority on ferns, Clive Jermy, encouraged me around 1965 to contribute to a journal under his editorship what we both envisaged as a short account of the extraordinarily destructive mid-Victorian passion for collecting and cultivating those plants, a passion peculiar to Britain. However, the material available proved to be so extensive that only book-length treatment was capable of doing the topic justice, and *The Victorian Fern Craze* (Hutchinson, 1969) was the eventual outcome. Essays V and VI recapitulate that story (with some updating), but in such different ways and degrees of detail that the inclusion of both was felt to be justified.

A third book to have generated some minor follow-ups is the history of the Botanical Society of the British Isles I was invited to produce in commemoration of its sesquicentenary. Entitled – decidedly over-sweepingly – *The Botanists* (St. Paul's Bibliographies, 1986), this included the salient fruits of an unusually arduous prosopography of that body's short-lived semi-ances-

tor, the Botanical Society of London, a research technique rendered necessary by the fact that most of the official records of that have failed to survive.
The difficulties that this presented are recounted informally in Essay VII,
while VIII draws attention to the extent to which at least one Metropolitan
body succeeded in its declared aim of attracting women as ordinary members
as early as the 1830s. The prosopography itself gave rise in turn to a number
of biographical by-products, two of which are reproduced here as XVIII and
XIX. Two further biographical pieces, XX and XXI, owe their existence in
part to the investigation of the BSBI's history more generally.

Much the earliest of the pieces in the volume, XVII, appeared in the
journal of what was then the Society for the Bibliography of Natural History.
This body originated in 1936 as a small coterie largely concerned with
establishing the precise dates of publication of scientific works in which
species had first been described and named, a matter of great moment to
taxonomists because of the rule of priority on which biological nomenclature
is based. By the 1960s, with that task largely done, that initial aim was
gradually altering into the study of the subject's past much more broadly, a
change of focus which culminated in 1983 in the adoption of a by then more
appropriate name, the Society for the History of Natural History, and the
retitling of its journal as *Archives of Natural History*. This transformation
solved an awkward dilemma that historians of science tend to find themselves confronted with: whether to publish in journals addressed to scientific
specialists but probably seen by few if any fellow historians or in historical
journals that few if any of those scientific specialists are likely to consult.
Thanks to the fact that taxonomy is unusual among scientific disciplines in
being necessarily much concerned with work carried out in the past, sometimes a very distant past, research on aspects of what I once proposed distinguishing as 'taxonomic archaeology' has led *Archives of Natural History* to
serve as a halfway house, attracting contributions from specialist historians
and professional biologists and geologists alike. It is because of this dual
readership that the journal has been the chosen medium for the majority of
the pieces reproduced in this volume.

An added attraction of that society and its journal is that they act as a
forum for specialists in many different aspects and branches of natural history. Historians, it has long seemed to me, have an important role to play in
revealing and emphasising the common roots from which the now innumerable specialisms and sub-specialisms have arisen during the last two centuries
at an ever-increasing rate. Although, as will be very evident from the pages that
follow, my own interests are mainly botanical, I have attempted from time to
time to examine natural history as a unitary whole, convinced that there are
many illuminating parallels and interactions between the separate studies of
which it is composed that would otherwise be overlooked. Five of the essays in
this volume (II, IX, X, XI, XII) have been endeavours in this direction.

Any collection of pieces published or delivered over a lengthy period must inevitably include a considerable amount of repetition. Audiences differ, and fresh discoveries and insights accumulate with the passing of the years. It has become conventional for the authors of volumes in this Series to apologise to their readers for this irritant, and I can myself but follow suit.

In closing, it remains only to thank the many friends and fellow researchers and, latterly, colleagues too who have helped in a variety of ways and given much-valued encouragement. In particular I would like take this opportunity of acknowledging the special debts I owe to Roy MacLeod and Bill Bynum for the key parts they successively played in drawing me into the academic world – the first in the form of a memorable term at the University of Sussex, the second for what has turned out to be an association of now many years' standing with the Wellcome Institute for the History of Medicine and in its recent reincarnation as the Wellcome Trust Centre for the History of Medicine at University College London. I hope some of the many benefits I have received as a result will be evident in these pages.

Winchester   DAVID ELLISTON ALLEN
December 2000

ACKNOWLEDGEMENTS

I am grateful to the following editors, societies and publishers for their permission to reproduce articles for which they hold the copyright: the Council of the Society for the History of Natural History (formerly the Society for the Bibliography of Natural History) (I–III, IX–XI, XV–XIX); Cambridge University Press (V); Intercept Ltd, Andover (VI); the Council of the British Society for the History of Science (VIII); the Council of the Linnean Society of London (XII, XIII); the editor of *Nature in Cambridgeshire* (XX); and the editor of the *Scottish Naturalist* (XXI). I would also like to thank afresh Mr R.J. Cleevely and Mrs Elizabeth Platts for the printing originally for private circulation of IV.

I

Walking the swards: medical education and the rise and spread of the botanical field class

ABSTRACT: Physic gardens expressly for teaching medical students to recognise herbs in the living state originated in northern Italy in 1543 and became a facility to which Europe's leading universities increasingly aspired. In default of one, the practice arose of taking students into the countryside instead; but that depended on there being a teacher who was also a keen field botanist. In the seventeenth century Paris, London and Edinburgh replaced Montpellier and Basle as the principal centres of this more informal approach, which eventually had one or two commercial imitators as well. When stricter qualifications governing medical practice in Britain induced a great expansion of medical schools there after 1815 student excursions were taken in Scotland to new heights of popularity and ambitiousness. Having originated in a need to protect future practitioners from being duped by their suppliers, field classes ended up by generating the publication of floras, a market for botanical collecting equipment and, above all, a simpler model for local associations of naturalists which liberated them from an inherited organisational straitjacket.

KEY WORDS: medical education – field class – medical botany – apothecaries – botanic gardens.

INTRODUCTION

Botany is today such a clear-cut and multi-faceted science in its own right that it is easy to forget that for most of its existence it has been but a branch of medicine – and a subordinate branch at that. For thousands of years the only justification for distinguishing different kinds of plants other than on account of whatever beauty they might possess was assumed to be their potential value therapeutically. The first person[1] known to have done so on any significant scale in the absence of that motive appears to have been a manorial steward in early seventeenth-century England, John Goodyer – whose training would have been an essentially legal one, not medical at all (R. T. Gunther, 1922). For long after that, though, botany remained in thrall to medicine and succeeded in achieving autonomy only very gradually and over a lengthy period. In so far as it was taught in universities, it tended to be assigned a place in the medical curriculum only grudgingly and then only as a component of materia medica, a subject notoriously hard to rescue from its intrinsically dry-as-dust character. This uncertain and marginal position reflected the fact that herbs were regarded as the province in the main of apothecaries and other more dubious kinds of practitioners, mere tradespeople without higher learning, for which reason no more than a smattering of knowledge on the subject was deemed either necessary or appropriate for intending physicians (Reeds, 1976, 1991). Lecturers on materia medica probably more often than not cared little about plants and were content to regurgitate uncritically what was written in the standard works, which in their turn were uncritical compilations substantially derived from revered ancient texts. It was proficiency in reading and understanding those texts that was rated all-important; compared to that, distinguishing plants in the living state was scarcely of much moment. There was the problem in any case that almost all the herbal species

I

were not in a good enough condition for their salient characters to be recognisable during the greater part of the academic year.

HIGH RENAISSANCE ORIGINS

The first breaks with that stultifying tradition took place in the second quarter of the sixteenth century in certain of the universities of northern Italy, seemingly through the influence of just one man. Luca Ghini (Figure 1), the son of a notary of Bologna, a city then within the domain of the Papal States, had graduated in medicine at the university there and in 1527 joined its teaching staff, initially as an instructor in *medicina practica*. Eight years later, perhaps as a result of displaying a botanical bent, he appears in the records formally designated as a lecturer on simples. The quality of the course he then developed

Figure 1. Luca Ghini (reproduced from Chiarugi, 1957).

on that subject apparently gained considerable renown, attracting students from many parts of Europe, including William Turner from England, and in 1539 he won promotion to a professorial chair (Sabbatani, 1923; Chiarugi, 1957; Keller, 1972). Though he was never to publish anything of significance, eventually handing over to Mattioli his material for an ambitious illustrated herbal he had never managed to complete, he was clearly outstanding as a teacher, doubtless through communicating his own enthusiasm for seeking out and putting names to as many different kinds of plants as he could find, an unusual interest up to that time.

It was apparently during the 1530s that Ghini was responsible for two teaching innovations that were both to prove extremely far-reaching. One was the encouraging of students to form reference collections of their own, by drying a specimen of each different herb, fixing it to a page of an album and labelling it with its name. The album was known as a *hortus siccus* ('dried garden'), a term which was to be supplanted much later by the rather snappier *herbarium*. There is evidence suggesting this practice was in use in medical circles at least a century and a half earlier (Sarton, 1947: 1177) and Ghini's adoption of it may therefore not have been original; he appears to deserve the credit, even so, for first introducing it as a teaching device. The three oldest herbaria known to be extant were all formed by men who were at one time students of his, and almost certainly it was through his example and perhaps even at his direction that these had their birth (Arber, 1986: 140).

It is Ghini's other innovation, however, that is the concern here. Presumably only too aware from his own personal experience of how unhelpful and often misleading the illustrations available at that period were as a means of recognising different herbs, he saw it as essential that students were shown the living plants as well. The easiest way of doing that would have been to take them into a nearby garden with a good selection of the relevant kinds, but no university yet had such a facility of its own and probably none of the private gardens in the city were sufficiently richly stocked. There was no alternative therefore but to go outside the city's walls into the countryside beyond. Plants could either have been collected there and brought back to the lecture-room for demonstration or the students taken out to see them *in situ*. While the second course was the ideal one, it had the drawback that it was time-consuming; it also required the teacher to have a reasonable idea beforehand of where best to go. Ghini is definitely known to have taken students out with him on occasion, but evidence is lacking on what scale or how formal a basis that was: it could have been his entire class or just a select one or two.

Despite having been promoted to a full professorship at Bologna, in 1543 Ghini succumbed to an invitation to move to an equivalent position at Pisa. That city was then newly part of the Grand Duchy of Tuscany and its ruler, Grand Duke Cosimo I di Medici, was keen to build up its reopened university. Deciding that it must follow Padua's lead in establishing a chair exclusively in Simples, the Grand Duke had initially had a try at luring Leonhard Fuchs, the author of by far the best herbal yet to have been published, but Fuchs had proved inextractable from Tübingen; baulked of a star researcher, he had settled for a star teacher instead. For Ghini the attraction must have been the chance to create the first-ever physic garden designed expressly to serve the needs of teaching. That a garden of such a kind had come to be seen as a pressing priority by others besides just him is shown by the fact that only two years after that ambition was realised by him at Pisa,[2] in 1543, not only was the establishment of a similar garden at Padua belatedly agreed to by the senate of

I

the Republic of Venice, but a third materialised at Florence, the Duchy of Tuscany's capital (for which reason Ghini had a major hand in that one as well).

After returning to his native city for what proved to be but a short-lived retirement, Ghini died in 1556. By then pupils of his had gone on to posts in universities in many other parts of Europe, where some had proceeded to copy his methods. Ironically, though, in the country of its birth the practice of taking students out into the countryside does not appear to have proved enduring, at any rate as part of the official teaching. It may be that the very fact of their having put resources and effort into creating teaching gardens led medical schools in Italy to assume that any instruction outside those had become superfluous as a result. That could explain why no such practice is heard of at Padua, even though the first prefect of its garden, Luigi dell' Anguinara, had acquired an enthusiasm for field botany from Ghini while a student at Bologna. It could also explain why Ghini's successor at Pisa, Andrea Cesalpino, another of his former students, is apparently not on record as having organized field classes there either. Yet even at Bologna, where there was bitter resistance to having a botanic garden till as late as 1568, it is not clear whether anything of the kind was kept up after Ghini departed to Pisa.

Shortly before Ghini's death, Ulisse Aldrovandi, another of his student converts and an all-round naturalist of a devouring acquisitiveness (Findlen, 1994), joined the staff at Bologna to teach logic; being medically qualified, however, he was later able to transfer to lecturing on general natural history, gaining a full professorship in that in 1561. For many years he was in the habit of making lengthy herbarizing expeditions during the vacations and he is known to have been latterly accompanied on some of these by students of his (Castellani, 1970). In the continuing absence of a botanic garden at Bologna field classes would have afforded the best and possibly the only means of identifying students with sufficient aptitude and keenness to make them suitable for such privileged attention (that at any rate was how Hooker was to recruit for his "long excursions" into the Scottish Highlands three centuries later), and that Aldrovandi was also pursuing that more formal mode of teaching can perhaps be inferred from this.[3]

MONTPELLIER

Luckily, as the flame was flickering out in Italy it was being rekindled in countries to the north and west, most notably at Basle and Montpellier.

Montpellier may well have been the first to blaze forth, in or just after 1550. Eleven years earlier Guillaume Rondelet, the son of a spice and drug merchant in that town, had returned to the university from which he had graduated on being appointed to a post in its medical faculty. A man of wide learning and culture, a dedicated and influential teacher who, like Ghini, never got round to publishing anything of significance, Rondelet had already gone much of the way to turning Montpellier into the foremost centre of botanical teaching in Europe – during a period, moreover, when that university was suffering repeated disruptions – when a court ruling stipulated that the subject was thenceforward to be taught practically as well as theoretically and required one of the doctors "to demonstrate visually the simples" and "to search for the said simples in the town of Montpellier and its surroundings" (Dulieu, 1966; Reeds, 1991: 59). Rondelet may perhaps have been behind this, for not only was he an enthusiastic field man but only a few months previously he had visited Padua and Pisa, meeting Aldrovandi and probably Ghini also and no doubt learning

I

of the latter's teaching innovations. Like Bologna, Montpellier had no botanic garden at that date, so the court ruling presented its medical faculty with the same two options that had confronted Ghini: bring the plants to the students or take the students out to see them. In this case a considerable body of evidence exists to show that the second solution was resorted to, but, in contrast to the pattern that was long to become the standard one elsewhere, Montpellier seems at first to have organised only lengthy excursions extending over more than one day. This preference may have been the price that had to be paid for having an experienced field botanist for a professor: Rondelet must long since have felt he had exhausted the flora in the immediate vicinity and hungered to explore areas further off. Possibly, too, the longer the excursion, the more likely it was to attract only the more committed of the students, the consequently smaller number being that much the more manageable. By their very nature, however, lengthy trips were more physically taxing for the leader, and it is no surprise to learn that by the time Mathias de L'Obel and Pierre Pena were students there, in 1565–1568 (Louis, 1980), Rondelet had largely delegated these occasions to two younger colleagues, Etienne Barral and his own son-in-law Jacques d'Assas, both of them apparently scarcely his inferior in knowledge and enthusiasm (Pena and L'Obel, 1571: 26, 312).

More enjoyable and profitable though they were for those leading them, however, than taking out a full class that included the reluctant and apathetic, long excursions presumably left a certain proportion of each year's students uncatered-for. Those who wanted to bother with only sufficient in the way of herb recognition to get by can hardly have helped but feel neglected. So no doubt it was for that reason that in 1575 and again the next year the students are recorded as having asked the faculty to pay for someone to lead them to look at plants "in the Montpellier countryside" in the days before the autumn lecturing began (Reeds, 1991: 75). Significantly, it was with "the whole flock of students" that François Ranchin was formally instructed by the faculty in 1592 to "investigate the plants themselves on some days of the week" (Reeds, 1991: 79). Excursions of such a frequency and inclusiveness imply the existence at Montpellier by then of field classes of the shorter type.

Montpellier's special tradition of lengthy excursions nevertheless continued. In 1595 Thomas Platter noted in his celebrated journal: "On the 13th of October ... I went botanizing with twenty other students, under the leadership of Dr. Ranchin ..., who was on horseback with some others of our party ...". Having counted on finding beds for the night in the town they had made for and found to their dismay that none were to be had, there was no alternative for them all but to sleep on the hay in a barn, Ranchin included (Anonymous, 1892: 208; Jennett, 1963: 49). Officially, it was one of the duties laid upon the holder of the newly established chair of Anatomy and Demonstration of Plants "to take the students out on botanical excursions during the summer", according to Platter (Jennett, 1963: 36). But the appointee to that, Pierre Richer de Belleval, a one-time student of Rondelet's, had effectively been imposed on the University by the king and enjoyed exceptional freedom of action, for in addition to the chair specially created for him and the assured directorship of a botanic garden that was to be established he was permitted to be absent on field trips for almost half the year. Consequently, excellent botanist though he was too, he was not available much of the time to take the students out himself. Nevertheless he does appear to have done so from time to time, to judge from a document of 1607, and "Discourses on various things for students when they are herborizing" was the title of a manuscript he was to bequeath on his death in 1632 (Reeds, 1991: 83–89).

I

BASLE

Given the amount of intellectual traffic taking place at that period between the universities of northern Italy and Montpellier and the great Protestant one at Basle, it was only a matter of time before field classes were introduced at the last of these too. As early as 1536 an anonymous professor, perhaps familiar with Ghini's practice at Bologna, in recommending a medical curriculum urged that the professors in summer "should lead the youths out, give the names of herbs to them and point out their properties"; but that was evidently no more than a description of an ideal model (a prototype of others that would surface later elsewhere) and seems to have been pursued no further (Reeds, 1991: 99, 104). It was not to be till 1575, well after the long excursions were in full swing at Montpellier, that any more is heard of instruction along such lines. In that year, as part of a recrudescence that the medical faculty was undergoing, a University statute ordained that "in spring and autumn one of the professors, in company with the dean, is to make an excursion with the medical students to see herbs in their natural habitats."[4] The doctors were to be paid a florin to cover the expenses of each trip, the students being expected to bring with them their own sustenance (Reeds, 1991: 110). As the faculty was headed at this point by a keen botanist in the person of Theodor Zwingler, it can probably safely be assumed that that statute was precisely conformed with. However, it was only after the appointment of Caspar Bauhin as the first professor of Anatomy and Botany, in 1589, that we can be sure that field teaching was indeed happening.

Another of the great figures of Renaissance botany, comparable in stature with Rondelet, Bauhin had had the good fortune to grow up in a circle of enthusiasts for the herbal side of learned medicine, not least with a father as well as an elder brother to share their expertise in that and give him every encouragement. After studying at Padua for a year and a half and then briefly at Montpellier too, he had returned to Basle to graduate and in 1581 embarked on medical practice. During the next eight years he combined that with privately teaching botany and anatomy, which, to judge from his personal passion for plant-hunting, probably extended to taking pupils out into the country with him. But it was only after his appointment to the University's medical faculty that his *herbationes*, as he termed them, became, according to his own account, a very regular part of his teaching: at the end of his life he was to claim to have taken students out in every month for over 30 years (Reeds, 1991: 117). It was expressly for them that he produced in 1622 a catalogue of the plants growing wild within walking distance of the city. Convenient in size for slipping into a pocket, this even had blank pages interleaved with the text on which to make notes. Sadly, Bauhin lived to see this made use of for only two years, and after his death botany at Basle began to die too, a process in any case hastened by the Thirty Years War and all the disruptions and adversities that accompanied or flowed from that.

OTHER CENTRAL EUROPEAN INITIATIVES

Well before then this mode of teaching had begun to be subscribed to, at any rate in theory, at other universities in the central parts of Europe. In 1576, one year after Basle's first official endorsement of the practice, the foundation statutes of the new Protestant university at Helmstedt, in the duchy of Braunschweig-Lüneburg, were particularly elaborate in their prescriptions for *herbationes*, requiring the local apothecaries (who were expected to attend these along with the students) to provide the professors with "a breakfast of Malmsey wine or preserves" *en route* to the countryside, while the students in their turn were to stand the cost of a little banquet in the evening as a way of thanking their teachers (Reeds, 1991: 6). Again, in 1602 the physician who endowed a new chair of Anatomy and Simples in the Jagiellonian University at Kraków desired a botanic garden to be established and the occupant of the chair to demonstrate herbs on certain days either in that or the fields ("*vel in campo vel in horto*") – and as the proposed garden failed in the event to materialise, that meant in the fields in practice. Unfortunately, though, the medical faculty proved indifferent to the benefaction and the person appointed to the post was someone so grand that it seems unlikely that he was prepared to stoop to this particular requirement (Czerwiakowski, 1864: 90; Szafer, 1969; Zemanek, 1993). It was all very well for detailed job descriptions of these kinds to be drawn up and issued, but until there chanced to be someone available with the requisite field knowledge and a liking, let alone a flair, for this less formal type of instruction, they were unlikely to achieve what was intended. This was to be a recurring problem, and it is clearly unsafe to assume that what was stipulated in statutes was therefore what transpired, even in part.

SHIFT NORTH-WESTWARDS

Shortly after 1600 a marked shift began to occur in field teaching's geographical centre of gravity. What sound like *herbationes* are heard of for the first time far to the north, in Sweden and Denmark. Significantly, the individuals responsible in each case had previously been at German universities, which suggests these were not spontaneous initiatives but the product of diffusion.[5] The Swedish initiative was that of Johannes Rudbeck at a private school he ran in 1610–1613 in Uppsala in competition with the university there (Eriksson, 1969: 33). The programme of one of its outings has survived. In Denmark, in more orthodox fashion, after appointment to a medical chair at Copenhagen in 1639 Simon Pauli instituted the teaching of botany and is said to have made excursions with his students (Anonymous, 1805), though on what scale and how formally is apparently unknown. In 1627 there were stirrings at last in the Netherlands too, at Leiden. In that year Adolph Vorstius, who as professor of Medicine and Botany was also *ex officio* prefect of the botanic garden, was urged by the Board of Curators of the University to take the medical students out into the country (Heniger and Sosef, 1989: 158). Vorstius had graduated at Padua and spent a long time there (Lindeboom, 1984), so ought to have been familiar with what was involved; possibly indeed the suggestion was his own. And that he may have made at least some token compliance is suggested by his subsequently adding to the published catalogue of the garden a list of the wild flora round about, for the benefit of those making botanical excursions locally. However, it is known that he increasingly defaulted on his lecturing within the garden, so even supposing he did supplement that by leading excursions beyond its walls, it is hardly likely that he persisted with what must have been regarded as a mere side-activity.

Leiden all along indeed was to be the conspicuous odd-man-out of the Continent's leading medical centres in this particular regard, despite having had a botanic garden from as early as 1587 and a run of able and distinguished botanists as its prefects – not all of whom had medical practices or teaching duties to distract them. When the Scottish naturalist Robert Sibbald was a student there in 1660, he repeatedly went over to Amsterdam and "herbalized in the downs and woods w^t the gard^{ner} of the medicine garden" (Hett, 1932: 58), such was the lack of any comparable opportunity, it would seem, at his own university. Nor do even the eminence of its medical school during Boerhaave's tenure of the chair of Medicine and Botany in 1709–1729 and the influx of scholars from all over Europe that resulted appear to have revived calls for anything more than the standard courses of lectures in the garden. Boerhaave delivered these conscientiously, but he had paid no attention to botany since his student days before being appointed to the chair in that (which merely chanced to be the one medical chair conveniently vacant for him); consequently he brought to his teaching of the subject no fieldwork background or knowledge of the local flora such as Rondelet and Bauhin had possessed (Lindeboom, 1968). Though his duties in other directions became multifarious and onerous, he could have delegated the taking of field classes to subordinates if he had only seen fit to instigate them. Very disappointingly, no tradition of field instruction seems to have taken root there or indeed elsewhere in The Netherlands, a country so much to the fore in the study of natural history in other ways.

SECOND WIND

The failure of the Dutch to respond, at any rate more than desultorily, can be seen as a symptom of the crisis of continuity that field teaching was faced with in the mid-sixteenth century. By then all those whom Ghini had inspired with his innovation at first or second hand were no longer around – Aldrovandi had died in 1605, Bauhin in 1624, Richer in 1632 – and no equally charismatic figures had emerged at their respective universities in their place. The Continent, moreover, was ablaze with religious strife and such foremost botanists as Turner and de L'Obel, who had personally experienced the pleasures of the field class tradition, and might well have passed it on, had been reduced to the status of refugees and failed to gain academic footholds. If the tradition was to recover that early impetus, it needed to acquire a fresh set of dedicated patrons.

Luckily, three new centres now arose to fill the hiatus and impart to the tradition an even stronger dynamic. These were London, Paris and Edinburgh. London led the way, some 70 years ahead of the others. And London's record of continuity was to be unbeaten anywhere: at least 214 years without a break, as against roughly a century and a half at Paris. Edinburgh began well, but fairly soon stumbled and failed to get back on its feet till the start of the nineteenth century – and then only fitfully at first.

LONDON: THE SOCIETY OF APOTHECARIES

The reason for London's remarkable persistence was that there, uniquely, one particular body had a vested interest in introducing field instruction in the first place and thereafter a mixture of pride and custom which kept on sustaining it. This was the Society of Apothecaries, one of the city's network of livery companies, which attempted to control entry to the various skilled occupations and maintain standards. The one area of expertise in which apothecaries could claim superiority over the other two rival sectors of medical practice with greater or lesser pretensions to learned status, the surgeons and the physicians, was the identification of herbs, knowledge of what each kind was supposedly effective for and adeptness in making preparations from them. This herbal expertise was also the chief way in which they could aspire to more than mere trade respectability and to be regarded as men of science. Not surprisingly, therefore, only a year or two after the Society hived off from its parent, the Grocers' Company, and assumed responsibilities for training its own apprentices, what were then called "simpling days" were being organised. These first feature in the Society's records in 1620 and by the 1680s, if not earlier, they were taking place monthly from April to September. An early by-product was a guide to the plants likely to be seen on various routes taken by the excursions, written by one of those appointed by the Society to conduct them, James Petiver. Entitled *Botanicum Londinense*, which suggests that it was modelled on Tournefort's Paris equivalent, this was published serially from 1710 in Petiver's own short-lived periodical, the *Monthly miscellany*, but apparently never completed.

The Society's senior counterpart, the College of Physicians, had no need of any comparable initiative, for its members, unlike their opposite numbers in Scotland and elsewhere, normally did not take apprentices. On the other hand there is evidence that that body too was already holding excursions, though ones of a different type, before the Apothecaries embarked on their training programme. In one of his herbals de L'Obel (1655: 38) mentions having collected a particular plant of interest *"in publica rusticatione sive exherbatione* [on a public field excursion or herbarizing]" in company with two luminaries of the College – and by naming those he enables the occasion to be dated to sometime in the years 1606–1610. A century later, as will be seen, the College of Surgeons in Edinburgh was also arranging "solemn publick herbarizings" expressly for its apprentice masters. It would appear that such events were a standard feature which the respective medical bodies had chosen to add to their existing armouries of ritual, perhaps in imitation of some Continental practice whose existence has yet to be uncovered by research.

The equivalent celebrations of the London Apothecaries were termed "General Simpling Days" (or, later, "General Herbarizings"). Instituted in 1633, they were gradually restricted to one each July and turned into a much more elaborate affair than any of the outings laid on for the apprentices (Wall *et al.*, 1963: 88). All the freemen of the society were expected to attend, incurring a fine if they failed to do so. The excursion itself was a comparatively lengthy one, spread over two days, and might be by coach to somewhere as distant as the middle of Kent. It was a set duty of the relevant office-holder, the Demonstrator of Plants, to go out a day or two beforehand and reconnoitre the ground. It was also his task to collect a sample of the more interesting herbs that the party met with for exhibition at the culminating highlight, the evening feast back at the Society's Physic Garden at Chelsea. At this, it was traditional for the main course to be a swan, which all present partook of as a kind of brotherly *agape*. It was further traditional for the Society's barge to be brought out in all its splendour on these occasions for conveying the Masters and Wardens along the river from their homes or shops in the city and then back again afterwards (its usefulness in this special connection had indeed been one of the arguments put forward for purchasing it in the first place (Burnby, 1994), just as the need to find somewhere to house it had determined the choice of Chelsea as the location of the Garden). One year the barge was even furnished with a band of musicians. Such touches show the lengths the Society was prepared to go to in its efforts to use this annual event as a means of reasserting its solidarity, of symbolically defining itself as a corporate entity. The General Herbarizing was a kind of embodiment of what the members liked to think was the ancestral essence of their craft. The halo it wore as a result cannot have failed to extend, at least in some part, to the ordinary excursions held for the apprentices – General Herbarizings-in-miniature, as they must have seemed – and thereby helped to ensure that those, similarly, were treasured and preserved.

LONDON: COMMERCIAL INITIATIVES

Enthusiastic outsiders were always welcome to join the Society's apprentices on their excursions and at one time or another every London field botanist of subsequent note appears to have availed himself of these opportunities. Indeed, until the nineteenth century hardly anything else of the kind existed in England on a regular and organised basis. The two known exceptions were both frankly commercial ventures, called into being by the growing demand for herbal tuition which the few medical schools yet existent were not in a position to meet.

The first of these ventures was a course on materia medica which George Fordyce, later senior physician of St Thomas's Hospital (and maternal grandfather of the great botanical systematist George Bentham), added in 1764 to one he had been giving on chemistry for some years already on a freelance basis. His lectures were extremely popular, attended by thousands of students during the three decades over which his teaching career extended, and being of the firm conviction that a good grounding in botany was essential for anyone entering medicine he occasionally carried instruction in that subject out into the fields (Curtis, 1941: 7). One of the keenest on those excursions was William Curtis, best remembered today for his magnificent folio, *Flora Londinensis*, and as the founder of the *Botanical magazine*. Curtis went on to hold the post of Demonstrator of Plants in the Society of Apothecaries, but after a five-year stint as that he resigned, ostensibly through pressure of work in the apothecary business he had inherited while still a student. A passionate naturalist, his heart was not in that, however, and the real reason was probably that he saw that an alternative, more congenial livelihood was to be had by setting up in competition with the Society. Even before taking his post with the latter, he had bought a small garden for the purpose of building up a comprehensive collection of plants indigenous to Britain (Curtis, 1941: 12) and this he now transferred to a site at Lambeth Marsh, at that time a village well to the south of the city. Opened in 1779 as the London Botanic Garden and aimed expressly at students, it offered subscribers the additional benefit of a well-stocked library on botany and cognate sciences. For ten years it appears to have modestly thrived there, but expiry of the lease, increasing pollution and the out-of-the-way location then combined to induce Curtis to move it to a much larger site at Old Brompton, in the grounds of a former tavern. There it was conveniently much closer for London's wealthier residents and was soon receiving the patronage of many of the nobility (Salisbury, 1810).

Whether up till then Curtis had taken his duplication of what the Society of Apothecaries was offering to the point of also offering field excursions is uncertain,[6] but a prospectus[7] survives from 1792 to prove that by that year at least he was hoping to make that a profitable sideline. In return for a fee of two guineas those signing on for the advertised "course of herbarizing excursions" were promised instruction from May to July in nearby Battersea Fields (a popular botanical hunting-ground of that period). They were also carefully assured that the period of study would extend to three or four hours, "never more", to be followed

I

by "a short frugal repast which will be regulated by the strictest rules of economy", taken at a table at which the lecturer would pronounce upon the specimens collected one by one. The stress laid upon the limited duration and the cheapness of the meal was clearly with hard-pressed students especially in mind; at the same time it could have been read as a dig at the expansive character of the occasions provided by the Society of Apothecaries. Their day-long outings were doubtless considered needlessly time-consuming by many, especially by apprentice masters loath to lose a pair of hands for such a period – to the extent that, despite the fact that the Society expected all its members who took pupils to send them regularly on its herbarizings, many probably actively discouraged them from attending (Burnby, pers. comm., 1987).

On Curtis's death in 1799 the London Botanic Garden passed to William Salisbury, a former student of his whom he had recently taken into partnership and whose drive and horticultural expertise he must have felt outweighed the lack of education that J. E. Gray was later to remark upon (A. E. Gunther, 1974: 46). About eight years later Salisbury moved the Garden yet again, this time to a six-acre site "nearer London" in what is now Cadogan Gardens, off Sloane Street. By instituting twice-weekly band concerts on summer evenings he quickly turned it into a fashionable place of promenade (Salisbury, 1810), while retaining its educational functions and adding a series of lectures on popular science.

In 1815 Salisbury's ambitions were raised considerably further when the Apothecaries' Act made the licence of the Society of Apothecaries the qualification that had to be obtained in future by any medical man wishing to engage legally in general practice in England or Wales (Holloway, 1966, 1970). The examination for that licence, a wholly oral one till 1840, naturally included, at the very least as one option, a test of candidates' knowledge of herbs, so a great surge in demand for instruction in that subject could confidently be anticipated. The medical schools not already covering it (and few were) therefore hurriedly recruited teachers with some botanical knowledge, men who were in such short supply that a medical qualification was not necessarily insisted upon. Salisbury was one of the immediate beneficiaries, taken on as *de facto* lecturer in botany at the joint school of Guy's and St Thomas's Hospitals and (according to J. E. Gray) at the small and private Maze Pond School opposite Guy's, apparently simultaneously. At both of these, as well as regularly in the pages of the *London physical and medical journal* and in a pocket-sized volume, *The botanists' companion*, which he published expressly in this connection, he advertised a programme of weekly lectures and – for an additional fee – monthly excursions in spring and summer which he was offering at his Garden and which, as he states (Salisbury, 1816: v), he had revived directly in response to the new Act.

That Salisbury's new programme was very much a market-oriented operation is shown by the repeated adjustments announced to the arrangements for the excursions: first they started from the Garden, then, more sensibly, at the particular place to be "herbarized"; similarly, they were shifted from Saturdays to Fridays and then again to Thursdays. Among those Salisbury managed to attract to them was the poet John Keats, then studying to be an apothecary (Evans, 1998). Another was the future head of the Natural History Department of the British Museum, J. E. Gray. It was while Gray and the rest of his class were waiting for one of these excursions to start that news arrived that Salisbury had been arrested for debt. Assuming this was some mere minor contretemps, the class elected Gray, as the most knowledgeable of their number, to act as temporary leader in his stead. It subsequently transpired, however, that the situation was really serious: the London Botanic Garden had outrun its capital. Salisbury was declared bankrupt and, according to the harsh practice of the day, was consigned thereupon to The Fleet Prison (A. E. Gunther, 1974: 47, 63; 1980: 202, 208). This was probably in 1817. Within two years Salisbury was busy publishing again, but it was too late for him to retrieve the Garden, which had to be sold and was then turned into a nursery. Reverting to a nurseryman himself, he returned to Brompton to live (Roberts, 1900), only to die not long afterwards, in 1823.

That was the end of Britain's last successful attempt at running field excursions commercially until recent years. It had needed a naturalist like Curtis to want a garden that operated on that basis to be a primarily educational venture and then to extend into that side-activity: after Salisbury there was no one with the special personal commitment to be prepared to persist with so doubtfully profitable a vision. As though to confirm that, a superficially identical venture was established in 1816 in an even more central location, in Regent's Park, but the two nurserymen behind it (Anonymous, 1816; Meynell, 1980) proved to have a purely horticultural intent. Though it later grew into a very substantial enterprise, secured royal patronage and even made a bid to take over the Royal Gardens at Kew, it was never to develop any extra-mural activity.

It would be pleasing to be able to demonstrate that Salisbury's pioneering of class excursions at London medical schools was responsible for inspiring, and not merely anticipating, those introduced by lecturers at several other ones in the years that followed – for example, by Edward Forbes at King's College in 1843 (Wilson and Geikie, 1861: 347), by Edwin Lankester at the Grovenor Place School (English, 1990: 52), by George Luxford at St Thomas's in that same decade (Luxford, 1849) and by Henry Trimen at St Mary's in the 1870s (Britten, 1896: 491).[8] Once again, though, these were the isolated initiatives of men who chanced to have a keenness for fieldwork themselves: they were not the product of institutional policy, and in each case the innovation doubtless petered out when the individual concerned moved elsewhere. By that time, as will be seen, field classes had become a well-accepted part of the medical curriculum at several of Britain's leading universities and there were ample models for copying even had there not been the longstanding one as well of the Society of Apothecaries. Forbes indeed stated explicitly that he had introduced the practice, "a new system in London", after becoming familiar with it during his years at Edinburgh.

PARIS

In contrast to London, the *herborisations* of the Jardin du Roi in Paris owed their hardly less prolonged existence to their having turned into a family tradition. They can be said to have had their origin in the appointment of Tournefort in 1683 to the curiously-titled post of "Sous-démonstrateur pour l'Extérieure des Plantes", presumably designed to ensure that he kept to his speciality of naming and classifying and left other aspects of botany to colleagues. By the 1690s Tournefort had unofficially extended his duties to taking out student parties every Wednesday to show them plants growing under natural conditions (Boerhaave, 1743). A flora of the environs of Paris, which he published in 1698, was divided into a series of chapters each describing a specific botanical walk, perhaps for the guidance of those students more particularly. When he resigned his post in 1700 in order to explore the Levant, the excursions may have ceased for a while; but in 1708 his protégé, Sébastien Vaillant, who had attended them as a newly-arrived surgeon at Neuilly and quickly impressed with his taxonomic flair, was appointed in turn to a sub-demonstrator post in the Garden and at his instance the *"herborisations publiques"* were continued. In his turn, too, Vaillant produced a similar guide to the local flora, *Botanicon Parisiense*, compiled over many years but published only posthumously in 1727.

Already by then the first of the remarkable de Jussieu dynasty held the principal post at the Jardin du Roi and had been able to contrive that the vacancy created by Vaillant's death was filled by his then scarcely botanical younger brother, Bernard de Jussieu. Bernard began unpromisingly by being brash and argumentative, but in time turned himself into one of France's foremost botanists and in particular proved an inspiring teacher. The conducting of herbarizings was officially one of his duties from the first, and over the years almost all of the leading figures in Parisian botany passed through his hands and no doubt also took part in these. Unlike their London equivalents, the excursions were expressly public occasions and for that reason they seem to have attracted visiting botanists from other countries more.

Bernard de Jussieu was the first of three members of the family who successively sustained these excursions at a high level of popularity for more than a hundred years in all. So central an activity of the Garden had they become by the time of Bernard's death that when his nephew Antoine-Laurent was appointed to the staff in 1793 it was to a post explicitly directed to that end in its title: "Botanique à la campagne". When Antoine-Laurent's son Adrien succeeded his father, in 1826, his title was wider still: "Professor of rural botany". By then transport had so improved that it was feasible to take parties considerably further afield than to such long-standing favourites as the Bois de Boulogne (Crestois, 1953: 78). A peculiarity of these excursions of Adrien, as a visiting English botanist was impressed to discover (Woods, 1843: 862), was the number of the Professor's friends who came along with the students, "eminent men of science, letters and arts, drawn and held by the charm of his conversation" (Decaisne, 1861). Fortunately, the students tended to be so full of questions that they received their proper share of attention from the leader nonetheless. Adrien de Jussieu indeed is said to have had all the virtues that this special kind of teaching calls for: "unrelenting patience, great presence of mind, much gentleness, a certain gaiety not allowed to descend into familiarity, ... a profound knowledge of the varied forms of the vegetation and a memory so sure that the professor cannot be stumped by a question sprung on him unprepared" (Decaisne, 1854).

Just as in London, the mainstream tradition in Paris eventually gave rise to at least one competing, freelance initiative. As in London, too, the person responsible for this was a former member of staff – in this case Michel Adanson, a pupil of Bernard de Jussieu who had left under a cloud. Long before, while a student at the Collège de France, Adanson had attended the excursions of the Jardin du Roi; so when he was thrown on his own resources and sought to earn a substitute livelihood by giving courses on natural history at his home, he drew on that experience to add a field dimension to them in 1773. In doing so he took advantage of his independence, like Curtis, to introduce some novel features. For a start, he limited the number on his excursions to ten, each of them carefully selected. As he was dependent on the fees, this can only have been in order to offer the 'plus' of individual attention. Secondly, he limited the walks to 1½ leagues (about 4½ miles, 7.25 km) at most, so that they took up only a morning and left the afternoon free for dealing with questions; this also allowed the particular area visited to be investigated the more thoroughly, a point on which Adanson was especially keen, for the courses covered natural history as a whole and were not limited just to botany. He further made a practice of taking his parties along

I

the same route twice each summer, to see how the vegetation had changed in the intervening period. A fourth innovation was to distribute cards beforehand detailing the itinerary followed and listing the plants likely to be seen (Nicolas, 1963).

By this period it seems to have become the norm all over Europe for field classes to be taken to the same few places year after year, along the same unvarying routes. This had the obvious advantage of ensuring that a sufficiency of different herbs of interest would be encountered but not so many as to cause mental indigestion – or some that the leader would be embarrassed not to be able to put a name to. At Uppsala, where Linnaeus instituted student excursions in 1762 (Figure 2), four years after attending those of the Jardin du Roi in Paris, Swedish botanists have found it possible to reconstruct with some exactitude where his parties regularly went from the lists of plants recorded. A species new to science was even found by a subsequent visitor, Friedrich Ehrhart, on veering off one of the paths just very slightly.[9]

Paris did not altogether have a monopoly of such occasions by then. An unidentified "licencié en médecine" (Anonymous, 1763) has left a colourful account of an excursion he went on at the University of Pau, in the foothills of the Pyrenees, when a student there in 1746, reminiscent of the fond recollections that were similarly to be penned by Edinburgh *alumni* a century later. A professor by the name of Camelinus had introduced a programme of purely recreational herborizations, each "une fête des plus brillantes", seemingly on the model of those of the Jardin du Roi – to judge from the fact that they were open to anyone interested and students made up only half the number who attended the particular occasion described. It was doubtless also the Jardin du Roi tradition that inspired Augustin-Pyramus

Figure 2. Linnaeus leading a student excursion. Imaginary scene by an unidentified Swedish artist.

de Candolle to revive field classes at Montpellier after his appointment to the directorship of its botanic garden in 1808. Ironically, he had been baulked of the chair of botany in the Jardin du Roi's new guise as the Muséum d'Histoire Naturelle thanks to the culture of nepotism that continued to hold sway there; otherwise it would have been the Paris excursions for which he had responsibility – though without the direct involvement, and consequently influence through them, that he was to have at Montpellier.

On later returning to his native city of Geneva, de Candolle is known to have continued to lead student excursions, though the only one of those of which a record seems to have come down was a ten-day trip into the neighbouring mountains in the early 1820s, with a select group of just a dozen instead of the multitudes he was accustomed to taking out at Montpellier. Among that dozen were his son Alphonse and the subsequent Irish pioneer of American botany, Thomas Coulter. The occasion was memorable for the delight with which they were received on arriving at their destination, where strangers were as rare as they were welcome. After being serenaded by the villagers, "we took possession of a fiddle and big drum", Coulter was to report to his sister, and after a tour of the market-place with those everyone took part in an open-air dance, rounded off eventually with choruses of Swiss national airs (de Candolle, 1862: 328; Nelson and Probert, 1994: 26).

EDINBURGH

At Edinburgh, the third of the centres with the lengthiest record of loyalty to field instruction in botany, there was again a close link with one botanic garden in particular. Of three separate institutions out of which the future Royal Botanic Garden emerged, the one initially of relevance to this story was a physic garden established in 1675 next to one of the hospitals for the benefit of the city's physicians and apothecaries. That this was being used for teaching their apprentices by 1683 is evident from a catalogue of the garden, *Hortus Medicus Edinburgensis*, produced in that year by its first "intendant", James Sutherland, and that on some of the many excursions he mentions in this having made in connection with his duties he was accompanied by at least some of these pupils seems quite likely. That likelihood is strengthened by the fact that, when under the terms of an act of the College of Surgeons in 1695 Sutherland undertook to teach their apprentices as well, he also undertook to wait upon their masters "at a solemn publick herbarizing in the fields four severall times every year" (Cowan, 1933: 30; Fletcher and Brown, 1970: 16). That these public herborizings did then take place on a regular basis would appear to be confirmed by one of Sutherland's successors, George Preston, having received an instruction in 1711 in almost identical words (Fletcher and Brown, 1970: 32). However, it does not necessarily follow that what the masters required to be arranged for themselves was considered necessary for the apprentices as well. Nor does it follow either that a duty laid down in the terms of an appointment was observed conscientiously or even at all.

No more, at any rate, is heard of excursions being organised from any of the Edinburgh gardens during the next hundred years. The most that happened was that one or two of the Principal Gardeners (as opposed to the Professors) who were also experienced field botanists took out with them on collecting forays some of the keener students of what by then was the University. John Mackay was one who is known to have done so in 1800–1801, during what proved an all-too-brief period on the staff before his death at only 30 ([Neill], 1804). By that time it was Edinburgh's geologists who were making all the running instead as far as formal instruction in the field was concerned. This was the work of Robert Jameson, the Professor of Natural History (excluding botany) for the 50 years from 1804, who had studied mineralogy under Werner at the Freiberg Mining Academy in Silesia and there imbibed his master's belief in the value of demonstrating direct from nature (Ritchie, 1952). Thanks to Jameson, field teaching came to be an accepted and even vaunted speciality of the Edinburgh scientific curriculum, enabling its eventual revival there in botany to take place as a matter of course.

OXFORD AND CAMBRIDGE

Regrettably, the English universities long remained uninfluenced by, perhaps even largely oblivious of, the developments in London and Edinburgh. Although Oxford acquired what was initially known as its Physic Garden as early as 1621, that was essentially a horticultural enterprise and, given the rudimentary structure of the University's medical teaching at that period, not envisaged as having any scientific function at first (Webster, 1986). The second of its superintendents, Jacob Bobart the younger, was in fact an active field botanist but sadly received no encouragement to provide instruction in that direction. It is true that the foundation statutes of Worcester College in 1698 prescribed a course in botany and laid down that its teacher was to take the students "four times into the fields, woods, and marshes to pick, collect, and distinguish plants", but those statutes were so unrealistically elaborate that it is credibly supposed they were drawn up merely to act as a bait for the intending benefactor (Daniel and Barker, 1900: 160). No more, at any rate, was heard of such a requirement, nor indeed was anything much heard of Oxford medicine as a whole during the century that followed (Webster, 1986). All through the years Oxford's record in the matter of field instruction was to be even more ignominious than Leiden's – and that despite the open-air classes in geology instituted in the early nineteenth century by William Buckland and the celebrity those gained far beyond the University.

For a long time Cambridge did scarcely better. Shortly after 1700 William Stukeley, Stephen Hales and some fellow students of medicine there are known to have made herborizing trips into the surrounding country "once or twice a week" (Lukis, 1882: 22, 39), but that was apparently of their own volition entirely.[10] There had been an abortive move by then to establish a botanic garden (Walters, 1981: 16) and in 1724 a Professor of Botany was even appointed: but, just as at Oxford, the impetus behind that 'greening' of the University was initially horticultural and the man appointed, Richard Bradley, lacked both qualifications and interest to lecture on the aspects of botany relevant to medicine. After three years a young habitué of the herborizings of the Society of Apothecaries, John Martyn, was therefore invited up from London to fill the gap with an appropriate course (Turner, 1835: 269). It is not clear whether he was expected to lead some excursions as part of that, but the fact that he produced at his own expense an updated version of Ray's *Catalogus plantarum circa Cantabrigiam nascentium* and distributed free copies of it to those attending his lectures makes it likely that it was to this occasion that his son ([T. Martyn], 1763) was referring in later recording that he "perambulated the country with his scholars, showing them the Cambridgeshire plants where Mr. Ray had described them to grow". That would have been second nature to such a keen field man as Martyn, but his presence at the University at that point was merely temporary and unofficial, so he could scarcely have inaugurated a lasting tradition. Though he did come back six years later, in 1733, this time as the occupant of the botanical Chair, it was not long before he ceased teaching altogether and returned to his practice in Chelsea, disillusioned by the University's continuing failure to fund a botanic garden as an earnest of its belief in the value of medical botany as a subject.

Very indirectly, though, Martyn was responsible for making Cambridge botany eventually field-conscious. This was by refusing to resign the Chair until his son was available to be appointed as his successor, in 1762. A botanic garden then at last became a reality and Thomas Martyn lost no time in producing a guide to the local flora, *Plantae Cantabrigienses*. A similar work had been conceived, ostensibly for the London area, by his father long before (J. Martyn, 1732), so there was evidently a family continuity in that as well. Yet how far the son's trail-laying had its desired effect remains unclear. No evidence can be found that his personal excursions round Cambridge were ever in the company of those who attended his lectures: he seems to have been a rare example of a field botanist who failed to link the classroom to the field.

DUBLIN

Though Oxford and Cambridge thus joined Leiden in demonstrating that field teaching was by no means necessarily an outcome of the acquiring of a botanic garden, that there nevertheless continued to be places where the two coexisted shows that the notion that they were functionally interdependent and reciprocally beneficial persisted in medical school thinking till well into the nineteenth century. Dublin's Trinity College, for long Ireland's sole degree-conferring institution, is one example. After 33 years of sustained pressure by its Professors of Botany T.C.D. eventually leased some land for a garden in 1806, entrusting the task of laying it out to James Townsend Mackay, the younger brother of the Mackay who had only recently revived the Edinburgh Garden's excursions before his early death. No evidence has been uncovered that that brother's initiative was ever copied by his long-serving Dublin opposite number, but that the College Board at least initially envisaged such a development is proved by a minute allowing the Professor at that time, Robert Scott, to omit one of the lectures he was required to give from mid-April to mid-July "if he chooses to conduct his pupils into the country in order to examine the native plants once a week" (Kirkpatrick, 1912: 210). The Board seems hardly likely to have specified this as an option had it not been presented as one of the associated benefits that the acquisition of a garden could bring.

THE BRITISH EFFLORESCENCE

Matters would doubtless have continued in British academia in this fitful and half-hearted fashion had it not been for the marvellous windfall of the 1815 Apothecaries' Act – and for the further chance that teachers of outstanding ability or at least charisma were found by the three universities that more immediately chose to respond to that. These were Edinburgh, Glasgow and Cambridge.

As the licensing system brought in by the Act applied only to England and Wales, it may seem odd that the premier universities of Scotland were so much to the fore in taking up the challenge. They had their position to maintain, however, as major training-centres for

I

the medical profession internationally and they could not afford to allow the many graduates they turned out surplus to Scotland's own domestic needs to be barred from going south of the Border to pursue their careers. Cambridge's output was puny by comparison, and its medical students mostly expected to become fellows of London's College of Physicians and thereby side-step the requirements of the Act; that it reacted so positively was due to the energy and foresight of John Stevens Henslow, an ardent naturalist who was tempted to switch from the Chair of Mineralogy to that of Botany in 1825. Edinburgh's recruit was similarly in a chair already, but it was merely from that of Botany at Glasgow that Robert Graham saw fit to transfer in 1820. In replacing him, Glasgow therefore acted much the most daringly by going for a man who not only had never previously held an academic post, but did not even possess a degree and had never so much as given a lecture: he was chosen purely on the strength of his rising reputation as a plant taxonomist and, surely not least, his personal dynamism. This was William Jackson Hooker, destined to leave that university with a knighthood even before moving on to revive the Royal Gardens at Kew, the achievement for which he is mainly remembered by history. That Hooker and Henslow came from outside medicine signalled the priority that was attached to securing men who would make botany their exclusive concern and not treat the subject, as had happened too often before, as effectively a sinecure. The fact that both had given evidence of an enthusiasm for fieldwork – even if in a sister science in Henslow's case – must also have been a weighty consideration. All three appointments, following one another so closely, can be seen as symbolising a collective break with the past, the coming-of-age of botany in Britain as an academic discipline in its own right.

Unlike Henslow at Cambridge, the other two were propelled from the first by a consistently strong student demand as well as by the system special to their universities whereby class fees were paid to the teacher direct. Dependent on these for their income, professors were under a strong inducement to win as many students as they could, and that in turn placed a premium on teaching that was not only good but somewhat theatrical even. For a botany professor, therefore, the opportunities for theatricality presented by field outings made those an obvious 'must', and both Graham and Hooker lost no time in building those into their courses. Graham had the precedent of Jameson's geological forays to take as a model, but Hooker may well have been more original. Both in due course were to give Henslow the benefit of their experience.[11]

Hooker's class excursions were limited to just three each summer. Two were on Saturdays and invariably to the same couple of botanical sites near the city (Huxley, 1918: 14), while the third lasted up to 11 days and went to some distant part of the Western Highlands. Initially held around the end of May[12] but later after the end of the summer session, the "long excursion" (as it was distinguished) saw Hooker come particularly into his own. A tremendous walker who could cover 60 miles a day with ease, he had already done much exploring of the Highlands before arriving as Professor and, thanks to that, evidently had no qualms about taking up to 30 students into remote and sometimes dangerous country. Not all of those students, moreover, were necessarily known to him, for the parties often included Edinburgh ones as well – though no doubt those were hand-picked and vouched for by Graham – and even on occasions a young botanist of promise who was not a student at all, such as the bryologist William Wilson, who was admitted to one party at the instance of Henslow. One or two older botanists, though, came along as well (G. A. Walker Arnott, a later occupant of the Glasgow chair, and H. C. Watson, who was to dedicate his *New botanist's guide* of 1835–1837 to Hooker, were particular regulars) and probably one reason for inviting them was that they helped to carry the burden of responsibility. On one of the first of these sorties the rarity of inns was anticipated by taking along a marquee in a covered wagon (Figure 3) and by buying food from crofters. On another occasion, like their distant predecessors at Montpellier, the whole party spent the night on a bed of heather on the floor of a cottage (Hooker, 1902; Huxley, 1918).

The pattern at Edinburgh was broadly similar, and the *esprit de corps* with which Graham, "genial hearty" (Wilson and Geikie, 1861), infused even his one-day outings found worthy reflection in nostalgic accounts published by several of his former students. From one of these (Thomson, 1854: 123–132) we learn that the party could consist of more than 50, most if not all medical students, which suggests that the entire class was expected to attend. This would have been important, for the apathetic were thereby exposed to the infectious jollity and enthusiasm of those converted already to the delights of field botanizing. As a result, as the membership lists of the relevant societies bear witness, a substantial cohort of the future British medical profession acquired a lasting interest in the subject and pursued it as a recreation.

Graham seems to have been slower than Hooker to start what similarly became institutionalised at Edinburgh as the "long excursion". Once into his stride, however, he far outdid Hooker in adventurousness, in 1827 going as far north as the mountains of Sutherland with some of his students and in 1838 to the west of Ireland even. Many of the remoter parts of the British Isles were explored botanically for the first time on these trips, the more interesting finds on which were reported punctiliously in the most appropriate

Figure 3. "A botanical encampment at the foot of Ben Voirlich. June 22nd. 1821": drawn by R. K. G. (i.e. Robert Kaye Greville (1794–1866)). This illustration appears to be a page extracted from a book or pamphlet, published by Glasgow Litho. Press, but neither the original artwork nor the original place of publication has been discovered. (Reproduced, by kind permission, from the library of M. Walpole).

I

scientific periodicals. Graham's successor, John Hutton Balfour, a rival to Hooker in energy and robustness, who was to continue the tradition for another 30 years and more and with possibly even greater élan, kept a series of diaries in which he recorded the details of every single excursion that he led (Balfour, 1902). From these it emerges that trains were regularly made use of for the day trips from as early as 1846, with steamers supplementing or replacing them as appropriate. By taking advantage of those, what an eyewitness once wonderingly described as a "botanical army" (Anonymous, 1850) was soon descending on places as distant as Kincardine and Aberdeen and returning the same night.

It was on one of the first of Balfour's "long excursions" that the party found their passage barred by the gillies of the local laird, the Duke of Atholl (Figure 4). This led to the newly-formed Scottish Rights of Way Society bringing a successful action against the Duke (Storer, 1991: 76), a case of historic importance which also gave rise to a celebratory song, "The Battle o' Glen Tilt", with which one of the medical professors was regularly to delight audiences for many years to follow ([Maclagan], 1873; Geikie, 1904: 177). On another of those occasions, this time an arduous ten-day tour of the mountains round Braemar, the party spent a night in a cave-like gap in a pile of rocks, keeping warm by making a fire from the juniper (Balfour, 1902: 190). Way back in 1835 Balfour had conceived the idea of a systematic survey of the vegetation of the Scottish hills and the "long excursions" were in large part his means towards achieving that; unfortunately, though, it still remained unwritten at his death. Not surprisingly – and entirely fittingly, given that the Edinburgh botanists had inherited the field class tradition from their brethren in geology – when that University at last acquired a chair in the latter in 1871, its first

Figure 4. The Battle o' Glen Tilt: Balfour and his students denied passage by the Duke of Atholl's gillies, July 1847. Drawing by J. Archer (reproduced from Maclagan, 1873).

I

occupant, Alexander Geikie, speedily introduced "long excursions" too (Geikie, 1924). The term was to be taken over also by the Geologists' Association and through that nation-wide body put into still wider currency.

Elsewhere in Scotland field teaching in botany became established much more slowly, contrary to what one might have expected. As early as 1800 something of the kind had been started at Marischal College, Aberdeen, by its Professor of Civil and Natural History, James Beattie the younger, but only as a vacation activity (Trail, 1906: 157), and presumably it did not survive his departure. One who attended his class was Robert Brown. In 1819, just after completing his medical studies at the rival institution, King's College, William MacGillivray advertised in one of the local newspapers a course on botany including short excursions (Ralph, 1993: 11), but nothing more was apparently heard of it and it must be presumed to have been a flop. Sometime before 1830 one of Aberdeen's ministers who was active in studying the local flora is known to have given classes on botany which attracted medical students and others (Dickie, 1860: viii), but whether those had a field component is uncertain. Things looked up a little in 1841 when MacGillivray returned, this time to Marischal College to Beattie's old chair, but though he "delighted in excursions, to which he welcomed those who would come" (Trail, 1906: 170), apparently rose to nothing of a structured nature. That had to wait for the creation by the University of a separate chair of Botany in 1860 and the arrival of the Aberdonian veteran, George Dickie, to fill it. The duties of the post included weekly excursions and these are known to have ranged as far as the hills above Braemar (Trail, 1906), but Aberdeen was never to rise to anything on the scale of Glasgow or Edinburgh. Nor does there appear to have been any other Scottish initiative that made much of an impact either. The only one indeed traced is that of Glasgow Mechanics' Institution, which in its successive guises down the years recruited as its Lecturer on Botany at different periods from 1849 onward a series of able local field men, who in turn made excursions a popular feature of their summer courses. One, James Ramsay, so afflicted with shyness that he "shrank from platform work", made up for that by proving "quite in his element in the field" (Sexton, 1894: 80). A predecessor of his, Roger Hennedy, later produced his *Clydesdale flora*, which eventually passed through five editions, as a field guide for his students. Hennedy had one rule in taking his classes out, it is recorded: "he would never accept an invitation from any of them to enter a public-house for refreshment ... He had his biscuit and a drink of water at a well, and thus preserved his perfect independence among his students" (Simpson, 1878: xviii). Hooker and Graham would not have approved.

At Cambridge Henslow laboured under the obvious disadvantage that there was nothing to compare with the Highlands lying within convenient reach. He had to be content, therefore, with just day excursions two or three times each summer term. These were in full swing by 1827 and steadily became so popular that Henslow continued to turn out to lead them long after he had abandoned the rest of his teaching in 1839 to attend to his duties as a country vicar in Suffolk (Crompton, 1997). Among those who went on the early ones,[13] apart from his faithful henchman C. C. Babington, were Charles Darwin and the future colossus of mycology, Miles Berkeley. Usually a stage-coach was hired for these occasions (anticipating uncannily the double-decker buses used there for the same purpose in recent times) but sometimes the party went down the Cam to the Fens on the conservator's barge and then made a long trudge on foot (Jenyns, 1862: 40). Henslow would halt to give a lecturette on any rarities encountered (Barlow, 1958: 60). Unlike their counterparts in Scotland, however, the outings were far from exclusively botanical: Henslow's interests in natural history ran very wide and devotees of various of its other branches also attended in sizeable numbers. That so many did so was a greater achievement than it sounds, for the excursions had to stand comparison with the spectacular open-air lecturers of the Professor of Geology, Adam Sedgwick, and the heady experience of as many as 70 horsemen galloping across open country to hear them.

Unfortunately, that period of large field classes at Cambridge proved all too brief. In 1835 the College of Physicians in London rescinded its statute permitting graduates of Oxford or Cambridge privileged access to its fellowships, and the number of students reading medicine declined dramatically in response (Becher, 1986: 24). Within ten years Henslow's students were down to about six a year. "Never was botany at so low an ebb in this place", his effective stand-in, Babington, had to write gloomily to Balfour in 1846 (Babington, 1897: 297). For many years thereafter Babington had to look to arts students with a taste for field botany for most of his clientele.

FURTHER SPREAD

Paradoxically, while field classes were enjoying popularity at the Scottish universities as never before, the Society of Apothecaries in London took the decision in 1834 to discontinue theirs.[14] The ostensible reason was the sprawling growth of the city and the much longer tramps rendered necessary to reach open country, but the true one almost certainly was that Thomas Wheeler, who had led the herbarizings with unexampled panache for the remarkable span of 42 years, had proved an impossible act to follow. As long as he had been willing and able to carry on, the Society had doubtless been content to see the tradition preserved, even though it must have been apparent to all by then that an ability to recognise native herbs in the wild no longer had practical relevance for the training of apprentices. The massive rise in imported drugs and the spread of proprietary medicines, manufactured on a large scale and distributed maybe through wholesalers to chemists' shops, had altered the trade out of recognition. Cheaper and less restrictive guilds were happy to play host to the new wave of competitors and increasingly the Society was being bypassed. Harsh trade realities had long since relegated its "herbarizings" to the status of a mere picturesque relic.

The Apothecaries' abandonment of the field was made to look all the more anomalous by the success the concept continued to have in penetrating higher education far and wide. In only the previous year it had been taken afresh to Switzerland from Bavaria: Louis Agassiz having been introduced to field classes by his botany professor, C. F. P. von Martius, when a student at Munich in the 1820s, now introduced them in his turn on taking up a professorship specially created for him at Neuchâtel. On later emigrating from there to the United States, he promptly made a similar innovation at the newly-established Lawrence Scientific School at Harvard University, where he was appointed a professor in 1848 (Lurie, 1960). Two years before that, Spencer Fullerton Baird, later of Smithsonian Institution fame, had instituted Saturday afternoon rambles at his *alma mater*, Dickinson College in Pennsylvania; to him, by a short lead, the credit has thus been claimed for inaugurating the first formal field teaching for college students in America (Dall, 1915: 145, 169). However, W. P. C. Barton, the nephew and successor of the Edinburgh-trained Benjamin Smith Barton as Professor of Botany in the University of Pennsylvania, is on record as having taught a course on botany there for five years from 1816 which included field trips (Sheets-Pyenson and Pyenson, 1999: 39), though what form those took has yet to be investigated.

The spread was more than just geographical. Field teaching percolated from the universities and the medical schools out to the very periphery of the educational system. Its arrival in the mechanics' institutes – the evening classes of Victorian Britain – has been noted already, and around 1880 what were inelegantly termed "botany trots" were made a feature of a small private agricultural college established near Salisbury at the instance of one of its founding staff, William Fream, a self-educated agronomist of subsequent great renown who had previously taught botany and geology at its better-known counterpart at Cirencester (Jones, 1983). In reaching the agricultural colleges field classes might be said to have found their ideal habitat. Those institutions, however, were themselves still almost as much of a novelty as imparting instruction out of doors was to them.

JUSTIFICATION

Any practice with such a lengthy, multi-national pedigree as this must surely have been accepted as serving some incontestably useful function to have proved so pervasive and enduring: it can hardly have owed it merely to the chance materialising in the right places at the right times of gifted teachers with a personal fondness for field botany. Why from the very beginning had it been thought desirable for students to be taken out of the lecture-room, and even out of the botanic garden once one of those existed, and be given the opportunity of familiarising themselves with a range of common herbs at first hand? Why were professors encouraged, let alone permitted, to spend so much time and trouble on such an activity?

The literature is so bare of remarks on this basic question that it can only be that the answer was so obvious to all concerned, at least in the early days, that it seemed unnecessary to mention it. Today, the common assumption is that students were being prepared for when they set up in practice and would need to collect the raw material for their medicines themselves. That that explanation is improbable, however, is well shown by the experience of the poet George Crabbe when he took time off from his Suffolk surgery for some recreational plant hunting. "His ignorant patients, seeing him return from his walks with handfuls of weeds, decided that, as Dr. Crabbe got his medicines in the ditches, he could have little claim for payment" (Crabbe, 1834: 34) – and his practice proved unprofitable as a result. There is admittedly one record of a Leiden-trained doctor dispensing herbs of his own collecting, but that was in the remoteness of eighteenth-century Orkney (Neill, 1806: 11), where the islanders were lucky to have the services of a medical practitioner at all. Otherwise it was out of the question for surgeons and particularly physicians to dirty their hands in that way, for to have done so would have been to trespass on the territory of their rivals, the apothecaries and the druggists, and to lower their standing to that of mere tradesmen. Insufficiently sensitive as yet to such distinctions, students on the other hand were unlikely to have been averse to making preparations for sale from the herbs they were being introduced to; however, as Reeds (1991: 6) has pointed out, that would have outraged their seniors by posing a threat to their livelihoods. Including herbal recognition in courses can therefore only have been for other reasons. One of those was no doubt a worthy if vague conviction that students ought to have some acquaintance at first hand with some of the different kinds of herbs they would be going to prescribe, even if they never so much as touched one again. Another, surely more cogent, was a concern to protect practitioners-to-be from being duped by their suppliers. Several seventeenth-century authors are so vocal on this second theme in their prefaces as to suggest that it was indeed a very real worry. Thomas Johnson, for example, in his *Descriptio itineris* of 1632, lays into those middle-men, the druggists, in no uncertain terms, belabouring them for their "supreme ignorance, which springs from carelessness or arrogance". "Almost every day in the herb market", he complains with some heat, "one or other of them, to the great peril of their patients, lays himself open to the mockery of the women who deal in roots. These women know only too well the unskilled and thrust upon them brazenly what they please for what you will ... The doctor relies on the druggist and the druggist on a greedy and dirty old woman with the audacity and capacity to impose anything on him!" (Gilmour, 1972: 101). Johnson provides several examples of the substituting of one kind of herb for another with a similar name, including that of a seriously poisonous species for one widely eaten at that time as a vegetable.

If those were the official justifications for sending students out into the fields, there were further ones that might have entered into thinking less explicitly. There was the baldly utilitarian argument, for a start, that excursions provided a means of extending the range of herbs on display in the botanic garden. Some, too, may have noticed that students tended to learn more readily in the relaxed conditions of a country saunter. The bonding effect on a class of what were usually stimulating social occasions as well could also have been pointed to. In universities at these earlier periods next to no sports were played and other opportunities for informal mixing tended to be rare or unknown. One cannot help noticing how the numbers on the day trips from Edinburgh leaped dramatically – to over 200 in one memorable instance – whenever the outing was to islands in the Firth of Forth or somewhere else with a general appeal. Lastly, those who organised and led these occasions were, as we have seen, more often than not keen field men themselves: they surely took pleasure in introducing others to the attractions as well as hoped to win converts to botany in furtherance of its climb to disciplinary autonomy.

DEMANDS ON LEADERS

It was not by any means enough, though, for a professor to know his plants or want to share his expertise: to be wholly successful as a teacher in the field he needed a range of other qualities besides.

First of all, his constitution had to be robust. Leading one of these excursions for even a day could be extremely exhausting. It was not just the distance covered but the sheer length of time the leader had to be unceasingly performing that was so gruelling. Before the days of trains and buses, if the rendezvous lay in the middle of a city (initially, the herbarizings of the London Apothecaries started from St Paul's Cathedral, for instance), the lengthy walk out to open country decreed forgathering at a dauntingly early hour, 5 or 6 o'clock being quite usual. That was scarcely a hardship for students accustomed to being up and about by such a time – at Edinburgh, around 1700, the lectures in the garden in summer were scheduled for an hour earlier even than that, to enable the apprentices to be back in their masters' shops by 7 a.m. (Fletcher and Brown, 1970: 29) – but it must have been a strain for the average professor. A typical pattern was then a two-hour trudge before breakfast at an inn, little or nothing at midday and then a large meal in the evening before the long walk back again. That evening meal was in some cases formidable in itself: at the University of Pau at least one excursion wound up at a local château, at which the party was regaled in great style by the marquise (Anonymous, 1763: 37). A century later Edward Forbes's classes from King's College London rounded off the day "with songs and lots of punch" (Wilson and Geikie, 1861: 347). The professor had to be on his mettle at these, all the more so if the practice laid down at Helmstedt was followed, whereby it was the students who had to pay for the meal by way of a thank-you to him for his efforts (Reeds, 1991: 6).

A further wearying factor was the constant chatter and questioning of so many young people. Parties commonly numbered 50 or so, though at Montpellier de Candolle regularly took out between two and three hundred – though some of those, in his view, came along only for the exercise (de Candolle, 1862: 233). Linnaeus coped with comparable multitudes at Uppsala, but he had the good sense to split them up into small groups for much of the day and allocate official tasks to select individuals: an "Annotator" to keep the record of what was found, a "Fiscal" to keep discipline, and so forth (Acrel, 1796).

Discipline could indeed be a problem on occasion. It has to be remembered that apprentices were normally bound at 13 or 14 and that even as late as the 1830s students in Scotland, for instance, went up to university around that age too. Apprentices were worked very hard and a day off in the country was liable to go to their heads, especially if they had no interest in the subject and had merely been compelled to attend by their masters. During the eighteenth century the Court of the Society of Apothecaries received complaints of "disorders frequently happening" on the herbarizings,[15] complaints which eventually gave rise to threats by masters to boycott them in future in view of "the irregular and indecent behaviour" of some of those attending, lest their own apprentices "be corrupted by such examples". The complainers were appeased by a general tightening-up, which included requiring the Demonstrator to produce a report on each participant and exclusion from the post-excursion dinner as the penalty for any receiving a bad one (Wall et al., 1963: 90). Naturalists are often shy and unassuming people, and however expert and enthusiastic the leader might be he was not necessarily any good at keeping order. William Hudson, the author of the much-valued *Flora Anglica*, was the particular Demonstrator who seemingly fell down badly in that respect and had to be replaced by someone of greater sternness.

But at least leaders were spared, until the last quarter of the nineteenth century, the added complication of the mingling of the sexes. Women first made their appearance on the Edinburgh excursions in 1870, when a group of 25 constituted more than a fifth of the total who turned out for a walk along the Fife coast (Balfour, 1902: 450). Those presumably belonged to the Ladies' Educational Association, which began fielding similar-sized parties for exclusive geological outings under Geikie's leadership two years later. Emboldened, in 1882 Geikie took more than half of this women's class on a week's course in the Isle of Arran, accompanied by his wife and that of a judge to act as chaperones. As an additional precaution, the course was held the week after the male students had completed one of their own and were safely off the island (Geikie, 1924: 201). Regrettably, no accounts appear to have been left of how these social delicacies were managed in botany, at Edinburgh or elsewhere. Though segregation was to prove unsustainable, its defenders nevertheless fought back doggedly. When J. H. Salter arrived as Lecturer in Biology at University College of

Wales, Aberystwyth in 1892, he initiated a scientific society among his students and led its members out on field excursions, sometimes with a picnic included. After only a year or two, however, apparently because of concern expressed about the dangers these presented to morals, for the purpose of field meetings the society was divided into male and female branches, each with its separate outings. Deprived of what had evidently been its principal attraction, the society expired within the next few months (Anonymous, 1894; A. O. Chater, pers. comm., 1998).

A good counter to boredom or indiscipline was some light-hearted fooling. It became the custom among the students of Bernard de Jussieu to try to puzzle him by producing flowers they had cunningly mutilated or by cutting the leaves of some plant into quite a different shape. On the Edinburgh excursions Balfour's assistant, John Sadler, used to provide entertainment with impersonations of the professor ("Alisma", 1918).

It was best of all if the leader himself was something of a showman or displayed a lovable eccentricity. What student could have failed to relish being led by the long-bearded Old Testament prophet that Balfour so closely resembled in later years? Or by Thomas Wheeler, who turned out in old age for the herbarizings of the London Apothecaries "with an old hat in one hand, and a botanical knife in the other, a pair of massive spectacles, and clad in an old threadbare black coat and waistcoat and breeches, and a pair of long leather gaiters" (Field, 1878: 142)? Not for nothing was he the cousin of a famous actress.

If a leader was incapable of providing that element of theatre himself, it could still be obtained by infusing some ritual. Probably no student excursions have ever enjoyed such a lavish helping of that as those at Uppsala in the 1740s. For these, the students adopted an unconventional, lightly-fitting suit of linen as a kind of uniform; whenever a plant of particular interest was encountered, a bugle was blown and everyone rushed to hear the great Linnaeus pronounce upon it; finally, when the time came to leave for home, the party marched back in a procession, with the leader at its head, to the accompaniment of horns and drums and repeated cries of "*Vivat* Linnaeus!". Such adulation hardly went down well with the professor's colleagues, who found him unbearably egotistical as it was, and the staider ones deplored the general informality as well (Acrel, 1796: 149; Lindroth, 1983: 61). Yet nothing worked so magically as turning a field class into a parade.

Not surprisingly, some professors overstrained themselves. Recalling his Sunday excursions for his students at Montpellier, de Candolle was to write: "I never knew fatigue comparable to that of these journeys, on which, apart from being on the go for 12 or 15 hours, under the hot sun of Languedoc, it was necessary to respond all the time to questions a hundred times repeated, to give unceasingly explanations on difficult points of science, and exercise over this mass of young people the surveillance necessary to ensure that no disorder took place ... On arriving home, I had scarcely an idea than to hurl myself into my bed". After one of those days he went down with quite a serious attack of fever (de Candolle, 1862: 23–24). As the obituarist of Adrien de Jussieu pointed out, on the western edge of Europe it was not only the long and testing distances that caused leaders to run risks with their health: it was also the frequent drenching they were liable to receive in unexpected downpours (Decaisne, 1854). But it was particularly the Scottish professors, with their forays into mountainous terrain lasting at least a week, who were inclined to put their physical powers to the test to a point little short of recklessness. Hooker and Balfour (whose nickname was "Woody Fibre") were both fortunately hardy in the extreme and so too was MacGillivray, who could regularly walk even the most energetic of his students

I

"into limp helplessness" (MacGillivray and Thomson, 1910). But Dickie, MacGillivray's successor, caught pneumonia the very first time he took students up into the hills, the subsequent complications from which eventually compelled his premature retirement (Trail, 1906). Graham, similarly, found one of his student excursions so exhausting that he believed it responsible for bringing on his final illness – though the real cause of that, it subsequently turned out, was a spinal tumour (Ransford, 1846).

SOME BY-PRODUCTS

Apart from their value educationally, field classes brought some benefits to the wider botanical community as well. In Britain, if not elsewhere, the sheer number of students involved in the decades after 1815 were large enough and regular enough to constitute a worthwhile market for makers of the obligatory field equipment: the plant-press, the botanical spade (or "spud') and the tin collecting-box (or vasculum). Thenceforward other botanists no longer had to have recourse to local craftsmen and have those made for them individually, at an inevitably higher cost. The Scottish universities, in particular, popularised the use of a sensibly far roomier type of vasculum, slung from the shoulder, in place of the small, hand-held models which botanists had carried previously and into which specimens mostly had to be squeezed to the detriment of their usefulness for study (Allen, 1959). This was such a radically improved version that Greville (1840) felt it deserved a name of its own and proposed designating it the "magnum".

The classes also generated purpose-made books: not only the guides to the local botanical walks that so many leaders from Bauhin and Tournefort onwards had produced, but also aids to identifying the plants of a country as a whole and framed with the needs of students particularly in mind. Hooker's *Flora Scotica*, published in time to be used on his second course, was a preliminary, half-way step in that direction; his subsequent *British flora*, nine years later, was so much better suited to the field than its expensive, multi-volume predecessors that it proved a considerable success commercially and went through eight editions.

Most importantly of all, the classes inspired, if sometimes indirectly, the forming of societies in which field excursions were newly given prominence or for which they were even the *raison d'être*. The earliest with this seeming parentage was the shadowy "*socii itinerantes*", a small coterie of fellow veterans of the herbarizings of the London Apothecaries who rode out under the lead of Thomas Johnson on exploratory tours of southern England in the years round 1630.[16] The latest may have been a student association founded at Edinburgh in 1823, suggestively soon after Graham's arrival there from Glasgow (though Jameson's field classes may equally well have been the determining influence,[17] particularly as the subjects covered ranged well beyond just botany). Known as the Plinian Society, this had weekly indoor meetings during the winter and excursions on Saturdays in summer. The accounts of these trips published in the Society's *Transactions* may well have been the model for those later produced by Balfour, who, significantly, belonged to this body in his student days (as also did Charles Darwin).

Through the Plinian Society the field class tradition accidentally struck gold. Three of the keener members went to live in Berwickshire on leaving the University and kept up the habit there of meeting from time to time for natural history outings. From these arose the idea of starting a club with such outings as its centrepiece, an idea that was carried

I

into being in 1831 (Elliot, 1871: 11–33). Although a number of societies of naturalists in different parts of Britain had been holding field excursions well before that time, it was not a practice followed by the more prominent ones which had come into being in most of the cities and larger towns. These had all blindly followed the contemporary fashion for learned institutions to model themselves on a classical academy, thereby rendering themselves both immobile and exclusive due to the formality and high expenditure inseparable from that way of proceeding. The achievement of the Berwickshire Club was to demonstrate that bricks and mortar were unnecessary for a body of naturalists to function productively and reputably: field meetings and published reports were alone sufficient. This structural simplification was exactly what the subject had been needing and the new, alternative model was seized upon with alacrity up and down the country, producing a liberating transformation in the way in which this group of studies organized itself throughout much of the Victorian era (Allen, 1987: 248).

Of the various branches of natural history, botany and geology were the two best fitted by their very character to come up with this transforming model, in as much as they were the only two sufficiently well-developed by the period in question that also found it practicable to investigate in the field in large groups. Geology, so fashionable and exciting in those years, might well have been the one that pulled that innovatory trigger, had it only become entrenched in the universities earlier. That the role fell instead to botany was thanks to the longer and stronger tradition that field teaching had in that discipline academically, an advantage which it owed to having been conceived within the womb of medicine and enjoyed down the centuries a protected position under that respected parent. It is to the botanical field class, consequently, that we have to look to find one of the basic roots from which natural history in the sense of a social entity has developed over the years.

ACKNOWLEDGEMENTS

This is an extended version of a paper given at a Wellcome Institute symposium, "The History of Botany and Medicine", in April 1998 and, in a more rudimentary form, at the 150th anniversary celebrations of Cambridge University Botanic Garden in July 1981. Still more rudimentary versions constituted the 1979 Sloane Lecture of the Faculty of the History and Philosophy of Medicine and Pharmacy of the Society of Apothecaries of London and the main substance of a talk at a joint meeting of the Pharmaceutical Society of Great Britain and the Botanical Society of the British Isles in February 1967 (summarised in the *Pharmaceutical journal* **198**: 290–291).

I am indebted to Nita Burnby for stimulating exchanges over the years in the light of her deep knowledge of the history of pharmacy and to her and to Malcolm Nicolson for scrutinising the paper in draft. I have Nicolson also and Charles Nelson to thank for putting me on to some out-of-the-way Scottish and Irish sources. Gareth Evans similarly gave invaluable help more particularly in clarifying William Salisbury's activities, and for bringing to my notice the Hooker–Hobson letter and the Aberystwyth excursions I have Anne Secord and Arthur Chater to thank respectively. I am further indebted to the late Douglas Whittet, Charles Webster, Max Walters and Janet Browne for their successive invitations to lecture on this subject, which have led me to keep probing more widely and more persistently than I surely would have done otherwise.

NOTES

[1] William Turner would have the prior claim were it not for his decade-long interruption of his clerical career to qualify in and then practise medicine. Already before that he had immersed himself in the herbals, possibly with medicine as an alternative career option in mind.

[2] It was long a matter of dispute whether the Padua or the Pisa garden was the earlier. The respective foundation dates established by the research of Chiarugi (1953) now appear to have received general acceptance.

[3] The same argument would have applied if Stresemann (1975: 16) had been correct in stating that Valerius Cordus made a botanical trip through Italy with some of his students from the University of Wittemberg, in the Electorate of Saxony, in 1544. That, however, was based on a misreading: Cordus is described – by Pierre Belon – as accompanied merely by two friends (Greene, 1909: 274; Delaunay, 1922). It is unlikely that field classes were in being at a German university as early as the 1540s, particularly as Cordus was unacquainted with Ghini before that Italian trip.

[4] The translation of the statute given here omits three words from the original Latin: "*in vicinos menses*" Reeds has read as "in the next months". But that not only seems meaningless in the context, but also requires the surely unlikely assumption that one of Europe's leading universities would have issued a document with legal force in which the accusative case is used instead of the ablative glaringly incorrectly. The explanation would appear to be that the text has undergone corruption. I am indebted to my colleague, Professor V. Nutton, for the suggestion that "menses" was originally "montes". On that reading the excursions were to be "into the neighbouring hills".

[5] Frustratingly little evidence appears to have come to light as to the existence or otherwise of field classes in Germany during the next 200 years. The only instance traced is at Göttingen, where Christian Wilhelm Büttner is known to have taken students out on excursions after becoming director of the botanic garden there in 1760. An account of one of those was published in *Hannover Magazin* in 1765; the party on that occasion numbered nine, of whom only seven were students (Hedge, 1967).

[6] In a letter to Curtis (now in the Curtis Museum, Alton) the Revd John Lightfoot refers to "yr. herbarizing excursions with your pupils." Unfortunately the year is missing from the date, and though Curtis (1941: 63) thought it probably 1783 he gave no reason for that conclusion. Lightfoot died in February 1788, so it must antedate the move to Brompton. It could, however, relate to Curtis's period in the employ of the Society of Apothecaries.

[7] A copy of the folio sheet in question is in the British Library (press mark 958.a.5(2)). It has been quoted from successively by Bacon (1913), Curtis (1941: 94) and Eastwood (1953: 158). Subsequently individual excursions were advertised in *The Times* (for example, in issue no. 2974 of 28 April 1794).

[8] But who can have been the "Dr. Wurzel", the professor of botany at one of the London medical schools, an excursion of whose class to Windsor was the subject of two satirical pieces in *Punch* in 1842 (1: 937, 257)? A reference to his attending a meeting at the College of Physicians makes the likeliest candidate Frederick John Farre, Censor of the College and Lecturer in Botany at St Bartholomew's Hospital in those years. There is a record of his taking students on a field excursion in the *Botanical gazette* 1: 319 (1849).

[9] G. Eriksson, pers. comm., 1983.

[10] Just as it also apparently was in the case of their contemporaries at Glasgow University, who similarly "made sallies out into the fields and fells" there (Threlkeld, 1726: preface).

[11] Hooker to Henslow, 14 April 1827 (f. 3); Graham to Henslow, 26 April 1828, Henslow Letters, Herbarium Archive, Cambridge University Library.

[12] Hooker to Edward Hobson, 8 June [1822], Department of Botany, The Manchester Museum.

[13] Henslow had lists of the plants collected on the earlier of his excursions printed and circulated, for the benefit of the students who attended. Examples of these survive in the library of the Linnean Society of London (*Opuscula* C 274 and C 278) and there is a complete set at Cambridge University.

[14] The Society has held herborizings on rare occasions since, but none expressly for students. At Apothecaries Hall there are photographs taken on one in 1902, when the party was led by the Master of the Society.

[15] Garden Committee minutes, February 1724, Society of Apothecaries MSS, Guildhall Library, London.

[16] The words "*socii itinerantes*" were employed by contemporaries with sufficient regularity to suggest that it was regarded as an established entity, albeit one without any formal structure, procedures or possessions. A Southampton apothecary indeed refers to it as a society (C. D. Whittet, pers. comm., 1985).

[17] Darwin, for one, was under the impression that Jameson was the founder (Barlow, 1958: 50).

REFERENCES

ACREL, J. G., 1796 *Tal, om Läkare-vetenskaps grundläggning och tillväxt vid rikets älsta lärosäte i Upsala.* Stockholm: J. P. Lindh.

"ALISMA", 1918 *Reminiscences of a student's life at Edinburgh in the Seventies.* Edinburgh: Oliver & Boyd.

ALLEN, D. E., 1959 The history of the vasculum. *Proceedings of the Botanical Society of the British Isles* **3**: 135–150.

ALLEN, D. E., 1987 The natural history society in Britain through the years. *Archives of natural history* **14**: 243–259.

ANONYMOUS, 1763 *Les botaniques, ou les parties de plaisir des étudians en médecine de l'Université de Pau, dans la recherche des plantes.* The Hague: Erialed.

ANONYMOUS, 1805 Account of Danish botanists. *Annals of botany* **1**: 405–407.

ANONYMOUS, 1816 *Curtis's botanical magazine* **43**: t. 1844.

ANONYMOUS, 1850 Botanical trip to Aberdeen. *Gardeners' magazine of botany* [**2**]: 40.

ANONYMOUS, 1892 *Félix et Thomas Platter à Montpellier.* Montpellier: Camille Coulet.

ANONYMOUS, 1894 College notes. *University College of Wales magazine* **17**: 22.

ARBER, A., 1986 *Herbals: their origins and evolution.* Third Edition. Cambridge: Cambridge University Press.

B[ABINGTON], A. M. (editor), 1897 *Memorials, journals and botanical correspondence of Charles Cardale Babington.* Cambridge: Macmillan & Bowes.

BACON, G., 1913 Lost London flowers. *Selborne magazine* **24**: 210–212.

BALFOUR, I. B., 1902 Botanical excursions made by Professor John Hutton Balfour, in the years from 1846 to 1878 inclusively. *Notes from the Royal Botanic Garden, Edinburgh* **2**: 22–497.

BARLOW, N. (editor), 1958 *The autobiography of Charles Darwin 1809–1882.* London: Collins.

BECHER, H. V., 1986 Voluntary science in nineteenth century Cambridge University to the 1850s. *British journal for the history of science* **19**: 57–87.

BOERHAAVE, H. (editor), 1743 Preface, in VAILLANT, S., *Botanicon Parisiense, ou denombrement ... des plantes, qui se trouvent aux environs de Paris.* Third edition. Leiden & Paris: Briasson.

BRITTEN, J., 1896 In memory of Henry Trimen. *Journal of botany* **34**: 489–494.

BURNBY, J., 1994 Some early London physic gardens. *Pharmaceutical historian* **94**(4): 2–8.

CASTELLANI, C., 1970. Aldrovandi, Ulisse, in GILLISPIE, C. C. (editor) *Dictionary of scientific biography* **1**: 108–110. New York: Scribner's.

CHIARUGI, A., 1953 Le date di fondazione dei primi orti botanici del mondo. *Nuovo giornale botanico Italiano,* new series, **60**: 785–839.

CHIARUGI, A., 1957 Nel quarto centenario della morte di Luca Ghini, 1490–1556. *Webbia* **13**: 1–14.

COWAN, J. M., 1933 The history of the Royal Botanic Garden, Edinburgh. *Notes from the Royal Botanic Garden, Edinburgh* **19**: 1–62.

CRABBE, G., jr., 1834 *The poetical works of the Rev. George Crabbe: with his letters and journals, and his life.* Vol. 1. London: John Murray.

CRESTOIS, P., 1953 *Contribution à l'histoire de l'enseignement de la pharmacie. L'enseignement de la botanique au Jardin Royal des Plantes de Paris.* Cahous: Coueslant.

CROMPTON, G., 1997 Botanizing in Cambridgeshire in the 1820s. *Nature in Cambridgeshire* no. **39**: 59–73.

CURTIS, W. H., 1941 *William Curtis, 1746–1799.* Winchester: Warren & Co.

CZERWIAKOWSKI, I. R., 1864 *Rys historyczno-statystczny Ogrudu Botanicznego Krakówskiego.* Kraków: Kraków Scientific Society.

DALL, W. H., 1915 *Spencer Fullerton Baird. A biography.* Philadelphia & London: Lippincott.

DANIEL, C. H. and BARKER, W. R., 1900 *Worcester College.* London: F. E. Robinson & Co.

DE CANDOLLE, A. L. P. (editor), 1862 *Mémoires et souvenirs d'Augustin-Pyramus de Candolle.* Geneva & Paris: Cherbulicz.

DECAISNE, J., 1854 Notice historique sur M. Adrien de Jussieu. *Bulletin de la Société Botanique de France* **1**: 386–400

DECAISNE, J., 1861 Jussieu, Adrien de, in HOEFER, J. C. F. (editor) *Nouvelle biographie générale* **27**. Paris: Firmin Didot.

DELAUNAY, P., 1922 L'aventureuse existence de Pierre Belon du Mans (part 1). *Revue du seizième siècle* **9**: 250–268.

DICKIE, G., 1860 *The botanist's guide to the counties of Aberdeen, Banff, and Kincardine.* Aberdeen, etc.: A. Brown & Co.

DULIEU, L., 1966 Guillaume Rondelet. *Clio medica* **1**: 89–111.

EASTWOOD, D., 1953 *Mirror of flowers.* London: Derek Verschoyle.

ELLIOT, W., 1871 Opening address. *Transactions of the Botanical Society of Edinburgh* **11**: 1–41, 193–255.

ENGLISH, M. P., 1990 *Victorian values: the life and times of Dr Edwin Lankester, M.D., F.R.S.* Bristol: Biopress.

ERIKSSON, G., 1969 *Botanikens historia i Sverige intill år 1800.* Stockholm: Almqvist & Wicksell.

EVANS, G., 1998 John Keats, poet and herbalist. *Herbs* **23** (2): 1–8.

FIELD, H., 1878 *Memoirs of the botanical garden at Chelsea* ... (edited by R. H. Semple). London: privately published.

FINDLEN, P., 1994 *Possessing nature: museums, collecting, and science in early modern Italy.* Berkeley, etc.: University of California Press.

FLETCHER, H. R., and BROWN, W. H., 1970 *The Royal Botanic Garden Edinburgh 1670–1970.* Edinburgh: HMSO.

GEIKIE, A., 1904 *Scottish reminiscences.* Glasgow: Maclehose.

GEIKIE, A., 1924 *A long life's work: an autobiography.* London: Macmillan.

GILMOUR, J. S. L. (editor), 1972 *Thomas Johnson: botanical journeys in Kent and Hampstead* (translated by C. E. Raven *et alii*). Pittsburgh: Hunt Botanical Library.

GREENE, E. L., 1909 *Landmarks of botanical history.* Part 1. Washington, D.C.: Smithsonian Institution.

GREVILLE, R. K., 1840 Directions for collecting botanical specimens and preserving them for the herbarium. *Annual report of the Botanical Society of Edinburgh for 1838–39*: 80–89.

GUNTHER, A. E., 1974 A note on the autobiographical manuscripts of John Edward Gray (1800–1875). *Journal of the Society for the Bibliography of Natural History* **7**: 35–76.

GUNTHER, A. E., 1980 The miscellaneous autobiographical manuscripts of John Edward Gray (1800–1875). *Bulletin of the British Museum (Natural History)*, historical series, **6**: 199–244.

GUNTHER, R. T., 1922 *Early British botanists and their gardens.* Oxford; privately published.

HEDGE, I. C., 1967 The specimens of Paul Dietrich Giseke in the Edinburgh herbarium. *Notes from the Royal Botanic Garden Edinburgh* **28**: 73–86.

HENIGER, J. and SOSEF, M. S. M., 1989 Antoni Gaymans (*ca* 1630–1680) and his herbaria. *Archives of natural history* **16**: 147–168.

HETT, F. P. (editor), 1932 *The memoirs of Sir Robert Sibbald (1641–1722).* London: Oxford University Press.

HOLLOWAY, S. W. F., 1966 The Apothecaries' Act, 1815: a reinterpretation. *Medical history* **10**: 107–129, 221–236.

HOLLOWAY, S. W. F., 1970 Significance of the Apothecaries' Act, 1815. *Pharmaceutical historian* **1**: 6–9.

HOOKER, J. D., 1902 A sketch of the life and labours of Sir William Jackson Hooker. *Annals of botany* **16**: ix–ccxx.

HUXLEY, L., 1918 *Life and letters of Joseph Dalton Hooker.* Volume 1. London: John Murray.

JENNETT, S. (editor), 1963 *Journal of a younger brother: the life of Thomas Platter as a medical student in Montpellier at the close of the sixteenth century.* London: Frederick Muller.

JENYNS, L., 1862 *Memoir of the Rev. John Stevens Henslow.* London: Van Voorst.

JONES, G. E., 1983 William Fream: agriculturist and educator. *Journal of the Royal Agricultural Society of England* **144**: 30–44.

KELLER, A. G., 1972 Ghini, Luca, in GILLISPIE, C. C. (editor) *Dictionary of scientific biography* **5**: 383–384. New York: Scribner's.

KIRKPATRICK, T. P. C., 1912 *History of the medical teaching in Trinity College Dublin and the School of Physic in Ireland*. Dublin: Hanna & Neale.

LINDEBOOM, G. A., 1968 *Herman Boerhaave. The man and his work*. London: Methuen.

LINDEBOOM, G. A., 1984 *Dutch medical biography: a biographical dictionary of Dutch physicians and surgeons 1475–1975*. Amsterdam: Rodopi.

LINDROTH, S., 1983 The two faces of Linnaeus, pp 1–62 in FRÄNGSMYR, T. (editor) *Linnaeus, the man and his work*. Berkeley, etc.: University of California Press.

L'OBEL, M. de, 1655 *Stirpium illustrationes*. London: Thomas Warren.

LOUIS, A., 1980 *Mathieu de l'Obel 1538–1616. Episode de l'histoire de la botanique*. Ghent & Louvain: Story-Scientia.

LUKIS, W. C. (editor), 1882 *The family memoirs of the Rev. William Stukeley, M.D., Vol. 1*. Surtees Society **73**. Durham: Andrews & Co.

LURIE, E., 1960 *Louis Agassiz: a life in science*. Chicago & London: University of Chicago Press.

LUXFORD, G., 1849 An occurrence of *Doronicum plantagineum* at Shooter's Hill. *Phytologist* **3**: 453.

MACGILLIVRAY, W. and THOMSON, J. A., 1910 *Life of William MacGillivray*. London: John Murray.

[MACLAGAN, D.], 1873 *Nugae canorae medicae: lays by the poet laureate of the New Town Dispensary*. Second edition. Edinburgh: Edmonston & Douglas.

MARTYN, J., 1732 *History of plants growing about Paris ... accommodated to the plants growing in Great Britain*. 2 volumes. London: Rivington.

[MARTYN, T.], 1763 *A short account of the late donation of a botanic garden to the University of Cambridge by the Rev. Dr. Walker*. Cambridge: privately published.

MEYNELL, G., 1980 The Royal Botanic Society's garden, Regent's Park. *London journal* **6**: 135–146.

[NEILL, P.], 1804 Short biographical memoir of the late Mr. John Mackay, Superintendent of the Royal Botanic Garden at Edinburgh. *Scots magazine* **66**: 95–99.

NEILL, P., 1806 *A tour through some of the islands of Orkney and Shetland*. Edinburgh: Constable.

NELSON, E. C. and PROBERT, A., 1994 *A man who can speak of plants. Dr. Thomas Coulter (1793–1843) of Dundalk in Ireland, Mexico and Alta California*. Dublin: privately published.

NICOLAS, J.-P., 1963 Adanson, the man, pp 1–121 in LAWRENCE, G. H. M. (editor) *Adanson. The bicentennial of Michel Adanson's "Familles des Plantes"*, volume **1**. Pittsburgh: Hunt Botanical Library.

PENA, P. and L'OBEL, M. de, 1571 *Stirpium adversaria nova*. London: Thomas Purfoot.

RALPH, R., 1993 *William MacGillivray*. London: HMSO.

RANSFORD, C., 1846 Biographical sketch of the late Professor Graham. *Phytologist* **2**: 572–573.

REEDS, K. M, 1976 Renaissance humanism and botany. *Annals of science* **33**: 519–542.

REEDS, K. M., 1991 *Botany in medieval and Renaissance universities*. New York & London: Garland Publishing.

RITCHIE, J., 1952 Natural history and the emergence of geology in the Scottish universities. *Transactions of Edinburgh Geological Society* **15**: 297–316.

ROBERTS, W., 1900 The London Botanic Garden. *Gardeners' chronicle*, series 3, **27**: 65–66.

SABBATANI, L., 1923 Alcuni documenti su la vita di Luca Ghini. *Atti e memoria della R. Academia di Scienze, Lettre e Arti (Padua)*, new series, **39**: 243–248.

SALISBURY, W, 1810 *Gentleman's magazine* **80**: 113–114.

SALISBURY, W., 1816 *The botanist's companion, or an introduction to the knowledge of practical botany, and the uses of plants*. London: Longman.

SARTON, G., 1947 *Introduction to the history of science*. Volume 2. Washington, D.C.: Carnegie Institution.

SEXTON, A. H., 1894 *The first Technical College. A sketch of "The Andersonian" and the institutions descended from it 1796–1894*. London: Chapman & Hall.

I

SHEETS-PYENSON, S. and PYENSON, L., 1999 Curricular value: natural history in early nineteenth-century medicine, in PYENSON, L. (editor), *Value: pondering goodness*. Lafayette: Center for Louisiana Studies, University of Southwestern Louisiana.

SIMPSON, W., 1878 Biographical sketch of Roger Hennedy, Professor of Botany, Andersonian University, pp xi–xxiii in HENNEDY, R., *The Clydesdale flora*. Fourth edition. Glasgow: Hugh Hopkins.

STORER, P., 1991 *Exploring Scottish hill tracks*. London: Warner Books.

STRESEMANN, E., 1975 *Ornithology from Aristotle to the present* (translated by H. J. Epstein and C. Epstein). Cambridge, Massachusetts & London: Harvard University Press.

SZAFER, W., 1969 *Concise history of botany in Cracow against the background of six centuries of the Jagiellonian University* (translated by W. Kulerski and H. Markiewicz). Warsaw: Central Institute for Scientific, Technical and Economic Information.

THOMSON, S., 1854 *Wanderings among the wild flowers*. London: Groombridge.

THRELKELD, C., 1726 *Synopsis stirpium hibernicarum*. Dublin: Davys.

TRAIL, J. W. H., 1906 Natural sciences in the Aberdeen universities, pp 147–200 in ANDERSON, P. J. (editor). *Studies in the history and development of the University of Aberdeen*. Aberdeen: privately published.

TURNER, D. (editor), 1835 *Extracts from the literary and scientific correspondence of Richard Richardson, M. D., F. R. S.* Yarmouth: privately published.

WALL, C., CAMERON, H. C. and UNDERWOOD, E. A., 1963 *A history of the Worshipful Society of Apothecaries of London*. Volume 1. London, etc. : Oxford University Press.

WALTERS, S. M., 1981 *The shaping of Cambridge botany*. Cambridge: Cambridge University Press.

WEBSTER, C., 1986 The medical faculty and the Physic Garden, pp 683–723 in SUTHERLAND, L. S. and MITCHELL, L. G. (editors), *The history of the University of Oxford*. Volume 5. (The eighteenth century). Oxford: Clarendon Press.

WILSON, G. and GEIKIE, A., 1861 *Memoir of Edward Forbes, F. R. S.* Cambridge & London: Macmillan.

WOODS, J., 1843 Notes of a botanical excursion in France, in the summer of 1843. *Phytologist* 1: 785–801, 828–834, 853–865.

ZEMANEK, A., 1993 The history of the Botanic Garden of the Jagiellonian University in Cracow, in ZEMANEK, A. and ZEMANEK, B. (editors), *Studies on the history of botanical gardens and arboreta in Poland*. Kraków: Polish Academy of Sciences.

II

Natural history in Britain in the eighteenth century[1]

INTRODUCTION

It is virtually a cliché that the eighteenth century was an age of transition. Nevertheless, like most clichés, it happens to be true. In a very recognizable way, the century started off feeling 'ancient' and ended up looking 'modern'. Its first twenty years or so seemed like a left-over from the previous era, a kind of morainic detritus abandoned in the retreat: indeed, historians today often speak of a 'long' seventeenth century which ended in Britain in 1714, with the arrival of the Hanoverians and the triumph of the Whigs. Then came the 'empty quarter', that middle period so depressingly inhospitable to detailed studies of every kind, yet so crucial for the gestating of new ways of looking at nature. Then finally came those wonderful last 40 years, bursting with new vigour, taking us into the Romantic Movement on the one hand and into the so-called Industrial Revolution on the other. Somehow 1760 feels closer in mood to 1860 than it does to 1700 or even to 1720. In those mysterious middle years Western Man suddenly grew up. In the fertile soil of scepticism a dispassionate distancing occurred, seemingly quite by accident. One result was that outburst of intellectual creativity that goes by the name of the Enlightenment; the other was a responsiveness to wild scenery and the birth of that empathy that lies at the heart of latter-day natural history.

Clearly, it was a century in which some very profound changes took place—against a backcloth which, confusingly, stayed much the same throughout. For until the closing years there is little of that sense of movement that the nineteenth century conveys: no repeated tides of reform, no ever-spreading railway lines thrusting their way through a virgin landscape, no obsession with Progress. Physically it is static, emotionally and intellectually it is dynamic.

DIFFICULTIES OF TRAVEL

The main reason for that stasis was the difficulty of moving around (on land, that is: on water it was a different matter). For the would-be traveller the only alternative to his own two feet was to be carried or drawn by horses, and owning or hiring horse-power was a privilege open only to a minority. Even the horse-propelled, though, were not that much better off, for roads were at best poor and at worst almost unbelievably frightful. Although the trunk routes increasingly came into the hands of turnpike trusts as the century wore on, the tolls levied by these long fed through into improvements in a few cases only. Responsibility for the upkeep of all the rest lay with each parish through which the roads passed, and the six days' unpaid labour which its surveyor of the highways was empowered to require of the parishioners for that purpose was liable to be obtained only by forceful individuals careless of their popularity locally. The consequence was that roads tended to be repaired only *in extremis*. Before that occurred, they had often deteriorated to the point of actual danger—in particular because of the unsuspected depth of the water that collected in their pot-holes.

Even when repairing did take place, the materials used were primitive and the surface they produced can rarely have been level. As a result, another of the miseries of travel was coach-sickness. Gilbert White is well known to have been one sufferer from this, which led him to undertake long, solitary journeyings on horseback instead. Yet that form of travel was not without dangers of its own, for in many areas the roads were infested with robbers and a lone rider who betrayed by the cut of his clothes gentlemanly status was sure to be an inviting target.

THE TAXONOMIC IMPERATIVE

Fortunately, to pursue natural history it was not essential to travel, or at any rate to travel very far. Even in southern England the more conspicuous sections of the local flora and fauna had still been but scantily investigated and there were notable discoveries waiting to be made virtually on every naturalist's doorstep. Any content to stay just within their own neighbourhood could be usefully occupied for many years, especially if, like Gilbert White, their primary interest was birds and they could therefore sit and wait for the rarities to come to them. For most naturalists, though, adding to science's stock of species constituted the greater lure, and to find those it was increasingly necessary to brave foreign parts—either by exploring Britain's remoter regions, in the footsteps of Ray and Willughby and Lhwyd, or by taking ship to distant lands, as Banks, most notably, was to do in due course.

The eighteenth century was the first great age of taxonomic description as a result. The drive to ransack the globe for its variety had originally been in the service of medicine: more and more now it was becoming an end in itself, an international competition to gather in as much as possible and to acquire the prestige of owning the richest collections. No longer was the accent on the useful or the merely curious: the aim now was to achieve comprehensiveness, to bring together under the eyes of science the entirety of Creation. As a result, under the sheer weight of novelty flowing in and requiring to be described, classification was falling into chaos. Latin names were long and cumbersome, insufficiently standardized and commonly applied to entities that their original authors had not intended. Worse, new names were continually being coined in ignorance, or even defiance, of the fact that the plants or animals that these were bestowed upon had received at least one name from someone else already. Descriptions in any case were often so inadequate, and the specimens on which they were based so fragmentary or poorly-preserved, that it was frequently impossible to be sure even what had been meant by them.

PRIVATE COMMUNICATIONS

Although collecting and describing were the sole concerns of almost all naturalists of that era, for the first two-thirds of the century the manpower was far too small for the size of the task that confronted it in this respect. Indeed, except in Europe's largest cities there were still too few naturalists even to gather together and form themselves into societies. In London, thanks to the programme of field instruction regularly laid on by the Apothecaries from 1620 or even earlier, a large enough bunch of botanists had contrived to emerge by the final years of the previous century to coalesce into a kind of club, meeting informally in one or more of the city's then numerous coffee houses (Jessop, 1989). In the 1720s a thoroughgoing society, albeit one in miniature and mainly composed of students, grew out of that self-same soil and briefly flourished (Allen, 1967).[2] By 1740 there were even enough collectors of butterflies and moths in and around the Capital to constitute a society too (Allen, 1966)—the first in a long series of all sadly ephemeral bodies to be devoted to that study until the Thirties of the century following. Collective activity, alas, just did not prosper: once such a grouping suffered some major setback, in particular the loss of its leading light, it was generally incapable of renewing itself. In the absence of any jointly-owned possession, such as a journal or a museum, to help cement it together, it was as easy and painless for members to slip away as it had been for them to enrol in the first place. It was only with the founding of the Linnean Society, in 1788, with famously valuable collections as its core, that this perpetual weakness began to be overcome.

In default of societies to belong to, naturalists were obliged to develop networks of correspondents instead. These were one of the century's most characteristic features. In as much as they substituted for papers read at meetings or published in printed volumes of transactions or proceedings, letters necessarily ran to some length; so keeping one's network fuelled entailed a great deal of time and effort, far more than membership of a society would have required, just as the outlay on postage must have considerably exceeded over time the cost of annual subscriptions. That very expenditure of trouble, however, served to ensure that letters received were commonly preserved, some of them even, with luck, like those of John Ellis (Savage, 1948) or Richard Richardson (Turner, 1835) or the several recipients of the *Selborne* correspondence, perhaps eventually to have permanency and general access conferred on them by being reproduced in print. On the whole, though, it was inevitably a private activity and an enormous amount of information, which other naturalists would have found of value or at any rate of interest, and which we today would dearly like to have as historical benchmarks, must have failed to be kept, discarded as too banal to be fit for anything but refuse.

PUBLICATION

Further penalties of isolation were the difficulty of knowing whether one's identifications were correct or observations original and the great expense at that period of purchasing the necessary works of reference—always supposing that those were known about or had yet even been written. Books of all kinds continued to be expensive (even a novel cost at least 7s. 6d., a large outlay in contemporary terms, as much as five meals in a tavern), because printing continued to be unmechanised and the people who could afford to buy them, or even want to read or consult them, were still relatively limited in number. For learned works that number was inevitably smaller still, and publication of those was normally practicable only by public subscription. The collecting of subscribers, moreover, was an onerous and expensive

II

process in itself, especially as it was customary for a list of their names to be included in the eventual book—a custom for which, all the same, later researchers have much reason to be grateful (and the fruits of which have by no means yet been exploited to the full).

The high price of books even so had one helpful side-effect: it kept them as desirable articles of luxury, enabling them to serve as status symbols for the affluent. As often as not a rich library was more the mark of a deep purse than evidence of cultivation and learning, a room with merely tasteful-looking shelves. Publishers sensed this and played on the weakness accordingly. The result was an emphasis on what would nowadays be termed 'coffee-table' books: books which, in the words of one contemporary, were "maide for pompe to fill a Library & more for outward show than reale use, . . . having very little within."[3] Such books sold, then as always, primarily on the strength of their illustrations, especially if those illustrations were coloured. And as there were few subjects that lent themselves so well to this as natural history, it consequently had the good fortune to develop an appeal commercially just at the period when more and more naturalists were producing book-length work that they wished to put into print. A reasonably workable compromise was the result.

That is not to say that the market for books on natural history that emerged was wholly or even mainly the product of what naturalists themselves chose to write. In the same way the purchasers of such works were very much more plentiful than the actual number of practising naturalists. This is something that we need to bear well in mind when we come across such deceptively bracing assertions as William Sherard's in 1720, that "Natural History of all sorts is much in demand,"[5] or Peter Collinson's in 1747, that works on natural history "sell the best of any books in England."[6] These statements do not refer to manuals of identification or even to the kind of recreational reading that naturalists write for one another; they do not necessarily refer even to books on the natural history of Britain. They merely tell us that the average library-builder was as keen then as ever on books with attractive pictures on reasonably elevating-sounding subjects.

Despite the great boost that the size and buoyancy of this 'popular' market in natural history books gave to the study in the stricter sense, it had two noticeable drawbacks.

Firstly, seductive illustrations came to be a *sine qua non* if a book of natural history was to attract a commercial publisher, regardless of the quality of the accompanying text. Some so-called authors were in reality just artists who relied on others to contribute the scientific 'meat', sometimes anonymously—legitimately in the case of Benjamin Wilkes's *The English Moths and Butterflies* (Whalley, 1972), illegitimately, because substantially plagiarized, in that of Eleazar Albin's *Natural History of Birds* (Stresemann, 1975: 48). Wilkes and Albin were both painters of miniatures by profession and presumably had no skill with the pen. But it is surely significant, even so, that it was their names alone that featured: the plates were what mattered, as far as the publishers were concerned. What is more, alas, the plates sold books even if they were badly done, so strong was the demand—at any rate initially. Albin was "as clumsy with the pen as with the brush and understood nothing of his subject" (Stresemann, 1975: 48) and the colouring in his plates has been described as child-like, yet his *Natural History of Birds* evidently sold well enough to allow it to run to three volumes spaced over several years (1731–38) and straight after that to go into a second edition. Later in the century, however, buyers seem to have grown more discriminating as competition intensified and standards rose, and illustrations had to be good if they were to 'carry' a learned text and make its publication viable commercially. John Latham's own, rather humdrum engravings for his *General Synopsis of Birds* (1781–85) presumably fell down in this respect, for a switch to a different publisher after the first volume suggests that its sales had proved disappointing. Latham may even have had to resort to subsidising the work to enable it to continue to appear. Clearly, he would have done better to have teamed up with a specialist illustrator. John Ellis was cannier when in the mid-1750s he sought to bring out his *Essay towards a Natural History of the Corallines*: he secured the services of Ehret, the country's foremost botanical artist, and the volume that resulted was to prove worth having for the superlativeness of the plates alone.

The second drawback was more subtle. Because naturalists in Britain, unlike those in other countries, had such comparatively little difficulty in getting learned texts published without the need for subsidy, they were tempted into opting to have their works brought out commercially in cases where this was contrary to their interests as scholars. To be sure of yielding a profit a book needed to be written in the vernacular—whereas if one's work was to have any real impact on the international world of scholars, it needed to be in the language of that world, which continued stubbornly to be Latin.[7] As late as the 1780s the poet George Crabbe laboriously prepared an account of the British flora in English, only to consign his manuscript to the flames on being ticked off by a don at Cambridge (the Vice-Master of Trinity) for "degrading such a science by treating of it in a modern language" (Crabbe, 1834: 134; Groves, 1906). Naturalists on the Continent, unaware of the market pressure that their counterparts in Britain were prey to, tended to think that authors like Latham, Pennant and Lightfoot were merely being arrogant or eccentric in publishing entirely in English, in the case of the first two even down to the names that they bestowed on the new birds they described (Stresemann, 1975: 55). In Latham's case, unhappily, this practice was to prove disastrous. Only three years after his *General Synopsis of Birds* had completed its appearance all his many new species were renamed in Latin by the German naturalist Gmelin. Belatedly hoping to retrieve matters, Latham rushed out a suitably Linnaeanized two-volume summary of that work, under the title *Index Ornithologicus*. But by then, alas, it was too late: ever afterwards the names have had to be credited to Gmelin, and Latham's pioneering labours have effectively been buried as far as posterity is concerned.

The difficulty of knowing which audience to address is common of course to all learned pursuits which have the good or bad fortune to attract a substantial popular following. Nonetheless it is salutary to be reminded that natural history authorship was dogged by this dilemma even in such early days.

WEAKNESS OF PROFESSIONALIZATION

The existence of that dilemma is the more ironic considering an amateur-professional dichotomy had not yet emerged by this period—nor would one emerge, indeed, till after half-way through the century following. The world we are considering was still

II

a world of amateurs, more or less exclusively. Until the establishment of the British Museum in 1753 and the first appointments ten years later of qualified scholars, like Daniel Solander and Charles Konig, to help curate its scientific collections, there were no posts of a permanent, full-time character by which a naturalist could earn a living. Everything else was either short-term or part-time or only unofficially employment for such a purpose—and except in the universities subject to the whims and idiosyncrasies of individual private patrons. It was the age of patronage and the age, too, of great private collections, and these two practices could reasonably have been expected to converge to yield niches for many a professional naturalist. Yet the extent to which that happened can only be accounted disappointing.

There were teaching posts, of course, but those were all part-time as well. The one of greatest consequence to the natural history world, though ostensibly its purpose was medical, was that of Demonstrator of Plants to the Society of Apothecaries in the Physic Garden at Chelsea. As part of the duties was to take out the Society's apprentices and make them familiar with herbs in the wild, the holders of the office necessarily had to be field botanists of competence. As such it attracted over the years men of such ability as William Curtis and William Hudson; but as it was open only to Freemen of the Society, and for them was at best a mere crutch financially, it can only be classed rather marginally as a professional position as far as natural history was concerned.

Three of the universities, Oxford, Cambridge (from 1724) and Edinburgh, each had Professors of Botany and Edinburgh and Marischal College, Aberdeen had Chairs of Natural History in whole or in part. Cambridge even had a Chair of Geology from 1731. But these titles are deceptive. These were not yet subjects in which students were examined: they were still generally regarded as little more than decorative, part of a wider, extra-curricular fringe of studies of which a would-be gentleman of cultivation could usefully equip himself with a smattering. Theology, Classics and Mathematics were what really mattered—in institutions which at this period, at least in England, were a mixture of finishing-school and seminary. At Oxford and Cambridge the college Fellows were the only people who really mattered, similarly. Unlike them, mere holders of professorships were permitted to be married, and could live far away for all anybody cared. Their posts were essentially honorific, worth having only for the status they conferred in the world outside and for the freelance commissions that flowed from that. Indeed, at the English universities (unlike the Scottish ones) they were taken so unseriously that they tended to deteriorate into sinecures. At Oxford, Humphrey Sibthorp allegedly gave just a single lecture in his 35 years in the Chair of Botany. At Cambridge, his opposite number, John Martyn, failed even to manage that for all but the first three of the 30 years of *his* tenure of the office, never so much as deigning to enter into residence. But at least Martyn had the excuse that the University refused to find the funds for the establishing of a botanic garden, without which the then accepted way of teaching botany was deemed to be impossible.

Yet at least it could be said for Martyn and Sibthorp that they were qualified for their positions: in other cases the two Universities simply plucked someone from quite another subject and left him to teach it as best he could. Behaviour of that kind is no more than we have come to expect of that shoulder-shrugging world of the eighteenth century; it comes as more of a shock, though, to find that it persisted well into the century following. As late as 1818 the Woodwardian Chair of Geology at Cambridge went to one of the dons in Mathematics, Adam Sedgwick, who at least had the candour to admit that hitherto he had never so much as turned a stone. Nine years later, similarly, Henslow was transferred to the Cambridge Chair of Botany from a post in Mineralogy, despite the fact that, as he was later to confess, his botanical knowledge was only very slight. By good chance both of these, as it proved, were excellent choices; but, clearly, things could have turned out altogether differently—as all too often they had in the past.

THE GREAT RECESSION

What had gone wrong with the universities in England? These were not the institutions that had bred and nurtured men of the towering stature of John Ray and Isaac Newton, less than a century previously. Nor, for that matter, was the Royal Society anything but a shadow of the great arena of inquiry and debate for which it had won such renown in its Restoration infancy. What had become of the shining start which that brilliant constellation of minds had given to subjects like natural history as the seventeenth century drew towards its close? There is a mystery here that calls out to be explained.

The decline set in as the new century was moving into its second quarter. As if worn out by all its exertions in the 60 years previously, the entire world of learning settled back, gave a great yawn and was soon fast asleep.[9] And not just in England either: in all the main countries of Europe the universities similarly went into retreat till early the next century—though in England the tendency was perhaps that much more extreme.

It is tempting to see some connection between this general abandonment of striving and the turning away from enthusiasm that equally occurred in religion. Europe as a whole had tired of all that fierce doctrinal quarrelling, which year after year, decade after decade, had plunged the continent into one long nightmare of anger and destruction. What it needed now was a rest; and in guarding against any fanning afresh of those mercifully dying embers, it was as if it was bent upon suppressing the slightest gleam of fervour in every other aspect of life as well.

'Slumbrous cynicism' are the words that have been used to characterize the eighteenth century's prevailing attitude to religion. But cynicism, too, and not so slumbrous, must surely have been induced by the peculiarly extensive web of corruption associated with the system of politics in force in Britain just at this period. The 40 years following the Duke of Newcastle's arrival in power as Walpole's Secretary of State in 1724 are notorious for the unparalleled degree to which patronage was used to advance the cause of one party and to solidify its position. Arrant jobbery and placemanship were extended down to the humblest levels of state and even much private employment, with the result that in the competition for office or preferment it was soundness politically that mattered rather than competence to perform the duties concerned. In such a system hierarchies based on ability are prevented from taking hold; would-be achievers, perpetually thwarted, eventually give up in disgust; all effort other than political effort comes to seem pointless. It is hardly an atmosphere in which scholarship flourishes.

II

It probably did not help, either, that around the same time the economy went into serious recession. For roughly 40 years, from 1725 to 1765, London's prosperity and population both stagnated (J. Landers, unpubl.). In the rest of the country matters were proportionately very much worse, so much so that the numbers of the rural poor thrown on to parish relief became so overwhelming that single parishes could cope no longer and resources had to be pooled in multi-parish 'unions' (Plumb, 1950: 20). In the Twenties the population of England and Wales actually declined, by about 1½%—though it rebounded in the Forties, with a vengeance (Wrigley and Schofield, 1981). In an age when most people in the middle levels of society were self-employed the general constriction in circumstances that these trends imply, and the pressures and worries accompanying them, can hardly have been conducive to the development of leisure interests (unless, that is, there is truth in the contra-cyclical notion that subjects like natural history flourish in times of adversity especially, when people seek them out as a balm and as a solace).

Whatever the explanations, there can be no doubting that during that very same span of years in which the economy of the country stagnated natural history stagnated too. By 1725 almost all the leading members of that group whose combined talents had given the subject such impetus in the period just before had either died or withdrawn from activity.[10] The only major figure now was Dillenius, busily compiling field handbooks of authoritativeness and excellence; but he was a foreigner who had arrived only recently and was therefore outside the general trajectory. As far as *native* hunters after species were concerned, a serious generation gap increasingly yawned. Not enough had been done to ensure a succession: suddenly there were far fewer naturalists around than there had been previously and the handful who persisted accomplished noticeably far less. Tellingly, two youthful recruits to the study during the desert years that followed each had to look to 70- or 80-year-old veterans as their principal instructors,[11] so almost completely had the flow of middle-aged field men given out.

The words 'field men' are used advisedly, for it was natural history in the traditional sense that had gone into recession: it was the people who got their hands and feet dirty who had departed from the scene in the main. Natural history as a tasteful pursuit of the leisured and cultivated, on the other hand, the natural history more especially of the upper classes, was very much in the ascendant, enjoying as never before a modishness that originated, like so much else that was tasteful or merely modish, in Europe's fashion centre, France. Manifested there above all in the extraordinary popularity attained by the writings of the Abbé Pluche and, subsequently, of Buffon, this was an indoor taste in essence: a posture of the salons (Mornet, 1911). Nature was something to be sampled from a distance, to be wondered at and argued about,[12] not something to be peered at indecently closely. Though the cultivated eye was learning at last to look beyond the garden wall and appreciate the gentler portions of the landscape that lay outside, it tended to be focused on nature only as a generality, unconcerned with its constituent details.

Whether it was that the upper classes had walked away with natural history and made it in their own likeness, or whether it was that the middle classes had temporarily lost their grip, what had occurred was a wholesale inversion. It is this which makes the mid-eighteenth century such treacherous ground for the historian of the subject and which has long rendered it so difficult to interpret.

It was part of a wider shift that scholars have detected in one field after another right across the whole spectrum of learning: a shift from empiricism to more speculative and fanciful approaches: a shift out of the corset of rigour to more relaxed modes of both thinking and seeing, nicely signalled by a fashion for more loosely-fitting clothes—and by the displacement of Baroque by the languidness of Rococo.

Although there is evidence of the switch in Britain as early as the Thirties, it was not until the second half of the Forties that there were signs that the vogue was well-established in the upper reaches of society. This is neatly shown by a sudden, five-fold jump in the course of that quinquennium in the share of space devoted to natural history in that leading general periodical, the *Gentleman's Magazine* (Baesel, 1974). By the late Forties, clearly, journalists had begun to realise that this was one of the subjects with which the average person of cultivation expected to be acquainted. It was in 1746, it will be recalled, that Collinson had reported that works of natural history "sell the best of any books in England." It was in 1746, too, that Daines Barrington's sister married a Herefordshire landowner, whose great friend, Benjamin Stillingfleet, thereupon came to live on the estate and took up the study of grasses with a view to advising on the improvement of its pastures (Ketton-Cremer, 1944: 102). It was even before that, sometime between 1741 and 1745 (Miller, 1986), that the Earl of Bute, later to be chief minister and mentor to the young George III, occupied his time in the political wilderness by similarly harnessing a taste for botany to the agricultural development of his property in Scotland (as well as by submitting the writings of Linnaeus to a pioneer critical appraisal).[13] It was in 1749 that the botanical artist Ehret discovered a lucrative demand for lessons in flower-painting among the daughters and wives of the nobility and gentry (Ehret, 1896). And it was by 1748-9 (Wilkinson, 1978) that sufficient wealthy subscribers had emerged—interestingly, no less than a quarter of them female—to allow Benjamin Wilkes to start bringing out serially his masterly paintings of *The English Moths and Butterflies* accompanied by a helpfully instructive text.

All through the Fifties the *Gentleman's Magazine* continued to pay natural history ever greater and greater attention. In the first half of that decade the percentage of its pages given over to the subject doubled yet further; by the second half they were taking no less than 17% of all the space (Baesel, 1974). But at that point the bubble burst: the fashion for the subject, it would seem, had finally run its course.

And is it sheer coincidence that it was precisely at this point that the older, empirical interest in the study began to show signs of resurfacing? Is it reading too much into things to see in the return of the middle classes the very cause of that waning of enthusiasm at the higher levels of society? By the Fifties the economy had more than recovered and in the ten years that followed it surged ahead, and continued to increase steadily for the remainder of the century. Better trade demanded better roads, and investment at last began to go into these, considerably improving the lot of the traveller. Christopher Hussey (1927: 101), the historian of the Picturesque, has noted how "the appreciation of scenery . . . increased in direct ratio to the number of turnpike acts"—and those grew almost fivefold between 1750 and 1790. In their wake came better maps, better horses and, perhaps most desirable of all, better coach springs. It was now that making tours, for no other purpose than to admire natural scenery, gradually became a comfortable proposition—and, in consequence, steadily more popular as a pastime. This introduced the countryside to large numbers

II

of people who had never properly stood back and looked at it before and tempted the more energetic even to leave their carriages and inspect its beauties on foot. That profound, immensely long-drawn-out and immensely complex process that goes by the name of the Romantic Movement, a sharpening and refining of the Western senses, began to be set in train as a result.

Two distinct attitudes to nature were now achieving a fruitful interpenetration: the hard and rational on the one hand, the soft and sentimental on the other. And in the merging of these two complementary approaches—the scientific and the aesthetic, the disciplined and the relaxed—there is to be found, surely, the explanation for the new quality that we begin to notice in natural history from this period: that "vivid, sensuous attentiveness" which Mabey (1986: 82) detects first in Gilbert White in 1761, in a long and detailed account of crickets which he penned for his private pleasure in that year. White, it seems, was one who had achieved a magical fusion of those otherwise contrary impulses, classical formality and genuine romantic feeling— an achievement which notably eluded his contemporary, the poet Thomas Gray, for example.

RECOVERY

And so finally we come to the great *risorgimento* of the last 40 years of the century: the marvellous rise to greater and greater popularity, almost even to cultural supremacy, of natural history as the kind of field study we have known ever since, as it emerged revitalised by the confluence of those two previously separate currents.

It was not quite the smooth upward path that the bare recital of events tends to lead one to suppose. Rather, it proceeded in a series of giant steps, each of them extending over roughly five years. The first took place in the mid-Sixties, the next in the second half of the Seventies, the third and final one ten years after that, in the second half of the Eighties.

The first step coincided with, and in large part was caused by, the impact at last in Britain of the ideas of Linnaeus. These had been rumbling for a long time on the horizon, and quite a number of naturalists in this country had considered them very seriously. Most liked the proposal that all organisms should bear just a two-word Latin name; many, though, were unpersuaded that the method of classifying plants by the number of their floral organs had sufficient intrinsic merit to warrant throwing over the well-established systems that attempted to group by natural affinities. Not surprisingly, those whose interests lay more in zoology, like Pennant, could see no benefit at all in switching to this rather quaint and frankly artificial method.

But eventually the barrage of Linnaean propaganda began to tell, particularly after the publication, in the Fifties, of the two mammoth compilations in which for the first time Linnaeus employed binomials consistently.

The *Species Plantarum*, the bible for the botanists, was first brought to general notice in Britain by a rave review (by Sir William Watson) in the *Gentleman's Magazine* at the end of 1754. In the very next year Israel Lyons took up field botany in Cambridge (Cooper, 1909) and at much the same time[14] the study gained another first-class convert in the person of John Lightfoot. These may simply have been coincidences, but the opposite seems much more likely. All the same a strong botanical current had been running in parts of England already, and we should not allow ourselves to be deceived by the Linnaeans into automatically assuming that all developments at this period were due solely to the influence of The Master.

Indeed, it is generally overlooked how extraordinarily slow was the progress made at first in Britain by the new Linnaean doctrine. Five whole years had to pass after that inaugural review before the first detailed exposition of the Artificial System for the general reader was produced (by Benjamin Stillingfleet, in his unappealingly-titled *Miscellaneous Tracts relating to Natural History, Husbandry, and Physick*). It was six years before James Lee, the Hammersmith nurseryman, published his *Introduction to Botany*, which was to prove particularly influential. It was eight years before there was the first fully-Linnaean handbook, William Hudson's *Flora Anglica*. It was nine years before any lecture courses at the universities were being given on the System. It was twelve years before a book on British fossils first used Linnaean binomials, fifteen before they were introduced to British entomologists and before they really came into currency among the country's collectors of Lepidoptera. Even after 23 years a local Flora (of the district round Faversham, in Kent) could still be published in which its author (Jacob, 1777) preferred to employ the pre-Linnaean names. People were set in their ways; books and other information circulated only slowly; there was a good deal of purely intellectual resistance to overcome as well. Allow for the time-lags produced by all those factors and it would have been only around 1765 that the first wave of Linnaeana arrived in the home of the average receptive reader.[15] And that was the year, we now know, in which Gilbert White embarked on his first serious work in natural history. One year later, we also now know, armed with copies of Stillingfleet and Hudson, he was busily compiling his manuscript 'Flora Selborniensis'. Did he realise, one wonders, how privileged he was to be the owner of a copy of that invaluable handbook of Hudson's? For by then it was already exceedingly hard to come by, the stock of that first edition having mostly been lost in a fire. When Rousseau was botanizing in England that same summer he had to be content with Dillenius's 1724 edition of Ray's *Synopsis*,[16] with its antiquated, cumbersome nomenclature. White, though, also preferred to use those older names, so perhaps the benefits of owning Hudson's work were altogether lost on him.

1766 is further hallowed as the year in which White's brother Benjamin was emboldened to strike out on his own as a publisher and bookseller and, encouraged by the latest surge of interest in the subject, to specialise in works on natural history. The very next year he was to publish Barrington's *Naturalist's Journal* and the year after that to start bringing out Pennant's *British Zoology* in its second, more complete, more portable, better-illustrated, no-longer-anonymous version. Thus did the two to whom the *Selborne* letters were to be addressed first arrive within Gilbert's orbit.

By 1775 Gilbert was reporting to his brother John: "Anything in the naturalist way now sells well" (Holt-White, 1901: 279). Soon he was telling him: "The love of such knowledge increases. Even bishops . . ., in order to recommend themselves, study botany." And William Curtis was finding that people "from the other end of the town" call at his London botanic garden "in their coaches to desire private lectures for grown gentlemen" (Holt-White, 1901: 311).

II

We are now on the second step. And by this time the numbers of naturalists have indeed become impressive. By 1775 there are even enough collectors of insects for the first comprehensive field guide, designed to slip into a pocket, *The English Lepidoptera* by Moses Harris, to achieve a wide and ready sale. Three years later the much-needed fresh edition of Hudson's national Flora, now greatly extended, caters similarly for the fast-swelling ranks of field botanists. As if to accompany it, the youthful John Walcott starts issuing a series of accurate engravings of the common British plants, at a suicidally low price to allow the parts to be purchasable by all but the poorest. A plateau of popularity has been reached, in which books can be written and sold at last with the ordinary, humble practitioner of the subject predominantly in mind—instead of the libraries of the wealthy.

It was time by now for naturalists to be collecting themselves into societies once again. And, lo and behold, in 1782 the first-ever ones in Britain to be all-embracing in their scope came into existence, within a few months of one another, in London and in Edinburgh.[17] Two years later J.E. Smith managed to purchase the library and collections of Linnaeus and soon after that there was a third body in being, the Linnean Society of London, which would long draw most of its strength from the enviable possession of those riches.

We are now on the third and loftiest of the steps. Natural history had attained such solidity that it had the self-confidence to take its continuance for granted and to begin to embark on long-term enterprises. And these were not only societies: in 1790 *English Botany* was launched, its authoritative text by Smith and its much-prized colour illustrations by James Sowerby. It would eventually run to 36 volumes and grace the shelves of just about every self-respecting library.

The years 1787–90 brought everything indeed to a triumphant climax, a climax for which its three star performances, so splendidly coinciding, seemed almost to have been saved up deliberately. The Linnean Society itself eventually emerged in February 1788 only after a gestation of twenty months or more. William Withering's *Botanical Arrangement of British Plants*, the most complete national Flora published up to that time,[18] the first volume of which appeared in 1787, was a largely rewritten version of a Latinized flop of eleven years previously. And *The Natural History and Antiquities of Selborne* finally entered this world in the autumn of 1788 only after years and years of deplorable shilly-shallying on the part of Gilbert White. It was as if History had decided for once to collude with Art, so satisfyingly well-timed was this culminating upyielding of creativity.

ACKNOWLEDGEMENTS

I am grateful to Roy Porter and David Knight for reading the text and making a number of helpful comments.

NOTES

[1] This is a slightly revised version of the opening paper at the Gilbert White Bicentenary Symposium, Selborne, 20 July 1989.

[2] This was not, however, the world's first formally-constituted society devoted to botany. One is known to have been in existence in Florence by 1716 and to have continued for nearly 70 years.

[3] Thomas Knowlton to Richard Richardson, 31 October 1736, in Turner (1835: 350) and Henrey (1986: 149).

[4] Stresemann (1975: 48) sees the progress achieved in taxidermy as one cause of the emergence of colour-plate books in zoology.

[5] Sherard to Richardson, 12 November 1720, in Turner (1835: 160).

[6] Collinson to Linnaeus, 16 April 1747, in Smith (1821: 18).

[7] An expensive compromise was a text in both Latin *and* the vernacular. In Commelin's *Horti Medici Amstelaedamensis Rariorum . . . Plantarum . . . Descriptio et Icones* (1687–1701) the two languages were printed in parallel columns.

[8] Nor is he known to have published any scientific work during that period. However, he did assist with the Botanic Garden.

[9] Medieval scholarship in Britain, for example, "underwent during the eighteenth century not a development but a reaction. These studies between 1730 and 1800 made no advance comparable to that which had been achieved in the previous seventy years. The stultifying of so promising a growth . . . was a phenomenon in the development of English culture which was very remarkable" (Douglas, 1939: 355). Again: "from 1705 to 1778 there was a period of relapse when the Earth-sciences lay stagnant and forgotten" (Davies, 1969: 95). A similar retrogression has been reported in several other fields. Porter (1977: 91ff.), apparently uniquely, has argued to the contrary as far as British geology was concerned; but at least one of his reviewers (J.D. Burchfield in *Isis* 1979, **70**: 317) found his case "strained and unconvincing."

[10] In just the same way the great tradition of Restoration historical studies came to an end as the last of its exponents died off one by one between 1710 and 1720 (Douglas, 1939).

[11] Joseph Dandridge acted as mentor to Benjamin Wilkes *ca* 1740, the Rev. John Bateman to his fellow Kent botanist Edward Jacob in the period 1734–44.

[12] Roger (1980) sees the gradual abandonment of the Cartesian philosophy as one of the two main reasons for the triumph of natural history (the other being the literary abilities of the writers on the subject). At mid-century in particular he discerns a dynamic antagonism in progress between the search for the causes of phenomena ('natural philosophy') and the mere description of what was found and observed.

[13] It is noteworthy that these experiments in agricultural botany preceded by some years Duhamel du Monceau's *Traité de la Culture des Terres* (1750), identified by Mornet (1907) as responsible for the '*Agromanie*' which gripped fashionable France in the years 1750–61. It was the methods expounded by Duhamel which Louis XV began to put into practice at the Petit-Trianon in 1754.

[14] Lightfoot states in the preface to his *Flora Scotica* (1777) that he had been pursuing field botany for over sixteen years prior to his tour of Scotland—which was in 1772.

[15] In 1763 Emanuel Mendes da Costa reported from London to the Rev. William Huddesford: "At present Natural History begins to revive somewhat in this capital" (Nichols, 1822: 475). That was also the year in which the *Critical Review* proclaimed that "Natural History is now, by a kind of national establishment, become the favourite study of the times" (quoted by Jones, 1937). These statements can be reconciled only by assuming that their respective authors understood two quite different things by the words 'natural history'.

[16] His copy of this was given to him by the Duchess of Portland (Leigh, 1977: 348). It is now in the library of Jesus College, Cambridge and shows that he laboriously updated it by entering the Linnaean names in the margins. At least he was luckier than his botanical contemporary in Guernsey, Joshua Gosselin, whose remoteness condemned him to have to rely for over twenty years on Parkinson's *Theatrum*, a herbal published over a century previously (McClintock, 1975: 25).

[17] Respectively, the Society for Promoting Natural History and the Society for the Investigation of Natural History (otherwise Societas Naturae Studiosorum Edinburgena). The latter was formed by students at Edinburgh University (for a full account of it see Allen, 1978). Significantly, Smith belonged to both, before moving on to launch the much more ambitious Linnean Society.

[18] Stephen Robson's *The British Flora* (1777) was the first botanical handbook aiming at a national coverage both written in English and presented on Linnaean lines. But Withering's work of ten years later was much more comprehensive and clearly enjoyed a far greater sale.

II

REFERENCES

ALLEN, D.E., 1966 Joseph Dandridge and the first Aurelian Society. *Entomologist's Record* **78**: 89-94.

ALLEN, D.E., 1967 John Martyn's botanical society: a biographical analysis of the membership. *Proceedings of the Botanical Society of the British Isles* **6**: 305-324.

ALLEN, D.E., 1978 James Edward Smith and the Natural History Society of Edinburgh. *Journal of the Society for the Bibliography of Natural History* **8**: 483-493.

BAESEL, D.R., 1974 *Natural History and the British Periodicals in the Eighteenth Century*. PhD thesis, Ohio State University.

COOPER, T., 1909. Israel Lyons. In LEE, S. (ed.) *The Dictionary of National Biography*. Vol. 12. London.

CRABBE, G., 1834 *The Poetical Works of the Rev. George Crabbe: with his Letters and Journals, and his Life*. Vol. 1. London.

DAVIES, G.L., 1969 *The Earth in Decay: a History of British Geomorphology*. London.

DOUGLAS, D.C., 1939 *English Scholars*. London.

EHRET, G.D., 1896 A memoir of Georg Dionysius Ehret, trans. E.S. Barton. *Proceedings of the Linnean Society of London, Session 1894-95*: 41-58.

GROVES, J., 1906 Crabbe as a botanist. *Proceedings of Suffolk Institute of Archaeology and Natural History* **12**: 223-232.

HENREY, B., 1986 *No Ordinary Gardener: Thomas Knowlton, 1691-1781*, ed. A.O. Chater. London.

HOLT-WHITE, R., ed., 1901 *The Life and Letters of Gilbert White of Selborne*. Vol. 1. London.

HUSSEY, C., 1927 *The Picturesque: Studies in a Point of View*. London & New York.

JACOB, E., 1777 *Plantae Favershamienses*. London.

JESSOP, L., 1989 The club at the Temple Coffee House—facts and supposition. *Archives of Natural History* **16**: 263-274.

JONES, W., 1937 The vogue of natural history in England, 1750-1700. *Annals of Science* **2**: 345-352.

KETTON-CREMER, R.W., 1944 *Norfolk Portraits*. London.

LEIGH, R.A., ed., 1977 *Correspondence complète de Jean Jacques Rousseau*. Vol. 30. Oxford.

MABEY, R., 1986 *Gilbert White: a Biography of the Author of The Natural History of Selborne*. London.

McCLINTOCK, D., 1975 *The Wild Flowers of Guernsey*. London.

MILLER, D.P., 1986 'My favourite Studdys': Lord Bute as botanist and scientific collector. In SCHWEIZER, K.W. (ed.) *Lord Bute: Essays in Reinterpretation*. Leicester.

MORNET, D., 1907 *Le Sentiment de la Nature en France de J.-J. Rousseau à Bernardin de Saint-Pierre*. Paris.

MORNET, D., 1911 *Les Sciences de la Nature en France, au XVIIIᵉ Siècle*. Paris.

NICHOLS, J., 1822 *Illustrations of the Literary History of the Eighteenth Century*. Vol. 4. London.

PLUMB, J.H., 1950 *England in the Eighteenth Century (1714-1815)*. Harmondsworth.

PORTER, R., 1977 *The Making of Geology: Earth Science in Britain 1660-1815*. Cambridge.

ROGER, J., 1980 The triumph of natural history. In ROUSSEAU, G.S. & PORTER, R.S. (eds.) *The Ferment of Knowledge: Studies in the Historiography of Eighteenth-century Science*. Cambridge.

SAVAGE, S., 1948 *Catalogue of the Manuscripts in the Library of the Linnean Society of London. Part IV.—Calendar of the Ellis Manuscripts*. London.

SMITH, SIR J.E., 1821 *A Selection of the Correspondence of Linnaeus and Other Naturalists*. Vol. 1. London.

STRESEMANN, E., 1975 *Ornithology from Aristotle to the Present*. Trans. H.J. & C. Epstein, ed. G.W. Cottrell. Cambridge, Mass. & London.

TURNER, D., ed., 1835 *Extracts from the Literary and Scientific Correspondence of Richard Richardson, M.D., F.R.S.* Yarmouth.

WHALLEY, P.E.S., 1972 *The English Moths and Butterflies*, by Benjamin Wilkes [1749], an unpublished contemporary account of its production. *Journal of the Society for the Bibliography of Natural History* **6**: 127.

WILKINSON, R.S., 1978 The death of Benjamin Wilkes and the publication of *The English Moths and Butterflies*. *Entomologist's Record* **90**:6-7.

WRIGLEY, E.A. and SCHOFIELD, R.S., 1981 *The Population History of England and Wales 1541-1871: a Reconstruction*. London.

III

James Edward Smith and the Natural History Society of Edinburgh

Among the many letters which his widow selected for inclusion in her two-volume memoir[1] of Sir James Edward Smith are three[2,3,4] written by him to his parents in 1782 while a medical student at Edinburgh University, in which he reports his founding there, with four or five friends, of 'a society for the prosecution of natural history'.

More than one latter-day reader has found these mentions tantalising. For any society devoted to natural history at so early a date, however insignificant, cannot but possess some historical interest. But when it also happens to have been the creation, at least in part, of the man who only six years later was to take the lead in launching the Linnean Society, this interest is considerably enhanced. For the moves that gave rise to that event were of no small import for the development of natural history in Britain, and the question inevitably poses itself whether this prior experience of Smith's of running a society helped to determine the form or course which this more substantial successor took.

Although it was merely a student society, the fact, too, that these were Edinburgh students ought to quicken the historian's pulse. For a notably high proportion of young men at that period who developed a fondness or – even more – a passion for natural history were steered into medicine as the logical professional outlet; and a notably high proportion of these in turn, and certainly of the most able ones, were sent to Edinburgh for at least a part of their training. Their common interest would have brought them together once there, and at least some of the friendships that resulted seem likely to have persisted into later life and may thus have influenced the direction of their subsequent scientific work.

One does not, in fact, have to search hard to find a natural history society referred to in the Edinburgh student records of that period. It is not obviously apparent, however, that this is the one mentioned by Smith in his letters. Student societies, notoriously, come and go; and on the face of things it is more likely that ones with different names represent different entities than that – as in this case – they are all one and the same.

It is this variety of names under which the society passed, as remarkable as it is bewildering, that has prevented it from achieving a readier identification. Even Smith himself seems to have been uncertain whether it was the 'Society for *investigating* Natural History'[5] or the 'Society for *the Investigation of* Natural History'[6]. The latter is the title that prevails at any rate in the more formal contexts, and it is thus presumably the one that the founders came down in favour of and by which they preferred the Society to be publicly known. In private, on the other hand, the members understandably reduced this to, just simply, 'the Natural History Society', and it is as that that it features throughout the rest of the Smith correspondence from as early as January 1784.[7] At some point the informal title eventually

III

took over, and by 1797 it was sufficient for letters to the Secretary to be addressed to: "ye Nat.H. society care of Messrs. Mudie & Sons booksellers".[8] To complicate matters still further, the Society had a Latin title bestowed on it as well — and it is by this alone that it is referred to in the one account of it ever to appear in print.[9] But even that title, too, was subjected to shortening, for, as is apparent from the printed rules[10], '*Societas Naturae Studiosorum*' should properly have been rounded off with '*Edinburgena*'. Not surprisingly, the less erudite among the members were rather unsure in their use of this and in at least one place the third word, '*Studiosorum*', has become corrupted into '*Curiosorum*' [11] (which some may consider a happier rendering in any case).

From the variety of references to the Society alluded to just in this discussion of the title it will be evident that the sources of information about it are a good deal richer and more numerous than has generally been supposed. We have the minute books; the rules-cum-membership list, amounting to a seemingly complete register of the 249 members down to 1802, giving each one's full name, date of election and home town, county or (in the case of overseas members) country; eleven volumes of the papers, or 'dissertations'[12], that every member in turn was required to deliver; quite a number of reports, albeit brief, in the Smith correspondence over a long period of years (1782–1803) on the Society's general condition; a few entries relating to it in the diary of William Thornton, now in the Library of Congress; and, not least, the printed Presidential Address of Richard Kentish in 1784 in which he provides, by way of an introduction, a first-hand account of its beginnings.[9] There can be few other early societies which we can hope to reconstruct as extensively as this.

That a student society could have kept going for as long as thirty years suggests that there were some special buttressing influences deriving from the character of the University itself. It is not difficult to identify what these might have been. The Scottish universities, unlike their English counterparts, were teeming ant-hills. Non-exclusive and cheap to attend, on the prevailing Continental pattern, they paid the price of these virtues in enormous classes and a near-absence of individual tuition. On top of this, with traditional Calvinistic rigour, students were worked very hard, there was little allowance for exercise or other recreation, and the social side of university life remained comparatively undeveloped. To fill this gap, from the 1720s onwards student societies consequently sprang into being, helped along by appreciative professors (and at least one Principal), who quickly perceived their value in countering the general amorphousness and anonymity as well as in serving a peculiarly effective means of supplementary instruction. Not a few students in later life, indeed, claimed to have learned as much through their membership of these societies as from the formal teaching in the lecture-rooms.

The impressive standard of discourse which these claims imply is probably only in part to be credited to the high sense of purpose characteristic of Scottish education. A more important influence must surely have been the above-average maturity of a considerable proportion of the students. Thanks to its late founding (in 1583) Edinburgh had escaped the medieval legacy which so held back the older English and Scottish universities, with the result that its teaching had a freedom from scholasticism and a strong vocational emphasis such as to give it a particular appeal to the professional classes — and by no means just those of Scotland. As the eighteenth century drew on, students from well-to-do English homes flocked there in ever-increasing numbers, many of them (like Smith) from the dissenting backgrounds which automatically precluded an English university. More and more of these, too, as the reputation of Edinburgh spread internationally, came just to round off studies which they had already substantially completed elsewhere.

III

Such students, clearly, had very little in common with the youths in their early teens, gauche and tongue-tied, lettered but hardly yet learned, who arrived from the Scottish schools to form the great majority. It was inevitable that a gulf should grow up between the two. And it was inevitable that the societies, or at any rate those of them with a scientific cast, should come to be identified pre-eminently with the older element (as shown by the disproportionately low number of Scots in those whose memberships have so far been subjected to analysis).[13,14] It was through this fact that they came to possess, as will be seen, some distinctly un-student-like characteristics.

Given such favourable conditions, it is surprising indeed that there was not a natural history society far earlier. The drawing-power of the Edinburgh School of Physic, to which is credibly attributed[11] the proliferation of scientific societies that manifested itself in the Scottish capital during the last thirty years of that century,[15] after was all well in evidence by the 1760s. Withering, Pulteney, Erasmus Darwin, John Sims, Thomas Yalden, even an ex-pupil of Linnaeus in the person of Adam Kuhn – these were just a few of the actual or potential naturalists which the English and overseas contingents contained in that period. In Archibald Menzies, George Fordyce and Robert Ramsay there would have been keen fellow spirits for them among the natives, while in John Hope and John Walker the later of them had the most stimulating of teachers who went out of their way to foster enthusiasm for the subject. Hope, the Professor of Botany and a dedicated expounder of Linnaeus from as early as 1763, yearly awarded a gold medal for the best herbarium formed by a student and delighted to dispatch his abler pupils to explore the natural history of the remoter parts of Scotland.

The explanation, one must suppose, is simply that the forming of natural history societies had not yet become an example to be copied from the wider world. The attempt in London in the Sixties to revive the Aurelian Society had failed after only about four years. Several English towns had spawned botanical societies, but these were all obscure and tiny. Until October 1782, when the Society for Promoting Natural History was founded in London, there was no body of any prominence, let alone one devoted (at least in theory) to the subject in its entirety.

By that time the University's fondness for societies had worked down to the areas of learning that were less directly vocational and traditional. A Society of Antiquaries, born in 1780, was almost bound to be followed by a society for the hardly less fashionable natural history. Models ready and waiting to be copied lay on every hand. It did not need much boldness or inventiveness to rise to what by then had become an almost blatant hint.

As Smith acknowledged, there were "four or five friends" associated with him in the venture.[2] These, the membership list suggests, were Jonathan Stokes, William Thomson and Richard Anthony Markham – all three of whom were subsequently to make some name as scientists – together with a student from Lincolnshire, Thomas Hardy, and the Swiss, Jean Stockar. But to describe these collectively as 'the founders', while strictly true, may give the misleading impression that their task was a more uphill one than was in fact the case. For as so often with natural history societies, the formal institution grew out of a pre-existing informal group.

The session of 1781–2, according to Richard Kentish (in that subsequent Presidential Address[9] already referred to), was "a year distinguished for the number of ingenious and learned men in this University." "A set of gentlemen from various parts of the world," he goes on, "whose parental climes differed more than their opinions, united for the purpose of mutual improvement in the different branches of natural history. Botany and Mineralogy were their chief pursuits, and to procure specimens of the different plants and minerals their intention. For this purpose they met, and unanimously went in quest of their respective objects."

Kentish continues, somewhat mysteriously: "Having for some time continued to amuse themselves in this manner, some circumstances occurred which made them desirous of meeting for the purpose of imparting their discoveries: accordingly they met at each others' rooms, and each in his turn entertained the rest with his success in collecting." Out of these meetings, Kentish appears to imply, the Society crystallised, more or less as a matter of course. There is thus no question of it having been created out of a vacuum, as Smith possibly intended should be thought. Smith's role, rather, was that of a catalyst – just as, four years later, down in London, he was to bring to a head the discontent within the Society for Promoting Natural History and lead a breakaway faction out of this to form the Linnean. What he contributed essentially was decisiveness: it was he who galvanised the ditherers, it was he who converted the desultory chat into organised debate. He was the scientific man-of-business – perhaps the first of this kind ever to concentrate his special talents on natural history's institutional development.

From this point on the accounts of Smith and Kentish tally. Dr. Walker, the newish Professor of Natural History, no sooner heard of the founding of the Society than he "offered up his museum to meet in, with the use of his books and specimens; and he begged to be admitted an ordinary member, which he accordingly was, and about seven young men besides".[2] The membership list shows that this was at the second meeting, on 5 April 1782. Among the "seven young men" were Kentish and Francis Buchanan – who, under the name of Buchanan-Hamilton, was to become celebrated for his work on the flora of Nepal. (Notoriety, by contrast, was Kentish's fate – through challenging to a duel a member of the College of Physicians whom he judged responsible for his failure to gain election to that body.[16])

Walker, the Professor, appears to have been the Society's mainstay. Having "no business to follow but natural history", Smith writes[2], he "is resolved to support it as much as possible". And clearly he lived up to this resolve, being a constant attender at the meetings and generally contributing to the discussions. John Hope, on the other hand, with heavy teaching duties, could spare much less time and was content to be enrolled as just an honorary member. Dr. Joseph Black, the Professor of Chemistry, who also put in at least one appearance, was accorded this status too. Their patronage and, still more, their presence obviously made all the difference: they elevated the tone and they evoked more painstaking contributions. After Smith had read a paper 'On collecting and preserving specimens of plants', it was, he reported home in pride, "debated on for three hours, and procured me much commendation from Dr. Walker and Dr. Hope".[3] The manuscript of that particular paper still survives (two copies of it in fact, one in London and one in Edinburgh) and its contents are certainly of interest – but hardly interesting enough to hold on to an audience for three whole further hours today.

From the first, and seemingly throughout the rest of the Society's history, the meetings took place once every week, from early November through to early May. They were held on a weekday evening and normally lasted around three hours. The proceedings opened with the calling of the roll, any member not being present to answer bringing upon himself a sixpenny fine. Visitors were admitted up to a maximum of four. The reading and discussion of the evening's paper then followed (originally there were two papers, but this was evidently abandoned as excessive), and after that such general communications as anyone present might see fit to make. Finally, there was a half-hour devoted to Society business, which every member was required to stay on for on pain of another fine of sixpence. The chief item of this was the reading out of letters of application for membership and ballotting on those applications already put through that ritual on the preceding occasion.

Early in each meeting an announcement was made of the subject of the paper to be given next time. To deter its author from defaulting, non-production of this was subject to a fine of quite exceptional steepness — one whole guinea no less. Everyone automatically joined the roster of paper-givers as soon as his membership had lasted eight weeks.

It must not be supposed that this profligacy with fines (seemingly without parallel, be it noted, in any of the University's other intellectual societies at that period [15]) was merely an ingenious way of putting the Society in funds. With an entrance subscription (till 1803) as ferocious as three guineas — and multiply that figure by twenty to arrive at its present-day purchasing equivalent — together with half a guinea by way of an annual levy there can hardly have been a need for any further money-raising. True, the Society sought to build up a library and a museum, and the first of these activities would not have been cheap; but even so it is difficult to believe that the purpose of the fining system was even primarily financial. Its purpose, rather, was surely to clamp the Society in a framework of iron. The discipline it succeeded in imposing thereby, embodied in a dazzlingly elaborate set of rules almost Mosaic in their sternness — and printed up in a special booklet, what is more, to intensify the impression of sacrosanctity — may well have been a further cause of the Society's unusually prolonged existence. Maybe, like some primitive tribe hemmed in with harsh taboos on every hand, it was awed, even cowed, into an enduring stability.

Fining was not the only method resorted to for dragooning back-sliders. Every new member was required to take a solemn oath, administered by the President, in the following words:

> "By inserting my name in the list of ordinary members of this Society, I promise and declare, that I will obey all its laws and regulations, and never consent to the alienation of its property, except with the consent of at least twenty members legally met."

Yet another bolstering effect was the very expensiveness of belonging — and, even more, 'of dropping out and then rejoining. High fees are a time-honoured way of conferring a sense of privileged exclusiveness, and even the annual half-a-guinea must have been a daunting sum for those many students whose presence at the University was contrived only through the proud Scots tradition of bag-of-oatmeal penuriousness.

Again, it is hard to credit that fees so high were essential. And certainly they accord ill with the traditional openness of natural history or with the desire to proselytise on the subject's behalf that one would have expected at that period. Probably the founders decided that only by a heavy commitment of money was a heavy commitment of time and effort obtainable as well. But there may also have been a further, more ignoble consideration. Eighteenth-century society had an obsession with rank, and it is unlikely that even student bodies would have been free from this — and least of all those recruited in the main from among the would-be physicians. It is abundantly plain from his writings, moreover, that Smith himself was particularly prone to this frailty. "Several men of genius and rank have petitioned to be admitted as ordinary members", we find him crowing to his father[2], "among whom are the Earls of Glasgow and Ancram, and Lord Dacre, son to the Earl of Selkirk — three young noblemen of fine parts and great fortunes". This sounds indecent to

modern ears, but it was of course the then accepted mode and the principle on which the
Royal Society no less than the new literary and philosophical societies were constructed in
conspicuous measure. Social standing and intellectual standing were still seen as necessarily
interdependent, and illustriousness in its composition still appeared the soundest guarantee
of a learned body's continuity. For even if they seldom or never turned up, members of
wealth and title could be counted on to act as a magnet for lesser, potentially more active
figures; they were also less liable to notice the expense of their subscriptions and so stayed
on contentedly for helpfully lengthy periods.

At the same time Smith was not without a weakness as well for a certain touch of
grandeur. In this, again, he was no more than reflecting that general penchant for flourish
and grandiloquence so characteristic of his century. To a latter-day observer the Edinburgh
Society, and no less the Linnean Society after it, has an overblown look: it regards itself too
loftily, its procedures have an extra-thick coating of ritual. But that, surely, is how Smith —
and doubtless his contemporaries in general — preferred to see Learning being conducted.
A certain elevation, it must have seemed, helped to induce the requisite *gravitas*.

There was a more basic way, however, in which the Society was able to satisfy this
appetite of Smith's. Towards the end of the first year, when thought was being given to a
full-scale constitution, he revealed excitedly to his father: "I believe we shall have four
annual presidents chosen; if so, I hope to be one of them."[4] He was not disappointed. He
had in fact presided unofficially over some of the meetings already, though, as he confessed,
"not . . . . without great anxiety" initially.[2] He quickly found that presidential chairs constituted his natural habitat, and he was scarcely ever to be out of one for the remainder of
his life.

Smith's years at university came to an end in the summer of 1783, less than eighteen
months after the Society's formation. Almost immediately he plunged into the affairs of
the Society for Promoting Natural History, successfully bid for the Linnean collections and,
not long afterwards, deployed these as the centrepiece of his breakaway Linnean Society.
Among the very first members of this were six who had been his comrades-in-committee
while at Edinburgh: William Thomson, by then a Lecturer in Anatomy at Oxford;[17] the
former Markham, now called Salisbury; the Sheffield physician William Younge, the companion of Smith's post-Edinburgh tour on the Continent; Francis Buchanan, by then in the
East; Jonathan Stokes, by then in practice at Kidderminster; and the son of Smith's old
botany professor, Thomas Charles Hope, by then Professor of Chemistry at Glasgow. Of
these, only Salisbury can be said to have impinged on these subsequent activities of Smith
with any force. In 1785, shortly after his leaving Edinburgh, an elderly lady whom he had
befriended left him a substantial fortune, at the mere price of changing his name bringing
him an estate at Mill Hill and freedom to devote all his days to botany and horticulture. For
long he and Smith kept in active touch; but eventually came the fell day when Salisbury
declared for the Natural System — which to Smith was tantamount to supping with the
Devil. A vicious quarrel ensued, and Smith proceeded to blacken his former friend's name
with all of that nauseating vindictiveness with which he was to hound several others besides
who dared to worship at that alternative altar.

Apart from these members, there is nothing else that the Linnean Society can be identified as having inherited from its predecessor unambiguously. The rules of the two bodies
have some suggestive similarities and there are apparently telltale resemblances in their procedures — yet these may be illusory, chance parallelisms resulting from a more distant com-

mon ancestry. All the same we may be sure that the experience as a whole was a profoundly formative one for Smith, and without it he would hardly have charged into the founding of a national society with such confidence at so very early an age.

The Presidency he had vacated at Edinburgh was filled for the next two winters by his friend William Younge. Francis Buchanan, with one more year to go, was available to keep Younge company; and when Buchanan resigned the following spring, Kentish was still on hand to take his place. There was thus a useful staggering of the inevitable departures of the original founding group, and this must have saved the Society during what would otherwise have been a dangerous period. For it is striking that for the next two years there is scarcely a single name in the membership list that is readily identifiable with anyone who later made a mark in natural history; and this strongly suggests an abrupt falling-off in drive and in standard of knowledge. Periodic bulletins to Smith from T. C. Hope would seem to bear this out. By July 1784, for instance, he had to report that Dr. Walker "is become rather a careless attender of your Society" – an ominous sign indeed – and that "at present its real Nat. Historians are but few in No." Moreover, Hope went on, "I think they are deviating a little from the first intention, admitting of all the subjects of Nat. Philosophy, which can hardly be prevented"[18]. On this second point a few months later he was more explicit: "The Nat. History now increases apace. The No. of members, *tho' not of Naturalists* [my italics], is considerable . . . ."[19].

Eight years later, when the next news came – from the pen of Arthur Bruce, a retired land agent from Dunfermline and keen field botanist who had been asked to take on the Secretaryship two years earlier – the story was worse. "I am happy to inform you that the Nat. History Society here still continues to flourish", Bruce opened, reassuringly; but "at present and for some time past, Chemical pursuits have very much engross'd the attention of Medical gentlemen at this University. And last winter along with the usual Dissertation on Natural History a Chemical Paper is also discussed weekly"[20]. The conclusion one naturally jumps to from this is that in the period that had elapsed since Hope's last report the Society had been increasingly infiltrated by chemists, culminating in their partly taking it over. But evidence from other sources suggests that matters were more complicated than this. Early in 1785, not long after Hope had written, a group of Joseph Black's pupils, in the full flush of the enthusiasm roused by his teaching, had banded together as a separate Chemical Society – the first, incidentally, exclusively devoted to that subject in the world.[14] Thirteen of those who joined this new body appear also in the membership list of the Natural History Society[13], some of them possibly continuing to belong to both, despite the heavy double outlay this would have cost them in subscriptions. Indeed, it may well have been this very duplication that proved the new society's undoing; for in 1788, after only three years, it apparently came to a sudden end[14]. Quite possibly what happened was a voluntary stand-down in favour of absorption by the longer-established (and conveniently more broadly-based) Natural History Society, with the instituting of a chemical dissertation in tandem with a natural history one as the agreed price of the merger.

In 1793 there came a further unpromising development: the Society recruited the last of its long trickle of members from the other side of the Atlantic (presumably because of the outbreak in that year of the War with the French Republic). The majority of these, twenty in all, had been from the British West Indies[21], but there were a noteworthy few besides from the United States. Caspar Wistar from Philadelphia, for example, joined in December 1784 and became one of the Presidents twelve months later – simultaneously with the

Presidency of the Medical Society — before returning to become (in due course) Professor of Anatomy in the University of Pennsylvania, President of the American Philosophical Society and immortalised through that beautiful genus *Wistaria,* which Nuttall named after him. The year following Wistar's arrival Samuel Latham Mitchill, also to become a leading pioneer in American science[22], joined him from New York. The year after that the University acquired Benjamin Smith Barton, likewise from Philadelphia. While at Edinburgh the 21-year-old Barton outdid all his contemporaries by publishing a pamphlet: *Observations on some parts of natural history: to which is prefixed an account of some considerable vestiges of an ancient date which have been discovered in different parts of North America.* Irritable and impetuous, he soon after betook himself from Edinburgh in a huff and obtained his doctorate instead at Kiel[23]. His contact with British naturalists, nonetheless, had been sufficiently stimulating and enjoyable to cause him to name his son after Pennant. A fourth American, a future son-in-law of Thomas Jefferson, Thomas Mann Randolph from Virginia, who joined just three weeks after Mitchill, is obscure by comparison; but he deserves mention for his unpublished dissertation, 'On the periodical appearing and disappearing of many British and Virginian birds'. This sounds as if it may be of significance for historians of migration studies in either country. Two other of the dissertations, both by West Indian members, might also be worth consulting while they are about it: 'On the migration of birds of passage', by John N. Nott of Jamaica, and 'On the emigration of swallows', by John Waddell of Demerara.

To help make up for this loss, signs of a better-quality intake from among the home students began in November 1791 with the election of none other than Robert Brown. (His dissertation, it is interesting to find, was 'On the botany of Angusshire'). By an odd coincidence, the very next person to be elected was the father of that other towering figure of nineteenth-century British botany, Charles Babington. In just over a year a further harbinger of promise joined them in the person of Robert Jameson. The future Lord Brougham, unexpectedly, turns up in the crop of 1795–6; but law and politics were to claim him, not natural history. Two others who came in around the same time were Fenwick Skrimshire[24] from Wisbech and Peter Roget[25] from London, who were both later to make their mark as entomologists — and the second, additionally, as author of the famous *Thesaurus,* in which his name continues to be commemorated.

Around then there also occurred a potentially serious calamity. The Treasurer, a Mr. Cuningham[26], was declared insolvent and as one immediate result the Society lost the whole of its funds. Luckily, wrote Arthur Bruce in April 1799, "their debits w^h were not very great are now all paid, but that is the most I can say"[27]. At the very least the building up of its library must have come to a halt, if only temporarily.

However, worse was to come. Some two years later the Society, Bruce was sad to have to report, "has undergone a very great change this winter. Its weekly meetings are almost wholly taken up in Experimental Chemistry, which at present sets aside many of its former pursuits."[28] So chemistry at long last had proved the cuckoo in the nest that it had been threatening to become.

Yet just at that point, when all seemed over, the natural history staged a rally. In 1802 there arrived a future President of the Geological Society (and father-in-law of Lyell), Leonard Horner. And three years later a major recruiting drive which extended beyond just students and professors brought in that pioneer of Highland botany, the elder George Don, who had lately become Superintendent of the Botanic Garden. That same year Arthur Bruce died and his place as Secretary was taken by a local printer and keen naturalist, Patrick Neill. Within a very short time, in May 1806, the new Secretary was sending Smith the cheering message that the Society "again begins to lift up its head". "We have but few members; but sometimes have good papers."[29]

That they had the chance at all of this revival, however – and it is to their credit that they seized it – was not due to the naturalists' own efforts. The humbling reality was that the chemists had come to the decision, not before time, to hive off afresh into a separate body of their own. This second Chemical Society appears to have been in existence by June 1800[30], and it is thus odd that Bruce makes no reference to it in his final letter. Its prime founders were evidently John Thomson, Brougham and Leonard Horner's brother, Francis[31].

After two more years Neill continued to be encouraged, pronouncing the Society "in a more flourishing state than it could boast for some years past", with several botanical members.[32] And this despite the launching, in January 1808, of the Wernerian Natural History Society of Edinburgh, which Smith had evidently assumed bound to have displaced its inevitably lighter-weight neighbour. Certainly this event did the Society one obvious harm, for Neill himself promptly left to become Secretary of the Wernerian. Here he made use of his dual experience to try to effect a merger and, on his own claim[32], nearly succeeded. In the end, though, he was forced to recognise that the two fulfilled different functions and would be better going their separate ways. The older one was essentially a debating society, and chiefly composed of students. "We could not pretend to alter so violently as to exclude these; and some of the best members of the New Society being *Professors* in the University could not, for obvious reasons, have joined us on the old footing."[32]

That is the last news from any of the insiders to have come down to us. For a time, it appears, the Society managed to ride out the squall of competition provoked by the very existence of the Wernerian, for four years later we find it still afloat. Yet the revival that it had experienced in its genuine natural history following had apparently petered out; for, when the end eventually came, in 1812, it was not the Wernerian (as one would have expected) that turned out to be its absorber but the Royal Physical Society of Edinburgh[33]. A last lurch to chemistry must have taken place: the cuckoo had finally ended up in possession of the whole of the nest.

ACKNOWLEDGEMENTS

I am indebted to Mr. G. R. Bridson and Mr. C. P. Finlayson for assistance in consulting the Smith papers in the library of the Linnean Society and the manuscript records in Edinburgh University Library respectively. I should also specially like to thank Dr. H. A. Torrens for pointing out the information on the successive chemical societies and the apparent significance of this, Dr. C. D. Waterston and Miss J. M. Sweet for first drawing my attention to the Society's records in Edinburgh, and Professor J. Ewan for, as always, putting at my disposal his unrivalled knowledge of early American naturalists and referring me to literature on those of them who were Edinburgh members.

NOTES AND REFERENCES

1 *Memoir and correspondence of the late Sir James Edward Smith, M.D.*, ed. Lady Smith. 1832. 2 vols. London.

III

492   JAMES EDWARD SMITH

[2] Smith to his father, 15 Apr. 1782: Smith Ms. 19, 29 (*Memoir*, Vol. 1, 44–47).

[3] Smith to his mother, 16 May 1782: Smith Ms. 19, 32 (*Memoir*, Vol. 1, 48–49). The date of this letter is given incorrectly as 4 May in Warren R. Dawson's *Catalogue of the manuscripts in the library of the Linnean Society of London. Part I.—The Smith papers* (London, 1934), 104.

[4] Smith to his father, 31 Dec. 1782: Smith Ms. 19, 65 (*Memoir*, Vol. 1, 63).

[5] Minute books, Vol. 1, fly-leaf (in Smith's hand), with date '1782'. Now in the Drummond Room, Edinburgh University Library.

[6] For example, at the head of two of his dissertations read before the Society, now in the Smith Mss. (39,1 and 39,39). The Society is also so titled in a letter addressed to him as President by the Earl of Buchan in 1783, accepting honorary membership (Smith Ms. 2, 170; *Memoir*, Vol. 1, 67).

[7] T. C. Hope to Smith, 12 Jan. 1784: Smith Ms. 23, 37.

[8] Arthur Bruce to Smith, 5 June 1797: Smith Ms. 21, 77.

[9] KENTISH, Richard. 1787. Introduction to an essay on the method of studying natural history; being an oration delivered to the *Societas Naturae Studiosorum*, at Edinburgh, in the year 1784. *Edinb. Mag.* **6**: 335–337. This important source has hitherto been overlooked.

[10] *Laws of the Society instituted at Edinburgh M. DCC. LXXXII, for the Investigation of Natural History.* Edinburgh, 1803. Copy in Library of Edinburgh History, Edinburgh Central Library, shelf no. B2507; photocopy in Drummond Room, Edinburgh University Library. According to Whitfield J. Bell, Jr. (1966. Medicine: foster mother of the sciences. *J. Am. med. Ass.* **196**: 50–54) there is an earlier edition dating from 1793.

[11] FINLAYSON, C. P. 1958. Records of medical and scientific societies in Scotland. II. Records of scientific and medical societies preserved in the University Library, Edinburgh. *The Bibliotheck* **1** (3): 14–19.

[12] The sequentially-dated set of these dissertations, now in Edinburgh University Library, evidently consisted of twelve volumes originally, but two are now missing. Along with them there is an additional, unnumbered volume containing dissertations of various dates down to the session 1812–13. There are also three duplicate copies of Smith's dissertations among his papers at the Linnean Society. A duplicate of another dissertation of his, 'On the *Florae Scoticae Supplementum*' (University Library collection Vol. II, 220), has recently been acquired by the Scottish Record Office among an extensive set of papers of John Hope deposited by Messrs. D. & J. H. Campbell, W.S., of Edinburgh.

[13] McKIE, D. 1961. Some notes on a students' scientific society in eighteenth-century Edinburgh. *Sci. Progr. Lond.* **49**: 228–241. This is the only study of the Society to have so far appeared in print.

[14] KENDALL, J. 1952. The first chemical society, the first chemical journal, and the chemical revolution. *Proc. R. Soc. Edinb.* **63A**: 346–358, 385–400.

[15] McELROY, D. D. 1969. *Scotland's Age of Improvement: a survey of eighteenth-century literary clubs and societies.* Pullman.

[16] BRITTEN, J. 1915. Richard Kentish. *J. Bot. Lond.* **53**: 179.

[17] A few years later Thomson ruined a career in Britain of brilliant promise, resigning from the Royal Society "for an offence which happily public opinion in this country never forgives", and was to spend the entire rest of his life in Italy and Sicily. Here he formed a valuable mineralogical collection, which he bequeathed to Edinburgh University on his death in 1806, together with an endowment now known as the Thomson Fund for Mineralogy. The minerals are now in the Royal Scottish Museum. See GUNTHER, R. T. 1939. Dr. William Thomson, F.R.S., a forgotten English mineralogist. *Nature* **143**: 667; WATERSTON, C. D. 1965. William Thomson (1761–1806) a forgotten benefactor. *Univ. Edinb. J.* Autumn 1965: 122–134.

[18] T. C. Hope to Smith, 22 Jul. 1784: Smith Ms. 23, 41.

[19] T. C. Hope to Smith, 22 Dec. [1784]: Smith Ms. 23, 47.

[20] Bruce to Smith, 2 Dec. 1792: Smith Ms. 21, 73 (*Memoir*, Vol. 1: 432).

[21] The first and most interesting of these was William Thornton, from Tortola in the Virgin Islands, elected in April 1782 and one of the Presidents from January 1783. That this was the subsequently famous American architect, inventor and civil servant of that name (1759–1828) is indicated by an exchange of correspondence he had with Banks in March 1786 concerning two ptarmigans and a mineral specimen he had sent him (*Supplementary letters of Sir Joseph Banks,* ed. Warren R. Dawson. *Bull. Br.*

Mus. nat. Hist., (Hist. Ser.) 1962, 3(2): 64). His correspondence and diary are now in the Library of Congress, and I am indebted to Dr. Ronald S. Wilkinson for searching these on my behalf for references to the Edinburgh Society. There proves to be only one relevant letter and the diary (which is partly in shorthand) unfortunately ceases in mid-May 1782. However, it contains sufficient to indicate that Thornton was active in the Society and had as particular friends among the members Robert Batty, from Kirkby Lonsdale (also an especial friend of Smith's) and the Swiss student, Stockar. His dissertation was 'On the preservation of birds'.

22 Mitchill returned to become Professor of Natural History and Botany in Columbia College. Primarily a chemist and mineralogist, his *Sketch of the mineralogical history of New York* (1798–1801) was among the first worthwhile contributions to the descriptive geology of North America – just as his list of the fish of New York State effectively inaugurated ichthyology on that Continent. Among those he encouraged were Torrey, Audubon and Rafinesque. For a full account see HALL, C. R. 1934. *A scientist in the early Republic: Samuel Latham Mitchill, 1764–1831.* New York.

23 Not Göttingen, as traditionally stated (WHITFIELD J. BELL, Jr. 1971. Benjamin Smith Barton, M.D. (Kiel). *J. Hist. Med.* **26:** 197–203). On his return Barton became Professor of Materia Medica, Natural History and Botany in the University of Pennsylvania. His *Elements of Botany* (1803) was the first American elementary textbook on that subject.

24 A founder member of the (third) Aurelian Society, 1801.

25 Council Member, Entomological Society of London, 1884. Also Secretary of the Royal Society, 1827, and author of one of the Bridgewater Treatises.

26 Thus Bruce's (none too reliable) spelling. Probably the James Cunningham, of Edinburgh, who joined on 26 April 1782 and was doubtless the 'Mr. Cunningham' whose garden Thornton records in his diary visiting that month, in company with his fellow-member Stockar "and a few others".

27 Bruce to Smith, 8 Apr. 1799: Smith Ms. 21, 82.

28 Bruce to Smith, 9 Feb. 1801: Smith Ms. 21, 87.

29 Neill to Smith, 9 May 1806: Smith Ms. 7, 170v.

30 THOMSON, J. 1859. *An account of the life, lectures and writings of William Cullen, M.D.* Edinburgh. (Introduction, p. 16.)

31 GRAY, J. 1952. *History of the Royal Medical Society 1737–1937.* Edinburgh. (p. 85.)

32 Neill to Smith, 17 May 1808: Smith Ms. 7, 175.

33 In the Conference discussion on this paper Professor D. K. McE. Kevan pointed out that at least during the early part of the present century the Royal Physical Society, despite its name, had a pronounced natural history orientation. Possibly this had been the case ever since the 1812 merger.

Shells, Collecting and the Victorians

The Victorians collected shells from quite a range of motives. Some of those were inherited ones, others were creations of their own. The same was true, broadly speaking, of Victorian natural history as a whole, but the weight of the cultural legacy that lay behind shells was an extra-large one and gave them a clear advantage in the jostling for favour when the new era began. Rather exceptionally, the collecting and study of them underwent no perceptible process of reinterpretation as the middle classes achieved their novel ascendancy. Conchology enjoyed a smooth continuum. It was one aristocratic pursuit which fitted extremely snugly into the new code of morals and manners, which was not felt to need knocking into a more appropriate shape. In so far as it underwent any alteration at all as the nineteenth century found its stride, that took the form of additions to its reach, which were the gift of advances in technology and of improvements in equipment.

As collectibles, shells have always had three great advantages: they are mostly decorative, they are relatively small in size (and so take up little space, at any rate individually), and they occur in a stimulating variety. Just like the postage stamps that would later topple them from their throne, they come in a colourful assortment of shapes and sizes, with their own equivalents of 'penny blacks' and 'Cape triangulars'; every country produces its own special kinds, some as common and spurnable as French Colonials, others as rare as Post Office Mauritius or one of nature's counterparts of an accidental misprinting; a beginner can start off with a presentable array, put together with his own unaided efforts and without any expenditure of money, while for the well-off connoisseur there is challenging scope for competing financially for the finest and scarcest. They are almost guaranteed to arouse the collecting instinct - that instinct which commonly starts to make its presence felt in the middle years of childhood, around the age of eight or nine. It was just at that age, we should not be surprised to learn, that one of the great British shell-collectors of all time, James Cosmo Melvill, is recorded as having first succumbed.

Yet as old as mankind as that instinct must surely be, as alluring as shells must all along have been to anyone who ever wandered along a beach, for eons upon eons it was an instinct that must have had to be largely repressed. Life was too much of a struggle for it to be permitted any but strictly utilitarian outlets. Shells could be used for personal adornment and for decorating more generally or even as currency, but collecting just for collecting's sake was firmly out : that had to be postponed until the necessary margin of leisure began to be enjoyed in certain cultures and at certain periods, more especially those which experienced much seaborne trade and contacts with areas that lay beyond normal reach. The Roman Empire was the natural birthplace for conchology, if that was indeed where its birth took place. Significantly, though, it was not until the sixteenth century and the re-emergnce of that key combination of a leisured class with close and plentiful access to imports from far-off lands that the pursuit enjoyed a resurrection. Significantly, too, it was in Holland, the leading sea power of the century that followed, with an extensive trade with the distant East Indies, that conchology then most firmly took root.

Alongside those specialist collectors of shells and nothing but shells there were at the same time, all over Europe, many more people, no less wealthy, who included shells in more general 'cabinets of curiosities'. Just as a display of *objets d'art* had come to be recognised as a mark of cultivation and good taste, a complementary display of **natural** objects, chosen either for their beauty or their mysteriousness, conferred upon its owner an aura of the *savant* - an impression, however spurious, of sharing in the learned quest for 'natural knowledge'. Shells featured in these cabinets in two quite different guises, respectively ancient and modern: as fossils on the one hand - those intriguing productions of very debatable origin - and as samples of nature's beauty, analagous to fine minerals, on the other. If the cabinets themselves were made of costly wood and lined in velvet, so much the better, for that served to emphasise the amount of wealth available for expending in this tasteful direction.

To some extent these two tendencies, the specialist collecting and the generalist connoisseurship, became interfused. The prestige to be gained from showing off beautiful possessions seduced at least some of the out-and-out shell collectors into going to great lengths to arrange their specimens artistically. Some again were tempted even to try to improve on nature and paid to have the duller kinds 'beautified' artificially. 'Shell-doctoring', as this was called, indeed developed into quite a trade in Holland, providing a living for numerous practitioners. Both then and later the purity of the drive to collect was at all times liable to be diluted and distorted by this wish to conform to the dictates of contemporary Taste - unfortunate though the effects of that could sometimes be.

The high reputability of collecting and the vaguely learned *cachet* shells had acquired as cabinet 'curiosities' were the two primary legacies to the Victorians from their predecessors. Three further, more minor ones can be identified as well.

First of these in time was the fashion for *rocaille*, the shell-like motif that became so ubiquitous from 1710 onwards. A central expression of the then modish Classicism (for the Ancient Greeks and Romans had been notably fond of shells as decorative items), the outburst of this at just that point in time may have been mere coincidence. However, a distinguished art historian, Dr Joan Evans (1931: 92), has gone on record with the claim that the trajectory of that fashion closely parallels the surges and falls in what by then had become a veritable shell-collecting craze - the '*conchyliomanie*', as it was being dubbed by the French. Like the 'pteridomania', the fern craze of the century following, with its suggestive echoes of the Gothic Revival, it may well have been that conchology had unwittingly fallen in step with a potent style trend in the visual arts. Whether this thesis holds water or not, the alignment of shell-collecting with such an emphatic expression of contemporary taste can only have helped it to appear that much more respectable.

A few years later there came the sea-bathing fashion, luring the affluent and the leisured down to Brighthelmstone or Weymouth and elevating those watering-places to an elegance that rivalled that of the inland spas. This brought about the first contact *en masse* between intelligent people of taste and the natural objects cast up on beaches. The most surprising product of that encounter was an interest in seaweeds, at first as the mere raw material for a handicraft but increasingly as the focus of scientific study, culminating eventually in several sumptuous monographs (Allen, 1996). Shells, though, predictably came in for attention too, and conchology acquired some prestigious reinforcements from the highest ranks of society as a result.

The third of these subsidiary legacies came from the high standing enjoyed by that top science of the immediately pre-Victorian period, geology. If it was socially acceptable to collect **fossil** shells, and even to be seen digging for them oneself in quarries or the newly-excavated sections of canals, then it was most certainly respectable too to be a collector of their present-day equivalents. Indeed, adding to knowledge of our contemporary molluscan fauna was doubtless smiled upon as potentially helpful to palaeontologists as well.

But that particular legacy can have been only an indirect and shadowy one at best. Indeed, it might not even be worthy of mention were it not for the fact that geology acted also as a prism through which were refracted, albeit very dimly, the rays of that enormously powerful source of contemporary cultural heat : romanticism. Unlike seaweeds, those fern-like adornments of rocks and stones with their inklings of the Sublime, shells were not in themselves romantic. The sea, of course, was, especially when it was boisterous, but it would be going too far to claim the same status for its miscellaneous contents. It was only when they featured as fossils, and thereby acquired a measure of romantic mystery, that that helpful mantle extended to mollusca. In that guise they could be seen as part of that terrible primaeval world of slime and shrieks and scaly monsters, that grisly world guaranteed to give rise to the most delightful shudders. Imagination grown rich on such a diet may sometimes have turned upon present-day shells and infused them into psudo-fossils: but, if so, that can only have been as a category mistake.

'Victorianism' tends to be thought of as a wholly novel set of attitudes and tastes which suddenly came into being in the 1830s and then survived more or less intact for another sixty years. In reality, as the history of shell-collecting illustrates so well in its own small way, it was for the most part little more than a distinctive stamp placed upon a random assemblage of habits and poses that had characterised the generation that immediately came before. In essence what the Victorians did was to take that assemblage over *en bloc*, superficially conserving it but, in fact, remoulding it in their own likeness. That likeness was the product of a widely-diffused austerity and restraint, a recrudescence of those traits which History has come to label 'puritanism', traits which were powered by an intense and even fanatical religiosity. That religiosity used up such reserves of emotional energy that there was too little left over for genuine aesthetic pleasure, resulting either in empty habits of response or in compensating over-concern with detail. It was no coincidence, as I see it, that the Victorian era opened with a fashion for microscopy, that so many naturalists in that first formative decade became suddenly entranced with the minutiae of nature (Allen, 1976: 129), exclaiming over mosses and beetles and the tinier Crustacea. Nor was it a coincidence, rather later, that the extraordinary craze for collecting and growing ferns closely paralleled the Gothic Revival in architecture (Allen, 1985). A special mind-set had developed that percolated everywhere.

The religiosity decreed that the worthwhileness of activities was to be measured in terms of the amount of moral uplift that they engendered. What had previously been quite innocent pursuits and pastimes - like shell-collecting, for instance - now had to be justified by that yardstick, both to oneself and to others. Natural history, which might have been dismissed as mere idle amusement, the plaything of atheistic aristocrats, luckily lent itself to reinterpretation as an outlet for 'natural theology': "through Nature up to Nature's God" - in the words of a favourite incantation of the period. (One even comes across those words employed as a kind of text on the herbarium labels of ultra-devout Victorian botanists.) It would hardly be too much of an exaggeration to claim that the Evangelical Revival and Nonconformism between them rescued natural history from lapsing into obscurity and even oblivion, infusing it with such a bracing self-confidence that its popularity has turned out to be enduring (at any rate among the Protestant nations of North-west Europe).

Perhaps the luckiest part of that accident was that collecting received religious endorsement. Collecting could of course be defended as necessary to science at that period, when the diversity of nature was still in the full flush of being uncovered and described, and at a time when public museums were only just coming into being and almost all entrants to any study still needed to rely on their own resources for putting names to species. Nevertheless many more people might well have preferred to investigate behaviour rather than push ever further forward the bounds of taxonomy had not collecting received such emphatic approval from society more generally. It was viewed by and large as a tasteful occupation, especially suitable for young people. It developed neatness; it encouraged perseverance; in theory it opened eyes to the beauties of nature and the challenges and wonders of science. It added interest to that necessary exercise, the Sunday walks. And, at the very lowest, it kept idle hands safely out of Satan's reach. We must also remember that a high proportion of the educated population still lived in the depths of the country or, at least, in quiet rural towns and villages, where alternative amusements were scarce for anyone without the wherewithal or taste for the standard rural sports. I have suggested elsewhere (Allen, *1996*) that the explanation for the striking number of maiden ladies who made a name for themselves in the unlikely field of algology may lie in the fact that patrolling their local beaches for unusual kinds of seaweeds was one of the few suitably decorous activities they were able to indulge in, marooned as they were in isolated seaside places, condemned to the narrowest of horizons. Doubtless this same environmental monotony gave rise to many accomplished female conchologists too, even though the potential for finding, in home waters, species, or even genera, new to science - and having these named after one - was very much slighter in the case of shells.

It was not only unmarried women, of course, who found in natural history collecting salvation from boredom. Two of the very few respectable middle-class careers at that period for men of a scholarly temperament were Medicine and the Church, and a high proportion of livings and practices were in country areas of comparative remoteness where kindred spirits were few. There is strong reason to suspect that one reason for that large number of Victorian clerical naturalists, so often remarked upon, is that an interest in the subject was actively fostered in their training colleges; for in many a rural parish an incumbent could expect to live out his days with barely another educated person to speak to and would be dependent on his own resources in the matter of recreation. For a man of the cloth few possible outlets in that direction were seemly, and natural history and the study of antiquities were the two most obvious choices, alike quietist pursuits redolent of the gentleman-scholar. Both also had the attraction that they encouraged a parson to get out and about his parish, arming him with pretexts, moreover, for penetrating its every part. Even a smattering of natural history knowledge, furthermore, could give him a conversational entrée into circles locally from which he might otherwise be barred. Even in recent years I have known of one newly-rural vicar who took up botany with the express aim of getting on terms with his farming parishioners by offering to identify weeds for them.

Yet, if natural history owed much to isolation, social as well as physical, paradoxically that was also a period when that isolation was also being very much reduced, most notably by the spread of the railway system from the 1830s onwards. That in its own way was richly productive of naturalists too. For it was thanks to the new steam trains that holidaying at the seaside now became practicable for the population at large, and greatly increased numbers consequently discovered for themselves the quiet pleasures of combing beaches for the tide's rejectamenta. That was not all gain, for those numbers were large indeed and the combing was liable to be overdone. Even before the Victorians crowded in there were warning signs that harm might result from this. As early as 1823, in a letter to one of the Sowerbys, a Belfast conchologist, James Cleland, can be found complaining that at the nearby resort of Bangor there were no longer limpets to be found, these having been "so much the fashion that the Visitors who frequented [that place], as Sea Bathers, during the last two summers, employed the children to collect them, and there is not one to be seen now" (Matheson, 1966). If over-collecting of that magnitude could happen at so comparatively early a period at somewhere so comparatively out-of-the-way, the damage visited later upon the coasts of southern England is likely to have been proportionately far worse. It must be counted fortunate therefore that shell-collectors were content to rely mainly on what the tides had thrown up on the open strand and refrained from seeking out the living animals.

It was this very **simplicity** that shells possessed as items to collect that surely accounted for much of the popularity of the pursuit. Unlike animals they did not need to be skinned or pickled, unlike flowers they did not need to be pressed and dried, unlike insects they did not need to be pinned and set. As one contemporary magazine pointed out, "there is no cruelty in the pursuit", which made it "a study peculiarly suited to ladies" - given that (the writer went on) "the subjects are so brightly clean, so ornamental to a boudoir". For women, too, shells shared with flowers the advantage that they could be collected without embarassment, for provided they were picked up off the foreshore - and did not have to be waded for or hammered off the rocks - they did not involve indecent postures or any stare-inducing equipment. It was only if there was a need to wander from that foreshore straight and narrow that problems were liable to arise. "When we first began Sea Weeds", the Berwickshire naturalist George Johnston once confessed to a correspondent, "my wife carried a larger muff than the present fashion would command, and many a heavy stone and well-filled bottle has therein been smuggled" (Hardy, 1892: 174). From the need for such subterfuges the ordinary shell-collector was happily immune.

There were two other features that distinguished Victorian natural history from the subject as it had existed before but which owed nothing to the special emotional character of the era.

Like the railways, one of these was the product of purely technological advance. In the 1830s great and progressive reductions in costs finally effected a printing boom which had long been artificially held back by designedly repressive taxes. A dazzling crop of popular magazines and handbooks immediately sprang up as a result, *inter alia* catering for the novice naturalist in a way that he or she had never known previously. It was not merely that works of reference that had lain out of reach before now became generally available and affordable: it was also that the literature as a whole altered in quality. Addressed no longer exclusively to scholars and to wealthy patrons of learning, it now stepped down from its age-old loftiness even to the point of becoming chatty. Loudon's *Magazine of Natural History*, hugely popular right from its launch in 1828, was the front-runner, and to some extent the exemplar, of a whole pack of other periodicals, almost all of them short-lived. For in those early days there were simply too many publishers and editors competing for a place in a still strictly limited natural history market - a market, moreover, which had to be wooed on as broad a front as possible if publishing was to be viable economically. The more sophisticated naturalists, with more specialist interests, found this situation chronically frustrating, for they badly needed alternative outlets for their observations and records to the limited number of journals produced by learned societies (which by definition had a closed circulation and frequently appeared only at lengthy intervals). The more natural history broke up into specialisms - and that process was under way very noticeably as the Victorian era opened - the more badly the need was also felt for journals that spoke to those specialist audiences alone. Those needs only started to be met as late as the 1860s, when the several major sub-communities (entomology, botany, geology, general zoology) had at last expanded to a size sufficient to render journals addressed to each one singly a tolerable proposition commercially.

Until that point was reached, publishing economics acted very helpfully to hold the various sub-studies together in a single, unitary subject, broadly conceived. Botanists were thereby forced to continue to take cognizance of what entomologists did, just as ornithologists were of geologists - to an extent that could only be regarded as healthy intellectually. At that period natural history was in any case much less tightly compartmentalised than it was later to become: many a naturalist was **both** a botanist **and** an entomologist, **both** an egg-collector **and** a geologist - and if not a follower of more than one pursuit simultaneously, then perhaps of several *seriatim*. People still tended to think of themselves as naturalists rather than as botanists, say, or geologists solely and specifically. Collecting, too, was a great binder: if you tired of one branch of nature, then you could readily start up in another, without feeling that this was a step of much significance. You merely altered the contents of what still probably remained the same set of drawers.

This lingering unity was further buttressed by the extent to which the various natural history sub-communities intermarried. In this respect the great Sowerby dynasty was merely one of several. Even without the special ties that bound together the descendants of the Clapham sect or so many Quakers, we do not have to dig far in Victorian natural history to find whole straggling networks of relations. In just one major society of the period, the Botanical Society of London, a truly national body with a membership drawn from all over the British Isles, **at least** one person in every seven has turned out to have been connected to one or more fellow members by blood or by marriage (Allen, 1986: 44). It was a world of quite startling smallness and intimacy.

One great benefit from that was that people knew what was afoot in related fields to a much greater extent than has tended to happen since. With more porous boundaries the different sub-communities consequently exchanged ideas more freely and were more inclined to borrow each other's useful innovations. One example of such borrowing was the adoption by conchology from botany of the Watsonian vice-county system as the basis for recording the distribution of the British non-marine mollusca, a scheme initiated in 1881 and masterminded by W. Denison Roebuck for the best part of half a century. This is of course one of the few other areas of natural history in which the subjects of study are as well-nigh stationary as plants; but would conchologists have got down to such a scheme, at any rate at so early a period, had there not been that botanical model to spur them to action first? Their record of alertness to useful possibilities in other fields is not, however, a very impressive one. When Broderip (1832) and Forbes (Herdman, 1923) began commending respectively rakes and dredges to them in the 1830s (in place of the long-established but less efficient trawls), those tools had been in use for other marine purposes for several decades already. Admittedly, though, until then their eyes had been firmly fixed upon the beaches and they had failed to realise the further rich potential harvest that lurked just off-shore.

The Victorians have come in for much mocking. And certainly in some degree they did rather invite this by taking their lives so extremely seriously. But what energy they had ! How marvellously inventive they were ! And what a magnificent natural history legacy they left to us in their turn !

REFERENCES

ALLEN, D.E., 1976 *The Naturalist in Britain. A social history.* London.

ALLEN, D.E., 1985 Natural history and visual taste : some parallel tendencies. In *The Natural Sciences and the Arts* [ed. Ellenius, A.], Uppsala.

ALLEN, D.E., 1986 *The Botanists : a History of the Botanical Society of the British Isles through 150 Years.* Winchester.

ALLEN, D.E., 1996 Fashions and crazes. In *Cultures of Natural History.* [ed. Jardine, N., Secord, J. and Spary, E.], Cambridge.

BRODERIP, W.J., 1832 *Hints for Collecting Animals and their Products.* London.

EVANS, J., 1931 *Pattern: a Study of Ornament in Western Europe from 1180 to 1900.* Oxford.

HARDY, J. [ed.], 1892 *Selections from the Correspondence of Dr. George Johnston.* Edinburgh

HERDMAN, Sir W.A. 1923 *Founders of Oceanography and their Work.* London.

MATHESON, C., 1966 G. B. Sowerby the first and his correspondents; Part II. *Journal of the Society for the Bibliography of Natural History,* **4** (5): 253-66.

A paper read at the Joint Meeting of the Conchological Society of Great Britain and Ireland, The Malacological Society of London and the Society for the History of Natural History, held at the Linnean Society, London, on 22nd October 1994, and privately printed in Manchester in 1996 for distribution to participants at that meeting. The author would like to thank Ron Cleevely and Bill Bailey for their assistance in printing.

V

Tastes and crazes

Fashions, in the strict sense, do not occur in intellectual matters, nor can they. For they are light-hearted products of imitation and show, necessarily transient and shallow in order to fulfil their function of expressing a merely temporary inclination or mood. They rise, they fall and in their turn are then replaced by something similar.[1] It is common to speak of intellectual fashions, but by that is meant no more than that some set of facts or a theory has caught on and become popular (and not necessarily only temporarily): being non-visual, it cannot serve as a vehicle for eye-catching display; being serious, it is not bound to be discarded once adopted too widely and persisted in too long.

Natural history, however, is not and never has been a purely intellectual pursuit. It has a considerable aesthetic component as well, of varying strength at different periods and in different individuals. Many people are attracted to it primarily for visual reasons, rather than to study behaviour, work out distributions or formulate concepts. Even in its most primitive manifestation, collecting, there can be a delight in shapes and colours and patterns which co-exists with the mere pleasure of acquisition or the sheer satisfaction of having the evidence for some additional item of knowledge.

Once this extra-intellectual interest goes beyond a certain point, natural history is liable to take on an additional dimension: to be drawn on for reasons that are purely aesthetic-cum-social, to become the prey of genuine fashion. At the extreme, the very subject itself may become the plaything of fashion, as happened in the eighteenth century and more especially in the Paris salons. More usually, though, one particular facet is fastened upon and inflated out of all proportion to its intrinsic importance as an area of study. Aspects of natural history which have some obvious potential as vehicles for symbolism are particularly vulnerable to being raided like this, and it is no accident that plants and shells have formed the subjects of the most salient instances that have occurred. In the words of one Victorian magazine, shells 'are so brightly clean, so ornamental to a boudoir', while the special attractiveness of plants, by virtue of their foliage no less than of their flowers, is in need of no

emphasizing. Both possess the additional advantage of easily recognized features which readily lend themselves to adoption as design
motifs, by which means they can become completely incorporated
into décor, totally abstracted from nature. Indeed, it may well be
that natural objects normally become the focus of powerful fashions
only if they are subtly in accord with the wider artistic expression
of a particular outlook associated with a particular span of years –
only if, in their own small way, they serve to reflect that elusive
entity, the 'spirit of the age'.

Conchyliomanie

Shells first became noticeably the subject of an elegant pursuit in
the seventeenth-century Netherlands. As early as 1607 artists there
were being commissioned to paint leading collectors of these with
choice specimens in front of them. Just like the postage stamps of
later generations, shells came in a gratifying assortment of shapes
and colours; many were pleasing to the eye and some even beautiful;
they were obtainable from all corners of the globe, but from many
of them only rarely and only with great difficulty; a beginner could
start with a presentable array, put together by his own unaided
efforts and without any expenditure of money, while for the connoisseur there was a challenging hinterland of scarcity, conferring
monetary value accordingly. For one of these Dutchmen, Pierre
Lyonet, shell collecting was indeed no more and no less than a
branch of art collecting, the finest specimens being purchased with
all the care and discrimination that went into his buying of paintings.
    By the early eighteenth century there were cabinets full of shells
to be found in the houses of the wealthy over much of Europe.
Two of the finest collections drawn from all parts of the then-
known world, were those of the London physician, Sir Hans
Sloane (1660–1753), and of an Amsterdam apothecary, Albert Seba
(1665–1736). Some of these cabinet owners went to great lengths
to arrange their specimens artistically (Figure 23.1) while others
went further still by trying to improve on nature's efforts by paying
to have individual specimens 'beautified' artificially (a fate similarly
visited in the next century on the tougher kinds of birds' eggs).
'Shell-doctoring', as this was called, developed into quite a trade
in the Netherlands, providing a living for numerous practitioners.
Yet a very much fatter living was to be had by the specialist auc-
tioneers: for collectors were continually dying, or simply tiring of
their hobby, or disposing of one collection preparatory to starting
all over afresh. At these sales impressively high prices, sometimes
even absurdly high ones, were increasingly reached as the pursuit
began to assume the proportions of a craze – the 'conchyliomanie',
as it was dubbed by the French.

V

Figure 23.1 A shell 'portrait' in the cabinet of a Dutch collector. Albertus Seba, *Thesaurus* (Leiden, 1758), vol. 3, plate 37.

Like the fern craze of the following century (of which more below), with its suggestive echoes of the Gothic Revival, the shell craze is under strong suspicion of having owed its super-normal vitality to acting as a side expression of a dominant trend in contemporary art. Indeed, one authority on the art of the period has gone so far as to claim that the craze precisely paralleled in its rises and falls the concurrent fashion for *rocaille*, the shell-like motif that became so ubiquitous from 1719 onwards.[2] However much truth there may be in that, it is certainly striking how suddenly the '*conchyliomanie*' came to an end: there was one final, immensely lucrative auction in 1757, that of the vast collection of the French ambassador at The Hague, the Marquis de Bonnac, and then prices abruptly dropped – and never afterwards recovered. 'All fashions end in excess', according to a dictum of the great couturier

Poiret, and maybe it was simply greed that did the shell collecting craze to death. Or maybe it was that the eyes of everyone in the salons had at last finally wearied of *rocaille* and of anything that resembled it.

Seaweeds

Closely akin to the shell craze, at least to the extent that it was similarly a product of the searching of beaches, was the somewhat later, but decidedly lower-key, fashionable concern with seaweeds. In this case, untypically, what began largely as an artistic vogue went on to open up a lasting field of serious study: more usually the reverse occurs, or the vogue and the study develop in tandem.

In 1751–2 John Ellis (1710–76), a London merchant active in botanical circles, began receiving collections of 'sea plants' and corallines from correspondents of his who lived on the coast. The reason for this is unclear, but it led him into making a pioneer classificatory study of those hitherto neglected groups, in the course of which he was to rediscover that corallines were animals, not plants (as generally supposed up till then) and, in a series of publications, to remove once and for all the misconception that they were an intermediate link between the two. This scientific work, however, had an unlikely by-product, for, apparently on a whim, he one day made a miniature seascape out of his specimens, giving this the modish name of 'grotto-work'[3] – in evident allusion to the then fashionable taste for caves, crags and ruins and their 'picturesque' accompaniment of greenery. The existence of this came to the knowledge of one of his scientist friends, the Rev. Stephen Hales, who thereupon asked him to make something similar for the Princess Dowager of Wales, to whom Hales was Clerk of the Closet.[4] After that a salon fashion seems to have arisen for this delicate type of fancy-work, a fashion which was to continue in some degree all through the century following (and to enjoy a revival in recent years as part of the taste for 'pressed-flower' pictures, in the guise of 'underwater scenes' in which seaweeds do duty as foliage).

It may have been this fashion and the demand for the necessary raw material that it generated that caused the Clerk to the Royal Society, Emanuel Mendes da Costa (1717–91), to write in those same months to a leading antiquary in Essex in the following (surprisingly peremptory) terms: 'Send me a small box of the seaweeds or corallines found on your coast. You have only need to lay them in a heap, damp as they are.'[5] About the same time a Mrs Le Coq, down at Weymouth, was likewise being pressed into service by that inveterate collector of almost everything, the Duchess of Portland; and presently quite a few others were joining in.

V

398

In the surviving letter-book[6] of Dru Drury, a wealthy London silversmith, are to be found, dated April 1764, some 'Directions given to Mr Warr, Cap. Mayle, etc. to be sent into Devonshire and Cornwall for Collecting Sea Weeds'. While still crudely minimal, these at least improved on Da Costa's by insisting that the specimens be washed in fresh water on being gathered, before being put moist into a box or barrel and packed very tight.

It was this very simplicity that seaweeds shared with shells (and, later, ferns) as items to take up and preserve that doubtless accounted for a good deal of their popularity with collectors. In this respect they were notably different from so many other items with which naturalists found it necessary to concern themselves. Like shells, too, seaweeds could be sought after without embarrassment, for provided they were picked up off the foreshore – and did not have to be waded for or hammered off the side of a rock-pool – they did not involve unseemly postures or any stare-inducing equipment. Once collectors left the safety of the foreshore, by contrast, they were liable to meet with problems. 'When we first began Sea Weeds,' the Berwick naturalist Dr George Johnston (1797–1855) once confided to a correspondent, 'my wife carried a larger muff than the present fashion would commend, and many a heavy stone and well-filled bottle has therein been smuggled.'[7] Not everyone, though, was willing to operate with such furtiveness. In the view of the no-nonsense Mrs Margaret Gatty (1807–73), 'any one really intending to *work* in the matter must lay aside for a time all thought of conventional appearances'. For her own forays along the edge of the tide she favoured a pair of boy's shooting boots, rendered waterproof with a thin coat of neat's-foot oil; above those merino rather than cotton stockings, and petticoats, also preferably of wool, that never reached below the ankle; over those a ladies' yachting costume (in her opinion, 'as near perfection for shore-work as anything that could be devised'); and, to complete the ensemble, a hat instead of a bonnet. Cloaks, shawls and all millinery she warned against as hopelessly impractical. Even she, though, otherwise dauntless though she was, was forced to admit that 'a low-water-mark expedition is more comfortably taken under the protection of a gentleman'.[8]

It was presumably because seaweeds were firmly associated in the public mind with a highly respectable kind of handicraft that so many women were emboldened to take up forming collections of them. Very much a minority fashion though this one remained all along, it was to become increasingly noteworthy for the prominence attained in it by that otherwise then so generally diffident sex. The fact that in its early stages the pursuit had gained a strong foothold among the landed gentry, and the male landed gentry at that, must also have conferred on it a certain social cachet which

no doubt provided them with additional encouragement. That aristocratic influx, indeed, temporary though it proved, appears at first sight an even more striking and unexpected feature of the fashion than the later prominence of women. Those were the years, though, in which the uppermost layer of society was deeply in thrall to the earliest manifestations of Romanticism, in which a taste for a feathery green covering of stone or rocks (as in the grottoes which provided John Ellis with a kind of code-word to flourish as a cover) was one conspicuous ingredient. The connection between the modish mediaevalism and the focus on seaweeds is well exemplified by the action of one of those landowners, John Stackhouse (1742–1819), whose Cornish estates included some marine frontage, in having a castle-like folly put up to serve as a base while he worked on this group of plants specifically. Some twenty years later, in 1795, his *Nereis Britannica* appeared as the outcome, one of several superb folios to be devoted to the subject by affluent enthusiasts at that period.

The women collectors were all much too self-effacing to contemplate such feats; indeed, with only one or two exceptions none of them were ever to venture into any form of print. How then did it come about that so many of them achieved a considerable measure of genuine botanical renown, ending up with new species and

Figure 23.2 Shore collecting: 'a low-water-mark expedition is more comfortably taken under the protection of a gentleman'. G. H. Lewes, *Sea-side Studies* (London, 1868).

even genera named after them? The answer to that question is to be found in the fact that most were condemned to lives of boring uneventfulness in small, relatively isolated seaside towns, in which a regular walk along the beach was one of the few kinds of outdoor recreation permissible. Short of dredging, an elaborate procedure which called for specialized equipment, the only way any collector had of acquiring specimens of the little-known kinds restricted to the deeper waters was to keep a watch on the beaches for any stray examples of them that happened to have been dislodged and cast up by storms. This elementary task was one for which such women were peculiarly well-situated. One by one, over the years, they were brought into touch as a result with specialists with monographs under way on these plants; and delighted to learn that their patrolling could be put to such wider and loftier ends, they scanned their local shores all the more diligently, periodically packing off by post consignments of their gleanings. In this way the seaweed fashion was to become the classic instance of the harnessing to the shafts of scholarship of what originally started out as no more than a tasteful diversion.

The fern craze

To a more limited extent such a claim could be put forward too in some mitigation of the greatest and ultimately most destructive natural history fashion of all: the Victorian fern craze.[9] A British Isles phenomenon more or less exclusively, this was remarkable both for the hurricane-like force of its impact when it eventually took off and for the length of the preceding gestation. In some form or other, though at very different levels of popularity, ferns were the subject of fashionable interest throughout the whole of the nineteenth century. This was primarily horticultural in its inspiration and expression and can truly be ascribed to natural history only very secondarily. It is the classic case in its turn of how natural history has always been potentially subject to the powerful gravitational pull of neighbouring cultural realms, the boundary between gardening and field botany being one that is particularly ill-defined and porous.

Like seaweeds, ferns originally caught the fancy of cultivated circles when Romantic tastes were beginning to stir, and almost certainly because of the similar appeal of their fronds when clothing old walls and weathered rocks. Unlike seaweeds, however, at the outset they were frustratingly lacking in diversity. The species found wild in Britain were few in number and the larger of those were unspectacular and in the main insufficiently unalike. People consequently looked to the wealth of ferns in the tropics for greater aesthetic enrichment. Unfortunately, though, until the closing

Figure 23.3 N. B. Ward's own personal fern-case, designed as a window of Tintern Abbey. Frontispiece to N. B. Ward, *On the Growth of Plants in Closely Glazed Cases* (2nd edn, London, 1852).

years of the eighteenth century hardly any of the tropical species had found their way into the hothouses of Britain, for the simple reason that till then no one had any idea how to raise ferns from spores and the vicissitudes of the sea voyages were generally fatal to the chances of successfully importing the living plants whether young or mature. Once the secret of spore reproduction was discovered and made known, in the 1790s, professional gardeners on the staff of some of the more horticulturally adventurous establishments started competing with one another in a race to grow the widest selection. Hothouses, however, were rich men's indulgences and that fashion seemed destined to be limited just to this tiny elite.

Then, early in the 1830s, the remarkable properties of more or less airtight glass cases were accidentally discovered by a London general practitioner, Nathaniel Bagshaw Ward (1791–1868). Wardian Cases (as they came to be called), the equivalent of today's 'bottle gardens', at last allowed living plants to be transferred without problems between regions with quite different climates; but, of more immediate importance, they provided micro-environments in which vegetation could flourish indoors (or on balconies) seemingly indefinitely, impervious to the fumes of the gas-lighting by then in increasingly general use. As the chief aim in having these cases was to brighten one's house with greenery all the year round, ferns were at once the favourites for this purpose, and would have been even had they not possessed a faintly Romantic resonance. At the same time glass at that period was formidably expensive, as a result of heavy duties originally imposed to help pay for defending the country against Napoleon, and that made ownership of such a case something of an extravagance. For a long time, therefore, this décor fashion stayed necessarily confined to the comparatively well-to-do.

Towards the end of the 1830s an enthusiasm for the native wild ferns arose in the ranks of field botany, at that time a suddenly fast-growing pursuit. For this, two books were mainly responsible, both by gifted freelance writers: *An Analysis of the British Ferns and their Allies* (1837), by George William Francis, which made up for a humdrum text with an attractive set of copperplate drawings, then a novelty in a work brought out at only a modest price; and *A History of British Ferns* (1840), by Edward Newman, which had first been published serially in a magazine and, despite making do with woodcuts, was written in a bubbling style which still reads irresistibly. Both books emphasized in their very titles that there was more scope than generally realized in learning to distinguish the relatively few native species and – as the justification for seeking these out was still primarily horticultural – in forming a collection of them on the garden rockery or, if Wardian Cases were beyond one's means, in the living-room under inexpensive bell-glasses.

As the botanists poked around in the lanes and coombes of the more westerly parts of Britain (where the damper climate gives rise to ferns in greater profusion), they began to light upon districts where some of the species had 'sported' with unusual frequency, putting out fronds with gross irregularities, sometimes of considerable beauty. The fashion for collecting the wild species was thereupon rescued from dying of banality by a fresh surge of enthusiasm for hunting and growing these 'varieties' (as they were called, though in strict scientific terms they were merely monstrosities). Handbooks duly appeared in response, in which the variants were given Latin names and described and the places in which they had been found were reverently listed.

Then, just after 1850, this obscure and decidedly recherché little fashion exploded all of a sudden into a craze of nation-wide proportions, of quite extraordinary vehemence. Every other person in the country, it soon began to seem, wanted ferns to grow in their gardens or in the rooms of their houses; and as the supply of exotic species was as yet strictly limited, it was the ones that grew wild in Britain that were inevitably the principal victims. As new handbooks were rushed out and existing ones hurriedly reprinted, nurserymen signed up agents on commission to scour the countryside for every fern of sale value that they could find. Fern touts meanwhile sprang into existence, hawking the roots of choice rarities in the streets of cities and even on the summit of Snowdon. Half-starved country folk, seeing to their astonishment a source of ready money growing all around them, joined in with no less abandon and even less discretion. Whole hillsides were stripped bare; woods were cleared of every frond; even private estates were invaded and plundered. It has taken the best part of a century for the native fern flora to recover.

There were two main causes for this huge, dramatic outburst, one obvious, the other less so. The obvious one was the arrival on the market of mass-produced sheet glass, consequent upon the repeal of the glass duties (after persistent, high-level lobbying) in 1845. Those duties had not only made that material unduly expensive: they had also discouraged technical innovation throughout the industry. The Crystal Palace, housing the Great Exhibition of 1851, was the immediate, stunning outcome. All at once everyone wanted their own miniature versions of that – and greenhouse manufacturers and glaziers proceeded to make fortunes as a result.

The other cause was a major switch in taste. As the leading trade magazine, the *Gardeners' Chronicle*, observed in a perceptive editorial in 1856, a liking for 'exquisitely beautiful foliage' was rapidly replacing 'merely gaudy flowers' in the public favour. The latter taste, by implication, was less sophisticated because less subtle. 'Lovers of plants', the editorial went on, 'begin to prefer graceful form to mere spots of colour . . . Dress, furniture, architecture, are all now moving upon the same road side by side' – in the direction of ornamental intricacy and the loving elaboration of detail. By no coincidence, 1851, the year of the Great Exhibition, had also been the year in which John Ruskin first championed the Pre-Raphaelites. In 1855, in the second edition of his *Seven Lamps of Architecture*, he had gone on to sound the opening trumpet-blast of what was to be the Gothic Revival.

It was not long before ferns were breaking out like a rash in almost every conceivable decorative medium. Meanwhile people pressed the actual fronds, fixed them on white paper and hung them up on walls in frames. They also arranged them in pleasing patterns, again on white paper, and then sprayed them with indian ink to obtain silhouettes of a pleasing delicacy – an accomplishment known as 'spatter-work'. This last was thus, ironically, a late by-product of the fashion, instead of its initiator, as the equivalent 'seaweed pictures' had been a century earlier.

So quintessentially were ferns sensed as embodying later-Victorian taste that they were still being taken from the wilds in horrifying quantities right up until the time of the First World War. By then, though, the fashion had become vulgarized, and was largely being kept alive by a commerce determined to squeeze from it every last penny. As if in obedience to the rules identified by fashion theorists, nurserymen ended up by offering the horticultural equivalent of 'hypertrophy', 'over-extension' and 'sartorial hysteria': fern varieties exhibiting such an extreme of deformity as to be tantamount to caricatures. When such a point is reached, it is a signal that a fashion has exhausted its stylistic possibilities before it has fully exhausted its social energy, with no alternative then left to it but to waste itself in flailing against a barrier as invisible as it must be impassable.[10]

Aquaria

There was one further major fashion which descended on British natural history in the mid-nineteenth century – with a similarly jarring abruptness and leaving behind it a similar trail of damage. In some ways a side-branch of the fern craze, it sprang from one of the same roots as that, was equally dependent on relatively cheap glass and essentially consisted of introducing into the Wardian Case movement and animation. Unlike the other fashions already described, however, it had no discernible stylistic associations or symbolical import: it seems to have been purely the product of a technical development. And although it was in part a décor fashion, that might well not have been the case had it not fitted into a niche prepared for it already by the fern craze. Much of the enthusiasm it engendered may have been owed, rather, to its sheer novelty and its impact as a curiosity.

The technical development in question was the extension to the animal world of the oxygenating principle which made possible the Wardian Case: the chemical effect produced by growing plants tightly enclosed in glass not only enables them to stay alive indefinitely, but also sustains any creatures that are placed in with them. Although Ward had taken this step himself as early as 1841, converting one of his plant-cases into what he called an 'aqua-vivarium',[11] he was not concerned to publicize it and it was not for another ten years that its existence was made generally known (in the official catalogue of the Great Exhibition). By that time a professional chemist, Robert Warington, had begun undertaking a series of experiments in which he succeeded in demonstrating, and reported in specialist journals with exemplary thoroughness, the scientific basis of the principle.[12] Additionally, he was able to prove that it held for salt water as well. After that it merely remained for someone with the necessary journalistic skill to alert the wider world to the exciting possibilities that this opened up.

Such a one quickly materialized in the person of Philip Henry Gosse (1810–88). Gosse wrote on natural history for a living and had already produced several of what was eventually to be a long line of beautifully illustrated books on the subject, some of which became bestsellers; he is better known today, though, as the oppressively religiose parent in that classic of autobiography, *Father and Son* (1907). Apart from his skill as a writer, his special contribution was to identify the 'aqua-vivarium' – or the 'aquarium', to which that had speedily become contracted – with the study of marine life more or less exclusively: for he chanced just at that time to have lighted upon the fauna of rock-pools and promptly succumbed to a passion for this. In his very next book, *A Naturalist's Rambles on the Devonshire Coast* (1853), he not only trumpeted his delight in that newly discovered miniature world, but also provided instructions on how to create a marine aquarium.[13]

Another nation-wide craze thereupon followed. All around the coasts rock-pools were pounced on and stripped of their inhabitants. Shops specially catering for the aquarist sprang up. The wealthy had palatial tanks erected in their drawing-rooms. Marine menageries pulled in the crowds in city after city and town after town.

But like all exaggerated fashions, this one had too much energy invested in it to be capable of lasting very long. Unlike the ferneries, though, aquaria were not expressive of Victorianism:

V

Figure 23.4 The marine aquarium. Engraving by F. W. Keyl in George Kearley's *Links in the Chain; or Popular Chapters on the Curiosities of Animal Life* (London, 1862), facing p. 111.

they bore no burden of symbolism that dictated that they should vanish once that symbolism lost its force. Aquaria have consequently continued in use down to the present day more or less uninterruptedly, though a good deal less ubiquitously and with that one-time halo of novelty long since forgotten.

For the scientific world there was one notable outcome: the renowned Stazione Zoologica at Naples, a bold speculative venture embarked upon in 1870 and the scene of much important work

V

at the cutting-edge of biology subsequently, was conceived on the assumption that it could be substantially financed from the fees charged for admission to a high-quality exhibition aquarium. Appropriately, the person engaged to build this was an Englishman, William Alford Lloyd, who owed his reputation and indeed his very career to the strong demand for the highly specialized form of construction work that the craze had engendered in Britain.

The fern craze, too, had its windfalls for science, albeit of a more modest character. They included the discovery of the value of spore characters for distinguishing between species, the proving of fern hybridity and the harnessing of nature-printing (a technique which the craze largely fostered) for the study of venation in fossil plants. Bud-propagation and apospory were similarly legacies to horticulture. All of these would doubtless have come to pass in time, but the intensity of focus that the craze induced caused such discoveries to be made much earlier than would otherwise have been the case. Whatever view one may hold of fashion as a process – and it has its admirers just as it has its detractors – there can be no denying that it does at least provide one good service to humanity in speeding up the adoption of useful practices and knowledge.

Further reading

Allen, D. E., *The Victorian Fern Craze* (London, 1969).
  The Naturalist in Britain: A Social History (orig. London, 1976; Princeton, 1995).
  'Natural history and visual taste: some parallel tendencies', in A. Ellenius (ed.), *The Natural Sciences and the Arts: Aspects of their Interaction from the Renaissance to the 20th Century* (Uppsala, 1985), pp. 32–45.
  'The Victorian fern craze: Pteridomania revisited', in J. M. Ide, A. C. Jermy and A. M. Paul (eds.), *Fern Horticulture: Past, Present, and Future Perspectives* (Andover, 1992), pp. 9–19.
Brock, W. H., '*Glaucus*: Kingsley and the seaside naturalists', *Cahiers victoriens et edouardiens*, 3 (1976), pp. 25–36.
Dance, S. P., *A History of Shell Collecting* (Leiden, 1986).
Rehbock, P. F., 'The Victorian aquarium in ecological and social perspective', in M. Sears and D. Merriman (eds.), *Oceanography: The Past* (New York, 1980), pp. 522–39.
Taylor, J. E., *The Aquarium: Its Inhabitants, Structure, and Management* (London, 1876).

V

489

Notes

1 For a review of this and related concepts see my essay, 'Fashion as a social process', *Textile History*, 22 (1991), pp. 347–58.

2 J. Evans, *Pattern: A Study of Ornament in Western Europe from 1180 to 1900* (Oxford, 1931), vol. II, p. 92.

3 Letter from the Revd William Borlase (15 February 1752), cited in S. Savage, *Catalogue of the Manuscripts in the Library of the Linnean Society of London. Part IV. Calendar of the Ellis Manuscripts* (London, 1948), p. 8.

4 J. Ellis, *An Essay Towards a Natural History of the Corallines* (London, 1755), pp. v–vii; J. Groner, 'Some aspects of the life and work of John Ellis', Ph.D. dissertation (Loyola University of Chicago, 1987), p. 143.

5 J. B. Nichols (ed.), *Illustrations of the Literary History of the Eighteenth Century* (London, 1817–58), vol. IV, p. 753.

6 Now in the Department of Entomology Manuscripts Library, Natural History Museum, London.

7 J. Hardy (ed.), *Selections from the Correspondence of Dr George Johnston* (Edinburgh, 1892), p. 474.

8 Mrs A. Gatty, *British Sea-Weeds* (London, 1872), vol. I, p. viii.

9 For a detailed account, with references, see D. Allen, *The Victorian Fern Craze* (London, 1969).

10 Allen, 'Fashion', p. 354.

11 S. H. Ward, 'On the growth of plants in closely-glazed cases', *Proceedings of the Royal Institution*, 1 (1854), pp. 407–12; S. Hibberd, *Rustic Adornments for Homes of Taste* (London, 1856), p. 7.

12 For a detailed account, with references, see C. Hamlin, 'Robert Warington and the moral economy of the aquarium', *Journal of the History of Biology*, 19 (1986), pp. 131–54.

13 He had already done this a few months earlier in a more specialized place: 'On keeping marine animals and plants alive in unchanged sea-water', *Annals and Magazine of Natural History*, ser. 2, 10 (1852), pp. 263–8.

VI

THE VICTORIAN FERN CRAZE: PTERIDOMANIA REVISITED

ABSTRACT

Raising ferns from spore, a late eighteenth-century discovery, made collections of the plants a feature of rich Englishmen's stoves, which many more people were enabled to copy by the invention in the 1830s of the Wardian parlour-case. Books by G.W. Francis and Edward Newman meanwhile inspired the forming of collections of the British wild species and, in due course, their frond variations. The slashing of the glass duties, the new craze for Gothic tracery and further appealing handbooks combined to fan this activity to craze proportions in the 1850s. Enormous damage to the native fern flora resulted, but there were some scientific and economic side-benefits.

INTRODUCTION

It is getting on for 30 years now since I carried out a study-in-depth (Allen, 1969) of that mysterious collecting epidemic that overtook the mid-Victorian botanical-cum-horticultural community. The idea had been to produce a paper for the *British Fern Gazette*, but I ended up with such a plethora of material that I found I had no option but to turn it into a short book.

A certain amount of additional material has inevitably come to light in the intervening years, but none of it has altered the picture in any major way. Of necessity, therefore, this account has to be a recapitulation, by and large, of what appears in my book.

THE EARLY DAYS

To see the craze in proper historical perspective it helps to start in the second half of the previous century. It was just after the middle of that century, and more particularly in its third quarter, that natural history - and above all field botany - effectively had its birth as a social phenomenon. Before that there were numerous individual workers in the subject, but they were too few and scattered to make up a coherent community, at any rate of an enduring kind. After that we find societies springing up on every hand, periodicals being launched, and soon even organised networks for exchanging specimens coming into being. Before, it was an essentially solitary pursuit; afterwards, it was increasingly a social one. By the 1830s field botany could claim to be a fashionable pastime among the upper and middle classes, and as such it was not only exposed to extraneous tastes and influences, but was also potentially capable of generating these in and of itself.

For a long time very few people took any special interest in ferns. For field botanists there were too few native species to constitute much of a collecting challenge and the group as a whole was one of those dull-seeming, greenish-looking masses, like the grasses and sedges, that tend to deter all but the most determined. For horticulturists and gardeners (at that period, of course, the two were not the same) there were also too few species available, whether native or exotic, to offer enough scope for specialisation. Bringing live ferns in from overseas was extremely hazardous; and it was not until the very end of the eighteenth century (in 1795) that the first major influx took place - in the shape of a cargo of 37 species from the West Indies, thanks to the supreme punctiliousness of Captain Bligh of Mutiny-on-the-Bounty fame.

Ironically, though, Bligh could have been spared all that great expense of care and effort; for in just the previous year his patron, Sir Joseph Banks, had brought to the attention of the Linnean Society the remarkable degree of success enjoyed by a surgeon in Jamaica in raising ferns there from spore. This was a certain John Lindsay, who had studied botany in the course of his medical training at Edinburgh. He was by no means the first person to manage this feat, but his success was the first to receive the necessary modicum of publicity.

Raising exotic ferns from spore thereafter gradually caught on as one of those competitive achievements that head gardeners at that period very much went in for. One of the leaders in this competition was the gardener to a member of one of the wealthy Quaker banking dynasties, Robert Barclay, of Bury Hill near Dorking in Surrey. Another was the gardener to Lord Fitzwilliam in

Northamptonshire. But the generally acknowledged champions were John Shepherd and his nephew Henry, the successive Curators of Liverpool Botanic Garden. By 1818 they had managed to raise as many as 53 species, many of them from tropical America. Before long, however, their efforts were to be massively overtaken by two other institutions with greater resources, one of them Kew, the other the great commercial nursery at Hackney in London built up by George Loddiges, a highly respected figure in the scientific circles of the day.

The renown won by those great collections of hothouse ferns has tended to obscure the fact that a few people were simultaneously pioneering the forming and raising of collections confined just to the hardy species native to Britain. Chief of these were a Nottinghamshire land agent and his wife, John and Meta Riley (Allen, 1978). In 1840 a lengthy monograph of theirs was read part-by-part before the Botanical Society of London, summarising what they were able to claim as *"the results of many years' personal experience"*, including cultivating every British species and studying minutely their specific differences. Another of their contributions to that Society in the same year was a paper entitled *On growing ferns from seed, with suggestions upon their cultivation and preparing the specimens.* Thus an interest in fern-growing had arisen, and was being actively propagated, quite independently of the main line of development that presently occurred in which the later, mid-century craze is identified as being rooted. A small-scale fashion (for the study and growing of British ferns and their varieties) would probably have come about in any event during those years, but it is hard to believe that it would have taken on the dimensions of a nation-wide craze had there not also been the invention in the meantime of the Wardian case.

The story of the accidental discovery by N.B. Ward, a general practitioner in one of the sooty, slum districts of London, of the ability of plants and other organisms to thrive in airtight glass cases, without any tending, is surely too well-known by now to need any detailing. Suffice it to say that it was made in 1830, subjected to extensive testing over the next four years with the aid of Messrs Loddiges (who already had portable greenhouses among their stock-in-trade), first revealed to the gardening public by the great Loudon in 1834, then gradually reported to the learned world, half-informally and very bittily, until eventually, a full 12 years after the discovery, Ward brought forth a definitive monograph. Though a keen field botanist and gardener himself, Ward, as the medical man he was, preferred to lay emphasis on the potential benefits of his discovery for public health, by purifying the air and improving the atmosphere in hospitals, and was seemingly uninterested in advancing his reputation or his finances as a result. Indeed, the grandest gesture in our direction he was ever to rise to was to move in his later years to the more salubrious environment of Clapham and there name his new home 'The Ferns'.

Happily, others came forward to act as Ward's spokesmen. One of them, Loudon, has just been mentioned. But probably more important and more lasting in their influence were two (Francis, 1837; Newman, 1840) who publicised the invention not, like Loudon, in a magazine but in books - and in books, what is more, devoted exclusively to hunting for, identifying and growing ferns: the first-ever ones, at any rate in English, wholly concerned with these plants apart from James Bolton's illustrated folio, *Filices Britannicae*, almost half a century earlier.

Little was known until very recently about the author of the first of these two books, G.W. Francis. An Australian descendant of his has now produced a biography of him (Best, 1986), and in the course of our joint research for that we succeeded in turning up a few extra facts. It transpires that at the time his book came out, in 1837, he was a teacher at a so-called 'gentlemen's academy', apparently run by his father, in a very unfashionable quarter of London. After unsuccessful attempts to switch to a botanical career, he compromised in the next few years by combining spells of schoolmastering with a prolific amount of freelance writing. At some point he appears to have acquired expertise in surveying, for a manual on that is one of the titles that stands to his name in the British Library catalogue and it was in that capacity that he was to obtain his initial employment on emigrating to Australia in 1849. But botany would out - and six years after landing he was busy establishing a botanic garden at Adelaide, the directorship of which he was to hold, with great distinction, till his death in 1865.

The chief appeal of Francis' little book was undoubtedly its fine copperplate engravings, at that period quite a luxury in a low-priced work (as they were much more expensive to produce than woodcuts). At the same time the text was highly competent botanically and, deservedly, a thousand copies were sold within two years (Francis, 1842) and a great many more later as it passed into three further editions. When writing it, though, Francis had presumably heard little as yet of Ward and his cases and there is no more than just a passing mention of them. Yet we know that he was fully alive by then to the great potential of the Wardian principle, for in an article he contributed near the end of his life to an Australian magazine (Francis, 1860) he revealed that in 1835, two years before his book came out, he already had in his London house *"a balcony enclosed with glass"*, in which he was growing plants *"from many countries ... not withstanding the smoky atmosphere around"*. Whether he owed the idea of that 'balcony enclosed with glass' to Ward - or at least to a report of Ward's discovery - he did not let on. But it is by no means impossible that a man of Francis' multifarious talents made the same discovery quite independently. For certainly we do know that a Professor of Law at Glasgow University, Allan Maconochie, did anticipate Ward, very precisely - though he failed to make known his discovery or exploit its potential (Maconochie, 1840).

By contrast, the author of the other book, which followed three years later, made no secret whatsoever of his indebtedness to Ward and his discovery. This was Edward Newman. Like Francis, Newman was an able journalist as well as a naturalist (though, unlike him, his main interest lay in entomology). Like Francis, too, he was only just then in the process of discovering his facility with the pen and of breaking away from a prior less-preferred career - in his case the rope trade. Already, *"for some years"* (as he let on in a letter to a relation), he had been cultivating British ferns, *"hoping to ascertain, with more certainty than at present appears to exist, the distinctions between one species and another"* (Newman, 1876). Then, in the autumn of 1837, while on a walking tour in the Welsh mountains, in his words in the introduction to the book, *"a desire came over me to learn the names of the ferns to be encountered. With this in view I gathered hundreds of fronds, and when I arrived at a quiet inn ..., I arranged them into supposed species"* - for he had no guide to their taxonomy with him, Francis' newly-published work having not yet come into his hands. *"Of every species I could obtain,"* he goes on, *"not only the fronds but the roots were carefully conveyed home,"* where *"I planted them with care, for the purpose of obtaining a more correct knowledge of the variations to which they were subject."* Although he had heard a great deal up till then of the difficulty of cultivating ferns, he was pleasantly surprised to experience none at all himself. Indeed, he was led to believe that *"there scarcely exists in the United Kingdom a plot of a few square yards in which the zealous cultivator might not accomplish everything he desired, and, with attention, cause the artificial to exceed in beauty the natural fernery; for the destruction by frost and wind, both highly injurious to ferns, may, with a little management, be completely avoided."*

After that personal *mise-en-scène* Newman devotes the rest of his lengthy introduction to a detailed and highly laudatory account of Ward's discovery. *"There is no limit to the application of this principle,"* he assured his readers, excitedly: *"instead of a jar, it is easy to construct in the window-sill, a box, extending through its entire length,"* in which the ferns will supply *"the most beautiful curtain or blind that could possibly be invented."* *"Extending the plan still further,"* he enthused, *"a large conservatory may be constructed or even a large garden, entirely inclosed with glass."* *"So great is the advantage of this plan, that the plants of tropical regions can now be cultivated in London with the most perfect success .... Plants in this way may be grown in a drawing room, without ever making the least litter or apparent untidiness, and without the trouble attendant on watering."* Indeed, *"if the cases were opened annually it would be sufficiently often."*

It was all most alluring; and not surprisingly, numbers of people quickly succumbed. What Newman had omitted to emphasise, however, was the great expense involved in acquiring even sufficient glass to constitute a modest case. This was because of crippling excise duties that had been imposed on that material to help pay for the war against Napoleon - and which governments had found it convenient ever since not to reduce. Consequently only the comparatively well-to-do could afford to furnish their rooms with cases of the kind that Newman advocated, everyone else having to content themselves with resorting just to bell-jars, which were sufficient only to cover a plant individually. Even so that very costliness of the parlour-case must have given it a certain air of exclusiveness and so helped to launch it as a fashionable item of internal décor; and before the thirties were out they were starting to be in evidence very generally .

THE FIELD BOTANISTS AND THE VARIETY HUNTER

Meanwhile Francis and Newman had quickly built up a following in quite another quarter: among field botanists. Coincidentally, the 1830s had witnessed an enormous increase in the numbers taking to that pursuit. Forming your own *hortus siccus* was the necessary means of entry into it in the absence at that period of public reference collections - and in any case was acclaimed as an admirably improving and even uplifting recreation, especially for young ladies. The Romantic Movement had opened people's eyes to the attraction of the Lake District and other mountainous areas, and in the course of thronging to these the botanically-inclined were drawn especially to their abundance of ferns, pressing them in their albums and bringing them home to form 'fern-rockeries'.

A select few went further. Quickly exhausting the very limited number of species that featured on the British list at that period, their competitive energies passed on to the frond variations that some of those species were found to sport. Confusingly, these variety-hunters, who came to regard themselves as a kind of élite, tended to reserve to themselves the title 'fern-collector', evidently regarding anyone who had not progressed beyond collecting the *species* as quite beyond the pale. The literature consequently needs reading carefully for that reason. For example, a paper by F.W. Stansfield entitled *Pioneers of the fern cult* (Stansfield, 1909), proves to be concerned with the pioneer *variety-hunters* exclusively (and it is, incidentally, far from complete in its coverage of the earlier ones). Restricting the term 'fern cult' to these is, on the other hand, entirely fitting; for they were indeed a coterie of veritable cultists, worshippers at the shrine of the great god Pteris - and waiting to snap up his occasional mistakes. It has often been claimed, and certainly it has been widely believed - and maybe it is in fact true - that our native species give rise to 'sports' far more frequently in the west of the British Isles than in any other parts of their European ranges, presumably because of some properties in the climate, or of the soil, peculiarly conducive to this. More puzzlingly, that proclivity to 'sport', though, tends to be far from uniform, some districts teeming with varieties, while others appear hopelessly devoid of them. Whether or not that is a geographical mirage, the product merely of intensive concentration on certain areas more particularly, it does appear to be the case that variety-hunting was long almost exclusively a speciality of the Irish and the British.

So everything might well have continued - but for three developments which by sheer accident occurred at much the same time and thus had a greatly magnified impact by operating in combinaton.

The most tangible of these was the appearance on the scene of a new author with a supreme mastery not only of the native species, but of their innumerable named varieties as well. This was Thomas Moore. In comparison with the other chief performers on the stage, Moore comes over as a colourless figure; but that may not be entirely fair to him: it may simply be that, unlike them, he moved for most of his life in just the one groove. A gardener by training, he had been talent-spotted by John Lindley and recruited to assist him in editing the *Gardeners' Chronicle*. He was eventually to be the co-editor of that periodical for 15 years and in consequence of that a leading force in horticultural circles, but at this point he was making the major step up in his parallel career as a botanic garden curator by taking charge of the famous Physic Garden at Chelsea.

He was to write several books on ferns, but the two most influential were to appear within three years of one another - both memorable dates in other connections. The first, *A Handbook of British Ferns* (Moore, 1848) was a miniature, pocket-sized volume (*"small enough"*, observed one reviewer, *"to be carried in a lady's reticule"*) but otherwise rather unremarkable. It was clearly written for a small, specialist, primarily botanical public, for which its one great attraction was its lists of the now fashionable varieties. Its impact may well have been magnified by the absence of any competitors, for the publishing trade had temporarily lost interest in the pteridological market and copies of Newman and Francis had by then become scarce.

Moore's *Popular History of the British Ferns and Allied Plants* (Moore, 1851) was a very different affair. One in a series of cheap illustrated handbooks on various branches of natural history brought out by the conchologist-cum-publisher, Lovell Reeve, it was aimed (as its title implies) principally at beginners. Its overwhelmingly attractive feature was 20 colour plates, from the hand of that great master of botanical art, W.H. Fitch. This placed it immediately in a class quite apart from all of its predecessors. Cheap colour printing had arrived providentially just at a time when the following for natural history in Britain was about to soar to renewed heights. But another, hardly less important feature of this second book was lengthy lists of localities where the species in question were on record as being found: a kind of pteridological Baedeker. This was almost guaranteed to start feet and fingers itching.

The second development took place somewhat earlier, in 1845 - but had needed time to have its effects. This was the repeal of the glass duties. The immediate consequence was a massive drop in price, bringing the new, greatly-improved plate glass at last within the average person's means. The Great Exhibition of 1851, in Joseph Paxton's dazzling Crystal Palace, was only the most conspicuous of the innumerable beneficiaries. In that very same year a reviewer was to write: *"We entertain no doubt about cold Fern houses becoming in time as common as greenhouses."* Suddenly, the way was clear for the Wardian case to plunge down market.

The third development was much less obvious, but probably the most far-reaching of the three. For it was nothing less than a switch in aesthetic taste. The *Gardeners' Chronicle*, in a perceptive editorial in 1856, seems to have been virtually alone at the time in drawing attention to this. Commenting on a report that the Royal Horticultural Society's Garden was to have a fernery, it saw this as nicely in keeping with what it termed *"that prevailing taste for exquisitely beautiful foliage which is rapidly replacing merely gaudy flowers in the public favour."* *"Lovers of plants,"* it went on, *"begin to prefer graceful form to mere spots of colour ... Dress, furniture, architecture, are all now moving upon the same road side by side, and are already unmistakably affected by the direction into which public opinion was guided by the Great Exhibition of 1851.*" That direction was towards the elaboration of detail. By no coincidence it was also in 1851 that Ruskin had first championed the Pre-Raphaelites. In 1855, in the second edition of his *Seven Lamps of Architecture*, he went on to proclaim salvation through Gothic, impressing upon his readers the great virtues of ornament and of capturing nature with the most close and faithful precision.

Ferns were vegetable Gothic: nothing else in nature so perfectly accorded with that new preference for curling lines and intricate detail. They consequently soon became a leading motif in decoration, turning up almost everywhere - on glass and china, on curtains and wallpaper, in needlework, on decorative tiles, even on wrought iron chairs and benches for the garden. They were of the very essence of mid-Victorianism.

Interestingly, ferns had been sensed as appropriate to Gothic architecture at an earlier period when the taste for Gothic was still confined just to picturesque ruins. Ward had erected inside the largest of his fern cases a reproduction of a window of Tintern Abbey, and Newman had not been able to resist something very similar among the vignettes that graced his 1840 *History*. It had evidently been a motif just waiting all along to find its way into the cultural mainstream.

What happened next is all-too-notorious. Everyone wanted fern-cases of their own and often fern rockeries as well - and the commercial world responded accordingly. Nurseries sprang up specialising in ferns, and because the demand was far too great to be satisfied by raising stocks from spore, they necessarily relied for the most part on what they could acquire from the wilds. A new occupation, professional fern-collecting, typically on a free-lance basis, was called into being, supplying not just the nurserymen (who tended to be discriminating in what they bought) but also the dealers in the big city markets (who bought ferns by weight, in bulk consignments). One such collector was later to boast to a botanist in Cornwall that he had recently dispatched up to London a whole truckload of royal fern roots, weighing over five tons. The easily-sold, more handsome species like that (the maidenhair fern was another) were naturally in the first line of grabbing. As always, too, the rarer ones were in demand because higher prices could be asked for them. But, alas, while those factors might have led to the depredation at least being selective, the knowledge that people were prepared to pay good money for these weeds that grew in abundance all around them quickly spread among poverty-stricken country folk, who proceeded to strip whole tracts of terrain of every vestige of their fern covering. *"The ferns in Arran are largely gathered"*, grieved Professor Balfour, resignedly (Balfour, 1870) - and he was probably not exaggerating. What the crowds of holiday visitors had left, the local cottagers and farm boys had helped themselves to.

Of course, there were protests. From landowners, who objected to the disturbing of their game preserves - to say nothing of the theft of what they saw as their property. From botanists, who saw not only the loss of prized local varieties, but feared even the total extinction nationally of the more precarious species. And even from fellow out-and-out collectors, who occasionally paused long enough to realise that at the rate things were going there would soon be nothing left. *"The poor ferns, like the wolves in olden times, have a price set upon their heads, and they in like manner will soon altogether disappear"*, wailed one of their number: *"We must have 'fern laws', and preserve them like game."* But she only half-meant that, for only a few pages later we read: *"I did what I advise other fern-lovers to do. I packed up a large hamper full, and sent it off by rail, home."* (Bellairs, 1865).

THE END AND THE LEGACY OF PTERIDOMANIA

Fortunately, all crazes exhaust themselves - and the more intense they are, the sooner that tends to happen. The 'pteridomania' (as Charles Kingsley (1855) dubbed it) lasted all through the fifties and the sixties and then eventually began to show signs of waning. Later writers, in looking back, picked out the early sixties as perhaps the peak of popularity. But even as late as 1901 Druery can be found tut-tutting about how painful it is in the autumn *"to see the baskets and hampers of wayside ferns which the visitors ... are bringing away."* (Druery, 1901). And six years after that a national newspaper was still credibly proclaiming that *"fern-lovers throughout the kingdom are waging a war with the fern grubber."* Such statements, it is horrifying to realise, were appearing on the very eve of the motorised era. Just imagine what would have happened if the craze had been kept up by the hordes who presently descended on the countryside from charabancs! Instead, as it turned out, they contented themselves with armfuls of bluebells. Ferns, luckily, were too inextricably identified with a musty Victorianism, by then on the way to being forcefully rejected. Even if it had not outlived its own inherent strength, the craze would surely have died from that even more fundamental switch in taste.

That long period in which ferns remained so abnormally in the forefront of interest left behind a number of valuable legacies to weigh against the destruction that was wrought. Our knowledge of the taxonomy and distribution of the native species was enormously enhanced, at a much earlier period than would otherwise have been the case. It was one of the leading variety-hunters who seems to have been the first to draw botanists' attention to the fact that "... *the spores of ferns, under a high power of the microscope, are almost an unerring diagnostic of a species"* (Wollaston, 1855). Other notable discoveries, of value to horticulture especially, flowed from the work of amateur enthusiasts: bud-propagation, apospory and fern hybridity, to name just the most salient. The art of nature-printing, which received so great a fillip from the boom in publishing on ferns, was later found to be an ideal method for the study of the venation in fossil ferns and for a long period constituted one of the central techniques employed in palaeobotany. The Wardian case, too, went on to greater and greater things, making possible the tea industry in India and the rubber industry in Malaya (to single out only its two best-known achievements).

But the most enduring legacy of all has proved to be the Society whose centenary we are gathered here to celebrate this week. It seems fitting to conclude with a vision of that by now well-known photograph (Fig. 1, opposite) of a group of members on an Annual Excursion c.1899. I like to think that I see in their faces a pride and a confidence as, on the threshold of a new century, they look forward to many more years of searching out and tending their "*plumy emerald green pets glistening with health and beadings of warm dew*" - in the immortal words of the incomparable Shirley Hibberd.

BIBLIOGRAPHY

ALLEN, D.E. 1969. *The Victorian fern craze: a history of pteridomania.* Hutchinson, London.

ALLEN, D.E. 1978. The first woman pteridologist. *Bull. Brit. Pterid. Soc.* 1: 247-249.

BALFOUR, J.H. 1870. *Account of botanical excursions made in the Island of Arran during the months of August and September, 1869.* Privately published, Edinburgh.

BELLAIRS, N. 1865. *Hardy ferns: how I collected and cultivated them.* Smith, Elder & Co., London.

BEST, B.J. 1986. *George William Francis, first Director of the Adelaide Botanic Garden.* Privately published, Adelaide.

DRUERY, C.T. 1901. *The book of British ferns.* Country Life & Newnes, London.

FRANCIS, G.W. 1837. *An analysis of British ferns and their allies.* Simpkin, Marshall, London.

FRANCIS, G.W. 1842. [Printed application for Professorship of Botany.] King's College London archives, "in letters", F14.

FRANCIS, G.W. 1860. The Wardian Case. *Farm & Garden*, 13 Dec. 1860.

KINGSLEY, C. 1855. *Glaucus: or the wonders of the shore.* Macmillan, Cambridge.

MACONOCHIE, A.A. 1840. On the use of glass cases for rearing plants, similar to those recommended by N.B. Ward, Esq. *Ann. Rep. & Proc. Bot. Soc. Edinburgh* Session **1838-39**: 96-97.

MOORE, T. 1848. *A handbook of British ferns.* Groombridge, London.

MOORE, T. 1851. *A popular history of the British ferns and allied plants.* Reeve, London.

NEWMAN, E. 1840. *A history of British ferns.* Van Voorst, London.

[NEWMAN, T.P.] 1876. *Memoir of the life and works of Edward Newman.* Van Voorst, London.

STANSFIELD, F.W. 1909. Pioneers of the fern cult. *Brit. Fern Gaz.* 1: 45-48.

WOLLASTON, G.B. 1855. *Lastrea filix-mas. Phytologist* (n.s.) 1: 171-173.

FIGURE 1. [Opposite] *A British Pteridological Excursion in the Lake District, c.1899 (reproduced by kind permission of Mr Fred Taylor).*
The participants are (from left to right): top row - *W. Wilson, J. Lovelady, W. Martin;* centre row - *W.B. Boyd, S. Hudson, J. Wiper, W. Troughton, J. Edwards, W.H. Atkinson, J.W. Walton, T. Garnett, J. Gott, T. Bolton;* bottom row - *G. Whitwell, Revd G. Gunn, W.H. Phillips, J.J. Smithies, C.T. Druery, W. Aldred, J.A. Wilson.*

VII

Bricks without straw: reconstructing the
Botanical Society of London, 1836–1856

(Edited version of an unpublished paper given in the seminar series of the
Unit for the History of Medicine, University College London, 20th May, 1987)

One of the reviews of my recently-published sesquicentennial history of the Botanical Society of the British Isles, *The Botanists,* expressed particular delight in finding that there is a national scientific body that has numbered among its leading members "a spy, a lady balloonist, a table tennis enthusiast and a concert singer". What the reviewer failed to make clear, however, is that those were people who belonged as recently as the 1930s and 1940s. A browse through the book's Appendix Two would turn up a no less colourful assortment from a hundred years earlier: a Queen's Messenger, for instance, an ice merchant, an umbrella repairer, a tallow chandler's assistant and the superintendent of a lunatic asylum. No fewer than five of the thirteen chapters of the book are in fact devoted just to the twenty years up to 1856 and represent the fruits of a specially intensive study of a short-lived ancestral body, the Botanical Society of London.

Those twenty years were, as we know, crucially formative ones for the natural history sciences in Britain, so any substantial society which flourished at that period, particularly if it flourished in the Metropolis, deserves to be looked into rather more than cursorily. Moreover, if it was a society that had as its effective head, almost throughout that period, so prominent and controversial figure as Hewett Cottrell Watson, then the case for investigating it is even stronger. To anyone interested in the history of nineteenth-century botany, however, it beckons for further and more enticing reasons: firstly, because there has long been a mystery why the Society collapsed; and, secondly, because that collapse chronically stunted the corporate development of the discipline in Britain, by leaving it cripplingly fragmented and without a Metropolitan focus – in sharp contrast to its sisters. As a result of the glaring hole left by the Society's disappearance, the various social segments of which the discipline was composed – the taxonomists and the experimentalists; the specialists in the higher plants and the specialists in each of the major cryptogamic orders (mosses, lichens, seaweeds and fungi); the Metropolitan botanists and the provincials – escaped being brought within the framework of a single unifying body, on the lines of the Botanical Society of America and of virtually all of the other botanical societies of Europe. That fragmentation continues to this day, and it may credibly be blamed on the small yet fateful stumble which befell British Metropolitan botany in the middle of that middle decade of the nineteenth century.

The only trouble is that the Botanical Society of London collapsed so completely and thoroughly that it has left behind few tangible relics of its existence. For a start, of its presumably once extensive administrative records, there is only a single item that appears to have come down to us. This is one of the minute-books, which somehow found its way into the custody of Kew and was subsequently donated to the Linnean

Society (as being a rather more appropriate home for it). A minute-book sounds rich in promise; but this one, unfortunately, could hardly be duller. For it contains only the official record of the business transacted in open meeting – the names of candidates for membership, donations to the library and herbarium, the titles of papers delivered – most of which is duplicated elsewhere in print. What are missing are the all-important minutes of the Council – or indeed any inkling, behind the bland official façade, of the debates and arguments that clearly raged both there and among the membership at large at various junctures in the Society's history. For of course, as always with learned societies, there is scarcely any flesh to be found on the bare bones of what it was thought fit to publish. What is more, the bones themselves are fewer even than usual. For after only one volume of printed *Proceedings* had been issued, it was found that that was more than the Society could afford, so it compromised by supplying reports of its meetings to a variety of outside periodicals instead. A remarkable number of these obliged at one period or another: eleven in all, it turns out, ranging from the *Literary Gazette* and the *Gentleman's Magazine* to the *Gardeners' Chronicle* and the *Botanische Zeitung*, though only four did so on any prolonged and regular basis. Every report in every one of these periodicals needs to be scrutinised by the historian, for they proved to be by no means all duplicates of one another. Some of the recipients cut what they were sent, some received accounts from obviously different hands. There are reports by clearly knowledgeable botanists, able to separate the ore from the dross and carefully discriminating in what they chose to pass on. And there are reports by journalistic hacks, who misspell botanical terms and the names of genera and species and even, in one extraordinary instance, jest about the inappropriateness of a particular member's name (Notcutt he had the misfortune to be called). Most, however, are seemingly the work of the Society's long-serving honorary secretary, whose handwriting unfortunately was not of the clearest. Only after an extensive exercise in collation is it possible to arrive at a reasonably coherent picture of how things were going from one year to the next.

This was not all that the Society put out about itself in print, luckily – though all too little of that further 'under-literature', essentially ephemeral in character, has chanced to be preserved. The British Library and the Botany Library of the Natural History Museum each hold a copy of one of the Prospectuses, that for 1843, to which is usefully appended a list of the Society's numerous Local Secretaries. The Natural History Museum also holds a copy of the inaugural Rules, as well as a catalogue of the terminal auction of the Society's effects. In Liverpool Museum a run of annual reports for the early years has accidentally survived among the papers of one of the members (together with the only-known set of instructions for preparing specimens for the Society's herbarium, clearly written by Watson, even though anonymous, and most valuably embodying many of his ideas on how the study of the distribution of British plants could best be forwarded). Most miraculously of all, there have survived at the Royal Botanic Gardens, Kew copies of the circular announcing the final winding-up meeting, preserved thanks to the fact that Watson utilised the reverse side of the surplus as rough paper on which to transcribe a list of Cornish plants that had been lent to him. Fortunately for posterity, Watson made rather a habit of that kind of thing. Some years ago I also discovered at Kew some specimens of Cotton-grass mounted on the back of what proved to be an early version of his will – a far more informative version, it transpired, than the one eventually filed for probate and now at Somerset House.

This additional miscellany of printed documents, while undeniably useful, does not take one all that much closer to understanding what was really going on within the Society. They are, for the most part, merely more bare bones. What one ideally needs are letters.

Watson, again fortunately, was a prolific correspondent and he is an important enough figure for his letters to have been thought worthy of retention. There are consequently largish collections of them at Cambridge, Edinburgh and Kew, written respectively to Babington, Balfour and the elder of the Hookers. They are splendidly waspish, often brutally frank, and valuably informative about his own role in the Society and what he thought of the other leading figures in it, but, frustratingly, they are silent on the internal politics except at the very end, when the Society was discovered to be deeply in debt and its demise seemed inevitable. What we need are some equally indiscreet letters by some of the other leading figures. But, sadly, there don't appear to be any – or any at least on anything more than routine administrative trivia. This cannot be entirely because none of those figures were comparable with Watson in scientific stature. And their letters might still have come down to us, even so, through the operation of two factors that are special to British taxonomic botany.

One of these is the superb comprehensiveness of the archives at Kew, the legacy of the practice of the two Hookers, who successively held the Directorship for over 40 years between them, of meticulously retaining and filing every letter that came in, however trite or marginally relevant it might be to the strict concerns of the institution. The British Museum, its counterpart, had no such policy, alas, nor indeed had one till comparatively recent years. There, the correspondence of the staff was regarded as purely a matter for the individuals concerned, and how far it was kept depended on their personal whims and habits. Even if they did keep it, they were free to dispose of it as they wished when they retired. That is how the Blacker-Wood Library in Montreal comes to own the correspondence of the Museum's bird expert of the years around the turn of the century, a collection of central importance for British ornithology's history. When the Natural History Museum was hived off in the 1880s, matters deteriorated even further, for in the new, exclusively scientific institution the nature of taxonomic research caused the emphasis to be placed very heavily on printed works. Sub-departments have been allowed archival autonomy, moreover, with the result that caches of letters to or from specialists in, say, ferns or mosses or diatoms are held far away from the Departmental or General Archives and instead alongside the collections to which they relate. Manuscripts have traditionally been treated on the whole as appendages of the herbaria, not as historical items in themselves. But that has been the cause of the other factor that I mentioned as special to taxonomic botany: in order to identify the handwriting on anonymous specimen labels, a magnificent collection of autograph letters has been steadily built up over the years. But, conceived as a working tool, this is kept in the middle of the General Herbarium and unfortunately the casual historical enquirer is liable to be left unaware of its existence.

In the absence of any letters to speak of other than Watson's, the only remaining hope of uncovering the Society's inner politics lay in identifying the social and intellectual affinities, and by implication the leanings, of the individual members. Changes in the representation of different kinds of people, particularly on the ruling Council, seemed likely to be indicative of changes in the dominant concerns, scientific and otherwise.

In other words, it was necessary to embark on a prosopography. I had employed this technique some years earlier to illuminate the character of a tiny, much earlier botanical society in London, and in that case I had been impressed by how much it was possible to discover about relatively obscure people at a period as distant as the early years of the eighteenth century. It seemed likely that the task would be that much simpler a hundred and fifty years closer to the present, by which time civil registration and the decennial Census were both in being. Even so, I was aware that this time I would be up against a membership of several hundred, many of whom might not be in the standard reference books, outstandingly good though those are in the field of botanical biography. To the best of my knowledge all other prosopographical studies carried out in the history of science have been concerned with reasonably prominent figures, all or most of whom can be run to earth in printed works, or at any rate professional registers, without all that much difficulty. But no one till now seems to have tried operating down to the much humbler level of gardeners and students or out to the extreme of such inherently elusive social categories as unmarried women of independent means. This was apparently virgin territory prosopographically – and not territory for the faint-hearted. Compared with the murkiness that has to be groped through down at these depths, those who compile collective biographies of bodies like the Royal Society of Edinburgh hardly know that they've been born.

What is more, prosopographers do at least normally start off with a complete list of the people they are proposing to study. But I had to begin by laboriously reconstructing one – and could never be sure that it was either complete or even fully accurate.

The basic problem was that the Society only ever got round to publishing a single membership list, and that was while it was still in its infancy, before the majority of the eventual members joined. Moreover, no addresses are given in this of those who lived in London, which makes some of them utterly impossible to trace. Even so, the minute-book that survives and at least one set of the published meeting reports give the names, and sometimes the town of residence too, of those elected to membership during much of the subsequent period. And there is a further way of discovering who belonged which is pleasingly special just to societies concerned with field botany. The Botanical Society of London, and at that same period its counterpart in Edinburgh too, made the conducting of annual exchanges of members' duplicate dried specimens the chief bait for joining. All field botanists in those days formed a private herbarium of their own, partly as a tool of reference, partly out of sheer love of collecting; and although far from all the Society's members went in for fieldwork, just under half of them did. Because botanical specimens, unlike zoological ones, lend themselves to being mounted on sheets of paper, the practice fortunately early set in of writing on these sheets, or writing on a specially-printed label glued or pasted on to them, details of where and when the specimens were collected and the name of the person responsible for doing so. Many thousands of specimens are known to have been distributed through the London Society's exchanges and sooner or later most of these have found their way into national or local museums. The earlier ones, conveniently, bear the Society's name on their labels, but that practice misfired (for reasons too complicated to go into here) and for the most part today that provenance can only be deduced as a result of careful detective work. Nevertheless, two or three herbaria exist which are identifiably of London Society origin in whole or at least in large part. By far the richest of these is Watson's, now preserved at Kew (and accorded there the exceptional honour of being kept together in a cupboard all of its own, instead of being incorporated piecemeal into the general collection). This is because Watson was invited to rescue the organization of the exchanges from chaos three years after their start and, in return for his enormous labours to that end (for sorting out the specimens to be distributed and deciding who was entitled to have what was a task of nightmarish proportions), he was allowed to take as much as he liked for his own personal collection.

From these herbarium labels, after a good deal of critical collation, it is possible to obtain a comprehensive picture of who was taking part, in what part of the country they lived (or, alternatively, where they had taken holidays) and how extensively they had contributed from year to year. Originally I had the idea of working out an 'index of activity' for every single member of the Society based on the award of points for frequency of participating in the exchanges, the number of mentions received in meeting reports, service as an Officer, on the Council or as a Local Secretary, and so forth; but I abandoned this, admittedly in some relief, as I came to realise that the information on these matters that one can put together is not only seriously incomplete, but also riddled with uncertainties. The meeting reports, in particular, turned out to be treacherous to use, for by no means all speakers or donors would seem to have been members. Similarly, non-members occasionally enriched the exchanges with specimens but without being distinguished as such in the annual lists of acknowledgments. Herbarium labels, too, fail sometimes to make clear that the named collector was not necessarily the distributor of the specimens – which may have been derived, without reference to the individuals concerned, from donation by a third party (most commonly the Botanical Society of Edinburgh, with which the London Society engaged in wholesale exchanges on a number of occasions). There is the yet further problem that one or two whose names feature repeatedly in accounts of the Society's activities are known – or at any rate are alleged by Watson – to have refrained from ever joining. This was presumably because they were in a position to enrich the annual exchanges with specimens of an especially desirable character and it was seen as impolitic to risk placing those valued contributions in jeopardy by pressing them to subscribe – for some of them may well have considered the Society beneath them.

While the Society was unusual in happily tolerating this fringe of non-members, it was by no means alone among Metropolitan bodies at this period in also being far from punctilious in ensuring that those who were enrolled continued to keep up their subscriptions. In startling contrast to usage today, it appears to have been standard practice then to allow backsliders a remarkable amount of leeway. Just as it was accepted that gentlemen took their time in settling bills and that no tradesman counting on their custom would risk causing offence by pressing too importunately for payment, so clubs and societies evidently saw it as tactless and improper to do other than leave it to members to behave honourably in this matter. Many members availed themselves of the excellent bargain involved in compounding their subscription at the time of joining, but for those who opted to pay annually it was all too easy to slip into arrears, through forgetfulness or otherwise. In one extreme case a fellow of the Linnean Society had his repeated failures to pay politely overlooked for the astounding total of 23 years. Stated membership figures are for this reason liable to be deceptive; and if the real situation was not reflected accurately in the annual accounts, a society could find itself in a severe crisis financially with little or no advance warning. The Botanical Society was only one of several that were eventually brought down, or at least had their survival temporarily imperilled, through this dangerously lax way of operating.

As that non-paying fringe was so essentially different in status, it seemed sensible to disregard it in compiling the list of candidates for biographical investigation. After then stringently pruning that of names that were doubtfully acceptable for various other reasons (in some cases because they were suspected of being misreadings), the total that remained came to 371. That was the overall number either known or believed on the balance of the evidence to have enrolled at some time or other in the course of the Society's 20-year existence.

Although a high proportion of the elections to membership are entered in the surviving records, very few deaths or resignations are. To complicate matters further, quite a number evidently allowed their membership to lapse and rejoined subsequently. So it did not prove easy to reconcile my year-to-year totals with the ones published by the Society in its annual reports. However, my 371 did reasonably tally with the total claimed in the last of these before the figures became demonstrably inaccurate, four years before the Society's end. Unfortunately, though, of that 371 no fewer than 29, or about 8%, still had to be classed as uncertain cases, in which full proof of membership is lacking.

371 is not all that large a number to deal with as prosopographies go. But in view of the fact that most of the individuals were likely to be more or less obscure, I needed this advantage. About half, I found, had entries in the standard biographical reference works; but as many of the entries in the most comprehensive of these, Ray Desmond's updated edition of Britten & Boulger, are very bitty and brief, this did not necessarily take one all that far. It was soon apparent that a great deal of delving in official and professional records, in local directories and in contemporary periodicals was going to be called for.

The easiest group to identify, and in fair detail, were the large number of medical men (of whom more in a moment). Most of these had taken the exam of the Society of Apothecaries, in order to obtain the licence to practise in England and Wales, and the Court of Examiners' entry books among that body's extensive records in the Guildhall Library normally give their date of birth and their parentage together with details of whom they had trained under and for precisely how long. However, that still leaves one in the dark about what happened to them afterwards. At the very least it was untidy not to know the year of their death.

I had set the year of birth and death, town of residence and occupation as my minimal target for biographical details. Anything I could obtain on top of these basics I welcomed as a bonus. Naturally I did my best to track down obituaries and memoirs, which were the richest source of all (and it was remarkable for how many there proved to be one or more of these), but in a great many cases there was no alternative to the drudgery of searching through year after year of names in indexes.

That drudgery was made very much worse by the appalling working conditions that obtained at that time at St. Catherine's House, where crowds of genealogists sweated elbow to elbow to find what they wanted in the large and unwieldy volumes – four to every year – that hold the indexes to the certificates of births, deaths and marriages from 1837 onwards. All too often the indexes proved insufficient in themselves and it was necessary to go to the considerable expense (and delay) of ordering a copy of the actual certificate. Sometimes, though, that did yield the bonus of an often interesting cause of death (typically tuberculosis or cirrhosis of the liver).

Luckily I soon found that it was possible to bypass St. Catherine's House in most cases for the purpose of establishing a year of birth. The dodge was to go instead to the Principal Probate Registry in Somerset House, which holds all the England and Wales wills since 1858. The indexes to these give the precise date of death and the address of the deceased. Armed with that information one could walk over to St. Catherine's House and, provided the death took place in the 1880s or later, look up in the registers there the age at which the person died. From that one could calculate the approximate year of birth (which I considered sufficient for my particular purpose).

The wills indexes proved invaluable for achieving a first identification in cases where there was no more than a bare name to go on – provided that name was not over-common. Most people of middle class status or above were in the habit of leaving wills by the period I was interested in (or, failing one, their next of kin applied for letters of administration) and the indexes are not so extensive, or their clientele so numerous, as to deter one from a systematic combing. With practice, I found I could cover 50 years in roughly 20 minutes. Although not strictly necessary, it often proved useful to go to the length of inspecting the will itself – at the cost of a trifling fee and only a little wait – for this sometimes yielded valuable information, in particular on family connections. In one case I was able to clinch an otherwise dubious identification on finding that the man in question included some natural history specimens among his bequests.

My other main hunting-ground was the search room in nearby Portugal Street, where the enumerators' books of the Censuses of 1841 and 1851 were consultable on microfilm. This usually entailed queueing for a reader, but the wait was usually worth it. For the Census gives age and occupation – in addition of course to the place of residence. But the snag is that unless you already know an individual's precise address, or unless he or she lived in a village, it can take hours trying to locate it. Even then the enumerators handwriting may be too faint to be legible and, even if it is not, you cannot be sure you have found the right person if the name is not all that uncommon. For that reason, I often found it worthwhile to establish the occupation beforehand, from a search of local directories. By far the best collection of these on open access proved to be at the Institute of Historical Research. Directories have the limitation, though, that they were compiled for commercial purposes and normally list only the gentry and the self-employed. That does not apply, though, to the nineteenth-century London directories, of which there was a fairly complete set, also on open access, in Buckingham Palace Road branch of Westminster Public Libraries.

If the impression I have conveyed is that prosopographical research consists in large part of slog and tedium, then that impression is all too correct. You do need great staying-power to get through these essential preliminaries (unless, of course, you are fortunate enough to be able to delegate them to one or more assistants).

Yet there are some delights to be had in this type of work. One is the lucky dip: the time when you take down the first volume in front of you out of fifty that you might equally well have tried – and there, first go, is the very person you were after. Another delight is the perfectly-aimed appeal for help. On almost every subject there is some person somewhere who has acquired a more or less encyclopaedic knowledge of it and as often as not is sitting on a massive mound of only partly-exploited data. The problem is coming to know of the existence of such people. I found it possible to take this ideal shortcut on just three occasions. On one of those I did, in the event, draw a blank; but at least I had the comfort of knowing that even if the expert in question could not find my member in his voluminous records on Sierra Leone, then there was no point in expecting to take that particular search any further. On the second occasion I spotted on the label of a specimen distributed through one of the Society's exchanges that a hitherto elusive member had used it as an opportunity for some discreet professional advertising by giving on it his occupation and address as well. By a stroke of luck he was a pharmacist – and I knew of someone with a comprehensive card index of past practitioners in that field. By return of post came a xerox of the man's obituary in an obscure journal in Australia. On the third occasion the bare name, which was all I had to go on, was a sufficiently unusual one to make it seem likely that others listed in the contemporary London directories as sharing it were more or less close relations. As they were in the silk trade, I thought it might be worth trying someone I knew had been toiling away for years on a history of that. Again by return of post came a photocopy of a family tree enabling me to identify my man exactly – even to the point of establishing that his initials had been wrongly transposed in the Society's records.

So much for how I put together my data. Now for something about what emerged.

The information from a prosopography comes in two layers. First you acquire a detailed, quantitative picture of the various social categories represented. Then beneath that surface you begin to spot patterns and movements in that social composition, or in the behaviour of various individuals, from which you hope to deduce tensions and motives.

Some of the social categories which the Botanical Society of London turned out to display were unexpectedly interesting.

In the first place, there were a startling number of women. Botany is, of course, traditionally thought of as a pursuit of particular appeal to the female sex, but that is quite a different matter from their being admitted to a national learned society in that era. After all, the Linnean Society stoutly refused to have women as Fellows till 1904 and the Geographical Society till as late even as 1919. However, the group which founded the Botanical Society was strongly progressive, even radical in its attitudes and it was determined to strike a non-discriminatory stance. To the astonishment of contemporary commentators, women were accordingly invited to join – and not merely to join, but to participate on almost exactly the same terms as men. It was not by any means certain, however, that women in any numbers would respond, and indeed, despite the considerable number who are known to have been active in the subject around that time, the response was to prove disappointing all along. In fact they probably never at any time comprised more than 6% of the total membership; a high proportion of those, moreover, were daughters of men who were prominent in scientific circles and who presumably therefore found this male world a good deal less intimidating than the great majority of their sisters. One must never forget the deep hidden array of social defence-works that discouraged their full-hearted involvement, not least the requirement that an unmarried woman be accompanied by a chaperone, and it is not altogether surprising that only one of them ever so much as produced a paper – and that seems to have been read on her behalf in her absence (and so disbelieving were the periodicals that a woman could possibly be its author that several attributed it to a 'Mr').

Even more unexpected than women was a sizeable contingent of lawyers – hardly the most likely of professions to encounter in a scientific society, nowadays at any rate. Excluding two members who qualified but never went on to practise, the Society attracted in its time eight barristers and seven solicitors – not far less than 5% of the total. What on earth were they doing there – assuming they were not just men with a dilettante interest in horticulture who had made a mistake about the Society's character? It was not until I happened to read Morris Berman's history of the early years of the Royal Institution, in which barristers were particularly prominent, that I understood the reason for the presence of this interloping element. In that period of Whig reform the fashionable thing for a progressive young man to be was a Benthamite Utilitarian. Jeremy Bentham had seen the legal system as the chief engine of progress and so it was with legal qualifications that the socially concerned therefore saw it as necessary to equip themselves, just as their counterparts in the 1930s were to equip themselves with degrees in Economics and in the 1960s to pour into Sociology. London in the 1830s must have had some resemblance to latter-day Washington – bristling with lawyers, who were more concerned with servicing the many lobbying committees than with practising the law as such. Like the early Royal Institution, the Botanical Society of London appeared to the reformists a suitable colony to annex: scientific knowledge was for them the key to civic improvement, and in botany there were topics such as the scandal of food adulteration, the potential of peat charcoal for use in sewage disposal or the cause of the disease then devastating the potato crops – all of them keenly debated by the Society on different occasions – to make this discipline seem amply relevant.

The sanitarian movement was well represented too among the pharmacists and medical practitioners, several of whom were among the pioneer public analysts and Medical Officers of Health. But the medical world was strongly represented in the Society for other reasons apart from that. Medicine and botany, those age-old twins, had not yet drifted apart – and indeed had been bound together all afresh by the 1815 Apothecaries' Act. This had had the effect of requiring any who wished to practise medicine in England or Wales to pass the exam of the Society of Apothecaries, which was renowned, *inter alia,* for the high standard it insisted upon in herb identification. As a result, wherever medicine was taught special courses had had to be added, and in many cases special teachers recruited, to provide a grounding in the elements of botany with this specific end in view. An entire medical generation thus found itself exposed to a subject it might never otherwise have encountered, and in the process the interest of not a few students was lastingly won. The lecturers in botany at various of the London medical schools were consequently well to the fore among the Society's earliest members and they continued to supply some of its most devoted adherents all through its life. Medical men indeed, of one stripe or another, constituted nearly a third of the membership in the inaugural period, though later, as the Society became better known in the provinces, the proportion sank to only a fifth. One striking feature, though, was the number of them, no fewer than eleven, who had qualified but never practised, being blessed, like Watson (and Charles Darwin), with sufficient independent means to abstain from a profession whose grisly contemporary methods so many found unbearably repugnant.

More difficult to account for is the surprising number of members who were grocers: six of them in all, plus a dead one's widow. This is a notably higher representation than of any other single trade. My guess is that there was a tacit social hierarchy in those days in shopkeeping, of which the 'clean' end, represented *par excellence* by the grocers and the wine merchants, ranked as the topmost tier. Priding themselves on a sub-bourgeois respectability, this tier would have striven hardest to identify with the tastes and the interests of the classes above, on which it also depended so largely for its custom.

Besides establishing members' occupations, I would dearly have loved to have known as well their denominational-cum-political persuasions. But that, of course, is a notoriously difficult kind of information to obtain; and I had to content myself with the knowledge that certainly 12%, and probably a good deal more, were broadly Nonconformist in their religious affiliation. Of these, Quakers and Unitarians were the most numerously identified.

The 6% who were Quakers – and, thanks to the unique comprehensiveness of the records at Friends House, that figure is a firm one – formed a noteworthy element for another, quite different reason: as a result of that sect's long tradition of in-marriage, a very high proportion of them were related. No fewer than 6 out of the 21, indeed, proved to belong to just one single great conglomerate of cousinhood. Yet though so particularly marked among the Quakers, that was a characteristic that extended through the Society much more generally.

Astonishingly for a national body – and its membership did come to have a genuinely country-wide coverage – no less than 15% turned out to be linked by blood or by marriage to at least one other member. To put it succinctly, one-seventh of the Society was interrelated. And that figure, it must be stressed, is only a minimal one; for spotting such connections is largely a matter of chance in cases where the surnames are different: several more may well have existed. Admittedly, in a few cases the connection was rather distant: second cousinhood or cousinhood-by-marriage. In one

VII

instance the brother of a member married the sister of another. But even so there were seven pairs of siblings, four pairs of brothers-in-law and three pairs of first cousins. In two cases both a father and one of his children belonged, in another two both an uncle and his nephew. But of membership by both a husband and wife there was only a solitary example.

This phenomenon has never been turned up before in a national society, at any rate in Britain, and probably never even suspected. It is doubtless to be explained in part by the well-known tendency for an interest in natural history to run in families, a tendency which was especially marked in the Victorian era. But probably more of the explanation is simpler even than that: in those days when families were very large and people saw a lot of their relations, it was easier for a member to recruit those to a society than it was to recruit anyone else. There may have been a certain element of kin-based power-manoeuvring, but, if so, it is hard to believe that it was more than slight. For I could find no evidence of anything on the lines of Arnold Thackray's "closely-knit, continually intermarrying, almost dynastic élite" which he has described as having dominated the Manchester Literary and Philosophical Society over a long period of years and which resulted in almost 5% of its membership and 25% of the available offices being drawn from just six Unitarian families.

One pleasing by-product of hunting for family connections was the discovery that quite a number of the Society's members belonged to families distinguished in literature rather than in science. They included the father and an aunt of Samuel Butler, the father of Gerard Manley Hopkins, a cousin of Robert Southey, and the father of the chief intimate and inspirer of Branwell Brontë. In 1850 the Society even acquired as a member a certain 'Miss Evans' of Coventry, whom circumstantial evidence suggests may have been none other than George Eliot.

This serves to underline the fact that science at this date had not yet emerged as a community apart. Nor was there as yet a discernible botanical profession. Throughout the twenty years of the Society's life professional botanists remained very few – though it depends a bit on how that term is defined. There were only four members who were full-time teachers of the subject (in whole or in part) in an academic capacity; but there were others who earned their living from it at a more or less scholarly level, as superintendents of botanic gardens, curators of museums or officials of learned society institutes. Even so, that group made up no more than 6% of the Society at most, and there is no indication that they acted as any kind of coherent interest group. Most of them, in any case, could probably not afford to travel up from the provinces for meetings and must have come into contact with one another rarely if at all.

Considerably more numerous than professionals in the strict sense were those in occupations in which some acquaintance with botany could be counted an advantage: pharmacists and druggists, nurserymen, florists and gardeners. Those employed in horticulture accounted indeed for almost as large a share of the membership as the strict botany professionals. There was additionally an element among that substantial group of members who were booksellers, stationers and/or printers who specialised in botanical literature, there were two members who lived largely by writing on the subject and two more who relied on patronage from this and related quarters for many of their commissions as engravers and artists. So there was quite a tail of what might be categorised as 'semi-dependent' professionals.

If there was no caucus of professionals, then, and no noticeable cleavage along some fault-line of family connections, what clash of interests was it that caused the society eventually to split – as we know it did (though only from an oblique remark by the ex-Curator, in an obscure entomological journal, some years later)?

The picture that emerged from a careful sifting of my data was a complex one but was broadly as follows.

Towards the end of the 1840s, after the Society had been flourishing for over ten years, a struggle for control appears to have developed between two conflicting coalitions. One of these, headed by Watson, identified the Society with the needs and aims of field botanists: either as the mere provider of a service which enabled them to enlarge and enrich their herbaria, or, more constructively, as a machine for gathering in data for the advancement of that Humboldtian approach which Watson advocated and popularised as 'topographical' botany. The other coalition comprised – on the one hand – the London clubmen, the non-collecting fraternity who wanted no more than somewhere to resort to before dinner for some chat and an interesting lecture, and – on the other – the committed ameliorists, those who saw the Society as one vehicle among many in the wider battle they were waging to bring about Reform.

It seems to have been tacitly accepted within the Society that residence in London was a *sine qua non* of election to the Council, presumably because experience had shown that no one who lived further out could be relied on to attend its meetings with the regularity desirable. Unfortunately, the majority of the field botanists, and certainly all the best ones, lived out in the provinces, so they were always liable to be seriously under-represented within the Society's counsels. This did not matter all that much as long as the London members broadly shared their interests; but when the Council began to fill up with public analysts, epidemiologists and sanitary engineers, and the topics chosen for the meetings began to reflect the concerns of such people more and more exclusively, the field men evidently began to get alarmed and organised a counter-attack. That, at any rate, is how I interpret the movement that occurred in the Council's composition at the margin – that is to say, who was newly elected to it each year and who went off on completing the maximum term. For this throws up a very suggestive pattern. Up to 1851 a significant proportion of the newly-elected were people for whom there is no evidence that they were ever collectors; after 1851 only a single such person can be identified. From around that date, too, all but one of the newly-elected who can be said to have had some standing as field botanists – six of them altogether – proved to have had one other feature in common: they had all moved to live in London very recently, even within a matter of months. That can surely only mean that the field botany faction, desperately short of eligible people to put forward in its campaign to regain control, was pouncing on the occasional provincial who arrived to settle in the Metropolis and urging him to stand for election. The rival faction would seem not to have been aware of what was happening – or maybe it had simply lost stomach for the fight by then and was content to cave in, for after 1850 the cause of Reform in mid-Victorian Britain had lost its momentum and was indeed in general retreat.

I could not have hoped to discern this pattern and what it seemed to imply had I not first built up `fullish biographical profiles which were able to add meaning to the bare statistics. Perhaps the greatest value of prosopography, despite the huge labour that the technique entails, is that it teaches one to visualise all the time the individuals who make up the composite categories that social historians are accustomed to frame and use for the most part as the basis for analysis. It makes one more aware of the numerous exceptions that in reality exist to the airy generalizations that one is always being tempted to indulge in. It can provide one with plenty of picturesque detail to enliven an otherwise all-too-humdrum narrative. It leads one down social alleyways it might never otherwise occur to one to explore. It can bring to light people whose presence would never otherwise have been suspected and sometimes enables one to add significantly to the biographies of leading figures – and that is the more likely to be the case, of course, the more formative the period one works in. The second quarter of the nineteenth century did prove to be a singularly fruitful choice in that particular respect.

In short, and to conclude, I ended up as an enthusiastic convert to prosopography. But I must warn anyone who may contemplate deploying the technique at a level that involves disinterring any considerable number of the lowly and obscure that one needs a great deal of time, a great deal of persistence and a reasonable ration of luck.

VIII

THE WOMEN MEMBERS OF THE BOTANICAL SOCIETY OF LONDON, 1836–1856

On 6 September 1836, George White wrote from Hatton Garden to T. B. Hall in Liverpool:

> I see by an advertisement that [there is] a proposition to form a Society to be called the Botanical Society of London—Its objects are the advancement of Botanical Science in general but more especially systematic and descriptive Botany—the formation of a Library, Museum & Herbarium—A meeting will be held at the Crown & Anchor, Strand, tomorrow evening & it is my intention to attend it—It has been proposed that *Ladies* should be admitted!!![1]

If the writer of those words lived up to his declared intention and did attend that or any other of the long string of inaugural meetings the Society held during the last quarter of that year, he would have been startled, perhaps even appalled to find how seriously that last-mentioned proposal had been taken. For on 3 November he would have found in the room at the Crown and Anchor Tavern (according to one report) 'a crowded assembly of both ladies and gentlemen'.[2] He would also have heard the founder of the Society, the nineteen-year-old Daniel Cooper, deliver a paper on the effects of light on plants, which (according to the same report) 'excited great interest, more particularly with the ladies'. A fortnight later the meeting was again 'numerously attended' and again it attracted a number of the supposedly unlearned sex, some of whom by then were 'members of the society' unambiguously.[3]

Exactly how many had joined by this stage is impossible to establish. The total subscribing membership at the time of the meeting following is known to have been thirty-eight,[4] and the address list that was published some eighteen months later shows only four women with dates of election in the inaugural period.[5] But it is possible that more had been elected during that eighteen-month interval and (as a sizeable proportion of the men undoubtedly did) subsequently failed to renew their subscriptions. All that can be said for sure is that women made up at least ten per cent of those who were regarded as the foundation members. By the time of the published list of February 1839, however, their share of the membership, by then doubled, had fallen to only six per cent; and in all probability it settled at around that level for the remainder of the Society's life.[6] In the absence of any further membership lists the evidence

This article is reproduced with the permission of the Council of the British Society for the History of Science. It was first published in *The British Journal for the History of Science* 13 (1980), pp. 240–254.

is merely impressionistic, but certainly there continued to be a goodly sprinkling of female names among the reported donors of specimens and books.

The presence at this period of women in such numbers in a learned society of national standing is joltingly at variance with two deeply established stereotypes: that women were excluded from the world of learning, and that only lone, very exceptional individuals (most notably Mary Somerville) went so far as pursue science actively. As so often, these are generalizations which, while broadly true, cease to hold good at the margins. In some of the natural history sciences, first in conchology and entomology, and later and more especially in botany, women were participants from at least the early eighteenth century. By 1836 their presence on the botanical scene was so ample and familiar that to admit them to the relevant societies must have seemed a logical development to all but the intellectually dishonest and the determinedly unenlightened.

Botany could break the rules because it had the great good luck to be in keeping with both of the contemporary alternative ideals of femininity. On the one hand it was able to masquerade as an elegant accomplishment and so found favour with the inheritors of the essentially aristocratic 'blue-stocking' creed, with its studied cultivation of an unintense intellectualism. On the other, it passed as acceptable in those far more numerous middle-class circles which subscribed to the new cant of sentimentalized womanhood: the 'perfect lady' of a repressive Evangelicalism. Aided by this double protective colouring it prospered accordingly.

At the same time the first murmurings among women against their social subjection were beginning to become noticeable. Most of these were confided to diaries or to friends in letters, but Anna Jameson's *Characteristics of women* dared to argue the case in public in 1833. Women's suffrage even featured fleetingly in the programme of the Chartist Movement when this made its appearance soon afterwards. Substantially responsible for this new aggressiveness were the Unitarians and the Quakers, those two sects which had long stood out in their unorthodox valuing of intelligence in women—in the same way as they were conspicuously to the fore in identifying with the advancement of scientific knowledge. As these twin concerns increasingly began to flow together, it was predictable that it would be into the scientific societies that the women would be most immediately thrust forward. It was predictable too that botany, the part of the battlefield where resistance could be relied on to be lightest, would experience the onset first, and that a strong sectarian contingent would be among those who achieved the eventual infiltration.

Even so, this initial encounter was a miniature affair. In the whole of the twenty years of the Botanical Society's existence the total number involved was probably very few more than 400. To be exact, 396 people have been traced,[7] who appear at some time in this period to have been subscribing members,[8] and of these, thirty-three were women. Only twenty-five of the thirty-three, however, can be identified with any degree of confidence. In the absence of detailed addresses women as a group are peculiarly difficult to locate in the contemporary records: even where their town or city of residence happens to be known, if this was at all large and their surname a comparatively common one, the task of identification is all but impossible without an occupation additionally to go on—and unhelpfully only one of the twenty-five worked for her living.

This non-employed status was one of several ways in which the twenty-five—at least—differed sharply from the men. Even the solitary exception was the unmarried co-proprietress of a small school for girls, the long holidays from which may have constituted the next-best thing to a job-free existence. Contrary to what one might have expected, none of the members were employed as school teachers in a subordinate capacity or as governesses: for a woman to belong to a learned society, evidently, was the hallmark of a copious leisure. Seemingly confirming this, of the six who had husbands one alone had children—and as the wife of a land-owner and high sheriff she was able to afford the ample help that also allowed her to write several novels.[9]   *

Compared with the men, too, the stations in life of the twenty-five were on the whole decidedly more elevated. Six belonged to the landed gentry (one being titled as well); another—though her immediate relations were clergy—was the niece and granddaughter of earls; another was the daughter of an admiral; at least three others had large family wealth in the background. Only the two Barnard sisters appear to have been in circumstances that were distinctly straitened, though Mrs. Gawler, as the wife of a parish clerk-cum-undertaker, is also unlikely to have been affluent.

Still more strikingly, most of the twenty-five were a good ten years or more the men's senior in age. Because of its minimal requirements in the matter of prior experience or knowledge, the Society had a membership that was singularly youthful overall, about a quarter being young men in their late teens or early twenties, partly reflecting the fact that many were medical students. A mere four of the twenty-five women, however, belonged to that age-group at the time they joined. Excluding two whose year of birth is unknown, the mean age of the women on joining —or at any rate at the time of first evidence of participating—was 42.7. From this one may conclude that by and large it was only those with the confidence of years who were available at that period for recruitment to a learned society. Even supposing it did not deter them intellectually, the meetings of such a body represented for women intimidatingly uncertain social country, to be braved with equanimity only by the most poised and experienced. In so far as the young and unmarried could be lured to them at all, this was possible only under close chaperonage. Lacking the informality, even gaiety, of the field excursions customary in comparable societies in later years, such occasions can hardly have afforded much opportunity for socializing, let alone served as a market-place for matrimony. Only two of the twenty-five in fact married during the years that they belonged to the Society and in neither case was this to someone known to have been a fellow member.

The high mean age of the women, admittedly, is in part accounted for by the inclusion of two octogenarians and a third member only slightly less advanced in years. As none of the rest were much over fifty at the time of their first appearance, one is led to suspect some special factor behind the presence of these three. Too frail, presumably, to take part in any of the Society's activities (and by the time they joined there was no longer a journal to be had in return for the subscription), perhaps they intended their membership to be seen essentially as a gesture. Survivors from a generation denied any comparable outlet in its own day for its intellectual ambitions, the daughters of an earlier generation that had had to make do with the contrived 'petticoteries' of Mrs Boscawen, Mrs Ord and Mrs Vesey, for them the emergence at long last of a national society that welcomed women must surely have seemed a milestone worthy of acclaim and more. Two of them, Miss Stovin of Chesterfield,[10] and Miss Hill of Braunton,[11] had first made a name for themselves among British botanists in the early years of the century. Since her sixties Miss Hill had been kept from further active work by ill-health; but Miss Stovin lost no time in demonstrating her solidarity by presenting sets of authentically named dried material; in addition she had parcels made up of surplus specimens from her rich herbarium. So, too, did the third of the veterans, Mrs Robinson of Fareham. Her background, however, was interestingly different: she had not blossomed forth as a botanist till her widowhood, but as the wife of a London grocer who had belonged both to the Linnean Society and to the ill-starred Royal Medico-Botanical Society she must have had more than her fill of enduring exclusion from the scientific life of the Capital.

Age and experience by themselves, however, seem not normally to have been enough to lead women to enrol. There was one further factor that clearly outweighed all the others in importance. Like Mrs Robinson, an impressively high proportion prove to have had a husband or a brother or a father or an uncle, or at the very least a cousin, who also had a well-developed interest in science, if not necessarily in botany. Family stimulus, in short, was the crucial motivating influence. As in other fields such as painting,[12] it almost invariably needed the extra stimulus of a shared family commitment to the same or some similar activity for a woman to overcome her diffidence, and all the insidious pressures of convention reinforcing this, if she was to step out into so male-dominated a milieu.

Mrs Riley of Papplewick, in Nottinghamshire,[13] the only one of the women members who rose to the height of contributing papers to the Society, is also the supreme example of the operation of this influence. Soon after she and her land-agent husband married, they jointly took up the cultivation and study of ferns—the substitute nursery, as it were, of a childless couple. Pioneer specialists in the native representatives of this order, their work eventually culminated in a comprehensive monograph embodying the results of growing side by side all the fifty or so then known British species, and observing 'with great care and attention' their distinguishing characteristics—an account of such length that when brought before the Society in May 1840 its reading had to be spread over four successive meetings. At least one periodical, the normally most reliable *Annals and magazine of natural history*, apparently unprepared to believe that a woman could be featuring in such a capacity,[14] attributed the authorship to 'Mr Riley'. But the *Literary gazette* assured its readers that 'the remarks are the result of the fair botanist's personal observation' and 'highly creditable and valuable'; the paper 'evinced extensive research and a thorough knowledge of the subject'.[15] Perhaps significantly, though, despite her consciousness of the honour,[16] she failed to come up from Nottinghamshire to deliver her paper before the Society in person. Nor did she do so on at least two other occasions when papers of hers were read: 'On the British genus *Cystea*', in November 1839, and 'On growing ferns from seed, with suggestions upon their cultivation and preparing the specimens', in the following August. Doubtless because of their less substantial character, both of these were correctly credited to her by the scientific press. Yet despite this evident acclaim, her adherence to this line of work, and even to botany at all, turned out to have been too shallow-rooted to survive the death of her husband when this very suddenly occurred not long afterwards. It had been the shared interest, rather than an urge for recognition for herself, that had apparently propelled her. Though she was to live on as a widow for fifty years more, there is no evidence that she ever studied ferns again.

In Mrs Riley's case it cannot have helped that she and her husband had worked in isolation, seldom coming into contact at first hand with other of the Society's members or—it would seem—with anyone else in the botanical world more generally. Her work therefore did not have the effect of enmeshing her in a net of scholarly relationships which might have held more lastingly.

With Miss Anna Worsley,[17] the next most impressive of the women members, the situation in this respect was notably different. Brought up in one of the leading Unitarian families of Bristol, which long played a prominent part in that city's intellectual life, she started off with the added advantage of having an ardent geologist for a brother. At first herself primarily an entomologist, her conversion to botany was possibly the result of the marriage of one of her sisters to an enthusiast for that study, the clerical father of the novelist Samuel Butler. A few years later a cousin distinguished himself by publishing a list of the plants of the Newbury district. She in turn then married, at thirty-seven, a fellow Unitarian who for some years had been her companion on plant-hunting expeditions. Though the marriage was childless, she was successful in passing on her interest to one at least of her nieces. One of the ablest women field botanists of her generation, she joined the Society within five years of its founding and continued as one of the most faithful supporters of its annual exchanges of specimens until the very end. Clearly a person of considerable intellectual powers (though known today only as a botanical artist), she might well have persisted in the study of her own accord; but at the same time there can be little doubt that her devotion to it was massively sustained by being woven so widely and continuously into her circle of relations.

Many of the rest of the twenty-five, similarly, came from scientific families—and several, what is more, from families with a demonstrable allegiance to one or more of the leading societies in particular. The backgrounds of these, in other words, decreed not merely sympathy for the pursuit of natural knowledge, but making some public and corporate expression of this. Brought up to be joiners, as well as doers, they were 'society women' in a very special sense. Miss S. B. Hawes, for example, counted among her uncles a chairman of the Society of Arts (another uncle was the engineer Brunel). The Misses Barnard were great-nieces of Sir James Edward Smith, the founder of the Linnean Society. The precursor of that body, the Society for Promoting Natural History, had had as one of its presidents an uncle of Miss Louisa Legge. Both the father and the father-in-law of Mrs Lloyd Watkins were Fellows of the Royal Society. The father of Mrs Atkins had been not only a secretary of the Royal Society, but also president of the Entomological Society and a vice-president of the Botanical Society itself.

Yet it must not be supposed from this that the membership of such women was merely a token one—or even passive. True, it was possible to belong and do no more than attend the fortnightly evening meetings and listen to the papers that were read and discussed or, one step further, consult the library, herbarium or museum. But the Society had another activity that required more positive participation: its scheme for the exchange of herbarium specimens. Although much inferior at first to the similar service provided by its almost exact contemporary and rival, the Botanical Society of Edinburgh, this underwent a great improvement after 1841 under H. C. Watson's meticulous supervision, and eventually became the chief justification for the Society's existence. However many of them may have patronized the meetings, it was as contributors to these exchanges that the women members were chiefly prominent—to obtain the benefits of which, very likely, had for the majority been their primary reason for joining.

Most people who interested themselves in botany at this period, professionals and amateurs alike, accepted that the forming of a personal reference collection was a necessary way into the study. What began for many, and for women in particular, as no more than a youthful pastime thus graded insensibly and conveniently into a reputable learned pursuit, making it possible for anyone possessed of those rudiments of knowledge required for the forming of a collection to wander almost without noticing into the domain of science.

Whether collecting which was so slightly directed towards the elucidation of taxonomic or phytogeographical matters may legitimately be classed as science must be debatable at best: the more important point in the present context is that its exponents were undoubtedly perceived by their contemporaries as having formally entered into the scientific community, the boundaries of which were by no means coterminous with those who were followers of the subject in its modern sense. Indeed, the standard of the Society as a whole was by and large so primitive, judged by present-day criteria, that internalist historians might be disposed to deny its very admissibility as science. Yet what is scientifically trivial may be historically significant. From the externalist standpoint important new trends often first make their appearance on the periphery: where othodoxy sits most loosely it leaves more room for the establishment of the cranky and disfavoured. Good ideas may germinate in poor soil as well as wrong ones. As George Basalla has observed,[18] externalists have been inclined to limit themselves to a social history of science defined by internalists; but once these institutional fringes of the subject attract their due share of attention, this situation must surely alter.

To judge from the frequency with which some of them took part in the exchanges of specimens, the women members encountered no discrimination in partaking of this activity. It did not of course involve face-to-face contact and it was in any case in the general interest that there should be as many contributors of material as possible. But whether this absence of discrimination extended to the meetings is less certain. Two or three of the women are recorded as having produced exhibits, but it is unclear whether they were induced—or allowed—to speak on them. No woman, to be sure, was ever a main speaker; we do not know whether Mrs Riley's failure to read her paper in person was due to prejudice or diffidence. Less ambiguously, and more predictably, no woman was ever elected to the Council or served as an Officer.

Formally, however, there was only one way in which the women members were treated differently. 'Ladies who are Members', ran one of the rules, '. . . have the right to vote by proxy at all General Meetings, having previously informed the Secretary in writing of their appointment of some gentleman, being a Member of the Society, as their proxy for the occasion'.[19] It is difficult to believe that the intent of this was other than supportive. No doubt it was believed that the women would be disinclined to attend the whole or part of any meeting that was to be given over to the transaction of business, particularly where this extended to matters of finance, and that some special provision was accordingly needed if they were to play the proportional part in the Society's democratic governance that their well-wishers planned for them.

For it was no accident that it was this society that had been the one to take the lead in giving such positive encouragement to women.[20] True, the Zoological Society had anticipated it by nine years in the mere fact of
* admitting them;[21] but that was a body of some grandeur, regarding itself (to quote its original prospectus) as 'bearing the same relation to Zoology that the Horticultural Society does to Botany',[22] and there can be little doubt that—as with the Horticultural Society—it was as elegant paraders through its grounds, not as scientific contributors, that the women were seen as deserving of this innovation. At any rate, the Zoological Society made no comparable play with this step in its literature, and there is no evidence that its example was looked upon as significant by contemporary progressive opinion. Certainly, in its learned aspects it shared essentially the same outlook and atmosphere as such other leading metropolitan societies as the Geological and the Linnean; and both of these, notoriously, remained stubbornly opposed to the admission of women for many, many years, only giving in as late as 1904 and 1919 respectively.

The Botanical Society owed allegiance to a very different quarter. Like the earlier British Mineralogical Society, the contemporary Entomological Club and the later Geologists' Association, it was one of that tangle of minor bodies which had gradually been springing up to cater for the large under-class of the scientifically inclined who, even if they had the intellectual attainments, could on social grounds scarcely hope for election to the major societies. In short, it was an organization of outsiders. And like its fellows, it reflected this in a self-consciously liberal stance that verged even on radicalism. A striking number of its members came from dissenting backgrounds, had marked philanthropic leanings, or were active in reformist politics. The largest and liveliest audiences at its meetings were for discussions of the part botany might play in solving topical social problems: the adulteration of food, the potato disease, the treatment of sewage. Besides its championing of women, the Society made itself distinctive by the deliberate lowness of its subscription (one-third that of the Linnean Society, for instance) and by the emphasis it placed—or at any rate, wished to be seen to be endeavouring to place—on mutual assistance.

It would be incorrect to call the Society unpretentious, for it was just because it set its sights above the manifest abilities of its leading members that it brought itself into a good deal of initial contempt.[23] But it was at any rate modest in its social ambitions. It aimed to be inclusive, not exclusive. It liked to think that it brought together those who practised— the 'practical botanists', as it termed them—as opposed to those who merely discoursed. It was part of that wider turning away from the pomp and lavishness and eighteenth-century grandiloquence which out in the provinces was currently being signalled by the displacing of the literary and philosophical societies and their spiritual descendants by the insubstantial, informal, inexpensive field clubs.[24] Above all, it was powered by that new confidence and faith in all-round progress that the passing of the Great Reform Bill had recently done so much to stimulate.

It was a society of outsiders from a scientific point of view as well. As if in deliberate defiance, it made up for its exclusion from the social mainstream by nailing its colours to a heterodoxy like other bodies of its kind. Just as its contemporary and half-sister, the Meteorological Society of London, energetically played with the view that climate was influenced by the planets,[25] so the Botanical Society aggressively espoused the 'natural system', the new scheme of classification still then in the process of pushing aside the 'artificial system' long doggedly defended by the disciples of Linnaeus. A society that saw itself as on the side of progress could hardly have been expected to choose otherwise; at the same time, even if the members had not been convinced of their correctness in this matter conceptually, they would surely have found in the struggle to dethrone a shamelessly contrived ordering of nature, so deeply identified with the 'Establishment' in their discipline, an emotional appeal which rang resoundingly in tune with their more broadly liberal sympathies.

In addition to this distinctive ideology and the stance of non-exclusiveness, the Society further took upon itself the distribution of enlightenment more generally. The Honorary Treasurer, John Reynolds, had been active in the founding of the London Mechanics' Institute, and several other members were prominent as scientific popularizers. Enlarging the audience, not screening it for the qualified and knowledgeable, was the prime concern of such as these. So in marked contrast to its loftier contemporaries, the new society threw itself open to all comers, with the sole hurdles imposed being proposing and seconding, followed by balloting on candidates[26]—and even those were in all likelihood mere formalities. A considerable throng with at best the slightest smattering of the subject was thereby let in. Many of these were the counterpart of the scientific generalists who had hitherto bulked so large in the literary and philosophical societies, and who were now trying to adjust to the onset of the age of specialization by joining a whole set of

VIII

specialist bodies in default of the pre-existing unitary ones. A kind of flotsam washing around the Capital's intellectual structures, this element was predictably much in evidence at the outset, if only because it was so readily to hand. But as the influx, particularly from the provinces, of the more genuinely botanical gradually rose, and the emphasis shifted to the interests of collectors and the taxonomy of the British flora, these bystanders dropped away.

Considering this exceptional openness, the number of women members the Society proved able to recruit must be accounted disappointing. The thirty-three were only a fraction of the total who were active in the field at this period. Hardly less disappointing was the fraction even of the thirty-three who achieved any prominence once they had joined. For those who had looked upon the Society's non-discrimination as a pioneering experiment that might bring about reform more generally, the response can scarcely have seemed encouraging. There was patently no shortage of female botanists of a calibre that made them likely candidates for such societies, yet all too few showed themselves prepared to take advantage of the opportunity in the one case where this had been extended to them more or less unreservedly.

This experience was all the more disheartening in that botany was the one intellectual pursuit above all others that was hailed and promoted on every side as ideally suited to women. It called for no craft skills apart from the extremely elementary (and domestically familiar) ones of pressing and drying; it required no expensive or complicated equipment; it involved no procedures that taxed the strength of or were liable to upset the tender-hearted; and though its terminology was at first sight forbidding, this could be mastered reasonably quickly given a little persistence. As long as it remained essentially a science of classification and distribution, it was most invitingly accessible—to anyone who was literate and who merely had the patience to gather and identify.

Moreover, since the later years of the preceding century, when the fashion for Sentiment had accidentally overlapped the fashion for botany inspired by the Linnaean System, the muddled belief had grown up that because flowers appealed aesthetically to women in particular, so the study of these was the counterpart intended by nature for women in the sphere of intellectual cultivation. So essentially feminine was botany felt to be that it was seized upon by emancipatory opinion as a chance to propel women in greater numbers into stretching themselves mentally. In 1796 Priscilla Wakefield in *An introduction to botany, through a series of familiar letters* (which went through eleven editions by 1841) was typical in hoping the subject would become 'a substitute for some of the trifling, not to say pernicious objects, that too frequently occupy the leisure of young ladies of fashionable manners, and, by employing their faculties rationally, act as an antidote to levity and idleness'.[27]

Ever since then the pathways into the study had been deliberately and profusely strewn with petals—so much so that it was the other sex, rather, that found itself having to struggle against a demoralizing stereotype. Increasingly, to take an interest in flowers came to be deprecated as unmanly: chasing after insects, hammering rocks, or shooting birds were, the adult world conspired to hint, the particular forms of involvement with the wilds appropriate to boys. The gradual sundering after the 1860s of botany's traditional conjuncture with medicine served to intensify this trend, by removing a robustly utilitarian pretext that had hitherto acted as a countervailing influence.

Botany, it must have seemed, was the great test case of feminine emancipation. If women did not shine in a field such as this, so superlatively tilted in their favour, what hope was there of their shining in any other? If their achievements here could not stand comparison with those of their male counterparts, what chance was there of closing the gap in environments much less sympathetic?

The Society itself apart, the scene unfortunately was hardly one of promise. Scarcely a single woman at this period ventured beyond botany's nursery slopes to the point of at least describing novelties or overhauling difficult groups. Only rarely could women be tempted into print at any length—and then almost invariably to produce comparatively simple and straightforward listings. Even the writing of county Floras, those supreme monuments to cataloguing stamina, contrived to yield only one solitary instance of female authorship—the Kirby sisters' rather indifferent *Flora of Leicestershire* of 1848[28]—in over a hundred years. Not until the arrival of the ex-governess Annie Lorrain Smith at the British Museum (Natural History) as an 'unofficial worker' in 1888 could botanical systematics in Britain boast a woman whose achievements were in the same class as those of the foremost of the men.[29]

The sad truth is that it made little enough difference how far the sympathizers went in lowering the formal barriers at this period. Welcoming women into a national society and making a fuss over those who responded were helpful contributions towards altering the general climate of antipathy; but as long as frustration at their exclusion from the world of learning was still so thinly shared,[30] there was insufficient fuel to power the needed collective thrust towards realizing themselves more fully. While they continued in thrall internally, the modifying of externals could have scant real effect. Until the scales began to shift more substantially, which was not to happen before the 1870s, moves like those of the Botanical Society of London were likely to do more for the morale of their male well-wishers than for the true deliverance of the women themselves.

VIII

The Women Members of the Botanical Society of London

APPENDIX

KNOWN WOMEN MEMBERS OF THE BOTANICAL SOCIETY OF LONDON

* Anna Atkins (1797–1871), of Halstead, Kent; novelist; wife of John Pelly Atkins, landowner; daughter of John George Children, VPRS, Keeper of Zoological Collections, British Museum. Elected 1839/40.

Maria Attersoll (1793–1877), of Weymouth; unmarried. Elected 1839.

Alicia Mildred Barnard (1825–1911), of Norwich; unmarried; sister of the next and of another member, Francis Barnard, of Great Yarmouth; great-niece of Sir James Edward Smith, founder of the Linnean Society. Elected September 1848.

Frances Kinderley Barnard (1818/20–1893), of Norwich; unmarried. Elected 1839/42.

Mary Beever (1802–1883), of Coniston; unmarried. Elected 1839/41.

Eliza Jemima Mary Branfill (1822–1907), of Upminster; sister of later prominent Essex ornithologist; in 1851 married Rev. Edward Francis Gepp, also a botanist; mother of two botanists. Elected November 1836.

Emma Farenden (1799/1801–1880), of Regent's Park; unmarried; schoolmistress. Elected July 1845.

Susanna Foster (1814–1847), of Luton; unmarried; Quaker; daughter of John Foster, chemist and druggist, also a botanist. Elected 1839/42.

Ann Gawler (1791–1844), of Lambeth; wife of James Longman Gawler, parish clerk and undertaker, also a botanist. Elected November 1836.

Amelia Elizabeth Griffiths (1802–1861), of Torquay; unmarried; daughter of Mrs Amelia Warren Griffiths, renowned algologist. Elected c1848.

Elizabeth Harvey (1797/9–1873), of Deal; unmarried; daughter of Admiral Sir John Harvey, noted conchologist. Elected November 1838.

Sophia Brunel Hawes (d. 1870), of Lambeth and Mortlake; Unitarian; daughter of Sir Benjamin Hawes, soap-boiler and MP for Lambeth; niece of William Hawes, FGS, twice chairman of Society of Arts; in 1848 married Charles Justin MacCarthy, Auditor General for Ceylon. Elected 1839/42.

Elizabeth Hill (c. 1760–1850), of Braunton; unmarried. Elected by 1846.

Louisa Frances Catherine Legge (1817/19–1893), of Wonston, Hants; niece of 3rd Earl of Dartmouth, president of Society for Promoting Natural History, etc.; great-niece of Countess of Aylesford, noted flower painter; in 1866 married Rev. Alfred Bishop.

Elizabeth Charlotte Moxon (1790–1884), of Twickenham; unmarried; sister of another member, Rev. George Browne Moxon, of Sandringham, and aunt of Norfolk botanist John Edward Moxon. Elected 1839/42.

Charlotte Perry (1805/7–1882), of Haslemere, then Godalming; unmarried; three sisters were also botanists, the eldest a close friend of Ann Gawler, q.v. Elected November 1836 (resigned 1844).

Margaretta Riley (1804–1899), of Papplewick, Notts; wife of John Riley, land agent. Elected 1839, elected again April 1847.

Mary Ann Thomasin Robinson (1775–1847), of Fareham; widow of Matthias Archibald Robinson, grocer, of Holborn, then Regent's Park, also a botanist. Elected September 1845.

'Miss Roods' (d. 1865 or later), of Bloomsbury; one or other of three unmarried sisters of Henry Crowhurst Roods, general practitioner. Elected 1839/42.

Frances Sawbridge (1807/1880), of Bath; unmarried; cousin of Henry Barne Sawbridge, FRS, the uncle by marriage of another member, Rev. John Frederic Bigge, of Northumberland. Elected c1844.

Margaret Stovin (1756–1846), of Chesterfield; unmarried; granddaughter of George Stovin, FRS, and second cousin of the leading botanist Richard Anthony Salisbury. Elected 1839/42.

Elizabeth Twining (1805–1889), of Twickenham; unmarried; cousin of another member, Thomas Twining, also of Twickenham; author and illustrator of several botanical works; originator of workhouse reform and a founder of Bedford College, London. Elected 1839/43.

Sophia Louisa Henrietta Lloyd Watkins (1802/4–1851), of Brecon; wife of Col. John Lloyd Watkins, landowner and MP; daughter of Sir George Pocock, Bart., FRS. Elected April 1850.

Sophia Elizabeth Caroline Windham (1811–1863), of Felbrigg, Norfolk; daughter of Frederick William Hervey, FRS, 1st Marquess of Bristol; wife of William Howe Windham, landowner. Elected 1839/42.

Anna Worsley (1807–1876), of Bristol, then Kenilworth; Unitarian; sister-in-law of another member, Rev. Thomas Butler, of Langar, Notts (the father of Samuel Butler, the novelist); in 1844 married Frederick Russell, of Kenilworth, also a botanist. Elected 1839/41.

NOTE: Except where indicated most, if not all, belonged to the Church of England. Where no occupation is indicated independent, non-employed status should be assumed. Places of residence are those during the period of membership *only*.

Unidentified members

Mrs Dennison, of London	Elected November 1836
Miss Evans, of Coventry*	October 1850
Mrs W. James, of Uxbridge	September 1851
Mrs W. Jones, of Woolwich?	c1849
Mrs Morgan, of Southsea	September 1851
Miss Nesbitt	1839
Miss Charlotte Wilkins, of Westbury†	November 1847
Miss Martha Wilson, of Belfast	August 1849 *

* Almost certainly 'George Eliot', the novelist (Mary Anne Evans, 1819–1880).

† Almost certainly the person of this name who d. 1876 in Bristol, aged 72, and whose legatees included two botanist cousins, Augustin Prichard and Rev. Augustin Ley.

NOTES

[1] Now among the T. B. Hall MSS in Merseyside County Museum. I am indebted to the Keeper of Botany, Mrs B. D. Greenwood, for bringing this letter to my attention.

[2] A. Heathcot, *Magazine of zoology and botany,* 1836, *1,* 502. The Society's original prospectus is quoted, ibid., as justifying the eligibility of women as members on the ground that 'there are many who have devoted their attention with success to this delightful study, and whose occupations often leave them much leisure for observation and research'.

³ *Athenaeum*, 26 November 1836, p. 835a.

⁴ Excluding (as throughout this paper) the non-subscribing categories of Honorary and Foreign Members.

⁵ *Proceedings of the Botanical Society of London*, 1839, *1*, 101–3. Only this one volume was ever published.

⁶ A report in the *Literary gazette* of the Anniversary (or Annual General) Meeting of 29 November 1837 asserts that this was 'very numerously attended, comprising many ladies, members of the Society'. But while there may have been 'many' present, the implication that these were all members is difficult to reconcile with the known figures. A journalist's misinterpretation seems probable.

⁷ Unexpectedly, this is considerably in excess of the total computable, with some estimating, from the Society's own year-by-year figures. The discrepancy is presumably due to many of those whose names feature in the reports never having enrolled formally. At least one person who rendered the Society much assistance over several years, the leading cryptogamist Thomas Taylor (1786–1848) is said to have come into this category (H. C. Watson to C. C. Babington, 27 March 1844; *Babington correspondence*, Botany School, Cambridge). The distinction between members and non-members is thus perhaps not one of much moment: the total of all who in some way contributed to its work would appear to be a truer measure of the Society's strength.

⁸ The principal sources of names are the 1839 membership list, lists of local secretaries appended to the early prospectuses, lists in the published meeting reports of those reading communications, exhibiting or contributing specimens, and data on labels in herbaria of gatherings identifiable as distributed through the Society.

⁹ Mrs Anna Atkins, of Halstead Place, near Sevenoaks.

¹⁰ For a fuller account see D. E. Allen and Dorothy W. Lousley, 'Some letters to Margaret Stovin (1756?–1846), botanist of Chesterfield', *The naturalist*, 1979, *104*, 155–63.

¹¹ A presumptive identification only. It is possible that the 'Miss Hill' listed in the Society's minute-book in 1846 as a subscriber to a portrait fund is not the collector of that name frequently referred to in the earlier literature.

¹² Germaine Greer, *The obstacle race*, London, 1979, p. 12: 'The single most striking fact about the women who made names for themselves before the nineteenth century is that almost all of them were related to better-known male painters'. In Greer's view, their motivation probably sprang from a desire to please and conform: they were not independent artistic personalities, with a self-generated determination to produce great art.

¹³ For a fuller account of Margaretta Riley see D. E. Allen, 'The first woman pteridologist', *British Pteriodological Society bulletin*, 1978, *1*, 247–9.

¹⁴ A much earlier precedent has recently been claimed for Mrs Maria Graham, afterwards Lady Callcott (1785–1842) as 'the first woman to have a paper published by the Geological Society'; see Valerie Appleby, 'Ladies with hammers', *New scientist*, 1979, *84*, 714–5. But while it is true that she features as the author of 'An account of some effects of the late earthquakes in Chili', *Transactions of the Geological Society of London*, 1824 [2], *1*, 413–5, this was merely an extract from a letter written by her to the vice-president and was not read before the Society—from membership of which its rules in any case excluded her.

¹⁵ *Literary gazette*, 1840, pp. 233, 314, 379.

¹⁶ As related by her obituarist in the *Nottingham daily express*, 20 July 1899.

¹⁷ For a fuller account see D. E. Allen, 'The botanical family of Samuel Butler', *Journal of the Society for the Bibliography of Natural History*, 1979, *9*, 133–6.

¹⁸ George Basalla, 'Observations on the present status of history of science in the United States', *Isis*, 1975, *66*, 467–70.

¹⁹ Copy in Department of Botany library, British Museum (Natural History), shelf-mark Obl. 22:58.

²⁰ Its Scottish counterpart, the Botanical Society of Edinburgh, doubtless moved by its example, also began admitting women in December 1836, nine months after the foundation date. But Miss Katherine Sophia Baily (from 1838 Lady Kane), of Dublin, author of a recent *Irish flora*, the one honoured on that occasion, had been joined by no more than two others by the end of 1838. And the rather grudging nature of the move that this much more sparing recruitment suggests was underlined by the Society's insistence in corralling them in a separate membership category of their own: women—and women alone—could only be Life members. Similarly, the British Association began formally admitting women to its Sectional meetings in 1837—though (significantly) only those for Geology and Natural History initially—but was not yet prepared to admit them to membership other than indirectly or on the same terms as men; see A. W. Thackray and J. B. Morrell, *Gentlemen of science*, forthcoming.

²¹ P. Chalmers Mitchell, *Centenary history of the Zoological Society of London*, London, 1929, p. 32. By a resolution passed in April 1827 women were formally admitted as Members on the same terms as

men. However, it was not till the end of the century that they became habitual attenders at the Scientific Meetings.

[22] John Bastin, 'The first prospectus of the Zoological Society of London: new light on the Society's origins', *Journal of the Society for the Bibliography of Natural History,* 1970, *5,* 369–88.

[23] On this see, for example, H. C. Watson, 'On the credit-worthiness of the labels distributed from the Botanical Society of London', *The phytologist,* 1847, *2,* 1005–15 (1008).

[24] P. D. Lowe, 'Locals and cosmopolitans: a model for the social organization of provincial science in the nineteenth century', University of Sussex M Phil thesis, 1978.

[25] G. J. Symons, 'The history of English meteorological societies, 1823 to 1880', *Quarterly journal of the Meteorological Society,* 1881, *7,* 65–98.

[26] A. Hume, *The learned societies and printing clubs of the United Kingdom,* London, 1847, p. 112. A two-thirds vote secured election.

[27] 10th edn., London, 1831, p.v. Quoted by Ann B. Shteir, 'Priscilla Wakefield (1751–1832): author, philanthropist, "respectable person" ', forthcoming.

[28] Even this seems to have depended crucially on the help and encouragement of a male botanical neighbour, the Rev. A. Bloxam. See Mary Gregg (*Née* Kirby), *Letters from my life,* London, 1887.

[29] D. L. Hawksworth and M. R. D. Seaward, *Lichenology in the British Isles 1568–1975, an historical and bibliographical survey,* Richmond, 1977, p. 26.

[30] Significantly, in Britain, unlike America, there was no tendency for women, in retaliation, to band themselves together in exclusive groups of their own, such as the Female Botanical Society of Wilmington in the 1840s, the Dana Society of Natural History of the Albany Female Academy in the 1860s and the later still Philadelphia and Syracuse Botanical Clubs. See Sally Gregory Kohlstedt, 'In from the periphery: American women in science, 1830–1880', *Signs,* 1978, *4,* 81–96. Similar bodies did make an appearance in Britain from the late 1880s onwards—but only in ornithology. British botany continued to be the exception in its non-discriminatory stance.

IX

The struggle for specialist journals: natural history in the British periodicals market in the first half of the nineteenth century[1]

INTRODUCTION

At some stage in its development every emergent field of learning tends to give rise to its own specialist literature. In these days we have come to take it for granted that this process does not necessarily have to start by taking the expensive route of print: some cheaper, less formal type of publication can serve until such time as the specialist audience has grown to the point at which the establishing of a journal becomes economic, either as the organ of a society large enough to be able to afford to meet its costs or else as the speculation of a commercial publisher. Today, copying machines of one kind or another allow fellow specialists to communicate with one another at minimal expense and without having to worry about attracting and satisfying a large paying readership.

Until these substitutes for print came along, life was hard for any group with a shared interest which felt the need to exchange information and opinions with more than just a preselected circle of private correspondents. Until late in the nineteenth century, and for most people until long after that, the one and only way in which written matter could conceivably be reproduced in quantity was by a laborious craft technique, and this by reason of that very laboriousness and the skill and training required—to say nothing of the raw materials—was unavoidably costly. That cost, moreover, was all the greater the smaller the number of copies required, which placed minority interests at a double disadvantage. True, a book with a limited appeal could always be published provided the necessary number of subscriptions could be obtained for it in advance, though so high a price might have to be charged that collecting these was liable to be as burdensome as it was prolonged. A specialist periodical, too, was always a viable proposition as long as there existed a society sufficiently sizeable and well-established to guarantee the requisite volume and stability of sales. A specialist periodical without such underpinning, however, was inherently much more problematical; for even if an adequate number of subscribers could be secured in the first instance, it was impossible to predict how many and how soon those would drop away or to have any real idea whether replacements for them potentially existed.

Despite those disadvantages, periodicals have always had some offsetting commercial attractions for publishers. With print runs pegged to subscriptions the risk of over- or under-producing is small compared to that in publishing most kinds of books. Production costs, moreover, are paid for in advance from the money received from subscribers—and that can be earning interest on deposit until the printer's bill comes in (Cross, 1984). Not altogether surprisingly, therefore, periodicals were being published speculatively in

IX

Britain as early as the late seventeenth century, some of them even catering for special interests (though invariably rashly).

Natural history was popular with book publishers in Britain through much of the eighteenth century, but it laboured under the handicap that its sales were seen as dependent on attractive illustrations. A periodical devoted to natural history was accordingly expected to have many of those too, which was bound to make it particularly expensive. The ideal one, indeed, was one that consisted almost wholly of colour plates, with a minimum of text. The *Botanical Magazine*, launched in 1787 by William Curtis, was to be the longest-lasting of several that were precisely that. It proved in fact highly profitable, on sales of around 2,000 copies on average montly (Curtis, 1941:74). Its title, however, is misleading, for it was a magazine only in the sense that it came out periodically: it was not a journal in the sense in which that term has come to be understood but, more correctly, a part-work.

THE FIRST JOURNALS

The first true journals in the field of natural history were almost all non-commercial enterprises, sponsored by one or other of the loftier bodies as those successively came into existence. With the Royal Society and its *Philosophical Transactions* as their model, they each early saw it as desirable, as well as a matter of prestige, to have an outlet for at least the more important material read before their members at their meetings. The Linnean Society's *Transactions* were the first to start, in 1791, to be followed by the Geological Society's in 1811, respectively three and four years after the founding of the parent body. The interval was shorter still in the case of the Cambridge Philosophical Society (which had the advancement of natural history as one of its declared aims on its founding in 1819), while the Wernerian Society launched its *Memoirs* in the very same year, 1808, that it broke away from the Natural History Society of Edinburgh to pursue an independent existence.

The societies could meet the need for journals only in part, however. Their 'house organs' were effectively exclusive to memberships that were themselves exclusive: only a relatively small proportion of the total following for their respective fields of interest was able to contribute and had access to what appeared. To qualify, papers had first to be read at one of the society's own meetings and the selection of those that it could afford to publish was decided upon by ballot, in which non-Fellows were likely to lose out. Even when lucky enough to be chosen, a paper could then take an agonisingly long time to appear, for such was the cost of printing at this period that an issue of the journal might have to be held over till the society's finances could bear it. Printing was only one part of the problem, moreover: the distributing of the copies was also a very protracted affair, for Fellows had to collect these by hand (or else arrange for others to do so on their behalf). As one of the Linnean Society's members was moved to complain, its *Transactions* tended to "come out at intervals too distant for the constant diffusion of knowledge that is necessary; they are too costly for general circulation; and are devoted to subjects too important to take in that subordinate but still valuable mass of information that is fitted only for the pages of a periodical journal."[2] As this last grumble reveals, there was a tendency for journals to be viewed as a second-best, as a somewhat inferior class of literature. In striking contrast to the present-day convention in science, it was in books that people expected to publish, and others to read, what more especially mattered. A periodical, however solid and learned, had difficulty in escaping the notion that it was, by its very nature, ephemeral and thus unsuited to material that was weighty and important enough to need to be available for continuing reference.

It early came to be realised that one of the most valuable functions a learned society could perform was to serve as a publishing co-operative, putting into print much that could never have appeared had it been necessary for the individual authors to meet the cost themselves. From that realization it was but a small step to a substitute, less formal group—a 'pseudo-society'—banding together for the sole and express purpose of bringing out a journal devoted just to its own particular focus of concern. Such an initiative was most likely to prove successful if the members of the group in question shared a certain theoretical viewpoint which they were hungering to voice. Coterie journals of this type early became a feature of German academic science, serving as the mouthpieces of individual professors and as outlets for the research of their students and disciples (Shils, 1968). The nearest British equivalent at this period was the *Zoological Journal*, founded in 1824 by some Linnean Society dissidents who wanted their debating of the then-fashionable Quinarian Theory reflected more fully and more speedily in print (Desmond, 1985: 159). The intellectual force behind that theory proved sufficient to keep the publication going for as long as ten years, and it closed its pages only when the main body of its supporters transferred their allegiance to the newly-founded Zoological Society of London and preferred not to compete with that body's monthly abstracts of its proceedings (Fish, 1976). Similarly, but in a more oblique way, Robert Jameson used the *Edinburgh New Philosophical Journal* (of which he became sole editor in 1824), just as he long used the Wernerian Society, to advance the cause of the geognostic system of Werner. As Jameson had studied under Werner in Germany, it seems more than likely that he derived this professorial tactic from his experience of how things were contrived in that country. The extremely limited development of any academic science in Britain at that period was almost certainly the only reason why more publications on this model failed to appear. For as soon as the situation in that respect changed, from the 1870s onwards, a flurry of coterie journals promptly materialised.

As well as the 'pseudo-society' there was the converse device of the quasi-Transactions. This was the eminently sensible one of buoying up a purely commercial periodical by making it the recognised outlet for one or more societies that lacked journals of their own. It was a development that arrived in the 1830s, as soon as a further layer of metropolitan societies of a less grand and affluent character began to come into existence. A typical example was the association of the *Microscopic Journal and Structural Record* with the Microscopical Society of London (Brock, 1989). Its founding editor, Daniel Cooper, in his eagerness to effect the marriage, went so far as to offer "to make the journal serviceable to the views of the Society" (Michael, 1895). The advantages of such arrangements, after all, were more on the one side than the other: an otherwise risky venture acquired the prop of a partly captive market and at the same time, hopefully, a steady supply of publishable material of the requisite specialised character. If the device was not resorted to all that widely, that was simply because even quite humble societies presently found it possible to rise to the luxury of publishing a series of Transactions or Proceedings exclusive to themselves (even if, in some cases, the members were able to obtain copies only by a separate payment on top of their subscription).

Despite the measure of protection from adverse winds that a journal gained by sheltering alongside a particular society or being tied to it officially, there were

IX

110   THE STRUGGLE FOR SPECIALIST JOURNALS

nevertheless some naturalists who viewed this dependence as too constricting and were unwilling to accept that it was necessary, convinced that a periodical of sufficiently high quality and with a sufficiently appealing mix of material could not fail to attract support enough to enable it to survive unaided.

Two who put this belief to the test, however, were all too soon proved wrong. Possibly deceived by D.H. Hoppe's apparent success just then with his *Botanische Zeitung* in Germany[3] (but overlooking the speedy demise there already of the *Annalen der Botanik*, the *Magazin für die Botanik* and the *Neue Annalen der Botanik* (Manten, 1980)), John Sims and Charles Konig[4] boldly started an English-language counterpart, the *Annals of Botany*, in May 1804 (Greene, 1958). Significantly, Konig had come to Britain from Germany less than five years before, having been engaged to work on the Queen's botanical collection in succession to J.E. Smith. It was probably he therefore who put the idea of a journal into the head of Sims, a fashionable London physician who by then had been editing for four years the lucrative *Botanical Magazine* and could well rise to the initial capital outlay. Though the two were nominally joint editors, most of the work seems to have been done by Konig: many of the contributions appeared over his name and he is known to have drawn the plates as well as produced the numerous translations of papers by leading continental botanists (Smith, 1969), this last a standard feature of commercial science journals of that era.[5] Other contributors included such eminent figures as Smith, Salisbury and Dawson Turner. The opening number was indeed extraordinarily impressive, with an authoritative survey of the recent European literature which extended to no fewer than 72 pages, followed by taxonomic and morphological papers, short notes and books reviews.

It was altogether admirable, but it could not possibly have survived without a heavy continuing subsidy, given the publishing economics of the period. Unsurprisingly, with only the second volume an editorial notice appeared announcing ruefully that, despite "so many flattering testimonials from botanists of the first repute", the journal would either have to be discontinued or its character changed in such a way as to render it cheaper to produce. Discontinuance proved in the event the harsh reality.

Konig was at first inclined to think that the very concept had been mistaken and that they could not have succeeded even had the marketing been handled by a bookseller.[6] Three years later, however, his optimism had recovered and he was claiming that the circulation "would certainly" have doubled, to some 500 copies, had only such a course been followed.[7] By that time he was bursting with ideas already for a successor, this time a quarterly to be devoted to natural history as a whole, not just to one of its branches. "The best plan, perhaps," he confided in a letter to Smith,[7] "will be to make it at first as light reading as possible, to proceed gradually *ad graviora*, and lastly, when the work is perfectly established, to consult nothing but the real advancement of the science, without minding the *Vulgus*." The types of material he envisaged including were much the same as those there had been in the *Annals of Botany* with the exception of reviews, which he had concluded few readers relished unless they were "severe and abusive"—"and I should not wish to gratify their taste", he added. A major innovation, on the other hand, was to be a section of miscellanea, featuring "accounts of museums, societies and their transactions, honors conferred on, and deaths of, naturalists, anecdotes etc." He confidently expected such a periodical, "if properly conducted", to attract at least 1,000 subscribers. He ended by inviting Smith to join him as editor and assume responsibility for the botanical contents. That was seemingly quite a sacifice, for botany was Konig's special field also; by

IX

THE STRUGGLE FOR SPECIALIST JOURNALS   111

that time, though, he had been appointed to the staff of the British Museum, where he had found it necessary to switch to mineralogy, and doubtless he no longer expected to keep up with the literature of his previous field of interest.

Though Konig wrote confidently of launching the first number in only a few months' time, his approaches to booksellers must have proved discouraging, for no more was heard of the venture. It was, in truth, only slightly less quixotic a brainchild than its predecessor, for the market conditions that would have enabled either of them to be at least partly feasible were still four decades off.

ECONOMIC BREAKTHROUGH

Salvation was on the horizon nevertheless. In the very same year that the *Annals of Botany* failed another German (with a surname, by a second coincidence, virtually the same as that of one of its editors), Friedrich König, had come to London in search of finance for his experiments on the application of steam-power to printing. Those experiments eventually bore fruit commercially eighteen years later, at the end of 1814, with the introduction of the cylinder press (Moran, 1973). By 1830 printing presses were able to produce up to twenty times as many impressions an hour as they had done two decades earlier. They had meanwhile also become simpler to use and able to produce better-quality work.

Papermaking had been revolutionized, similarly. In 1804 the Fourdrinier brothers had acquired the English patent for a French invention which enabled a continuous sheet of paper to be made on an endless wire cloth operated by rotary motion. Three years later what was essentially the modern continuous papermaking machine, which still goes by their name, was built for them and thereafter went into production (Coleman, 1958).

These technological advances combined to make possible long and fast print runs at very much lower prices. Riding on their backs came a no less wonderful bounty of technical improvements in the reproduction of illustrations: first wood engravings, then engravings on metal, finally the far cheaper lithographs. Rudwick (1976) has pointed out how especially important this last chain of developments was for the natural history sciences, with their traditional concern with configurations that could not be conveyed adequately in words. It was no accident that one of the first of any publications for which lithography was used was the *Transactions* of the Geological Society.

The full benefits of the new technology did not flow through to publishing economics, however, till a considerably later date. This was entirely because of a set of particularly oppressive taxes, originally imposed to help pay for the wars against Napoleon and subsequently kept in place by one Chancellor of the Exchequer after another. Of these, the one that bore down hardest on journals was the excise duty on paper. This was estimated to account for between a fifth and a third of the cost of producing a monthly or quarterly of 80 pages (Wiener, 1969: 13). Publication at such infrequent intervals was effectively forced on periodicals by the application, from 1819, of a no less onerous stamp duty to any that appeared more often—or that sold for less than sixpence (Wiener, 1969: 4). They all consequently remained too expensive to be bought by any but the well-to-do. On the other hand they were spared the further imposts on advertisements and newsprint with which other sectors of the publishing industry had to contend, and that may well have had the effect of making them more attractive as commercial speculations than might otherwise have been the case. Overall, though, the profitability of publishing was severely held in check by the weight of this burden, which by keeping prices artificially high depressed sales and prevented the great expansion in readership which the concurrent rises in national prosperity and national literacy fully entitled the industry to expect. The principal sufferers, though, were newspapers, the sales of which hardly increased at all in proportion to population in the twenty years after Waterloo. That above all infuriated radicals, who credibly saw these so-called 'taxes on knowledge' as having the secondary aim of clipping the wings of political agitation. Their long-drawn-out campaign on this issue eventually met with partial success in the 1830s, when a weak Administration, needing the support of reformist votes, greatly reduced all of the taxes in question. Though not the one of prime concern politically, the paper duty was not overlooked, though it was not until 1836 that it was lowered by as much as half (Brown, 1985, 1992; Collet, 1933).

By then the railway age had arrived, bringing the promise of sizeable reductions in distribution costs as well. At the start of the next decade there would be reasonably fast train services out of London as far as Newcastle upon Tyne to the north and as far as Bristol to the west. The remodelling of the postal services quickly followed. A Parliamentary Select Committee was persuaded in 1839 that it was volume of business, not the distance an individual letter or parcel was conveyed, that ultimately mattered, and in the next year abruptly lower uniform national rates were introduced for all inland mail. That this cut by three-quarters the cost of sending a single sheet between London and Edinburgh indicated the magnitude of the impact that this alone must have had on journal economics. Postage costs had in fact been especially crippling for this sector of publishing, for apart from the correspondence incurred with contributors and the dispatching of proofs and offprints the practice of charging by weight rendered each individual copy of a journal a formidably expensive item. It was only when Rowland Hill introduced a special book rate in 1847 that this last handicap was substantially removed (Brock, 1980; Brock and Meadows, 1984).

LOUDON'S EXAMPLE

As so often with major new departures, it required an outsider to demonstrate the possibilities that this series of developments had begun to open up. John Claudius Loudon, the person who now arrived on the scene to fill this role, was a man of quite exceptional industriousness even by nineteenth-century standards. A landscape gardener by training, his never-idle pen and a bubbling fascination with novelty soon led him into architecture on the one hand and into the compiling of encyclopaedias on gardening and farming on the other. Keenly attuned to the interests and tastes of the newly-comfortable middle classes, in 1826 he exploited the gap in the market for a periodical devoted to the practical side of horticulture. The resulting *Gardener's Magazine and Register of Rural and Domestic Improvement* (to give it its full title) quickly proved a resounding success. Started off, warily, as a quarterly, it was soon doing well enough to be brought out monthly and earning Loudon the immense profit annually of £750 (Loudon, 1845), equivalent to about £20,000 today. This success was all the more impressive in view of the fact that the breakthrough in publishing economics had not by that time extended to the fiscal and distribution aspects: the wave he rode was a technological one purely and simply.

Brimming over with confidence now and with a gardener's interest in botany already, Loudon saw a *Magazine of Natural History* as the appropriate next addition to his stable. Brought out in the spring of 1828, this was boldly made a bi-monthly from the first, the aim being to go monthly once it was established. The publishers, Longman & Co., ingeniously retained stereotyped plates, thereby allowing extra copies to be produced on demand.

Initially, this magazine too proved a conspicuous success, the first few issues selling over 2,000 copies each (Sheets-Pyenson, 1981a, 1981b). Once again, it seemed, Loudon had hit upon exactly the right formula, a formula indeed not very different from that envisaged twenty years earlier by Konig for his own abortive natural history journal but with more of an emphasis on items likely to appeal to the less experienced. The style, deliberately, was informal and chatty.

In view of the state of natural history in Britain at that period, however, it was dangerous for a periodical devoted to that field to be seen to succeed so spectacularly. There was too much material known to be in search of publication and there were too many people who fancied it as their mission to see that material into print. It was a period, moreover, when a scatter of paid practitioners of the subject was at last beginning to emerge, but practitioners earning for the most part such derisory salaries that there was anything but a shortage of willing and well-qualified part-time editors.

Predictably, therefore, a rush of imitators of Loudon's magazine promptly appeared, a considerably larger number than the market could accommodate, as it almost equally promptly turned out. Only some of these were devoted to natural history exclusively, others being general science periodicals and one or two attempting a coverage even wider than that. The *Analyst*, for example, which began coming out (unusually, from a Midlands base) in 1834 and which published some competent natural history matter, sounded from its sub-title virtually omnivorous: 'a Quarterly Journal of Science, Literature, Natural History and Fine Arts'. The *Magazine of Science and School of Arts*, launched anonymously in 1839 under the editorship of an able botanist, G.W. Francis, and printed by his brother, was another with a wide reach—though evidently successfully, for by 1842 it was far outdoing Loudon by selling 3,000 copies monthly (Best, 1986: 16). By contrast, the *Edinburgh Journal of Natural History and of Physical Science* seemingly did itself no good by publishing with the exceptional frequency of every fortnight and with the added inducement of an exceptionally low price. Though edited (and probably largely written) by the well-regarded William MacGillivray for a more affluent naturalist proprietor, Captain Thomas Brown, it petered out in 1840 after a life of less than five years (MacGillivray, 1910: 115).

In a situation of frantic jockeying for position only a slight error could prove a journal's fatal undoing. The worthy and the unworthy perished alike. In the allied field of medicine and health, in which a closely similar state of affairs was occurring (Peterson, 1979), it has been calculated that new periodicals were coming on to the market in the period 1828–39 at the rate of rather more than four a year on average; yet more than two out of every three of those new arrivals died within two years, almost half of them even in their first twelve months (Loudon and Loudon, 1992). Comparable calculations are precluded for natural history because of the gradation of the field into other areas of knowledge, but its experience was almost certainly not dissimilar. The literature of the period abounds with titles that ceased to be heard of again only a short time after announcing their appearance.

One likely cause of trouble was the existence in certain cases of both a naturalist editor and a naturalist proprietor—such as the Edinburgh duo of MacGillivray and Brown noticed already. As there were no such things as editorial boards and referees at this period,[8] the potential for suicidal squabbling over the character of the contents is only too apparent. Disagreements over strategy between street-wise commercial publishers and scholarly but unworldly editors or proprietors was a yet further possible cause of journal fatalities.

Thanks to the recent studies by Susan Sheets-Pyenson (1981a, 1981b, 1981c, 1987), we know that personality clashes were not necessarily the reason for failures, however: in at least some cases elementary mistakes in marketing were merely to blame. The most usual of these were pricing too low, publishing too frequently, paying the editor too much, being over-lavish with plates and ordering too long a print run. But even if those hazards were all avoided, a journal could still be laid low if its aim veered off-target in the most crucial aspect of all: the kind of material placed before the readers. After Loudon chose to delegate the editorship of the *Magazine of Natural History* in 1831 to his young assistant, John Denson, a gardener with an interest in field botany, circulation fell off badly, allegedly because "facts fresh from the field" had been supplanted by "dry, musty, closet-hatched speculations". More accurately, it had probably contracted a disease to which would-be 'popular' periodicals were peculiarly prone in the natural history field: 'learned drift', a tendency to turn ponderous and earnest, however lightweight their proprietors or editors wished them to remain. The infection was due to the shortage of well-informed naturalists with the necessary light touch who were willing to keep sending in the kind of material wanted. Such contributors were greatly outnumbered by those who wanted an outlet for their records or their theories—an alternative to the journals of the societies, in other words. Loudon seems to have arrived at the mistaken belief that the fault lay with Denson and that what was needed was an editor better qualified to discriminate and to obtain the kind of material best capable of bringing back the subscribers who had dropped out. If so, he made an even worse mistake in recruiting (in 1836) Edward Charlesworth, a competent geologist but a believer in controversy as the answer to falling circulation. That policy, however, was soon shown up as ill-conceived, for sales sagged even further—in no small part, it was said, because of Charlesworth's "contentious and vitriolic outbursts" (Sheets-Pyenson, 1981b).

THE ONE EXCEPTION

At the same time there was a section of the natural history community which longed for journals of precisely the kind that the more commercially-minded proprietors struggled to avoid. It was for these more scholarly naturalists that the *Magazine of Zoology and Botany* was expressly devised by three northern heavyweights, George Johnston, P.J. Selby and Sir William Jardine, and was first published in that same year, 1836, in which Loudon was desperately shuffling editors.

The subsequent history of this newcomer has recently been pieced together in unusually rich detail (Brock, 1980; Sheets-Pyenson, 1981a, 1987; Brock and Meadows, 1984), thanks to the survival of its successive publishers' records. From the very start it seems to have been the victim of misjudgements on three separate fronts: it had higher distribution costs through being based in Edinburgh instead of London; it was deemed necessary to offer certain leading figures payment for their solicited contributions in the belief that those would not otherwise be forthcoming; and the content was too preponderantly zoological—to the extent that it was a specialist journal in all but name.

After two years it had lost its trio of proprietors the very sizeable sum for those days of £400. Determined to persist but recognising that corrective action was needed, in their inexperience they identified the chief weakness as the poor coverage of botany. Johnston had a good knowledge of that subject but lacked the eminence in it necessary to secure material of the desired high quality, so it was clear to them that their number had to be augmented by a botanist of the requisite standing brought in from outside. The obvious choice was the recently-knighted W.J. Hooker, then still Professor of Botany at Glasgow University and thus conveniently at hand. Hooker, moreover, was a seasoned editor by then but known to be sustaining with difficulty two specialist botany journals of his own,[9] which otherwise amounted to awkward competition. However, he proved to want to try persevering with those, and by the time he was ready to abandon the lamer of them and throw in his lot with the *Magazine of Zoology and Botany* it was in such deep trouble that the decision regretfully had to be taken to cease publication.

The latecomer to the feast having arrived only to find the table being cleared now proceeded to arrange for it to be laid all afresh. With characteristic drive Hooker went down to London and prevailed on his friend, Richard Taylor, a down-to-earth commercial publisher who was also a noted scholar in his own right, to relaunch the title on the intended broader basis. As an inducement, Hooker undertook to take on a new and separate section to be devoted to botany in return merely for a regular number of complimentary copies and reimbursement of his postal expenses.

Conceded full financial control and a free hand, Taylor remodelled the journal in the light of his experience of editing David Brewster's *Philosophical Magazine* and publishing the *Transactions* of both the Royal and Linnean Societies. By adding some geology in addition to the extended treatment of botany (and thereby justifying a change of title to the *Annals of Natural History*) and by reducing costs in a variety of ways—in particular by employing for a pittance his illegitimate son, the university-educated William Francis, as sub-editor—he gradually managed to retrieve the situation. He succeeded in this, moreover, despite the early loss of Hooker, who, offended by Taylor's failure to accord botany the separate section that he had been given to expect, used his lack of remuneration as a pretext for switching his loyalty back to his own, still-surviving competitor, the *Journal of Botany*. A windfall in May 1840 more than made up for that, however. This was the chance to acquire (for £100) the by then badly ailing *Magazine of Natural History*, along with the rump of subscribers it had succeeded in retaining. Renamed yet again as a result, as the *Annals and Magazine of Natural History*, under this combined banner the journal turned out in the end to be the only one devoted solely to natural history to emerge alive from that murderous free-for-all of the 1830s. Generations of taxonomists have had much reason to be thankful for that survival ever since.

NEWMAN'S COMPROMISE

If Taylor had shown that it was possible for a scholarly journal to be viable in this field commercially—provided it was run with his exceptional discipline and skill—he nevertheless seemed to have demonstrated also that this could be achieved only if it was addressed to naturalists as a whole. Although the *Annals and Magazine of Natural History* was to revert to being an essentially zoological enterprise, the breadth implied by its successive titles and the expansion in coverage apparently required to effect its refloating initially disguised the true extent of Taylor's achievement. The depressing inference seemed to be that journals catering for just one section of the natural history community remained out of reach for the foreseeable future unless dependent upon a society (or some similar institution).

Experience in Germany, that trend-setting country for nineteenth-century scholarship, was hardly less discouraging. True, after one journal after another devoted just to botany had turned out to be short-lived, Hoppe's *Flora* had managed to keep going since as far back as 1818; but that was probably achieved only with the aid of surreptitious subsidies (Leussink, 1981). And there was no comparable stayer there in zoology—*Ornis*, C.L. Brehm's fond hope of 1824, having proved unsustainable after a life of only three years (Stresemann, 1975: 304, 310).

The great surge of enthusiasm for entomology in England in the 1820s (Allen, 1976: 101–103) had predictably given rise to the idea of a journal exclusive to that pursuit, but J.O. Westwood's 'Entomological Miscellany' had never progressed beyond the stage of a prospectus. In that corner of the field even the device of harnessing a specialist journal to a relevant society did not appear to be the answer either; for the close symbiotic relationship which the six years older Entomological Club developed with its offshoot of 1832, the *Entomological Magazine*—so close that the editorship was apparently treated as one of the duties of the Club's successive honorary curators (Mays, 1978: 35)—failed to endow it with more than six years of a fragile existence. The founding of the much more substantial Entomological Society of London in 1833 might have been its salvation, however, had that body not decided, after much deliberation, to publish a journal of its own—to the bitter disappointment of the keenest of those curators-cum-editors, Edward Newman. Newman indeed went so far as to resign from the new Society's Council in protest, and took every opportunity to snipe at it in the pages of the *Entomological Magazine* (Shaw, 1980).

This unhappy interlude had nevertheless brought on to the scene the person who was now to demonstrate to the would-be publishers and purchasers of journals for natural history's minorities that their resigned acceptance of the market's supposedly unbeatable economics had been needlessly premature.

A lifelong naturalist of unquenchable enthusiasm as well as a born journalist of exceptional flair, Newman was at that time in his early thirties and discontentedly employed in the rope trade. Finally breaking free from that and realising his true vocation, he proceeded to buy a partnership in a small firm of printers. The owner of this, George Luxford, was himself a botanist and a writer of ability (Trimen, 1876). Consequently, when in the following year, 1841, Newman bought him out, Luxford was the obvious choice to edit a new monthly for him, the *Phytologist*, to be published by the firm, an initiative perhaps occasioned by the news that the recently-founded Botanical Society of London could not afford to sustain a journal of its own.[10] Having been baulked of the prop of its entomological sister three years earlier, Newman was not the sort of man to miss the same opportunity twice. Though the *Phytologist* was never to prove successful commercially (Trimen, 1876) and its circulation latterly was perhaps even as low as 200 copies,[11] Newman persisted with it for as long as 13 years. That its discontinuation coincided with Luxford's death (Newman, 1876) doubtless encouraged the belief that he did so merely out of loyalty to his former partner, but contemporary letters reveal that he was in fact anxious to see it carried on and made vain attempts to interest at least two leading botanists, H.C. Watson[12] and J.G. Baker[13] to take over the editorship. The real reason why he so stubbornly preserved it (presumably by cross-subsidy) was that it fitted into a wider plan and its survival was necessary to prove the correctness of a conviction of his own on which that plan was based.

The conviction may well have arisen even prior to his entry into publishing, but it must surely have been reinforced by the position in which he accidentally found himself very soon after that event. For the reason why he did not edit the *Phytologist* himself—though he contributed its annual, very thoughtful editorials—was that a year before its launching he had taken on that role for another new journal brought out under his auspices, the *Entomologist*, and because that dealt with the subject that was always closest to his heart, it had the first call on his energies. The *Entomologist* was effectively a mere retitling of the *Entomological Magazine* which he had been editing just previously, but its existence meant that he had two journals in play concurrently, each catering for a separate minority. Any other publisher at that period would surely have merged them; but Newman's deep personal involvement in the natural history community apparently led him to believe that such a strategy was no longer essential. While it might be convenient commercially to assume that there was still a single entity, natural history, with a readership sharing tolerably similar concerns, the reality more and more was that the subject had broken up into a series of substantially self-contained branches, a process which was likely to be irreversible. What is more, the tremendous growth in following that field natural history had enjoyed in Britain in the previous fifteen to twenty years had so increased the sizes of these sub-communities as to suggest that a series of specialist journals for them might be feasible commercially at last. Newman's perception, however, went beyond the simple, even banal fact that "all naturalists like works confined to the particular science in which they take most interest," as he observed in a letter to Hooker in the spring of 1841:[14] he had spotted that the breaking up of the subject's former unity had an implication that promised to alter journal economics. "The purchasers of . . . the numerous magazines of Natural History" were having to pay "two-thirds of their subscription exclusively for the benefit of others", and he had become convinced that that was a major reason why almost all of the broad-spectrum journals had lacked success (Newman, 1846). He forbore to add that the *melée* of the 1830s had helpfully eliminated almost all of the competition by then and that the paper duty had now been halved, with the result that the risks were markedly lower than previously.

In January 1843 he set out to prove his point further by introducing the *Zoologist*— though he immediately weakened his case by killing off the *Entomologist* and incorporating that in it. With a coverage that consequently embraced two of the most popular aspects of natural history, namely birds and insects, while also not neglecting other forms of animal life as well, he was thus attacking on a fairly safe broad front. The reception given to this new journal nevertheless surprised even him. A year later he was able to report that it had "met with most unequivocal success. Contributions have poured in from all parts of the kingdom in a manner, I believe, wholly unprecedented in the annals of any other Natural-History Magazine: indeed, so great, so overwhelming is the supply, that I have lately been unable to publish more than half the communications I have received." More important, though, sales were continuing to grow—and to help them along, he presently took the step of extensively distributing a circular seeking more subscriptions (Newman, 1844). Ten months later still he was crowing about the increasing demand even for the earlier issues, "contrary to the usual fate of periodicals, the earlier numbers of which almost invariably remain a dead weight on the hands of the proprietor, until they are eventually sold at a price scarcely equivalent to that of waste paper" (Newman, 1845). Another year further on sales were growing at an even faster rate, with particularly marked leaps in the north and west of the country (Newman, 1846). The *Zoologist* was indeed to prove Newman's one really lasting success—which was just as well, for it was the journal that undoubtedly mattered to him most. He was to edit it personally for no fewer than 33 consecutive years, ending only with his death in 1876, and for 40 further years after that it continued to lead an independent existence.

IX

Newman delighted in twitting his rivals, in particular Richard Taylor, for surrendering their journals to "conservative dullness", to what he saw as "prescriptive technicalities and chartered obscurities" (Newman, 1847). It always seemed to him pointless, not least because it was so commercially inhibiting, to duplicate what the learned societies published, in what he was once pleased to call their "unreadable and cumbrous tomes" (Newman, 1832–33). The policy he pursued with his own publications was one of "letting his contributors determine and make the style and character",[15] following Loudon's practice of printing just about everything sent in, however trivial, trusting to the good sense of the natural history community to filter out the worst absurdities and errors. Like all the best journalists, he knew instinctively what his readers were likely to find of interest—which was, broadly speaking, what he himself found of interest too.

His touch was not always sure even so. The *London Geological Journal*, which he brought out in 1846, with a view to completing his quiver, proved a short-lived disaster. Significantly, it dealt with a subject which he knew little about personally. Nevertheless, that he was right to steer clear of too staidly scientific an approach was only too quickly confirmed by the fate of a would-be, more scholarly rival to the *Phytologist*, the *Botanical Gazette*, with which Taylor and Francis vainly sought to go along that same specialist road in 1849. An initial print run of 550 was quickly shown up as wildly optimistic, an actual sale of a mere 200 causing the venture to be abandoned after only two years (Brock, 1980). Matters were probably not helped by the fact that the proprietor and editor, Arthur Henfrey, Lecturer in Botany at St George's Hospital, had little interest personally in the areas of the subject that most of the journal's potential readers favoured, being primarily an enthusiast for plant physiology and similar experimental aspects.[16]

THE MARKET CONQUERED

It was only twenty years later on, in the 1860s, and more particularly in the middle of that decade, that the day of the specialist commercial journal can truly be said to have arrived in British natural history. By that time a number of further fiscal and technological improvements had led to a second wave of significant cost reductions, and it is tempting to identify that as the causal factor. The final abolition of the stamp duty in 1855 had been followed by that of the duty on paper in 1861, while the raw material cost of the latter began to fall considerably after 1857 as a result of the exploitation of esparto grass (Wiener, 1969).

It was perhaps no coincidence, therefore, that April 1856 saw the launch of yet another of Newman's bright-and-breezy periodicals, the *Entomologists' Weekly Intelligencer*. Edited by the affluent H.T. Stainton, the sponsor already of an eminently successful Christmas publication, the *Entomologists' Annual*, and priced at only a penny, this was at first intended, as its name implied, as an up-to-the-minute bulletin on what insects were around, to appear during the collecting 'season' only. However, it speedily acquired such a large,[17] eager and vociferous following that both editor and publisher were forced to change their plans and bring out a stop-gap, appropriately called *The Substitute*, to satisfy the hunger of its readers during the winter months as well. Thereafter it was decided to publish the *Intelligencer* all through the year, on which basis it was carried on until 1861 (Capper, 1898; Classey, 1957). Its absence was then so keenly felt that a replacement, the *Weekly Entomologist*, was quickly brought out by T. Blackburn, a collector in Cheshire. Costing twice as much, this lasted for a further 26 issues before petering out in its turn two years later (Classey, 1957). It may be that the *Intelligencer* had come to its seemingly most untimely end through some difference of opinion between Newman and Stainton; for it looks suggestive that in 1864, the very next year after its successor folded, Stainton ✳ promptly re-emerged to become 'editor-in-chief' of a more up-market product, the *Entomologist's Monthly Magazine*, for Newman's rival, John Van Voorst. Evidently stung by this invasion of what he regarded as very much his personal patch, Newman thereupon retaliated by reviving his *Entomologist*, transferring to it all the material relating to the insect world from the by then overflowing *Zoologist*—so much so that double numbers were frequently having to be resorted to—and proceeded to edit the two journals in tandem for the remaining dozen years of his life. Like the *Zoologist*, this new one was also to thrive for many years subsequently.

Simultaneously, and seemingly quite independently, there was a parallel renewal of activity on the botanical front as well. In 1855 Newman had sold the title of his by then defunct *Phytologist* to an antiquarian bookseller who was the leading specialist of the day in botanical works, William Pamplin. Pamplin had installed as editor a Chelsea school-master, and long-time field companion of his, Alexander Irvine, who succeeded in making the new series lively but at the same time outdid even Loudon's Charlesworth in the degree to which he tried to stoke up that liveliness with provocative editorialising and acrimonious comment. One of his frequent veiled targets was H.C. Watson, whose habit of merciless criticism had made him numerous enemies. For five years Watson was content to treat Irvine's shafts with a contemptuous aloofness, dismissing this successor to Luxford's worthy namesake as beneath serious notice. Eventually, though, the disservice he saw being done to botany by its unchallenged existence drove him to draw up plans for an alternative, respectably scientific monthly. So set was he on this that he was fully prepared for the costs to be double the returns and to have to make up the difference out of his own, far from deep pocket. He proposed to call it the 'British Botanist' and had sent out two prospectuses and lined up Newman as its printer and the ex-Curator of the lately-deceased Botanical Society of London, J.T. Syme, as its editor when a strong potential competitor unexpectedly emerged (Allen, 1986: 71). This was a second *Journal of Botany* (no relation of Hooker's earlier periodical of that name), which the German botanical explorer Berthold Seemann had been encouraged to bring out as an English-language counterpart to his widely-admired *Bonplandia*. Although the promises of support that Watson had laboriously collected thereupon melted away and Pamplin also used this development to close down his loss-making *Phytologist*, even with its resulting near-monopoly[18] Seemann's journal nevertheless barely managed to stay afloat in the first years after its launch in 1863, having run through two successive publishers (Robert Hardwicke and Lovell Reeve) and with its circulation stuck at a mere 250[19] by the time the next decade opened. On that showing no one would have predicted that it would survive—as in the event was to prove the case—for almost 100 years further. Unaccountably, the support for journals among botanists was not nearly so strong as it was among entomologists, even though the respective sub-communities seem to have been of much the same size.

No one would have ventured to forecast a long-term future, either, for the *Geological Magazine*, yet another offspring of those same, ultra-fertile mid-sixties. Launched, like the *Entomologist's Monthly Magazine*, in that auspicious year 1864, under the editorship of Henry Woodward of the British Museum, in just the same way as its birth-mates in entomology and botany this edged out a more populist predecessor, in its case the *Geologist*, with which Newman had eventually filled that embarrassing vacancy in his journal stable and which S.J. Mackie had very successfully[20] edited for him during the previous six years.

That these new, more earnestly scientific, more professionally-oriented journals should all have arrived on the scene in a sudden bunch was symptomatic of more than just a shift in publishing economics: they betokened a change in the make-up of British natural history itself. Suggestively, their appearance coincided with the advent as well of major specialist societies, most notably the Geologists' Association and the British Ornithologist's Union, which for the first time did not depend for their national status on being rooted in and identified with one or other of the capital cities. By the 1860s natural history's several sub-communities had expanded in size to the point where they could at last count on self-sufficiency in the open market for periodicals. In future, free-standing journals tailored to their particular interests might still give rise on occasions to anxiety, but at least it would no longer be a story of general, continual, nerve-wracking precariousness.

ACKNOWLEDGEMENTS

I would like to thank G.D.R. Bridson, Professor W.H. Brock, Professor W.F. Bynum and Professor Susan Sheets-Pyenson for helpfully commenting on this paper in draft. I am particularly grateful to the first-named for drawing my attention to several additional references and for bringing to bear his unrivalled expertise on the dates in the Appendix.

NOTES

[1] This is a much-expanded version of a paper given at the 9th International Conference of the Society for the History of Natural History, April 1994, which in turn was an expansion of one contributed to the symposium on "Publications" at the 17th International Congress of History of Science, Berkeley, 1985.

[2] N.A. Vigors to W. Kirby, 1 October 1822: reproduced in Freeman (1852: 372).

[3] The *Botanische Zeitung* managed to keep going from 1802 till 1807 (Leussink, 1981).

[4] Strictly, Carl Dietrich Eberhard König, but after settling in England he always used this anglicised version of his name.

[5] As Loudon and Loudon (1992) have pointed out, the widespread practice at this period of reprinting articles from other publications, including overseas ones, was not regarded as plagiarism or as in breach of copyright, but seen as a compliment to the author and publication in question.

[6] Konig to J.E. Smith, 9 October 1806, Smith Correspondence, vol. 23, f. 95, Linnean Society of London.

[7] Konig to J.E. Smith, 3 October 1809, Smith Correspondence, vol. 23, ff. 98, 99.

[8] The concept of an editorial board goes back to Henry Oldenburg and the *Philosophical Transactions* in the seventeenth century, but it was still surprisingly rare even for the leading societies to buttress the judgement of their editors with this device. Even in the medical field there was probably only one British journal in the first half of the nineteenth century, namely that owned by the Royal Society of Medicine, which went so far as to have papers refereed. This began in 1843, two dozen Fellows of the Society being appointed to act in this capacity (Loudon and Loudon, 1992).

[9] These were his *Journals of Botany*, effectively a continuation, from 1834, of the short-lived (1829–33) *Botanical Miscellany*; and the *Companion to the Botanical Magazine* (1835–7).

[10] The Botanical Society of London, for ideological reasons, was unwilling to countenance a subscription rate that would have made this possible (Allen, 1986: 22). It published one volume of *Proceedings* in 1839 and then gave up.

[11] H.C. Watson to C.C. Babington, 12 January 1849, Babington Correspondence, Department of Plant Sciences, Cambridge University.

[12] Watson to Babington, 16 February 1861, Babington Correspondence.

[13] J.G. Baker to W. Wilson, 23 August 1854, Wilson Correspondence, Department of Botany, the Natural History Museum.

[14] Newman to Sir William Hooker, 27 March 1841, Hooker Correspondence, Incoming Letters, vol. 16, letter 290, Royal Botanic Gardens, Kew.

[15] Watson to Babington, 8 December 1851, Babington Correspondence. The words quoted were written of the *Phytologist*.

[16] According to Busk (1860), Henfrey supported the *Botanical Gazette*, "I believe at his own risk, with zeal and perseverance, for two or three years, when, finding that, like almost all strictly scientific periodicals in this country (to our shame be it spoken), it could be carried on only at a loss, he was reluctantly compelled to discontinue it." Evidently Taylor and Francis acted in this instance as no more than the printers and distributors. Henfrey was not wealthy enough to be able to pay the subsidy required, which accounts for the abruptness with which the journal folded. Had he only had warning, H.C. Watson confided to C.C. Babington (16 October 1852, Babington Correspondence), he would have offered Henfrey £50 or £100 for the copyright and subsidised and edited it himself.

[17] Within two years its circulation was averaging 600 (Editorial to no. 78: 201).

[18] Following the demise of Pamplin's *Phytologist* Irvine went on to edit the short-lived (1863–5) *Botanists' Chronicle*, a penny monthly distributed with Pamplin's catalogues of second-hand books.

[19] Watson to J.G. Baker, 14 January [1871], Baker Correspondence, Botany Library, the Natural History Museum.

[20] According to Ellegård (1957: 28), the *Geologist* attained a circulation of around 1,000 copies, a very impressive figure for the period.

REFERENCES

ALLEN, D.E., 1976 *The naturalist in Britain. A social history*. London.

ALLEN, D.E., 1986 *The botanists. A history of the Botanical Society of the British Isles through 150 years*. Winchester.

BEST, B.J., 1986 *George William Francis, first Director of the Adelaide Botanic Garden*. Adelaide.

BROCK, W.H., 1980 The development of commercial science journals in Victorian Britain. In MEADOWS, A.J. (ed.), *Development of science publishing in Europe*, 95–122. Amsterdam, New York, Oxford.

BROCK, W.H., 1989 Patronage and publishing: journals of microscopy 1839–1989. *Journal of Microscopy* **155**: 249–266.

BROCK, W.H. and MEADOWS, A.J., 1984 *The lamp of learning: Taylor and Francis and the development of science publishing*. London.

BROWN, L., 1985 *Victorian news and newspapers*. London.

BROWN, L., 1992 The British press, 1800–1862. In GRIFFITHS, D.(ed.), *The encyclopaedia of the British press 1422–1992*, 24–32. London.

[BUSK, G.], 1860 *Address of . . . the President, together with obituary notices of deceased members . . . of the Linnean Society*. London.

CAPPER, S.J., 1898 A short sketch of entomological serial literature in Britain. *Entomologists' Record* **10**: 54–64.

CLASSEY, E.W., 1957 The weekly entomological periodicals of Great Britain. *Entomologist's Gazette* 8: 216–217.

COLEMAN, D.C., 1958 *The British paper industry 1495–1860*. Oxford.

COLLET, C.D., 1933 *History of the taxes on knowledge: their origin and repeal*. London.

CROSS, N., 1984 The economics of learned journals. *Times Literary Supplement*: 1348.

CURTIS, W.H., 1941 *William Curtis, 1746–1799*. Winchester.

DESMOND, A., 1985 The making of institutional zoology in London 1822–1836. *History of Science* **23**: 153–185, 223–250.

ELLEGÅRD, A., 1957 *The readership of the periodical press in mid-Victorian Britain*. Göteborg.

FISH, R., 1976 The library and scientific publications of the Zoological Society of London: part I. *Symposia of the Zoological Society of London* **40**: 233–252.

FREEMAN, J., 1852 *The life of the Rev. William Kirby*. London.

GREENE, S.W., 1958 C. König and J. Sims' *Annals of Botany*, London. *Journal of the Society for the Bibliography of Natural History* **3**: 319–320.

LEUSSINK, J.A., 1981 A short history and bibliographical analysis of the journal *Flora (Regensburg)* . . . Part I. The editors. *Taxon* **30**: 375–392.

[LOUDON, J.], 1845 An account of the life and writings of John Claudius Loudon. In LOUDON, J.C., *Self-instruction for young gardeners* . . . London.

LOUDON, J. and LOUDON, I., 1992 Medicine, politics and the medical periodical 1800–50. In BYNUM, W.F., LOCK, S. and PORTER, R. (eds.), *Medical journals and medical knowledge: historical essays*, 49–69. London and New York.

LOUDON, J.C., 1830 *Magazine of Natural History* **3**: preface.

MacGILLIVRAY, W., 1910 *Life of William MacGillivray*. London.

MANTEN, A.A., 1980 The growth of European science journal publishing before 1850. In MEADOWS, A.J. (ed.), *Development of science publishing in Europe*, 1–22. Amsterdam, New York, London.

MAYS, R., 1978 *Henry Doubleday. The Epping naturalist*. Marlow.

MICHAEL, A.D., 1895 The history of the Royal Microscopical Society. *Journal of the Royal Microscopical Society*, ser. 2, **15**: 1–20.

MORAN, J., 1973 *Printing presses: history and development from the fifteenth century to modern times*. London.

[NEWMAN, E.], 1832–33 Introductory address. *Entomological Magazine* **1**: 1–4.

NEWMAN, E., 1844 *Zoologist* **2**: v–vi.

NEWMAN, E., 1845 *Zoologist* **3**: vi.

NEWMAN, E., 1846 *Zoologist* **4**: v–vi.

NEWMAN, E., 1847 *Zoologist* **5**: v.

NEWMAN, T.P., 1876 *Memoir of the life and works of Edward Newman*. London.

PETERSON, M.J., 1979 Specialist journals and professional rivalries in Victorian medicine. *Victorian Periodicals Review* **12**: 25–32.

RUDWICK, M.J.S., 1976 The emergence of a visual language for geological science 1760–1840. *History of Science* **14**: 149–195.

SHAW, J.G., 1980 Patterns of journal publication in scientific natural history from 1800 to 1939. In MEADOWS, A.J. (ed.), *Development of science publishing in Europe*, 149–176. Amsterdam, New York, Oxford.

SHEETS-PYENSON, S., 1981a From the north to Red Lion Court: the creation and early years of the *Annals of Natural History*. *Archives of Natural History* **10**: 221–249.

SHEETS-PYENSON, S., 1981b A measure of success: the publication of natural history journals in early Victorian Britain. *Publishing History* **9**: 21–36.

SHEETS-PYENSON, S., 1981c Darwin's data: his reading of natural history journals, 1837–1842. *Journal of the History of Biology* **14**: 231–248.

SHEETS-PYENSON, S., 1987 The effect of changes in printing technology on the development of natural history sciences during the nineteenth century. In McNALLY, P.F. (ed.), *The advent of printing: historians of science respond to Elizabeth Eisenstein's 'The Printing Press as an Agent of Change'*. McGill University Graduate School of Library & Information Studies, Occasional Paper No 10: 21–26.

SHILS, E., 1968 The profession of science. *Advancement of Science* **24**: 469–480.

SMITH, W.C., 1969 A history of the first hundred years of the mineral collections in the British Museum, with particular reference to the work of Charles Konig. *Bulletin of the British Museum (Natural History), Historical Series* **3**: 235–259.

STRESEMANN, E., 1975 *Ornithology from Aristotle to the present*. Trans. H.J. & C. Epstein. Cambridge, Mass. and Loudon.

TRIMEN, H., 1876 Edward Newman. *Journal of Botany*, **14**: 223–224.

WIENER, J.H., 1969 *The war of the unstamped*. Ithaca, N.Y.

APPENDIX

BRITISH JOURNALS REFERRED TO IN THE TEXT

The Analyst, 1834–9
Annals of Botany, 1804–6
Botanical Gazette, 1849–51
Botanical Miscellany, 1829–33; continued as (Hooker's) *Journal of Botany*, 1834–42; as
    London Journal of Botany, 1842–8; as *Hooker's Journal of Botany and Kew Garden
    Miscellany*, 1849–57
Botanists' Chronicle, 1863–5 (privately circulated only)
Companion to the Botanical Magazine, 1835–7
Edinburgh Journal of Natural History and of Physical Science, 1835–40
Edinburgh New Philosophical Journal, 1826–54; new series 1855–64 (when incorporated
    in *Quarterly Journal of Science*)
Entomological Magazine, 1832–8
The Entomologist, 1840–2 (when incorporated in *The Zoologist*, q.v.); revived 1864–1973
Entomologists' Annual, 1855–74
Entomologists' Monthly Magazine, 1864–
Entomologists' Weekly Intelligencer, 1855–61
Gardener's Magazine, 1826–43
Geological Magazine, 1864–
The Geologist, 1858–64
Journal of Botany, British and Foreign, 1863–1942 (when incorporated in *Annals and
    Magazines of Natural History*, q.v.)
London Geological Journal, 1846–7
Magazine of Natural History, 1828–40 (when incorporated in *Annals and Magazine of
    Natural History*, q.v.)
Magazine of Science, and School of Arts, 1839–49; continued as *Magazine of Science and
    Artist's, Architect's and Builder's Journal*, 1850–2
Magazine of Zoology and Botany, 1836–8; continued as *Annals of Natural History*,
    1838–40; as *Annals and Magazine of Natural History*, 1841–1967; as *Journal of
    Natural History*, 1967–
Memoirs of the Wernerian Natural History Society, 1811–39
Microscopic Journal, and Structural Record, 1841–2
Philosophical Magazine, 1798– (with variations in title)
Philosophical Transactions of the Royal Society, 1665–
The Phytologist, 1841–54; new series 1855–63
Proceedings of the Botanical Society of London, 1839
Transactions of the Geological Society of London, 1811–56
Transactions of the Linnean Society of London, 1791–1875; continued as separate
    botanical and zoological series till 1955
Weekly Entomologist, 1861–3
Zoological Journal, 1824–35
The Zoologist, 1843–1916

X

THE EARLY PROFESSIONALS
IN BRITISH NATURAL HISTORY

'Professional' is one of those sponge words—like 'culture' or 'fashion' or, for that matter, 'natural history'—which tend to be used in a confusing variety of senses. On the whole such words normally serve us best by being left in this convenient vagueness. But there come times when we want to look more closely at the concepts for which they do this rough duty and when we therefore have to start by carefully defining terms. This is one of those occasions.

Clearly, when we speak of 'profession' in the context of science, we understand by it something rather different from the classic extreme represented by the law or medicine. Quite a number of sociologists and historians of science in recent years have made the attempt to spell out precisely what this is. Most of these attempts, however, have been aimed at delineating the modern, highly sophisticated world of scientific research and have consequently arrived at definitions which are too tightly-drawn to fit the earlier, less developed versions which fall short of professionalization in this full and ultimate sense. By their criteria what the historian of early nineteenth-century science in Britain is concerned with is semi-professionalization at best. A less demanding definition, such as one that has been put forward by a specialist in that period (Berman, 1974), therefore seems appropriate. This definition requires 'professionals' to be basically "a group of practitioners of a discipline whose practice of this is their major or entire source of income, on which their livelihood depends and which may come from a regular salary or from fees charged for services rendered." But to merit the term fully, this definition requires them also to share a special collective consciousness, notably about standards of what constitutes expertise. Oddly, in British science this sense of a common identity was established very early, yet full professionalization was achieved extremely late (Shils, 1968). What was missing in this country were the opportunities for full-time research careers on the scale which scientists in France enjoyed from as early as 1795 thanks to their extensive employment by the State. So advanced were the French in this respect that priority has been claimed for them in the evolving of a true professionalized science (Crosland, 1969:ix; 1970); but it has been objected that, as they lacked as yet the further crucial feature of institutional provision for scientific training, this can hardly be (Ben-David, 1972). Germany, therefore, wins the prize for this particular race. There, incontestably, a full professionalization came into being, well before anywhere else, through the teaching of science in universities in which it had come to be accepted that the duties of a professor explicitly included research.

2

Why did Britain lag? How did it come about that, even as late as mid-century, 'science' in this country continued to mean for most people "a random and casual familiarity with natural phenomena, rather than a theoretical grasp of a subject acquired through disciplined study" (Berman, 1974)?

The favoured explanation is that science, like so much else in British life, was in thrall to the ideal of the leisured gentleman amateur. Here uniquely, Berman has suggested, the natural trend to professionalization was chronically blocked on account of the operation of an overriding social process of a kind technically known as 'hegemony'—that is, the exercise by one section of society (or, alternatively, one nation) of a purely cultural supremacy as a kind of displaced substitute for the exercise of power politically and economically. On this view British science, though by that time mainly a pursuit of the middle classes, danced to the off-stage tune of the more influential, leisured upper layer.

But superimposed on that basic cause there may have been another, important contributory factor. Those areas of science which happened to achieve the greatest popularity at that period, namely those broadly classified as natural history, happened also to be those most amenable to study by amateurs. By over-identifying with just this one limited part of the whole, the new generation of scientific enthusiasts—that much more forceful and committed wave of people for whom Kargon (1977) has usefully coined the term the 'devotees'—fixed the idea of science too firmly in their own image. It thus came to be accepted that what such amateurs did was, broadly speaking, what science was all about.

These novel, sophisticated amateurs brought to the subject an intensiveness and a standard of expertise which could well be mistaken for those of professionals.[1] Indeed it is tempting for historians of science to see in them the obvious missing stage in what ought otherwise to have been a natural linear sequence leading up to professionalization in the fullest sense. But that is to assume that amateurs *ought* to evolve into professsionals and that professionalization is a necessary and desirable development in itself. To an American, accustomed to a society in which the drive to professionalize has had a special cogency because of the value of occupational distinctions in countering the 'melting-pot' amorphousness, a reluctance to abandon amateurism might well seem unnatural and perverse. In the British context, however, this has never been a ridiculous position to take.

For provided a study does not call for facilities that are prohibitively expensive or require techniques that can be performed only by teams, there is no *prima facie* reason why the professional should be regarded as having the advantage. This is especially true in a field like natural history; but it is equally true in such other observational sciences as meteorology and astronomy, to which the amateur has continued to make a contribution of significance wherever a tradition of the worthwhileness of his efforts has similarly managed to survive (Meadows & Fisher, 1978).

In fields such as these the reason why a professional normally has the edge over an amateur today is only partly the extra depth of expertise, theoretical and manipulative, that he will ordinarily have acquired as a consequence of an academic apprenticeship: it is also, quite simply, the far greater time and energy that he is able to devote to his work. Yet this has not always been the case. We tend to forget that it is only comparatively recently that the self-supported, full-time amateur scholar was rendered more or less extinct, with an abruptness and completeness rivalling those of the dinosaurs, by the onset of a deleterious economic climate. A hundred and fifty years ago probably few people would have imagined that matters in this respect would alter so drastically. And there is no scientific reason why the change should have taken place at all: it is through quite extraneous historical factors that it has happened.

From the standpoint of the early nineteenth century what appears today as the triumphant rise of the professional might well be viewed, rather, as an ignominious downfall from Paradise. For what could be more ideal than to spend all one's days immersed in one's favourite pursuit, consciously nudging the limits of accepted knowledge, communicating with and respected by the leaders in one's field—and not to have to trouble about money or a career, about students or administration, about the importunities of the public or the jockeying of colleagues? What could possibly be better than to be a Lyell or a Darwin, or even a Waterton or a Dovaston—or, failing their amplitude of means, at least an H. C. Watson, with his monkish austerity and enclosed dedication? For in truth one did not need all that much to achieve independence and still retain the standing of a gentleman. It is misleading to think only of those sweeping lawns and those battalions of servants: Watson's cabbage-patch of a garden and his solitary housekeeper were enough for those prepared to cling to Eden the hard way.

No one in their senses would have voluntarily exchanged that freedom for the life of a professional, with all its embarrassments and pressures. For that generation, in any case, to seek to earn one's living from something like natural history did not rank as following a profession as that word was generally understood: it was almost tantamount, rather, to running off to sea or joining a circus—a mad gesture by the foolhardy or the desperate. Professions involved expensive training and were exclusive by definition. Once qualified in one of these, a man could expect to be his own master or have other people to order for most of the time at least. But a naturalist? He could expect only to cling to the outermost margins of respectable society and to be sat upon and snubbed. It was anything but a desirable prospect for a person of gentle birth.

Indeed, looked at in a brutally objective light, the mere fact of being in paid employment of any kind could be said to be inherently demeaning, whatever the circumstances. To be paid is to be constrained, to enter into a state of submission in at least some degree. However far away in the background, the money that employs is the power that potentially distorts. However noble the pursuit, it is contaminated inescapably in so far as it is dependent on the sordidness of lucre. The market-place, necessary though it may be, is in all ways and at all times a subtly lowering influence. Our grandparents' grandparents were absolutely right, surely, to fend it off as long as they possibly could.

X

Naturally, their amateur status was preserved only at a price. They tended to work in comparative isolation—not merely geographically, but at a certain social distance as well, with the result that they were exposed too seldom to bracing critiques. Free from pressure to give proof of their abilities, they could dawdle over their research or postpone its completion indefinitely. And they were over-prone to change, dropping an interest before they had written it up (or at any rate published on it adequately).

But their professional contemporaries could be just as ill-disciplined too. The continual interruptions of administrative life were liable to sap consistency of effort. The need to pursue outside earnings to supplement the pittances that passed for salaries could lead to the squandering of research energy. The very richness of the collections ever on hand could produce a fatal lack of focus. Too many opinions raining down, too many bright new theories, too much distracting gossip: just as the amateur was at risk from working so largely on his own, so for the professional there was the contrary danger.

Yet, despite these very good reasons for resisting professionalization, the first half of the nineteenth century saw natural history starting to succumb. Despite being the area of science in which pre-eminently the amateur could sparkle, paradoxically this was the one area in which the number able to make their living by it seems to have grown most and fastest. As so often, the sharply different experience of natural history has been conveniently disregarded, it would appear, by those mainly responsible for the received historical picture.

The reason why natural history was thus so atypically advanced was the growth in the number and extent of its collections, public as well as private, living as well as dead. The fashion among the wealthy for forming these had gradually given rise to a minor associated industry in which explorers, showmen, dealers, and taxidermists all found niches of a greater or lesser degree of lucrativeness. The wish to have the specimens correctly named scientifically brought in turn a growing demand for the expertise of naturalists.

There were various ways in which this could be tapped. The simplest was to engage appropriate experts to come on visits to one's house or even to stay there for a protracted period. An early instance of the latter, probably the earliest occasion of all on which a naturalist was engaged full-time in Britain expressly for his scientific services, was the bringing over from Germany of Johann Jakob Dillen, otherwise Dillenius, by William Sherard in 1721. It was on just this same pattern that the young Linnaeus was later to be employed by Clifford at De Hartekamp. It may be significant that in both these cases it was foreigners who were chosen: perhaps this was because to have a foreign expert resident in one's house conferred a certain cachet. Foreigners, moreover, had no obvious place in the host country's class system and so raised fewer problems about where they should be located within the household. Home-grown naturalists, if of gentle birth, had to be given some recognised status if their presence was not to be misinterpreted: they therefore tended to be smuggled in under the guise of some more ordinary domestic office. Thus the Duchess of Beaufort tried to lure Sherard to Badminton as nominal tutor to her son, while the Duchess of Portland, more successfully, caught Lightfoot in her toils by appointing him as her personal chaplain.

Unless these great private collections were broken up and dispersed on the death (or bankruptcy) of their owners, most of them eventually found their way into the custody of the State. There, if they were not to deteriorate irreparably, to the point of political scandal, they demanded at least a modicum of curation from an always grudging Treasury. And as their potential for enlightening the masses, over and above their more obvious role in furthering scholarship and research, gradually came to be appreciated, this increasingly pointed to the recruitment of permanent officials with the requisite specialist knowledge. That these would be highly-qualified scholars, however, not all of whom would have the mainstay of private means, does not seem to have been realised: for the salaries were pitched at a level with barely-educated clerks or even caretakers evidently in mind. These almost invited derelictions of duty while supplementary earnings were having to be sought.[2]

Indirectly, and probably unwittingly, the State was itself responsible for producing some of this trained corps of specialists. This came about through the voyages which governments were increasingly talked into sponsoring for reasons of foreign policy or because of their general utility to navigation. Exploring and natural history had by this time a long-established relationship, and such voyages consequently presented naturalists with opportunities for widening and deepening their experience which they could hardly have come by otherwise. Through this same means so many ships' officers were able to equip themselves with serviceable extra skills that 'naval science' came to be seen as an avenue for career advancement (Knight 1974; 1976:109), and for ships' surgeons to double up as naturalists thereby became in turn respectable and official. There was a naturalist appointed to the *Beagle*, it has recently been pointed out (Gruber, 1969), quite apart from Captain Fitzroy's better-known gentleman companion.

Such back-door means of obtaining government support were temporary expedients at best, though. The State gave permanent employment only to those accepted as unavoidable if the national heritage was to be safeguarded— in theory at any rate (for the Geological Survey,[3] the great exception, was seen as a finite, short-term undertaking, requiring its staff to be merely on contract). All of these permanent posts natural history owed, directly or indirectly, to the benefactions or influence of Sloane and Banks. The British Museum, the provider of the majority, had taken on Solander as early as 1763; but it was not until 1807, when the new Keeper of the Natural History Department, George Shaw, was provided with an assistant in the person of the able Charles Konig, that the staff in this sphere began to grow. Three decades later it had reached half a dozen, with some temporary appointments as well (Gunther, 1975, 1980; Stearn, 1981).

By that time other museums were beginning to appear in London and to create additional openings, though none of these could rise to more than a couple of naturalists at most. There was the notable collection of the East India Company, for instance, which employed the man effectively responsible for procuring it in the field in the first place, Thomas Horsfield (Desmond, 1982). There was the Hunterian Museum of the Royal College of Surgeons, which afforded a ledge for zoologists with leanings to comparative anatomy—thereby, through twenty-six years, sustaining Richard Owen and, from 1843, an Assistant Conservator as well, J. T. Quekett. There was a small museum at the new King's College, which required another, albeit less qualified, naturalist curator. And later, from 1851, there was the Museum of Practical Geology in Jermyn Street (the ancestor of the present-day Geological Museum). In addition, the several metropolitan societies offered a selection of full-time and part-time posts as curators, secretaries or librarians. The pay that went with these varied considerably, depending on each society's size and standing; but it was normally enough to attract a competent naturalist, provided he was able to supplement it with some lecturing and journalism and, if part-time, he could obtain one or more similar appointments and hold these in plurality.

Out of London, too, there were quite a number of posts to be had superintending the affairs and collections of the literary and philosophical institutes, which had been springing up in most of the cities and larger towns. But these by comparison were insecure (for the institutes tended to be shakily funded) and there were far fewer opportunities for holding them in conjunction with other related work, so they rarely acted as career stepping-stones. Only when, later in the century, the new municipal corporations began taking over these collections and conferring on their curators the security of local government employment, did prospects in this quarter improve.

Botanic gardens, of which there were more than is generally realised, yielded further jobs. Only rarely, as at Kew and Chelsea, were the top posts at these seen as essentially scientific; but several attracted as superintendents men like David Moore (at Dublin) and William Baxter (at Oxford), who, while gardeners by training, also proved themselves botanists of some accomplishment.

In botany, indeed, the range of opportunities was noticeably greater than in other branches of natural history for, apart from the powerful helping hand of horticulture, its still-lingering place in the medical curriculum ensured that there had long been chairs in this discipline at the older universities. To these, moreover, had lately been added (thanks to the unforeseen outcome of the 1815 Apothecaries Act) numerous teaching appointments in the London and provincial hospital schools.

In other respects, higher education was almost a desert for would-be professional naturalists. At the universities there were no posts subordinate to those of the professors, and in so far as chairs existed in natural history subjects nowhere had more than three of these. At Oxford and Cambridge, such appointments were in any case largely honorific: a livelihood came from the Fellowship of a college. Until as late as 1869, when the celibacy requirements began to be lifted, teaching at those universities was mainly a job for young clerics before they moved out to a parish. Henslow's career is typical of this. That Oxford and Cambridge nevertheless produced several

outstanding figures of a distinctly greater permanence—Buckland and Sedgwick, Babington and Newton—was no more than a series of lucky accidents.
These were dons who chanced to be naturalists: natural history was hardly
the means by which, strictly speaking, they gained their living.

At the Scottish universities matters were rather different; for the professors
there were mainly dependent on the class-fee paid to them by each student
directly (Morrell, 1976:63), so that a man like Jameson or Graham or
MacGillivray who attracted a large following by the excellence of his teaching
could much more rightly be classed as a natural history professional. On the
other hand, his status was more akin to that of the freelance public lecturers
(like Robert Bakewell and Gideon Mantell). Like any freelance, too, he had
to go on working when even into his dotage, as Jameson was forced to do
("that old brown dry stick" as Darwin was to recollect him), in the absence
of any financial crutch.

Such a situation made for a negligible turnover, which further narrowed
the chances of a career academically. The new London University chairs,
from the late 1820s, and subsequently the string of Irish ones widened the
field encouragingly; but even so vacancies continued to be rare and the level
of the salaries disgraceful. Academia was patently not one of the fronts on
which progress looked at all hopeful.

Baulked of employment in any of these directions, a naturalist might still
scrape together some kind of a living right out on the periphery. Three
botanist exemplars of this must suffice. William Gardiner, an umbrella
repairer in Dundee, found there was money to be made collecting the
Highland plants on commission and in 1844 he decided to make a full-time
trade of this (Anon., 1847). G. H. K. Thwaites, a Bristol accountant,
abandoned that career in 1846 and, styling himself 'Botanist', for the next
three years apparently supported himself by lecturing on the subject. Failing
then in the fierce competition for one of the new Irish chairs, he applied for
and obtained the post of Superintendent of the Botanic Gardens in Ceylon—
a useful reminder that, if all else failed, there were often posts to be had in
the more remote areas of the Empire. Pursuing a lower trajectory, F. Y.
Brocas, apparently an unsuccessful medical student at first, subsisted on a
medley of temporary posts which included the Assistant Librarianship of the
Linnean Society and cataloguing a wealthy botanist's books; additionally he
offered for sale sets of named British mosses and wrote the odd hack work
for publishers. Later, in 1857, he purchased at auction most of the stock of
duplicates left by the Botanical Society of London following its collapse and
set up in business enduringly as a dealer in herbarium specimens.

Men like Gardiner and Brocas, one suspects, braved the hazards of earning
their livelihood from natural history for the simple reason that they expected
no more of it financially than they could expect from anything else. Besotted
with the subject, they would probably never have been able to settle to
anything more orthodox. But there were others whose venturing down this
path would doubtless never have occurred at all had they not been forced
on to it involuntarily. These were the men who had suffered some adversity
and either had no alternative, in the absence of any other marketable skills,
but to turn their leisure interest into their profession or else seized upon this

as an opportunity to make the necessary fresh start in a more appetising direction.

These 'refugee' professionals fell into three distinct groups. First, there were those who came from backgrounds that were comparatively humble and who, having lost one livelihood already, could thus see no more risk in natural history than in starting up again in their previous occupation. J. G. Baker, a grocer-cum-draper in Thirsk, lost in a fire both his home and his business; but by then, luckily, he had made a national reputation as one of the best of the up-and-coming botanical systematists and before long the younger Hooker sensibly snapped him up for the new post of First Assistant in the Kew Herbarium (Foggitt, 1933). No less fortunate was the Cheltenham druggist James Buckman, after going bankrupt in 1844:[4] his reputation as a naturalist was sufficient to secure him the Professorship of Botany and Geology at the Royal Agricultural College, Cirencester. By contrast, Robert Bakewell, who went bankrupt much earlier as a wool stapler, in 1810 turned to freelance lecturing and writing, largely on geology—maybe because posts were then far fewer. Poor Edward Blyth, though, reduced to penury by the failure of his Tooting pharmacy, could land nothing better than the Curatorship of Vertebrates in the Calcutta Museum, a vilely paid appointment in an even viler climate (from which he was to be invalided home twenty-one years later).

The second group owed their arrival in the subject professionally through having had to abandon some other, much more paying line of work for reasons that were other than financial. Almost all of these were refugees from medicine, that cognate calling which also usefully provided the nearest approach at that period to a professional qualification in natural history. Almost all, too, made the switch because of some physical disability. Chronic asthma, for example, in the case of Arthur Henfrey, deafness in that of T. Rymer Jones.

The third group is much the most interesting, not least because the adjustment its members had to make was very much more drastic. These were the *rentiers manqués*: men of a wealthy and propertied background whose upbringing had led them to expect a life of leisured ease and who had seen no cause to take out even the standard insurance policy of professional certification. Edward Forbes and J. G. Children, two of their number, did at least go to university but had shrunk from anything so vulgar as taking a degree. Forbes was contentedly lingering on there, pursuing his private researches on a slender allowance from his father, when the family's money was suddenly all lost in an Isle of Man bank failure and he was left as its sole support. The chair of botany at King's College London, which he managed to obtain, carried an emolument of less than £100 a year, so he was forced to take on simultaneously the Geological Society's (better-paid) Curatorship (Wilson and Geikie, 1861). For Children, the equivalent catastrophe was the failure of the Tonbridge Bank, in which his father was a partner. Better-connected than Forbes but, unlike him, without any scientific reputation, he was lucky enough to be taken on to the British Museum staff through the influence of the Marquess of Camden. That post, however, was in the Department of Antiquities: it was only some years later that he was transferred to the Natural History Department, allegedly against his will, because his real interest was chemistry (Gunther, 1978). His becoming a professional naturalist was thus doubly involuntary and fortuitous.

Other members of the group had less cataclysmic experiences. The elder Hooker, atypical in that his plight was not an inherited one, decided to go in search of a botany professorship when the brewery in which he had sunk a large part of his patrimony was going seriously downhill and looked like having to be sold (Allan, 1967: 75). De la Beche discovered that his family estate in Jamaica was falling into debt and looked to geology for a substitute source of support (McCartney, 1977: 28). But he did so only surreptitiously and no one seems to have realised that the empire he proceeded to hack out of the Ordnance Survey jungle had a private economic motive for its foundation. (Murchison, similarly, began studying geology in the wake of a financial crisis (Secord, 1982); but in his case money did not prove sufficiently short to push him into turning professional.) William Swainson's story was far less happy. His first, vain attempts to turn professional—on the strength of his extensive fieldwork overseas—were undertaken, like De la Beche's, merely with a view to "adding to a small independence" (Swainson, 1840: 346). These amounted to applying for positions at the Liverpool Royal Institution and the British Museum. Then, as with Forbes and Children, things turned abruptly glacial: his naturalist father died, his annual allowance of £200 thereupon ceased and the money that consequently came to him proved far short of what he had been expecting. His response was to try to earn his living as a writer on natural history. When that eventually failed, he emigrated to New Zealand, in despair.

More such instances will no doubt come to light just as soon as the leading figures of the period have had their personal financial circumstances looked into more closely.

The men in this third group would never have even thought of turning professional but for the accident of their misfortune. For to take paid employment, even as a respected public official, was in the circles in which they moved to cross a social Rubicon. "Gave my first lesson for a guinea", the painter Ford Madox Brown noted in his diary in 1855, adding wryly "and am no longer a gentleman" (Surtees, 1981). Natural history was a highly respectable leisure pursuit, but to follow it for money was to commit a kind of suicide.[5] Worse, to be seen to have accepted employment, with all its attendant indignities—instead of at least retaining autonomy as a freelance—made the drop in status all the greater and the more painful.

An outcast among his previous social peers, the reduced gentleman was hardly less welcome in the circles to which he had descended. For below a certain level he was the half-unwitting inflicter of severe role-cum-status anxieties at the same time as he was the sufferer from them. Like a rather grand governess in a household of newly rich he would have left his superiors, no less than the outsiders he had to deal with, uncomfortably unsure how he should be treated. For a man of scholarly bent in such a situation employment would have been tolerable only in institutions where fellow-scholars were numerous enough to ensure that scholarly values prevailed. Everywhere else would have been outer darkness. There was thus a kind of

10

plimsoll line below which the would-be professional of gentle birth could not allow himself to slip: beyond that point it was preferable to abandon the idea and settle for a different livelihood altogether.

Although it has long been fashionable to denigrate the system that then obtained of filling jobs by patronage, this did have the great advantage of letting in the occasional person who was well worth having but who would certainly have been excluded in later days as more or less unqualified. This was to prove of the greatest importance in this proto-professional period, if largely by accident. For it resulted in placing in key positions several men of the highest calibre, such as De la Beche and the elder Hooker, whose backgrounds were such that they were able to talk on level terms with the civil servants with whom increased funding for their institutions had to be negotiated. They consequently had success where more orthodox professionals are unlikely to have been heeded. They thereby advanced the professionalization of the subject doubly: they brought about an increase in the number of the posts available and they raised the general standing of scientists in government.

Yet these pioneering achievements of the proto-professionals were to prove almost completely irrelevant to the professionalized science which eventually arrived in Britain in the third quarter of the century. For it was not in government but exclusively in the universities (as in Germany) that that fuller scale of development was achieved. The new academic disciplines which emerged in that process, moreover, roundly rejected systematics and the field and had as little as possible to do with that other professional community which antedated their existence.[6] The professional natural history of the early nineteenth century has, in consequence, continued down into the present, with its character substantially unchanged. *Si testamen requiris, circumspice...*

NOTES

[1] Indeed, as pointed out by Dr M. J. S. Rudwick (pers. comm.), rather than stressing the professional/amateur dichotomy at this early period it might be more fruitful to devise a classification of the different levels of amateurs. Reingold (1976), like Kargon, has made a start at this; but his contrasting of 'researchers' and 'cultivators' does not seem to me to go far enough.

[2] Holders of government posts at that period seem often to have treated them remarkably cavalierly in any case, in the older, cynical eighteenth-century manner. John MacCulloch, for example, while nominally employed full-time as Chemist to the Board of Ordnance in 1807-11, simultaneously practised medicine on the side (Cumming, 1980: 156). George Shaw, similarly, shamelessly used the British Museum's time for writing books for his own private profit.

[3] The Geological Survey did not afford employment to more than a mere seven scientists until after 1856: its great expansion came in the two decades that followed (Flett, 1937).

[4] I am indebted to Dr H. S. Torrens for this information.

[5] De la Beche was regarded as tainted once he had accepted paid government employment and sneered at as a 'jobber' behind his back (Porter, 1978: fn.69).

[6] Although in geology the academic intrusion was less forceful, the impact of professionalization was similarly disruptive. Just as taxonomists continued to work on as before impervious to the new biological culture, so the older fieldwork tradition doggedly persisted in geology: "academic degrees—and especially higher degrees—remained essentially irrelevant for research geologists right up to the First World War" (Porter, 1978). O'Connors & Meadows (1976) have also

X

pointed out the extremeness of the exception which geology presents: in this science, they emphasise, the divergence of the professionals from the amateurs did not occur till after the Second World War.

REFERENCES

ALLAN, M., 1967 *The Hookers of Kew 1785-1911*. London.

ANON., 1847 William Gardiner the botanist. *Chambers's Edinburgh Journal* 7: 248-251.

BEN-DAVID, J., 1972 The profession of science and its powers. *Minerva* 10: 362-383.

BERMAN, M., 1974 'Hegemony' and the amateur tradition in British science. *Journal of Social History* 8: 30-50.

CROSLAND, M. (ed.), 1969 *Science in France in the Revolutionary Era described by Thomas Bugge*. Cambridge, Mass. and London.

CROSLAND, M., 1970 The rise and decline of France as a scientific centre. *Minerva* 8: 453-454.

CUMMING, D. A., 1980 John MacCulloch, F.R.S., at Addiscombe: the lectureships in chemistry and geology. *Notes and Records of the Royal Society* 34: 155-183.

DESMOND, R., 1982 *The India Museum, 1801-1879*. London.

FLETT, J. S., 1937 *The first hundred years of the Geological Survey of Great Britain*. London.

FOGGITT, T. J., 1933 Annals of the B.E.C. II. Recollections of the Thirsk Botanical Society. *Report of the Botanical Society and Exchange Club of the British Isles* 10: 289-297.

GRUBER, J. W., 1969 Who was the *Beagle's* naturalist? *British Journal for the History of Science* 4: 266-282.

GUNTHER, A. E., 1975 *A century of zoology at the British Museum through the lives of two keepers, 1815-1914*. London.

GUNTHER, A. E., 1978 John George Children, F.R.S. (1777-1852) of the British Museum. Mineralogist and reluctant Keeper of Zoology. *Bulletin of the British Museum (Natural History), Historical Series* 6: 75-108.

GUNTHER, A. E., 1980 *The founders of science at the British Museum 1753-1900*. Halesworth.

KARGON, R. H., 1977 *Science in Victorian Manchester: enterprise and expertise*. Baltimore and Manchester.

KNIGHT, D. M., 1974 Science and professionalism in England, 1770-1830. *Proceedings of the XIVth International Congress of the History of Science* 1: 53-67.

KNIGHT, D. [M.], 1976 *The nature of science*. London.

McCARTNEY, P. J., 1977 *Henry De la Beche: observations on an observer*. Cardiff.

MEADOWS, [A.] J. & FISHER, T., 1978 Gentlemen v. players. *New Scientist* 79: 752-754.

MORRELL, J. B., 1976 The patronage of mid-Victorian science in the University of Edinburgh. *In* TURNER, G. L'E. (ed.) *The patronage of science in the nineteenth century*. Leyden.

O'CONNORS, J. G. & MEADOWS, A. J., 1976 Specialization and professionalization in British geology. *Social Studies of Science* 6: 77-89.

PORTER, R., 1978 Gentlemen and geology: the emergence of a scientific career, 1660-1920. *Historical Journal* 21: 809-836.

REINGOLD, N., 1976 Definitions and speculations: the professionalization of science in America in the nineteenth century. *In* OLESON, A. & BROWN, S. C. (eds.) *The pursuit of knowledge in the early American Republic*. Baltimore and London.

SECORD, J. A., 1982 King of Siluria: Roderick Murchison and the imperial theme in nineteenth-century British geology. *Victorian Studies* 25: 413-442.

SHILS, E., 1968 The profession of science. *Advancement of Science* 24: 469-479.

STEARN, W. T., 1981 *The Natural History Museum at South Kensington: a history of the British Museum (Natural History) 1753-1980*. London.

SURTEES, V. (ed.), 1981 *The diary of Ford Madox Brown*. New Haven.

X

12

SWAINSON, W., 1840 *Taxidermy; with the biography of zoologists, and notices of their works*. London.

WILSON, G. & GEIKIE, A., 1861 *Memoir of Professor Edward Forbes*. Edinburgh, London and Cambridge.

XI

On parallel lines: natural history and biology from the late Victorian period

INTRODUCTION

At this distance in time it is difficult to appreciate the full immensity of the shock that the world of natural history experienced as the nineteenth century drew towards its close. There had been an earlier shock, when Darwin had eventually unveiled his theory of evolution, but during the two decades that had elapsed since then the profound implications of that had been more or less adjusted to. For most naturalists it was the second shock that was the more deeply upsetting, for it affected them personally in a much more direct way, challenging their *amour-propre*. Suddenly, they found themselves being told that what they had all along been accustomed to think of as useful and even in some cases valuable scientific work was no longer of very much moment and, worse, ought for preference to be abandoned and a quite different approach adopted in its stead.

The pronouncements to this effect were hard to ignore, inasmuch as they emanated from a quarter that the natural history world was used to respecting and looking up to for much of its intellectual leadership. Unexpectedly, this quarter had become populated by a novel breed of professionals, with interests and attitudes that were alien and even hostile to the traditional ways of investigating nature. For almost two centuries by then there had been a few individuals lucky enough to be able to earn their livelihood from natural history, and the number of those had gradually been increasing. But on the whole those professionals differed from amateurs merely in the fact that they were paid to apply their expertise on a full-time basis: their outlook and their objectives were essentially the same as everyone else's. Moreover, their status was rarely as enviable as amateurs imagined, for most were employed in posts that involved much dull administrative routine and were so ill-paid that additional income had to be earned on the side, which left little enough time and energy for research. The Geological Survey was the one conspicuous exception to that generalization (Porter, 1978; Secord, 1986). The only advantage that many of those proto-professionals enjoyed over the general run of amateurs was continuous access to a large and high-quality reference collection; but even in that they were not necessarily better off than some of the amateurs of independent means, who, if they did not own such a collection themselves, were free to make their home conveniently close to one and consult it on a regular basis provided they had the necessary standing as a scientist.

The supreme example here is George Bentham, who early abandoned a legal career to spend his days in the herbarium at Kew turning himself into a world-class systematist (Jackson, 1884), with a published output of such stunning dimensions that professionals even today marvel at it. Yet it was not necessary even to have a large collection at hand for an amateur to achieve a great reputation if he was content to rely on the observations of others and weave grand theory out of them—as Darwin so matchlessly demonstrated.

What is too easily forgotten today is how very little natural history had changed all through the nineteenth century and indeed for a century or two before that. Through all that time it had enjoyed a lasting consistency and stability. Collecting techniques in entomology, for example, involved a set of equipment in the mid-eighteenth century almost identical to that in use 100 years later—and basically similar to that of even 100 years later still (Wilkinson, 1966). Until the 1950s field botanists still carried a collecting-tin, the vasculum, identical except in its larger size to the candle-boxes which their predecessors had resorted to within the life time of Ray, two and a half centuries earlier (Allen, 1959; 1965a). As ever, the standard and accepted way into natural history in any of its aspects was to form a personal collection, and how best to preserve what one had collected was the subject of a tried-and-tested lore that had been passed on from one generation to the next. By and large the natural history world lived for and by collecting: it was a passion in itself, but one which could be justified to the extent that it widened knowledge of the diversity of the natural world and stimulated the amassing of records, out of which distributions could be worked out or other patterns of behaviour pieced together on a steadily growing scale. The great aesthetic pleasure to be had from mapping distributions was one of the special discoveries of the nineteenth century, at first by geologists and then by botanists. Although working one's home district had its limits, once all the species had been found there one could move on to collecting their varieties and aberrations; or one could exchange specimens with fellow collectors and so begin to extend one's reach nationally or even beyond; or one could specialise in some particularly difficult or neglected group and eventually produce a pioneer monograph. There always seemed to be more than enough waiting to be done. The task of describing the diversity in nature and logging how far it extended appeared to be one of almost infinite duration, stretching into a very distant future.

That assured sense of the intrinsic immutability of the study of nature was reinforced by the relatively small amount of change which had also occurred in everyday life through most of the nineteenth century. By 1900 the clothes people wore would still be broadly similar to those that had been worn at the start of the Victorian era. Social divisions and sectarian cleavages continued to hold as firmly as ever. Health had improved only marginally. The currency was miraculously stable. You knew where you were, and you could take your time adjusting to such few major innovations that came along to intrude on the long-familiar scenery.

ACADEMICIZATION

What naturalists had overlooked were the radically different approaches to investigating nature that were liable to emerge once there came into being sizeable groups of

XI

scientists on the staff of universities. Apart from being employed to teach, academics are expected to push out the bounds of knowledge in every possible direction. They are recruited not for a specific, probably long-lasting, even routine set of duties, as in a government research establishment: they are free-ranging scholars in very open competition, ever on the look-out for untouched territory to colonise. Prestige comes to the propounders of refreshingly novel ideas or techniques. To persist with a traditional furrow, even if aiming to transform that almost out of recognition by widening and deepening it, is to risk being categorised as an unhopeful pedestrian in academia's unending race. Even worse, it may leave one appearing to be engaged on what any reasonably gifted amateur might equally be able to undertake.

The suddenness of the shock that was visited upon the natural history world from this quarter would have been far less extreme if only more had been aware of what had been happening already, for quite some time, in Germany. In that country, perhaps because of its fragmentation into so many independent and in some cases minuscule states prior to its unification in 1871, the medieval guild system for apprentices had persisted as the model for higher education. Just as an apprentice trained under a master for a set period of years and was required to produce a 'masterpiece' as culminating testimony to the standard of skill he had achieved, so a student was assigned to a particular professor and laboured under him for a comparable period of years on the scholarly equivalent, a doctoral thesis. This system chanced to be highly conducive to the production of academic research. Students had to undergo a much more rigorous and extended training than was customary in other countries' universities, and they constituted a continuing pool of committed workers on which the holders of the established teaching posts could draw to assist them in their own particular areas of investigation. Out of this there arose in time substantial pyramids of scholars, each constituting a distinctive research 'school', its members pursuing a cluster of closely-related topics and publishing the products in a journal founded, and maybe edited, by the professor for the express purpose of serving as his particular 'school's' outlet and giving an identity to its achievements (Shils, 1968; Farrar, 1975; Ringer, 1979).

Even as early as the eighteenth century Germany boasted more than 30 universities, each funded, in one way or another, by their respective parent states. This exceptional number reflected the fact that there were so many proudly independent polities, which vied with one another in the amount of patronage they bestowed on the arts and learning, sharing as they did a culture outstanding for its high seriousness. One result was that scientists in the German universities had numerous laboratories made available to them at a period when the rarity of those was being keenly felt everywhere else, permitting a much earlier development of experimental approaches. Add to that the higher salaries of their professors and their relative freedom from political or religious pressures and it is not surprising that from the 1830s onwards Germany became the greener grass that frustrated academics in other countries increasingly eyed with envy, and it was increasingly reckoned important to study at its universities, not least as an additional career qualification. Typical of many a British scientist who trained at that period, Sir Peter Chalmers Mitchell (1937: 112) was later to recall that

from the early eighties to the early nineties Germany for me was first and foremost the land of zoology. The battle for the theory of evolution had been won, and biologists were engaged chiefly in working out the pedigrees of living things . . . From almost all the main universities of Germany there was

XI

a vast output of zoological work. To read German and to know Germans were necessary parts of education and research in zoology . . .

Though no other country developed a research culture on so wide a scale so early, Germany was not unique in fostering one with state subvention. France was no less forward in doing so, but there things were centralised and for long dependent on the fitful patronage of the king. As early as 1666 what was tantamount to a state research institute, the Académie royale des sciences, was established under the auspices of Louis XIV. The members of this were paid to sit on the premises and carry out investigations, contribute to the Académie's twice-weekly debates and advise the Crown on appropriate technical matters (Stroup, 1990). After the Revolution this was carefully continued as a civil service establishment, in the same way that the Jardin du Roi underwent a reincarnation as the Muséum d'Histoire Naturelle. But instead of then seeking to diffuse that research culture via the universities, the French preference was for propelling it more directly through a series of specially-created élite institutions, the *grandes écoles*, all located in the capital, Paris. These received the cream of resources for research and, although they concentrated on technology and tended to leave the life sciences to the universities, it was a policy that kept the latter group of disciplines academically stunted in France for considerably longer than might otherwise have been the case (Fox, 1973; Crosland, 1975).

It was Britain, however, that was the laggard pre-eminently. Scotland, admittedly, had a university structure and a national culture conducive to the teaching of science, in which Edinburgh in particular famously long outshone its counterparts in England. Unfortunately, though, professors there were so heavily dependent for their livelihood on class fees paid direct to them by their students that that acted as a strong disincentive to the introduction of additional courses, for those were likely to compete for what was assumed to be a fixed pool of student money and so push down earnings. New academic disciplines, such as the experimental life sciences, were consequently frozen out till they had become so much the norm internationally that they could be resisted no longer (Morrell, 1973; 1977). In England, though, the problems went deeper. There was not only no tradition there of supporting universities from public funds, whether national or local; it was also most unlikely that national opinion would even have countenanced that, given how deeply the doctrine of *laissez-faire* had put down roots. Not that the old-established universities wanted to change in any case. They saw their role as essentially a teaching one, and as such, reserved for their long-traditional clientele of future Church of England clergymen and such sons of the rich as wanted at the very least to equip themselves for intelligent conversation. That being the case, they saw no reason to broaden the curriculum and introduce science as other than a voluntary extra. Dons who were able and active naturalists themselves (such as Charles Babington and Alfred Newton at Cambridge) could be highly effective in turning individual students into better-disciplined, more thoughtful amateurs who would go on to do better amateur work after they went down, but that influence was brought to bear mainly informally. The new secular colleges, in London, Manchester and elsewhere, on the other hand, while in principle more open and innovative intellectually, in practice were too tightly constrained financially to have money to spare for anything but the most meagre in the way of research facilities.

It was not the fault only of *laissez-faire* that science achieved such a belated recognition in Britain in the concrete form of jobs. Historians have credibly identified a further, more subtle factor at work. This was the taboo—one can only call it that—against undertaking work for money which the upper layers of society obstinately subscribed to. To take—or, worse, live by—paid employment in any but a small handful of acceptable professions was to consign oneself to a social limbo. Men of gentle birth with a recreational attachment to science turned to that for a livelihood only *in extremis*, typically when the family fortunes ran low or gave out unexpectedly (Allen, 1985). The best thing to be, by common consent, was a leisured amateur. That credo was buttressed as far as natural history was concerned by the aristocratic aura that still clung to the forming and ownership of great collections. Even if one had collected none of the specimens oneself, those continued to entitle one to be considered a person of cultivation and learning. One of the first things many a Victorian manufacturer or merchant did on becoming rich was to take a short cut to this emblem of status by buying up other people's collections in the salerooms and then presenting the amalgam as their own.

In other words, natural history was so deeply embedded in the collective British mind as the kind of science that it was socially respectable to pursue that alternative approaches were excluded from consideration for a substantially longer period than in the other leading Western countries (Berman, 1974). Nevertheless experimental, laboratory-based disciplines increasingly began to find advocates in British universities, as the massive output of German research in those stimulating new directions flooded the learned literature. What was later to be seen as a landmark event was the promotion of the Natural Sciences Tripos at Cambridge to an honours degree in its own right in 1861, after its introduction as an option 10 years earlier. But it was only in 1872 that the New Biology (as its protagonists challengingly proclaimed it) achieved its first major institutional breakthrough, when the Natural History Department of the School of Mines, the ancestor of Imperial College, acquired space for a teaching laboratory and at once became a breeding-ground of preachers of what one of the most fervent of them regularly spoke of as "the cause" (Green, 1909; Bower, 1938). It had in fact come to be seen by them as a crusade. The entrenched resistance of British academia to curricular change had predictably produced an almost fever-like frustration. Had that change only been spread over a period measured in decades, as in Germany, and thereby been assimilated reasonably gradually, the tensions it inevitably gave rise to would surely have been only comparatively slight. But the abnormally long time it had been blocked in Britain had the result of compressing it into just a few years. The dichotomy which now overtook the life sciences was consequently all the sharper and assumed the character of a rift.

By the 1880s exponents of the laboratory disciplines were firmly in the ascendant in universities in both Europe and America (Cittadino, 1980), and the adherents to taxonomy and the like were being increasingly reproved for not moving with the time and generally treated with disdain. Within academia there was much bitterness in places where elderly professors, doggedly loyal to the approach they had devoted their life to, refused to release rooms for additional laboratories or allocate departmental funds to the purchase of much-wanted equipment (Bower, 1938). Outside academia, on the other hand, the pre-existing community was simply bypassed. Even if it had felt the inclination to adapt and seek to ingest the new areas of knowledge now being opened up, very few of its members could have managed to do so. For the new approach was effectively out of reach for most, by reason of the specialised training and access to costly equipment it required—to say nothing of the bafflingly unfamiliar terminology that had to be mastered. Most in any case lacked the experimental urge which was basic to the New Biology (Keeney, 1992).

In an odd way, though, it was convenient for the laboratory community to have that other community continuing in existence. The very fact that there was a quite different approach to investigating the natural world which was so largely identified with amateur endeavour gave the experimentalists the opportunity to emphasise their distance from that and so underline their status as out-and-out professionals. Some of them indeed felt it necessary to go so far as to pour public scorn on what that other community persisted in doing. In 1880, for example, a lengthy editorial in America's *Botanical Gazette* berated it for "spending much valuable time in getting together material that has already been collected, or is not important enough to justify the trouble" (Keeney, 1922: 128). In similar vein, at the 1906 meeting of the British Association for the Advancement of Science Professor F.W. Oliver attacked Britain's two main institutions devoted to taxonomy for standing aloof from "the ordinary botanical current" and for their failure to retain a sufficient research following to justify the substantial share of taxpayers' money lavished on the housing and upkeep of two such vast collections, which, in his view, ought therefore to be merged (Oliver, 1907). Ironically, or maybe significantly, Oliver was the son of a distinguished taxonomist himself. It could be that conflict between the generations was to some extent a factor that entered into the contentious mix; more certain, though, is the particularly provocative contribution made by one or two renegade amateurs, of whom L.C. Miall was the most egregious example in Britain (Baker and Bayliss, 1985), who laid about their erstwhile brothers-in-the-field with all of the convert's special extremism. What might otherwise have stopped at the level of teasing—the one lot ridiculed as "worm-slicers", the other derided as "bug-hunters"—took on an extra edge of maliciousness, descending in some instances into the verbal equivalent of acid-throwing.

THE NATURALISTS' RESPONSE

Many naturalists, engrossed in their collecting and record-compiling, seem barely to have noticed what had happened and continued calmly on their way. Some others did notice but simply shrugged their shoulders and turned their backs. Still others, however, began to be demoralised: to see and hear what they had hitherto supposed to be useful scientific work dismissed as no longer of interest deprived them of their rudder and their intellectual bearings. Here is one of them, an expert on the taxonomy of microfungi, writing sadly in one of the natural history journals at the time: "The glory of the field naturalist has departed. The biologist or physiologist is the hero of the hour, and looks down with infinite contempt upon the luckless being who is still content to search for species. 'Tis but the swing of the pendulum, the fashion of the day, and like many another fashion, 'Made in Germany'. Soon will come the inevitable reaction." But Grove (1892) was wrong, of course. This was no passing fashion: the New Biology had come to stay.

XI

As that realisation increasingly sank in, many amateurs cast around for compromises, for some middle way in which their efforts would be accounted progressive in the eyes of what was at last a self-consciously distinct community of professionals.

The most salient of these compromises, well-intentioned though it was, did lasting damage to natural history. This was the innovation in primary school teaching which went by the name of 'nature study' (and to which one could wish those two words had been inseparably fixed for evermore). It originated in America, as part of the new heuristic trend in education, which gave it an extra momentum (Jenkins, 1981; Keeney, 1992: 136–145). In essence a boiled-down version of the New Biology, it substituted for the previous classroom staple of forming and labelling collections the study of developmental processes. That was fine, even praiseworthy, as a method of instruction; unfortunately, though, it largely succeeded in replacing the popular image of natural history with one indelibly associated with schools and juvenilia. It was an image natural history would not entirely manage to shake off until after the Second World War.

Another attempted compromise tackled the problem from the opposite end, by retaining the tradition of fieldwork but turning it in a more dynamic direction. Ecology, another newly-emergent discipline with promising academic credentials, seemed at first to be the answer here. As that initially arose in Britain and France in the 1890s it took the form of a branch of geography, being principally concerned with broad-brush vegetation mapping (Tansley, 1947; Sheail, 1987). Several of the ablest among the amateur field botanists then became enamoured of the phytosociological approach which had taken root on the Continent (where it has continued to dominate plant ecology ever since), for in distinguishing and tracing the distribution of plant associations they were able to put to effective use their taxonomic expertise. In that respect, indeed, they were able to show up the ecological academics, whose many mistakes in identification continually riled them.

Unfortunately, though, ecology was another light that failed. By the time of the First World War academic ecologists in Britain had found the elaborate Continental classification of plant communities hard to apply in the more fluid environment of the Atlantic fringe, and in their disillusionment they adopted a physiological approach instead. That at once pushed ecology out of the domain of the amateurs. As one of their number subsequently recollected:

... from the beginning of our field work the question *why* kept intruding itself, becoming more insistent and more clamorous as time went on . . . So it came about that the glorious days of primary survey, when we ranged free over moor and mountain, to a great extent were superseded . . . Weapons of greater accuracy were required. Six-inch map, binocular and pencil were replaced or at best reinforced by instruments for measuring the amount and variation of light, heat, moisture . . . The use of a biological laboratory was a necessity, as well as a full knowledge of the methods of physiological research . . . [and] new concepts not easy to grasp and sometimes obscured by a formidable terminology. (R. Lloyd Praeger, quoted in Lowe, 1976.)

Although a sprinkling of amateurs stayed and persevered and there were to be gallant attempts, like the long-running *Biological flora of the British Isles*, to effect a reunification, ecology has remained obstinately, dauntingly technical, latterly adding statistics to its series of excluding fences.

In so far as there has been a reconciliation, or at least a *modus vivendi*, between ecology and the world of the great majority of amateurs it has occurred under the banner of nature conservation. That has necessarily brought the two close together again, albeit as allies rather than collaborators in the true sense, and it has proved to be one major new direction in which amateur naturalists have found for themselves an important and satisfying substitute role. At the same time that has by no means displaced the older tradition of alpha taxonomy and the logging of records, even though collecting has largely fallen from favour except in some areas of zoology.

Apart from conservation there has turned out to be a second way, a purely scientific one, in which amateurs can play a useful role without compromising their traditional stance as field observers. Uniquely, this is a role they stumbled upon themselves, more or less by accident. It derives from the fact that amateurs, unlike professionals, have become relatively very numerous and well distributed around whole countries (though by no means as evenly as everyone could wish). Provided they are set appropriate tasks and given well-focused encouragement and direction, they can take advantage of their very numbers to act as a data-collection mechanism on a scale comparable with the kind of surveys routine in epidemiology, yielding results that could otherwise be obtained by professionals only with the expenditure of a great deal of time, effort and money (Campbell, 1950).

In one sense this method of collective research goes back to the questionnaires sent round to country parsons and others by eighteenth-century naturalists and antiquaries, to elicit information about the natural and man-made 'curiosities' of the various parishes. By the turn of the nineteenth century this same method was being employed to compile a rough gazetteer of where the rarer wildflowers were to be found in the different counties of England and Wales. This had no hope of being properly systematic or achieving the thoroughness of a modern guidebook, but it may have opened eyes to what might be accomplished if and when naturalists were spread around considerably more thickly.

That necessarily greater thickness had arrived in Britain by the 1820s. It was then that H.C. Watson hit upon the idea of building up a more precise knowledge of plant distribution in England, Wales and Scotland by inducing collectors all around those three countries to send in their duplicate specimens to a central repository on the promise of receiving parcels of equivalent desirability in return—on the lines of a commodity exchange (Allen, 1965b). This idea was presently taken up by the two national botanical societies, in London and Edinburgh respectively, that came into existence just around that time. One of those, the London society, made such a success of what it called its annual 'distributions' that these provided much of the basic data for Watson's successive attempts at a geographical compendium of the British vascular plant species, culminating in his devising the vice-county system and popularising the use of that through his culminating work, *Topographical botany*, in 1873–4. Among the several other branches of natural history to follow that botanical lead were the students of the land and freshwater Mollusca, at the instance of W. Denison Roebuck. From that crude beginning, with its still awkwardly large and non-standardised mapping unit, has descended the present-day series of national schemes to map the flora and fauna of the British Isles in terms of the squares of the Ordnance Survey National Grid. By other routes other European countries have arrived at comparable terminal destinations.

That line of work has been an impressive achievement and in the main an amateur one. Yet another form of collective research has in its own way been no less productive and successful. This originated in the need by ornithologists to tackle their most conspicuous unsolved mystery: migration. Again, someone had a bright idea. All around the coasts of the British Isles a great chain of lighthouses and lightships had come into being. If only the occupants of those proved willing to keep a careful record of the numerous birds that were known to dash themselves to death against those powerful beams, then it seemed likely that much of value could be learnt. On being approached, the keepers proved in the event both co-operative and diligent (Gurney, 1880); and as the years went by so much data accumulated that it eventually made a backbreaking job for the one member of the research team to whom the writing-up had been delegated. Because of his exacting standards, that particular scheme lasted 33 years in all, from the pilot launch in 1879 to the publication of the eventual book (Clarke, 1912).

The British Association had nursed that work along, assisting it with modest grants. The ornithologists' own national society, the British Ornithologists' Club, now took over and in 1906–14 lined up a fresh corps of observers, inland as well as on the coasts this time, to report on the arrival dates of summer migrants. By then birdwatching—as opposed to bird-shooting—had begun to attract a very large following, and the numbers were great enough to suggest large-scale enquiries might also now be feasible on topics without such an obvious appeal as migration. These started in 1908 and steadily increased in ambitiousness and momentum until, by 1931, well over 1,000 people were taking part (Allen, 1976). On the back of that wave of enthusiasm it then proved possible to float a permanent, self-supporting body to keep this particular line of work in being on a continuous basis. This was the British Trust for Ornithology. Subsequently, after some vicissitudes, that embryo was to develop into the sizeable research institute of today, the substantial contracts it wins from government agencies being testimony enough of the scientific value of the collective enquiries, from nest counts to ringing, that it goes on sponsoring and sustaining.

This achievement in ornithology demonstrated for the first time, at least in British natural history, that purely amateur research could evolve spontaneously into a measure of professionalization—without the intercession of the state or of academics. Such a feat would not have been possible unless that particular branch of natural history had risen to a level of popularity sufficient to yield the necessarily large number of committed, reliable recorders. It may be that no other branch of the subject will ever be able to engender comparable 'minimum density potential'. There have since been many other examples of full-time corporate entities being brought into being in natural history as the result of amateur effort: the Field Studies Council for one, and innumerable initiatives on the conservation front, from the Royal Society for the Protection of Birds to the county wildlife trusts and their proliferation of reserves. But those have all arisen from other considerations and had other objectives in view: they have not sprung directly from research activity. So far, the British Trust for Ornithology would seem to be unique. It well illustrates how careful we need to be not to equate the professionalizing of a field of learning with its academicization. These are two distinct processes which by no means necessarily coincide.

XI

REFERENCES

ALLEN, D.E., 1959 The history of the vasculum. *Proceedings of the Botanical Society of the British Isles* **3**: 135–150.

ALLEN, D.E., 1965a Some further light on the history of the vasculum. *Proceedings of the Botanical Society of the British Isles* **6**: 105–109.

ALLEN, D.E., 1965b H.C. Watson and the origin of exchange clubs. *Proceedings of the Botanical Society of the British Isles* **6**: 110–112.

ALLEN, D.E., 1976 *The naturalist in Britain: a social history*. Allen Lane, London.

ALLEN, D.E., 1985 The early professionals in British natural history. In Wheeler, A. and Price, J.H. (Eds) *From Linneaus to Darwin: commentaries on the history of biology and geology*. Society for the History of Natural History, London.

BAKER, R.A. and BAYLISS, R.A., 1985 The amateur and professional scientist: a comment on Louis C. Miall (1842–1921). *Naturalist* **110**: 141–145.

BERMAN, M., 1974 'Hegemony' and the amateur tradition in British science. *Journal of Social History* **8**: 30–50.

BOWER, F.O., 1938 *Sixty years of botany in Britain (1875–1935): impressions of an eye-witness*. Macmillan, London.

CAMPBELL, B., 1950 Co-operation in zoological studies. *Discovery* **11**: 328–330.

CITTADINO, E., 1980 Ecology and the professionalization of botany in America, 1890–1905. *Studies in History of Biology* **4**: 171–198.

CLARKE, W.E., 1912 *Studies in bird migration*. 2 vols. Oliver and Boyd, Edinburgh; Gurney and Jackson, London.

CROSLAND, M., 1975 The development of a professional career in science in France. *Minerva* **13**: 38–57.

FARRAR, W.V., 1975 Science and the German university system, 1790–1850. In Crosland, M. (Ed.) *The emergence of science in Western Europe*. Macmillan, London.

FOX, R., 1973 Scientific enterprise and the patronage of research in France, 1800–70. *Minerva* **11**: 442–473.

GREEN, J.R., 1909 *A history of botany: 1860–1900*. Clarendon Press, Oxford.

GROVE, W.B., 1892 The happy fungus-hunter. *Midland Naturalist* **15**: 158–161.

GURNEY, J.H., junr., 1880 Migratory birds at lighthouses. *Nature* **22**: 25–26.

JACKSON, B.D., 1884 The late George Bentham, F.R.S. *Journal of Botany* **22**: 353–356.

JENKINS, E.W., 1981 Science, sentimentalism or social control? The nature study movement in England and Wales, 1899–1914. *History of Education* **10**: 33–43.

KEENEY, E.B., 1992 *The botanizers: amateur scientists in nineteenth-century America*. University of North Carolina Press, Chapel Hill and London.

LOWE, P.D., 1976 Amateurs and professionals: the institutional emergence of British plant ecology. *Journal of the Society for the Bibliography of Natural History* **7**: 517–535.

MITCHELL, Sir P.C., 1937 *My fill of days*. Faber, London.

MORRELL, J.B., 1973 The patronage of mid-Victorian science in the University of Edinburgh. *Science Studies* **3**: 353–388.

MORRELL, J.B., 1977 The rise and fall of Scottish science. *The Times Higher Education Supplement* 8 April: 15.

OLIVER, F.W., 1907 Botany in England. *Report of the British Association for the Advancement of Science* **1907**: 733–738.

PORTER, R., 1978 Gentlemen and geology: the emergence of a scientific career, 1660–1920. *Historical Journal* **21**: 809–836.

RINGER, F.K., 1979 The German academic community. In Oleson, A. and Voss, J. (Eds) *The organization of knowledge in modern America, 1860–1920*. Johns Hopkins University Press, Baltimore and London.

SECORD, J., 1986 The Geological Survey of Great Britain as a research school, 1839–1855. *History of Science* **24**: 223–275.

SHEAIL, J., 1987 *Seventy-five years in ecology: the British Ecological Society.* Blackwell Scientific, Oxford etc.

SHILS, E., 1968 The profession of science. *Advancement of Science* **24**: 469–480.

STROUP, A., 1990 *A company of scientists: botany, patronage, and community at the seventeenth-century Parisian Royal Academy of Sciences.* University of California Press, Berkeley, Los Angeles and London.

TANSLEY, A.G., 1947 The early history of modern plant ecology in Britain. *Journal of Ecology* **35**: 130–137.

WILKINSON, R.S., 1966 English entomological methods in the seventeenth and eighteenth centuries. *Entomologists' Record* **78**: 143–150, 285–292.

XII

The biological societies of London 1870–1914: their interrelations and their responses to change

The years between the outbreak of the Franco-Prussian War and the start of World War I were years which witnessed a tremendous acceleration in scientific discovery and activity. For science in Britain especially, and for biology here in particular, they constitute a period that is characterized by a certain underlying unity and that is sharply bounded at both ends by events so profound and far-reaching in their effects as to make it a more real entity than most such constructs of chronology. Its starting-point, indeed, is marked in this country by a milestone which is scarcely less conspicuous, and certainly of a much more readily perceived significance, than the opening of a new and decisive bout for dominance over the European land-mass. For 1870, very conveniently, also chanced to be the year of W. E. Forster's Education Act, which not only ushered in at last an education system underwritten by the State but required at the same time the new Elementary Schools that were to be created to include in their curriculum a grounding in science. Just two years after that, the Natural History Department of the Royal School of Mines moved from its cramped location in Jermyn Street to more spacious quarters in South Kensington; and there, released at last by the provision of a laboratory, Huxley forthwith introduced his historic crash-course in the elements of biology for the first of those who were going to have the task, in turn, of introducing the subject into the schoolrooms. During the eight years that followed, the flower of a whole academic generation passed through this South Kensington filter, as imbibers of the course or, more important, as its expounders, and went on from there to instil in the universities, in the training colleges and in the schools the new experimental approach and the novel theoretical concerns that gave to the then incoming tide of learning an appearance sharply different from all that had preceded it.[1]

By the year 1870 it is thus by no means anachronistic to speak of the *biological* societies of London — rather than of its societies of natural history. Though it would be some years yet before they would feel the full impact of the growing professionalization, 'biology' was coming into use increasingly as a handy collective term for a natural history confined just to zoology and botany, now that geology, the traditional third member of the sisterhood, was beginning to grow away as it was beginning to grow up — and would soon cease to be generally thought of as belonging to the same family at all.[2]

Yet despite the ferment that zoology and botany were undergoing intellectually, on the whole this was a quiet and rather uneventful period structurally for the societies that represented them in the metropolis. After the intensely competitive years earlier in the century, the 'Twenties and 'Thirties more particularly, when a layer of new bodies had thrust their way into being and those that already existed lived under the ever-present threat of breakaway moves by discontented factions, the scene had become comparatively settled. Disregarding for the moment the several, unpretentious bodies that had appeared in the suburbs, the ones which had survived that period of turbulence now numbered essentially four. In order of age these were the Linnean (founded back in

1788) the Zoological (a semi-offshoot of that[3] in 1826), the Entomological[4] (another Linnean offshoot, in 1833) and the Microscopical[5] (born six years after that, in 1839). All identified themselves with London in their titles. In addition, there were of course various societies that concerned themselves with medicine, but although those concerns were in large part biological that was a world quite apart and for that reason they can justifiably be excluded from consideration. Similarly, while there was also a steadily-growing chain of further national societies with a more specialized focus (the Conchological in 1874, the Mycological in 1896, the Ecological in 1904...), and one or two of those perhaps had some claim to be classed as metropolitan in so far as their activities were predominantly London-based,[6] they were too markedly different in character from the major, propertied societies and were too far removed from the centre of the stage to count sufficiently in this particular context.

Of the four, the Zoological Society was far and away the largest, starting off the period with a subscribing membership of around 3000 and finishing up with nearly 5000 by 1914. But then it was — as it still is — a remarkable triple cross: part scientific society, part research institute and part public spectacle. Reflecting this, a high proportion of its membership was no more than nominally scientific, subscribing essentially for access to the zoo on privileged terms.

Next in size at the opening of the period was the Microscopical, rather unexpectedly. This had over 400 Ordinary Fellows by 1870 and another 200 more twenty years later. Yet subsequently, as we shall see, its membership was to plunge to make it the smallest of the four by far.

In third place came the Linnean, doggedly preserving its commitment to the whole of natural history in its antiquated eighteenth-century sense. With a subscribing membership of around 500 at the start of the period, this was to remain much the most static, its numbers fluctuating between 700 and 800 for a full half-century from 1883.

By contrast, the Entomological expanded very markedly — but with the advantage of starting from a much lower base. It began as easily the smallest, with little more than 200 subscribing members, but by the close of the period it was nearly two and a half times that size, with well over 500.

Nineteenth-century membership figures, however, must be treated with some reserve. Learned societies in that era were quite extraordinarily reluctant to remove the names of defaulters from their lists. A gentleman met his debts, the contemporary code insisted — and to intimate otherwise was the mark of the lowest type of tradesman. In consequence membership registers, both published and unpublished, tended to be more than a little misleading and are not to be read as statements of the strict position such as we are accustomed to read into their present-day equivalents.

The differences between the four societies in size are in no way accounted for by the differences in the cost of belonging, for it was the two with the higher subscriptions which had the largest memberships (at any rate at the end of the period). These, the Linnean and the Zoological, had closely comparable rates, £3 annually in both cases on top of an admission fee of £5 in the case of the Zoological and £6 in the case of the would-be slightly grander Linnean. In sharp contrast, the Entomological asked less than half as much: a mere guinea to enter and then two guineas yearly. The

Microscopical came in between (though only just), charging two guineas for admission and then the same amount on an annual basis.

These rates were of a striking and enviable stability, in all four societies remaining quite unchanged throughout the period we are considering — and indeed for very many years after it. The Linnean and the Entomological did not find it necessary to raise their subscriptions till the steep inflation just after the end of the First World War, and the Zoological held out against an increase till even as recently as 1958 — and even then it was approved only after a prolonged and acrimonious battle.[7]

Crisp

Although the rates bore some proportional relationship to the societies' respective financial commitments, there was a considerable element of symbolism in them as well. This was a chief reason, quite apart from the stability of the currency, why they were kept undisturbed for so long. They functioned in part as symbols of corporate good health, a standing testimony to competent stewardship of the society's affairs. They also functioned, more importantly, as symbols of the particular social level which the respective societies saw themselves as attaining. The Linnean and the Zoological, creatures of an earlier era, continued to make a point of recruiting in the aristocracy and for long, like the Royal, had preferred to be headed by men more distinguished for their social position than for any particular scientific accomplishments. Status in the wider world beyond science mattered much to them: they were, in effect, just learned appendages of that exclusive stretch of the metropolis that we know as 'Clubland'.

The Entomological was entirely different. One of that brood of new bodies hatched out by the middle classes when they invaded the cultural life of the Capital in strength in the 'Thirties, it was notable from the first for its relatively informal atmosphere, for its general air of youthfulness, and for the great extent to which its members were practising naturalists and not mere posturing *dilettanti:* as William Swainson put it, there was "no *quackery* in its composition".[8] The ill-fated Botanical Society of London had been preponderantly youthful too and proud of its non-exclusive character and of the fact that most of its members were practical exponents of the subject, similarly.[9] Bodies such as these sprang from a separate tradition and are best seen as merely the centrally-positioned flagships of the great fleet of natural history societies and field clubs that flourished out in the suburbs and in the provinces beyond.

Stainton

The scientific community that the four major metropolitan societies catered for was predominantly a zoological one, it will have been noticed. It is true that botany had no internal chasm to compare with that which early caused the entomologists to adopt an existence quite apart from the other followers of the science (and the hiving-off of the students of birds, as the British Ornithologists' Union, in 1858, had made this disunity of zoology doubly apparent). But the lop-sidedness was also the result in large measure of a historical accident. In the great formative period for corporate science in the metropolis, the 'Twenties and 'Thirties, two specialist societies for botanists had indeed arisen here. One, the Botanical Society of London, gradually attracted to itself most of the abler field botanists scattered throughout the country and grew to reasonably impressive dimensions (ultimately, with about 250 subscribing members, much the size achieved by the Entomological at the opening of the 1870s), but it foundered after twenty years from an insoluble conflict of aims compounded by maladministration.[10] Its most valuable activity, the postal exchange of herbarium specimens, was fortunately kept up and operated within the framework of a small, unambitious club; but although this was run from London for a time later in our period, it subsisted without premises and can hardly be ranked as metropolitan. The other, with a confusingly similar name, the Royal Botanic Society, was essentially a horticultural body and had as its *raison d'etre* a large botanic garden inside the Inner Circle of Regent's Park.[11] Initially this establishment was seen as a potential rival to Kew, the royal gardens having declined into a rather run-down state; and there were active plans to build it up into the national centre for botanical science that Kew had earlier given promise of becoming. To this end the Society began amassing herbaria and even came within an ace of being left the enormous Fielding collection which in the end went to Oxford.[12] Then, unluckily for the Society's hopes, Kew acquired Sir William Hooker as Director and the backing, at last, of Her Majesty's Treasury; the botanical community thereupon switched horses and the Regent's Park establishment reverted to its pristine horticultural purity.

The disappearance of these two societies left a hole in the scientific life of the Capital which has never been more than partly filled since (for although the body that was to evolve into the Botanical Society of the British Isles became permanently London-based from 1939, it has never seen itself as specifically metropolitan and has never organized a regular programme of meetings there). With nowhere else to go, the botanists necessarily piled into the Linnean, tilting even more disproportionately in their direction a society that had already forfeited its proper share of the zoologists to its latecoming rivals.

Ever since the separate societies for zoology and botany had come into being the role of the Linnean had indeed been problematical. Its acquisition of the Linnean collections had had the effect of making it unduly inward-looking, over-content to fill the role of custodian of a shrine. By the 'Forties it had become tightly exclusive, insecure financially and moribund intellectually. There was a dearth of papers for reading at its meetings and the meetings themselves were but thinly attended. On one occasion no more than five Fellows were present apart from the President and the Secretary.[13] Absurdly, papers were not allowed to be discussed, for fear of provoking controversy of the kind that regularly racked — but also animated — the contemporary Geological Society; and the evenings tended to deteriorate as a result into (as Edward Forbes wryly put it) "but sleeping draughts".[14] By 1851 the condition of the Society was such that an anonymous reviewer in the leading botanical journal of the day, the *Phytologist,* was driven to voice the regret of "all right-minded men of science to see it sinking, as it were, into a state of lethargy and inanity". It was, he declared, in a "mesmeric coma", and he went so far as to express the hope that "the somnolency which at present oppresses it may not be the sleep of death".[15]

At that point, luckier than it deserved, the Linnean acquired a man of uncommon drive and vision as its President. This was Thomas Bell, a dental surgeon who had gravitated to the Chair of Zoology at King's College London. During his eight years in office Bell shook the Society back to life and propelled it in a variety of new directions.[16] One of these he eventually got round to in 1858. In that year, in his

28

Presidential Address, he deplored what with hindsight could be seen to have been the near-suicidal action of the Linnean's zoologists in helping off the ground the scientific side of the fledgling Zoological. He acknowledged, however, that that new society had had the irresistible attraction of a much greater financial ability at the time to advance their branch of science. The unintended results of those breakaways of twenty-five to thirty years before was that the separate activities of the four metropolitan societies that now catered for zoology were carried out at a combined expense which would be very much lessened if only they could be brought together under the aegis of a single body.

Bell

He stopped short of proposing an outright merger: that, he must surely have recognized, was by then hardly practical politics. More surprisingly, he rejected even the next-best solution: an arrangement whereby members of the other societies could join the Linnean on preferential terms. Instead, distinctly lamely, he came up with the suggestion that the other three societies should communicate to the Linnean such papers as might be especially suitable for publication in its *Journal* or *Transactions*.[17]

Nothing came of this, but it was a promising augury of a closer moving-together. In the meantime, no doubt, there was a good deal of discussion off-stage (though how extensive this was, and what form it took, we shall only know when the history of these societies has been pushed beyond published matter and internal records into the underworld of private papers). Certainly, there were key individuals who straddled two or more of the societies and were thus favourably placed to help things along. William Yarrell, an extreme case, had been simultaneously Secretary of the Zoological and Treasurer of the Entomological, and in the second of these capacities he latterly doubled up as Treasurer of the Linnean as well. Some years after his death H. T. Stainton, the virtual mainstay of the Entomological, served a five-year term as Zoological Secretary of the Linnean. Similarly, Frank Crisp was both Secretary and Editor of the Microscopical while also Treasurer of the Linnean. It is all too easy to forget this persisting, and surely influential, cross-membership. We badly need a prosopographical study to establish how widely and how deeply it reached.

In 1854 the Government purchased Burlington House from the Cavendish family for the express purpose of accommodating a number of the leading metropolitan societies. Originally only four of them were earmarked for this precious, rent-free privilege, namely the ones that were occupying space in Somerset House which the Treasury coveted for housing the Registrar General and his staff. Two years later, however, it was agreed that the number could be extended to include the Linnean.[18] It was lucky for the Linnean that the Zoological was irremovably tied to its menagerie, while the Entomological and the Microscopical, for their parts, had too specialized an image and clearly ranked lower in mere seniority and substance. But all these other three could have made good use of the Burlington House premises nonetheless,[19] and it cannot have been without some pangs of guilt that the Linnean moved into its palatial new residence in the spring of 1857. That this was just one year before Bell made his Presidential overtures is probably not a coincidence. The Linnean must surely have sensed that it owed it to its less fortunate sisters to offer them some share in the benefits of this publicly-funded windfall.

Even so, nine years had to pass before any sharing of the Burlington House rooms materialized. Already by then, for quite some time, the Zoological had found its Scientific Meetings were being noticeably less well-attended and its thoughts had turned to running a joint programme with one or more of the other societies instead. In the event it did not go quite this far: for the winter session of 1866–7 it chose to hold its meetings indeed in the Linnean's rooms, but it timed them for alternative evenings to those of the Linnean, with the aim of attracting members of both societies to each. Alas, however, the experiment was not a success,[20] the meetings had to revert to their previous venue in Hanover Square, and the Zoological and the Linnean thenceforward permanently turned their backs on one another.

The involvement with the Entomological was more wholehearted and more enduring. In that same year, 1866, hard-pressed for accommodation, the entomologists jumped at the offer of two rooms on the Linnean's ground floor (together with the use of the main meeting-room for the reading of papers and showing of exhibits). Their library, however, necessarily had to be left behind, in rented premises in Bedford Row, and this was both a severe inconvenience and a drain financially.[21] The arrangement, even so, lasted for as long as ten years; and it culminated in a request from the Entomological for some more thoroughgoing mode of affiliation. Stainton, who was the Linnean's Zoological Secretary by then, almost certainly had a major hand in this —but the suspicion is unconfirmable from at any rate the Linnean minutes. Matters

30

were carried by the Entomological to the point of a general referendum of its members, from which it emerged that a large majority favoured an arrangement whereby its Fellows would constitute a special new category in the Linnean, under the name of "Entomological Associates". At that point, for some reason, the negotiations foundered. The minutes of both societies are annoyingly unrevealing, but the best guess as to what went wrong is that of their respectively official histories:[22] at the last moment it turned out that the Linnean had no space for the Entomological's extensive library — and that for the entomologists was a *sine qua non,* quite conclusively. In the summer of 1875, accordingly, they found alternative refuge with the Medical Society of London, in Chandos Street; and there they were to remain for the fifty years that followed.

Yarrell

Fired by the example of its two elder sisters, the Microscopical, too, in turn had a mild flirtation with the Linnean. In 1867 it applied to use the Linnean rooms as well; but this time the Linnean felt obliged to demur, taking the view that any more societies on its premises would overstrain its staff resources.[23]

With just a little more vision, just a little more persistence, it is hard not to believe that a workable federal structure for the nation's biologists might well have come out of all this. As a result, instead of the fragmentation that has continued down to the present, there might have been achieved the enviable near-unity of the geologists and the chemists. Whether this would have been beneficial to the scientific development of the subject depends on the view that one holds about the role of learned societies in that process. Some might maintain that the socializing currents should be allowed to swirl and coalesce where they will, that it makes little difference how the field is segmented corporately — or even how minutely. On this view, the Linnean may be forgiven its prolonged period of inertia: it is sufficient that a forum continued to exist within easy walking-distance of Pall Mall (or within a quick tube-ride of South Kensington or Kew), where useful papers were delivered and discussed and whence publications of value regularly appeared.

On the other hand, benefits must surely have flowed from, at the very least, a pooling of resources. More funds could thereby have been made available for assisting young researchers of promise; expensive library duplication could have been avoided; more cross-fertilization between the different disciplines could have been induced. A wider role in safeguarding the interests of the emergent profession could have saved the trouble of concocting the Biological Council many years later — just as the Institute of Biology, equally, would have been superfluous if only responsibility had been assumed for controlling the standards of entrance. An 'umbrella' serving to shield, and to co-ordinate the work of, the vast army of amateurs throughout the country could similarly have made unnecessary the sadly short-lived Council for Nature (so pale an imitation of the Council for British Archaeology).

Although it was strictly speaking on the threshold of the period with which this paper is concerned that this abortive coming-together of the four societies took place, it scarcely needs stressing that the experience fundamentally determined the pattern of association among the biologists in the metropolis throughout the decades that followed. By the time our period begins, the 1870s, a situation that had been briefly and encouragingly fluid had set dauntingly hard, seemingly unbreakably. The legacy handed on to the generation that came after had to be accepted, broadly speaking, as it was. There was no going back.

There was no going back for the further reason that the individual societies presently had their attention diverted — inwards, to certain new developments which were subjecting them to increasing strain.

The principal source of strain, and certainly the longest-lasting, was the often grating intrusion into these hitherto peaceful preserves of mainly leisured gentlemen-amateurs of a greater and greater number of the new class of thrusting university professionals. Natural history had been accustomed to a small sprinkling of men who earned their living from the pursuit for fifty years and more; but except in that fact, these had scarcely been any different in their interests and outlook from those otherwise placed. The professionals who now were appearing came from a faster-moving world, where they were thicker on the ground and where there was a far greater number of posts to compete for, which induced a more intense ambitiousness. Perhaps more importantly, though, their interests were sharply different. They were not merely devoted to aspects of the subject well removed from the traditional fare of systematics, and trained in specialized laboratory techniques accordingly; they were even, in some degree, positively opposed to systematics, despising it as a largely worked-out vein, a hopelessly dreary backwater. Nor was this an opinion that they liked keeping to themselves.

As one would expect, in the official histories there is scarcely a hint of the tensions that must have arisen from the colliding within the societies of these two antipathetic sub-cultures. Even had the histories been written in a more incisive mode, considerations of tact would doubtless have kept their authors from giving attention to a topic so domestically uncomfortable. For much the same reason, the published literature carries next to no references to it either. All we have to go on at present is the bare, external evidence provided by the membership lists and the content of the publications — and to try to infer the degree of pain from a mere reading of the temperature charts is too indirect a way of enquiry to be reliable.

The Zoological, the only one of the four societies to operate on the relevant scale, had the added complication of an increasing number of professional biologists on its own staff. This had major consequences politically, for every extra one of these who was recruited could be expected to side automatically with the Executive Secretary in his long-running battle with the Council to devote more resources to strengthening the Society's scientific work. Those who were opposed to this policy thus had an interest in resisting the enlargement of the scientifically-qualified staff. For many years the Executive Secretary himself had been the sole full-time employee in this category. Then, in 1865, at the instance of Huxley, who was keen to see the collection put to more use for research purposes that were not merely taxonomic, a special committee was set up to oversee what happened to the corpses of the animals that died and, to further its work, a new post was created with the title of Prosector. The first holder of this was James Murie, of Central African fame, an anatomist of great proficiency even though he was to prove, both there and subsequently at the Linnean, painfully difficult as a colleague.[24] About the same time another scientist was smuggled in, under the guise of a library clerk, in the person of R. Bowdler Sharpe, already an ornithologist of distinction.[25] (Later, after the First World War, the no less able F. Martin Duncan was to be secured by this same, unlikely route.[26]) In 1903 a third official scientific post, that of Pathologist, was added as part of the outcome of a general shake-up;[27] and after that, helped no doubt by the current of the time, there was at last a flood of further appointments, raising the total to ten by 1928.[28] But achieving these still seems to have called for a certain amount of camouflage. Julian Huxley records in his memoirs being approached by the then Executive Secretary, Chalmers Mitchell, in or around 1916 and asked if he would be interested in becoming the Superintendent of the Gardens — a post for which a qualified scientist was not really necessary. "As this was mainly concerned with looking after the feeding and health of the animals, and I had no experience in such matters," Huxley decided to resist the suggestion.[29]

The Zoological could afford the luxury of this expansion thanks to the fact that the number of visitors to the Zoo was soaring and the finances of the Society as a whole were benefiting correspondingly. The Entomological, too, in its own much more modest way, had entered a period of prosperity and growth, helped by the many new posts in the applied areas of its subject and the influx of extra members in consequence.[30] The Linnean, on the other hand, was much less well placed. Other, more specialized societies were now springing up, with a greater appeal to the younger professionals with their more narrowly-focussed concerns;[31] and a generalist body, relatively expensive to belong to besides, was especially vulnerable to competition from such quarters. The best it could rise to, however, by way of a defensive move was to abolish the admission fee for those under 35.

But if the Linnean was under pressure, this was nothing to the plight of the poor Microscopical. Contrary to what one might have supposed, the general swing in the universities and schools to work based on the laboratory had not been to its advantage. A

R. Bowdler Sharpe

society identified with an instrument rather than with a particular scientific discipline seemed almost an irrelevance to the new generation of professionals, and matters were made worse by the fact that by around 1880 the light microscope had arrived at its peak of resolution.[32] By 1913 membership had slumped to less than two-thirds of the mid-'Eighties level — and it was not to clamber back to that till after the Second World War.

There was another change in the composition of these societies at this period that was also a cause of a good deal of tension—or in one of them, at any rate. This was the enrolment at last of women, in not insignificant numbers. Unlike the pain that the new professionals gave rise to, the pain from this source is in one case amply documented, doubtless because it was temporary and acute instead of mild and persistent: a toothache rather than rheumatism.

Peculiarly, and most uncharacteristically, the Zoological had been prepared to admit women as Fellows (and on the same terms as men) ever since 1827, a few months after its founding. But this liberal policy does not appear to have been taken advantage of to any noticeable extent and was probably introduced merely with the privileged hours of access to the menagerie in mind. At any rate it was not until the closing years of the century that the Society's Scientific Meetings began to attract women as habitual attenders[33] — and that the rules permitted this doubtless came as quite a shock to the more benighted of the male Fellows.

With the conspicuous exception of the short-lived Botanical, which went out of its way to recruit women members and made quite a fuss of the few brave ones who responded,[9] all the other metropolitan learned societies of substance remained aloof, with varying degrees of explicitness. The ever-unpompous Entomological might well have been an exception, had there only been the women entomologists wishing to join; and certainly, when at length the first trickle of these appeared, in 1890, this society absorbed them without apparent friction — at least if the total silence on the subject in its official history is any indication.[34] The Microscopical, on the other hand, as if in keeping with the intermediate status that its rates of subscription affected to express, at first contrived to meet the problem by steering an exactly middle course. Ludicrously, from 1884 right up until 1909 (when sanity eventually won) women were allowed to be elected as Fellows and pay the necessary fees but they were not allowed any of the rights or privileges of membership.[35]

But it was left to the Linnean to set the really deplorable example in this (though, even so, it hardly behaved any worse than, say, the Royal or the Geological). Its long tradition of exclusiveness — and perhaps also its location, in the very heart of 'Clubland' — made it an obvious resister, even though its preponderant concern with botany, the one science traditionally best disposed towards women, might have been expected to have led to a countervailing current of tolerance. In this struggle that now took place the women who made the running were indeed botanists in every case: the opposition, one suspects, came much more strongly from the zoologists.

The first shots were fired at the end of 1886, when requests began to be received for particular women to be allowed to attend particular meetings in order to hear the reading of papers of which they were the co-authors. This was something the Council graciously felt able to permit. Fourteen years later, however, in April 1900, battle was joined in earnest when a Mrs Ogilvie Farquharson, author of a book on ferns, widow of a leading Scottish expert on diatoms and by this time a committed feminist ironclad, submitted a petition arguing for the election of duly qualified women as Ordinary Fellows, with all the rights of existing members. The petition was returned with a brutal discourtesy. When she persisted, the Council decided that it was "more than doubtful whether the Society's Charter could be held to apply to women" — and, much to their glee, they were upheld in this view by legal opinion.

Not to be put off, Mrs Ogilvie Farquharson returned to the attack. With the help of male sympathizers among the Fellows, enough signatures were secured to compel the Council to take notice; a committee was appointed, then a general referendum held and finally a Special General Meeting called to put the matter to the vote, the 'ayes' proved to outnumber the 'noes' by a completely decisive 54 to 17; and so at last, in November

1904[*], the names of sixteen women were put forward confidently for election. Only fifteen of them, however, were successful: Mrs Ogilvie Farquharson, for her pains, was humiliatingly blackballed. Though she was successful when she applied again four years later, she died, alas, before she had the opportunity to savour her triumph to the full by registering as a Fellow in person.[36]

The first ladies

It would be wrong, and seriously misleading, to complete this account of London's biological societies without making some mention of the other world of humbler, wholly amateur bodies which flourished outside the central area. Or rather, mainly did so: the Quekett Microscopical Club was one exception, founded in 1865 as an offshoot of another, similar body, the Society of Amateur Botanists. The latter did not last long, but the Quekett is happily still with us, continuing to cater for the beginner and to maintain the informal, unoppressive atmosphere that its founders looked for as a change from the comparative loftiness of the Microscopical.[37] Such deliberate unpretentiousness was the hallmark of all the societies in this consciously lower layer — that and low subscriptions too (typically 5/- to 7/6d), reflecting the facts that they needed only modest premises (if they needed premises at all) and that the great majority of their members were anything but affluent. Essentially they were the strongholds of

---

[*] Editor's note; The first U.K. Parliamentary election in which women were eligible to vote was 1918 — But they had to be over 21 and householders or married to householders. Otherwise they had to be over 30!

the lower middle classes — the small tradesmen, the elementary schoolteachers, the skilled artisans — and they were generally recognized as such. Many of their members had a better knowledge of their subjects than many of those elected to the grander Big Four and carried out, and even published, much more and much better scientific work; but they felt more comfortable in these simpler settings, which were in any case conveniently close to their homes and jobs.

It was to the constraints of geography that most of these societies owed indeed their original existence. Until the Underground began to be electrified, from 1890, travelling any great distance across the Capital tended to be relatively very slow and there was not much temptation to forsake one's home area for the centre, especially after a hard day's work. In the early part of our period, accordingly, we find London neatly parcelled up into a whole series of societies for the different points of the compass. Almost all of these were exclusively or heavily entomological, reflecting the exceptional popularity of insects then among natural history collectors and the greater need felt in this field for a regular circle in which news could be exchanged and prize specimens exhibited. In one guise or another three of the societies, remarkably, survive today. The best-known, the South London,[38] almost petered out a few years after its founding in 1872, when a rift occurred over the vulgarizing of the Society's so-called "First Great National Entomological Exhibition", which, thanks to heavy publicity, drew the astonishing attendance of over 70 000 during the fortnight it remained open. Fortunately, the membership numbers recovered (reaching well over 200 by 1890) and on the strength of this a journal was launched successfully. Gradually the Society's reputation spread and many non-locals began to join, eventually in such droves that it turned into a national body in all but name. A major reason for this was the large number of leading amateurs who found the old-established Entomological increasingly too technical as the new breed of professionals moved in, and who found the South London virtually as handy and altogether more agreeable in atmosphere. The rise and rise of the British Entomological and Natural History Society (as it has eventually come to be known, in the last few years) is indeed the principal surface sign of the tensions that accompanied the amateur/professional change-over.

The other two survivors, the City of London and the North London, have come down to us through a merger (which took place in 1914). Their joint offspring is that present-day colossus, the London Natural History Society. The histories of these two are less colourless than usual, thanks to the splendidly unabashed way in which they chose to blend their learned activities with others of a more secular hue. These included an annual Cycle Run, held over a long weekend, and (in 1907) a subscription dance in aid of funds — which, alas, raised a mere five shillings.[39] Best of all, one gave rise to a hockey club composed exclusively of its members. The wife of one of these played in goal, "where", it is recorded, "her long skirt was very useful."[40]

And that is a salutary, closing reminder that learned societies, however humble or however lofty, are not just mechanisms for the exchange and sifting of knowledge, for the amassing and maintenance of reference collections and libraries, for the publishing of the results of research. Certainly, they have these functions — functions which on the whole they perform with quiet efficiency and in the process relieve the State of a massive expenditure that it would otherwise have to incur itself. But they are also —

societies, in the fuller meaning of the word: social entities, communities in miniature, in which friendships are cemented, animosities aroused and reputations formed. Without them, Scientific London in these years would assuredly have been a very much duller as well as a very much poorer place.

NOTES

[1] J. Reynolds Green, A *History of Botany in the United Kingdom . . .,* London and Toronto, 1914, pp. 528-539.

[2] D. E. Allen, 'The lost limb: geology and natural history', in L. J. Jordanova & R. S. Porter (Eds), *Images of the Earth,* Chalfont St. Giles, 1979, pp. 200-212.

[3] The founding of the Zoological was on the independent initiative of Sir Stamford Raffles, but that section of the Linnean's members who constituted the latter's near-autonomous Zoological Club made a major contribution from the first, filling three of the most important executive posts (John Bastin, 'The first prospectus of the Zoological Society of London: new light on the Society's origins', *Journal of the Society for the Bibliography of Natural History,* 1970, 5, 369-388).

[4] Since 1933 the Royal Entomological Society (though incorporated by Royal Charter in 1885).

[5] Since 1866 the Royal Microscopical Society.

[6] For example, the Malacological Society, founded in 1893, which had "of London" in its title and held its meetings in the Capital. However, it possessed no premises and used those of the Linnean on a fee basis.

[7] Zuckerman, 'The Zoological Society of London: evolution of a constitution', in Zuckerman *et al., The Zoological Society of London 1826-1976 and beyond,* London, 1976, pp. 14-15. Admittedly, the raising of the subscription (to £8) was coupled with the far more contentious proposal to divide the Fellowship into scientific and non-scientific classes.

[8] William Swainson, A *Preliminary Discourse on the Study of Natural History,* London, 1834, p. 317.

[9] D. E. Allen, 'The women members of the Botanical Society of London, 1836-1856', *British Journal for the History of Science,* 1980, *13,* 240 254; *The Botanists.* A *History of the Botanical Society of the British Isles through 150 years,* Winchester, 1986, Ch. 2.

[10] Gertrude Foggitt, 'Annals of the B.E.C. 1. 'The Botanical Society of London', *Botanical Society and Exchange Club of the British Isles report for 1932,* 1933, 10, 282-288; Allen, *The Botanists,* Ch. 5.

[11] Guy Meynell, 'The Royal Botanic Society's garden, Regent's Park', *London Journal,* 1980, *6,* 135-146.

[12] H. B. Fielding to Sir William Hooker, 9 Feb. and 18 Mar. 1842; W. J. Hooker Letters, Royal Botanic Gardens, Kew.

[13] Sir Joseph Hooker, (Hooker Medal acceptance speech), *Proceedings of the Linnean Society of London,* 1898, *33* (and quoted in *Journal of Botany,* 1898, *36,* 489).

[14] Forbes to H. C. Watson, I March (1843), C. C. Babington Correspondence, Botany School, Cambridge.

[15] Anon., *Phytologist,* 1851, *4,* 264.

[16] A. T. Gage, A *History of the Linnean Society of London,* London, 1938, pp. 48-49. Significantly, Bell had already served as President of the Microscopical, in 1844-46.

[17] ibid., p. 58.

[18] ibid., p. 50.

[19] The Microscopical, for example, had for many years met in the rooms of the Horticultural Society in Regent Street, for an annual rent of £20. In 1856 it was on the look-out for a new home, as shown by its move then to King's College (A. D. Michael, 'The history of the Royal Microscopical Society', *journal of the Royal Microscopical Society,* 1895, Ser. 2, 15, 1-20).

[20] H. Scherren, *The Zoological Society of London,* London, 1905, p. 144; P. Chalmers Mitchell, *Centenary history of the Zoological Society of London,* London, 1929, pp. 112-113.

[21] Gage, op. cit., p. 60; S. A. Neave & F. J. Griffin, *The history of the Entomological Society of London, 1833-1933,* London, 1933, p. 36.

[22] Gage, op. cit., p. 72; Neave & Griffin, op. cit., pp. 40-42. The Council minutes of the Linnean Society (2 April, 7 May and 3 Dec. 1874) provide no fuller details.

[23] Gage, op. cit., p. 61

[24] Mitchell, op. cit., pp. 267-271.

[25] ibid., p. 109.

[26] ibid., p. 111.

[27] ibid., p. 277.

[28] ibid., p. 285.

[29] Julian Huxley, *Memories,* London, 1970, p. 230.

XII

[30]Neave & Griffin, op. cit., pp. 52, 62. A graph analysis of the Entomological's membership by a statistician President, C. B. Williams, published in its *Proceedings,* Ser. C, 1947, *12*, 66-67, shows that the increase during the years 1880-1914 was a remarkably steady one.

[31]Or with interests for which the existing societies did not cater. Thus, the Malacological was founded because the shell-collectors who comprised the Conchological had little or no concern with the anatomy of the creatures within.

[32]G. L'E. Turner, *Are Scientific Societies Really Necessary?,* London, 1976, p. 4 (reprinted in Turner, *Essays on the History of the Microscope,* Oxford, 1980).

[33]Mitchell, op. cit., p. 32.

[34]On the other hand in the even more informal North London N.H.S., which was concerned with entomology almost exclusively, women members were admitted (in 1893) not without some opposition and one resignation at least (L. J. Tremayne, 'The North London Society in 1892 and onwards', *London Naturalist,* 1958, 6-8) .

[35]Gage, op. cit., p. 86.

[36]ibid., pp. 87-90

[37]J. R. Ramsbottom, 'The Society of Amateur Botanists and the Quekett Microscopical Club', *Journal of the Quekett Microscopical Club,* 1931, Ser.2, *16*, 215-230.

[38]M. J. James, *The New Aurelians. A Centenary History of the British Entomological and Natural History Society,* London, 1973. See also F. Stanley-Smith, 'The history of the "South London" Society', *Proceedings & Transactions South London Entomological and Natural History Society* for 1953-54, 1955, 55-74.

[39]L. G. Payne, 'The story of our Society, part I', *London Naturalist,* 1947, 3-21.

[40]C. L. Collenette, 'The North London Society in 1907', *London Naturalist,* 1958, 8-9.

This is a somewhat condensed version of a paper originally given in February 1982, in one of a series of Royal Institution historical symposia on the 'architecture' of scientific activity in the metropolis between 1870 and 1914.

XIII

Changing attitudes to nature conservation:
the botanical perspective

CONTENTS

INTRODUCTION

Botany is handicapped in the nature conservation stakes for the reason that it is not possible to be cruel to plants, strictly speaking. Sentient creatures can be seen to suffer pain, or may at least be believed to do so, and are thus prone to arouse that powerful emotion, pity. When human consciences revolt, they tend to revolt first of all against human beastliness and only far later against what amounts to mere lack of thought for others. To the non-scientific, destroying a plant is a sin against aesthetics at worst; but killing an animal is that and more, an indulgence in an altogether baser level of behaviour. There is an ethical dimension available to would-be preservers in zoology that can never be available to their counterparts in botany.

EARLIEST INITIATIVES

Even so there were moves to protect wild plants much earlier than might have been supposed. Indeed, if the import of one document is what it can be interpreted as being, the first of these long antedated the moves made in any other branch of natural history. This is a note written by John Ellis to Daniel Solander in 1762 and which recently came to light in the Linnean Society's archives (Anon., 1986). It reads: "You may let Mr Collinson and Mr Fothergill know that Mr Webb will assist them in getting a clause put into an Act of Parliament to make it Transportation to steal curious plants." The 'Mr Webb' referred to is Philip Carteret Webb, the antiquary and politician best known for the leading part he played in Parliament's counter-attack against the agitations of John Wilkes. A keen horticulturist as well, he was in the habit of inviting Ellis to stay at his country seat and advise him on the propagation of the rarer exotics that he had procured for his stoves (Savage, 1948: 4, 59). It may thus have been garden plants, rather than wild ones, that the proposed piece of legislation was intended to protect. All the same it is rather shocking, and a sad commentary on the conventional ferociousness of the age, that leading naturalists, some of them even Quakers, could contemplate a penalty so draconian as deportation to the Colonies for that comparatively venial offence.

But landowners could also act positively, on the side of enlightenment, in certain special circumstances where their actions cost them nothing. Thus we read that when one of the woods in Killarney was about to be felled around 1804 its proprietor, the Earl of Kenmare, gave instructions that all the trees of the great speciality of that district, *Arbutus unedo*, were to be left untouched (Weld, 1807). Perhaps significantly, that was at much the same time as orders were also given to leave unmolested a solitary pair of gulls which had stayed behind to breed on the South Stack, near Holyhead, after all the other sea-birds had been scared away by the disturbances accompanying the building of the lighthouse there (Stanley, 1838: 234–236). It was the period, too, of Sir William Pulteney's abortive Bill aimed at the suppression of bull- and bear-baiting in Britain, of the founding in Liverpool of a short-lived Society for Preventing Wanton Cruelty to Brute Animals, and of the publication of an article that dared to attack even hunting (Fairholme & Pain, 1924). Even botany could well have been a beneficiary, however slightly, of that primordial, all-too-brief, humanitarian wavelet.

COLLECTING AND ITS MODERATORS

A quarter of a century later sentiments of that kind re-emerged, as one strand in the ideology of the great coalition of progressives which arrived at power and influence with the passing of the 1832 Reform Act. Even metropolitan science was not immune from that pervasive liberal current. In 1836 a group of obscure outsiders, drawn disproportionately from ameliorist circles and from the Nonconformist sects (Allen, 1986: 43), banded together as the Botanical Society of London and defiantly set about admitting to their ranks anyone at all who professed an interest in the subject regardless of their means or social background or depth of knowledge—and, astonishingly for the time, not even excluding women. A body that was prepared to be so tolerant in its recruiting could be expected to be broad-minded in other ways as well; and it is no surprise to find that its founder and Honorary Curator, Daniel Cooper, a medical student barely then out of his teens, lost no time in giving vent to some impressively modern-sounding views. Speaking of Battersea Fields, for example, he deplored the fate that he predicted was bound to descend upon it soon, "when railroads extend into this, the metropolitan Botanist's favourite locality, overturning and obliterating some of nature's choicest productions" (Cooper, 1839). With this great increase in destruction hauntingly in mind, he felt bound to remonstrate with the "many botanists of the present day [who] are not content with collecting one, or even half-a-dozen specimens, more particularly if the plant is of uncommon occurrence." "I have known instances", he protested, "where whole species have been uprooted by the eagerness and avarice of the collector." Yet "if the plants are *annuals* it is doing injustice to the rising generation of botanists" (by which he meant that they were thereby deprived of the chance of obtaining examples in their turn for their herbaria); "if they are *biennials* or *perennials*, surely collecting the portion above the earth in most instances is sufficient . . ." (Cooper, 1838).

It is good to know that such cautionary words were being preached as long as a century and a half ago to that step-parent of today's Botanical Society of the British Isles. It would be even better if we knew that they had been taken to heart. Unfortunately, though, that was altogether too much to expect of field botanists in the 1830s. Discouraged perhaps, Cooper never returned to the theme in any of his later published writings and there is no evidence—though that evidence is admittedly fragmentary—that these matters were ever raised again at a meeting of the Society.

One decade further on, however, there were noticeably more protesting voices—and some of those belonged to people who were, or had been, members. The Rev. C. A. Johns, for instance, author of those classics, *Flowers of the Field* and *A Week at the Lizard*, ended a short paper on Cornish plants in what was then the most widely-read of the botanical periodicals, the *Phytologist*, by reserving to himself "the right of withholding information about those which are found only in small quantities from all travellers who collect for either of the Societies for the Extermination of rare British Plants" (Johns, 1846). By that satirical title all his readers would have understood him to be referring to the Botanical Societies of London and Edinburgh, both of which had become well-known for the respective services they ran for those of their members who wished to engage in the exchange of herbarium specimens. These services undoubtedly fostered over-collecting, for the size and quality of the parcel a contributor received in return depended on how much, and especially how much out-of-the ordinary, he himself had sent in. When the discovery of a species new to the British flora was announced, all the exchanging members inevitably clamoured to have an example for their herbaria; and the more conscientious the Societies were in trying to meet their members' requests, the more recklessly they were inclined to behave. In 1842, for example, no fewer than 300 specimens were sent in of the rare umbellifer *Bupleurum falcatum* from its newly-known Essex station. At that rate, as must have been apparent to even the most obtuse, the population could hardly last.

Probably it was no coincidence that only a few months later a letter appeared in the *Phytologist* under the heading "Remarks on the threatened extermination of rare plants by the rapacity of collectors". "I frequently caution brother botanists on this head," wrote its Westmorland author, but "seldom get more than a smile in return" (Haslam, 1843). He would have been heartened, however, had he known how widely his attitude was coming to be shared by then. Unfortunately, though, the complaining was all being done at the local level, so its extent failed to be realized. In Berkshire, for instance, one local Flora-writer was bemoaning the "many Botanists springing up around us", as a result of which "some few of the rare plants are becoming nearly extinct owing to the constant visits and pilferings for specimens"—though digging up and carrying off for gardens and, even more, wholesale raids by herb collectors were the cause of still worse damage (Lousley, 1964). Further north, in Worcestershire, the discoverer of a new rarity pronounced himself "almost afraid to indicate the exact locality, lest a file of men" from his local natural history society "should reduce the whole colony to mummies" (Lees, 1843). In Gloucestershire, however, the boot had passed to the other foot and it was the local society that was taking the lead in ensuring moderation; for we read that when the Cotteswold Naturalists' Field Club paid their respects to a colony of the Pasque flower (*Anemone pulsatilla*) in 1847, "only a specimen or two were allowed to be carried off, so as not to deprive this spot of so lovely and rare a tenant by useless devastation, an example of delicate forbearance which all collectors would do well to imitate" (Fletcher, 1946: 3). One year earlier, the equivalent of that club on Tyneside had gone one better and even written two special rules to that effect into its inaugural constitution (Goddard, 1929: 56). The Tyneside Club, like the Botanical Society of London, was a self-consciously liberal body in the stance it adopted more generally, and so it is to be expected that it should have been ahead of the rest of the field in fastening upon itself such scrupulous behaviour. Nevertheless it is noteworthy that liberalism in this particular direction no longer took the form merely of a homily preached by a single high-minded individual, but had progressed to a code of conduct which, at least in theory, was subscribed to collectively.

MID-VICTORIAN SHOCKS

But just as the vanguard in ornithology had begun to set aside their fowling-pieces and take to bird-watching through spy-glasses (Allen, 1967), only to have their good example presently lost to sight under an avalanche of trigger-happy newcomers armed with ever-cheaper and ever-more-efficient guns, so these first, faltering steps by the more enlightened section of the botanical community were also now to be rendered vain by a comparable inrush of heedless outsiders. The middle years of the 19th century were on the whole years of regression—and years of shock.

In botany that shock largely came from the extraordinary craze for collecting and growing wild ferns. What had previously been a little-noticed, somewhat esoteric specialism suddenly exploded in the 1850s into a virtual mass pursuit. The primary cause was the advent of cheap plate glass, which brought within the range of the average middle-class pocket those long-prized miniature conservatories that went by the name of Wardian cases. And ferns were favoured for these apparently because they were so perfectly in keeping with the then dominant aesthetic canon, that taste for exquisiteness of detail which found its supreme expression in the reproducing of Gothic tracery (Allen, 1969, 1985).

The havoc wrought by the craze was so sudden and drastic that it seems to have left field botanists stunned. Whole districts were effectively stripped of every plant that bore a frond. The choicer species were sent up to the markets in

London by the wagonful. There were even touts selling the rare Holly Fern (*Polystichum lonchitis*) on the very summit of Snowdon.

It was perhaps because most of the damage done by fern-collectors was so obviously attributable to rampant commercialism or to poor country folk who could hardly be expected to know better that the outcry from field botanists was so markedly subdued. They doubtless felt that they were powerless to intervene, that their numbers and their voices were far too small to have any hope of making an impression. In any case all too many of them were guilty themselves of raiding the wilds for their herbaria. Morally, they were not on strong ground when it came to remonstrating with the non-scientific.

There were, it is true, one or two among the fern-collectors who occasionally experienced some pangs of guilt; but the pangs did not last. Here, for example, is one of them, in just such a momentary fit of conscience:

> It seems cruelty so entirely to destroy the habitat of any Fern: yet, if the present rage continues, I see no hope of any known species being allowed to remain in its old haunts. The poor Ferns, like the wolves in olden days, have a price upon their heads, and they in like manner will soon altogether disappear. We must have 'Fern laws', and preserve them like game (Bellairs, 1865: 77).

But only a few pages later that same author can be found uttering this: "I did what I advise other Fern-lovers to do: I packed up a large hamper full, and sent it off by rail, home."

It may have been partly out of revenge for this humiliating invasion they had had to endure in the name of the world of gardening that the field botanists, in a remarkable display of unity, mounted an attack of great fierceness in 1864 on the Royal Horticultural Society. In that year the Council of that body, in what it no doubt supposed was a laudibly public-spirited move, announced a national prize competition for the best county collections of dried British plants, with the avowed aim of encouraging the spread of an interest in scientific botany. Much to its surprise, the field botany 'establishment' responded in outrage. The columns of the learned journals speedily filled with angry letters and a series of 'round robins' signed by most of the subject's leading figures descended in quick succession on the Council's unwitting heads. "The year 1864 will be remembered as the last year of the existence of most of the rare plants of the British flora" was one of the more extreme reactions. "Every genuine lover of botany", thundered the *Botanists' Chronicle* in an editorial, "already laments the growing tendency to the extinction of our botanical rarities, through the selfish greed, not of real botanists (who greatly regret the loss of even a single species, and are generally careful to leave enough for their successors), but of the race of mere collectors, who have no true interest, either in plants or in science" (Anon., 1864). It was these 'mere collectors'—money-grubbers, surely, tempted by prizes—that the botanists persuaded themselves would be the main people recruited by such a competition. In the event that does not seem to have been the case, and the fears expressed proved largely groundless. Simply giving voice to them, however, had had the effect of putting new life into the cause of protection in the ranks of field botany. It was evident now that the advocates of moderation were no longer an isolated few and might indeed be at last even in the majority.

CONFLICTING AIMS

Unfortunately, having managed to come that far, right-thinking opinion proceeded to rest there. No one among the subject's leading figures saw fit to act the crusading champion. Nor, as ill luck would have it, did botany possess at that time a national society of its own of sufficient size and standing to provide the necessary corporate backing and embodiment. The scene was dominated by the exchange clubs—and in the eyes of the protectionists those were irremediably tainted.

For many years yet, therefore, anything that could be achieved would have to be achieved by individual initiatives, without any co-ordination centrally. An example of one of these, far ahead of its time, was the action of the Wiltshire botanist, the Rev. T. A. Preston, in obtaining the lease of a certain marsh at Oxford purely so as to safeguard its flora (Anon., 1905). Possibly this was the first-ever nature reserve in Britain to be purposely acquired—as opposed to those landed estates whose owners, like Waterton and Dovaston, needed to do no more than confer on them sanctuary status. And considering how many wealthy people there were in the ranks of natural history at that period, it is remarkable that more people did not use their purses in the service of their wishes. Certainly, if they were botanists, they can hardly have failed to perceive the importance of conserving habitats no less than of campaigning against the picking and uprooting of species. Indeed, it seems to have been a botanist who was the first to call in print for the establishment of reserves by the State in Britain. This was a future Director of Kew, W. T. Thiselton-Dyer, writing in the *Academy*, one of the general intellectual periodicals of the day, in 1873. It would be "well worth the attention of an intelligent government", he suggested, "to preserve spots of primitive land-surface of which the vegetation was especially interesting." Probably it had been the opening of the Yellowstone National Park in America the previous year that had put that notion into his head. But in *laissez-faire* Victorian Britain it was a notion that must have seemed to his readers impossibly Utopian.

That habitat-buying did not catch on can doubtless be blamed on the mesmerizing success British ornithologists had had in carrying protectionist legislation on to the statute book. Even though the Wild Birds Protection Act of 1880 had serious defects, it shone like a beacon for naturalists as a whole and presented itself as an achievement to be emulated. Thereafter the way forward was sensed to lie through Parliament and the preponderance of effort came to be concentrated on lobbying to that end.

About that time, in 1885, the Selborne Society was formed, with the preservation of wild plants as two of its five declared main objects (Blackmore, 1985). Though birds were all along to claim most of its attention, this was to be the first of a whole series of bodies, not all of them so enduring, whose exclusive concerns were educating the public in the ways of moderation, publicizing threatened destruction and campaigning for more and more effective legal measures. In the continuing absence of a specialist botanical society of properly national status it was to these bodies that botanists who shared such concerns now mainly looked.

By the turn of the century opinion had crystallized in favour of a Native Plants Preservation Bill; and it was in his capacity as the Selborne Society's president that that grand old man of British protectionist legislation, Lord Avebury, was turned to with a view to taking soundings about whether this was considered desirable or feasible (Boulger, 1902). Consciously modelled on the Wild Birds Bill of some 20 years before, like its predecessor the proposed measure gave rise to a good deal of discussion as to the species which merited a place on the schedule for special protection. One who was consulted, W. A. Shoolbred of Chepstow, urged that all the ferns should go on to it with the exception only of Bracken (Allen, 1980). To wiser minds this smacked of overkill and seemed likely to result in the general ineffectiveness of which the ornithologists had complained since the Act of 1880. Instead, they preferred the suggestion, made to one of them by—it is interesting to note—the Secretary of the Society for the Protection of Birds, of abandoning the goal of legislation, with all its disappointments and uncertainties, and concentrating on acquiring particular portions of the countryside and thereby ensuring that the flora of these was *ipso facto* preserved (Boulger, 1902). It must be a matter for lasting regret that the financial and functional collaboration that that suggestion betokened between the world of botany and the world of ornithology never in the event took place.

What did take place was the founding, a few years later, in 1912, of a further body altogether, spanning the whole of natural history, with the acquisition of just such areas as its central and express concern. Enough is included in this volume already about the SPNR and its pioneering work to make it superfluous to dwell on them afresh. The noteworthy contribution made by a botanist, G. C. Druce, the autocratic Secretary-Treasurer of the Botanical Exchange Club, should, however, be stressed. Seven years before, in the course of a learned paper on the flora of Berkshire, Druce (1905) had bewailed the threat to the continuance of many local species presented by the ever-increasing invasion of the countryside by building. The fern-collector, too, he added, "is devastating our copses". "How long", he asked, "will naturalists be content that birds only should be protected from such mischievous marauders?" Though a notorious collector himself, he was substantially to expiate his sins by subsequently taking the leading role, with characteristic energy, in compiling for the SPNR the list of candidate sites reckoned to be of prime importance botanically (Sheail & Adams, 1980). He was eventually to benefit that Society even further by leaving it half the residue of his estate, a sum so very considerable that the Society's annual income was trebled as a result (Sheail, 1976: 66).

During those years, ironically, Druce was placed in an increasingly embarrassing position by the rising chorus against collecting from the many less scientific members whom he had recruited to the Botanical Exchange Club, a name which consequently suited it less and less. "I am really *glad* to hear there are so few Exchange members", wrote one of them to him, aggressively, in 1913 (Allen, 1986: 108). So strong was the groundswell on that score that the BEC would surely have been turned into botany's principal protectionist vehicle, had it only been less ethereal and possessed a constitution under which such an object could have been formally asserted. That was not to be feasible, however, until after Druce's death, and it was only in 1935 that a rule to such an effect was eventually adopted by it.

The running was accordingly left to a miscellany of other bodies. Alongside the SPNR and the Selborne Society there were now appearing further ones with

XIII

strictly botanical aims: Flora's League (from 1925), the Society for the Protection of Wild Flowers and Plants (from 1930) and the Wild Plant Conservation Board (from 1931), this last an offshoot of the Council for the Preservation of Rural England. Products of the great new wave of concern for the countryside aroused by the horrors of the charabanc era, all of these did useful work of a mostly low-level, educational sort. One, the Society for the Protection of Wild Flowers and Plants, even went so far as to turn 20 acres of Wanstead Park into the first of an intended series of sanctuaries for the preservation, and cultivation, of native wild flowers. But so far as securing legislation was concerned, their efforts led precisely nowhere. The earlier idea of a private Bill, which the outbreak of the First World War had abruptly put paid to, was revived to the extent of having one drafted—but it raised too many misgivings and never in the end made its way to Westminster. In default of that, attention came to be concentrated on seeking to persuade county councils to introduce by-laws on the subject or enforce the ones that many had in being already (six of them indeed from as long before as 1910 (Webb, 1925)). But for all the activity, the cause of protection, let alone of conservation, was not noticeably much advanced in those inter-war years (Sheail, 1976, 1982).

POST-WAR ADVANCES

The rest of the story is fairly well-known and need therefore be only briefly told.

The crucial breakthrough occurred, most unexpectedly, in the middle of the Second World War, in the context of the framing of a national plan for post-war land use. Nature reserves, at last, were taken on to the political agenda and thereafter the momentum proved unstoppable. Plant ecologists, notably in the persons of A. G. Tansley and E. J. Salisbury and corporately in the shape of the British Ecological Society, now took the lead, as had long been more appropriate, and conferred a professional scientific dimension (Sheail, 1982). The establishment of the Nature Conservancy in 1949 lay at the end of that particular trail. It would be difficult to exaggerate how much British field botany has owed to the Conservancy's existence and to that of its twin successor bodies. Apart from producing a great volume of rigorous research they have served as a kind of sea-wall around which the voluntary movement has been able to consolidate. For the BSBI, in particular, the Conservancy proved itself an essential ally, first in substantially co-funding the Society's pioneer Distribution Maps Scheme in the 1950s and then in establishing in its wake the Biological Records Centre.

Yet even before the Conservancy had its birth that long other stream of initiative, the more defensive tradition of safeguarding particular species or localities and the fighting of threats to them, had also finally found its way into a more substantially scientific setting. In 1947 the Botanical Exchange Club symbolically changed its name, and as the Botanical Society of the British Isles symbolically signalled, in turn, the shedding of its collecting-ridden past by setting up, 2 years later, a standing committee expressly concerned with conservation. That commitment was to take the Society into the many and varied developments that have since occurred on the national conservation front (Milne-Redhead, 1971). It was to take it into a long, arduous and expensive fight through Parliament in a vain attempt to save the flora of Upper Teesdale from the building of the reservoir at Cow Green (Gregory, 1971). It was to take it into framing, during the second half of the 1960s, a new and updated Wild Plant Protection Bill—which, though it proved on that occasion abortive, later won through in the guise of the Conservation of Wild Creatures and Wild Plants Act of 1975, and, more definitively, of the Wild Life and Countryside Act of 1981. Most recently of all, it has taken it into the setting up of the Conservation Association of Botanical Societies along with the securing of the appointment, albeit so far on a short-term basis only, of a full-time Conservation Officer under the aegis of that body. Out of this, given time, will perhaps emerge a counterpart for botany of the Royal Society for the Protection of Birds. Compared with the wondrous progress achieved in ornithology, botany's track-record has not been all that impressive, it must be owned. Yet maybe the time has arrived now when the tortoises will do some catching up on the hares.

ACKNOWLEDGEMENTS

I would like to thank Mr D. H. Kent for permission to draw on his unpublished study of the 1864 R.H.S. prize competition, and Mr F. H. Brightman and Mr N. F. Stewart for bringing to my attention certain data that I would otherwise have overlooked.

REFERENCES

ALLEN, D. E., 1967. J. F. M. Dovaston, an overlooked pioneer of field ornithology. *Journal of the Society for the Bibliography of Natural History, 4:* 277–283.
ALLEN, D. E., 1969. *The Victorian Fern Craze.* London: Hutchinson.
ALLEN, D. E., 1980. The early history of plant conservation in Britain. *Transactions of Leicester Literary and Philosophical Society, 72:* 35–50.
ALLEN, D. E., 1985. Natural history and visual taste: some parallel tendencies. In A. Ellenius (Ed.), *The Natural Sciences and the Arts:* 32–45. Uppsala: Almqvist & Wiksell.
ALLEN, D. E., 1986. *The Botanists.* Winchester: St. Paul's Bibliographies.
ANON., 1864. On the impending eradication of rare British plants. *Botanists' Chronicle, 5:* 33.
ANON, 1905. The Rev. Thomas Arthur Preston, F.L.S. (1833–1905). *Journal of Botany, 43:* 362–364.
ANON., 1986. What's new about conservation? *Linnean, 2(1):* 5–6.
BELLAIRS, N., 1865. *Hardy Ferns.* London.
BLACKMORE, M., 1985. *The Selborne Society: its Origin and History.* London: Selborne Society.
BOULGER, G. S., 1902. The preservation of our indigenous flora, its necessity and the means of accomplishing it. *South-eastern Naturalist and Antiquary, 7:* 28–35.
COOPER, D., 1838. On the advancement of local botany in the environs of London. *Magazine of Zoology and Botany, 2:* 163–170.
COOPER, D., 1839. On the distribution of plants in Battersea Fields, Surrey. *Proceedings of the Botanical Society of London, 1:* 22–25.
DRUCE, G. C., 1905. Additions to the Berkshire flora. *Journal of Botany, 43:* 14–25.
FAIRHOLME, E. G. & PAIN, W., 1924. *A Century of Work for Animals.* London: John Murray.
FLETCHER, T. B. 1946. *The Cotteswold Naturalists' Field Club 1846–1946.* Gloucester: Cotteswold Naturalists' Field Club.
GODDARD, T. R., 1929. *History of the Natural History Society of Northumberland, Durham and Newcastle-upon-Tyne, 1829–1929.* Newcastle: N.H.S. of Northumberland, Durham and Newcastle-upon-Tyne.
GREGORY, R., 1971. *The Price of Amenity.* London: Macmillan.
HASLAM, S. G., 1843. Remarks on the threatened extermination of rare plants by the rapacity of collectors. *Phytologist, 1:* 544–546.
JOHNS, C. A., 1846. A few notes on Cornish plants. *Phytologist, 2:* 725–726.
LEES, E., 1843. New habitat for *Lepidium Draba. Phytologist, 1:* 679–680.
LOUSLEY, J. E., 1964. The Berkshire records of Job Lousley (1790–1855). *Proceedings of the Botanical Society of the British Isles, 5:* 203–209.

212

MILNE-REDHEAD, E., 1971. Botanical conservation in Britain, past, present and future. *Watsonia, 8:* 159–203.

SAVAGE, S., 1948. *Catalogue of the Manuscripts in the Library of the Linnean Society of London. Part IV.—Calendar of the Ellis Manuscripts.* London: Linnean Society.

SHEAIL, J., 1976. *Nature in Trust.* London: Blackie.

SHEAIL, J., 1982. Wild plants and the perception of land-use change in Britain: an historical perspective. *Biological Conservation, 24:* 129–146.

SHEAIL, J. & ADAMS, W., 1980. Worthy of preservation: a gazetteer of sites of high biological or geological value, identified since 1912. *Univeristy College London, Discussion Paper in Conservation, 28.*

STANLEY, E., 1838. *A Familiar History of Birds*, 2nd edition. London: John W. Parker.

WEBB, W. M., 1925. Plant protection. *Journal of Botany, 63:* 273–275.

WELD, I., 1807. *Illustrations of the Scenery of Killarney and the Surrounding Country.* London.

XIV

The lost limb: geology and natural history

'Whatever became of geology?'

The question may seem absurd, yet it is a far from unreasonable one for a historian of natural history to ask. For what finally solidified some two hundred years ago into a generally-accepted trinity, an inescapable conjoining of the science of the earth with the sciences of the two kingdoms that make up its modern covering, is manifestly now no more. Geology has continued to flourish; yet in the course of the past century, slowly and unobtrusively, it has slipped out of touch with zoology and botany to the point where communications with them have become all but lost.

Oddly, hardly anything seems to have been written on this massive and far-reaching split. Historians of science have focussed their attention on the internal development of the individual disciplines and have had no eyes for their external contours and their macrocosmic positioning. Yet the way in which disciplines are ordered—or rather seen as ordered—in the wider landscape of learning is surely important in itself. There is a mental cartography at work here which preconditions the extent to which a discipline receives influences from its neighbours. If a science is thought of as closely allied to the one we follow ourselves, we make more of an effort to keep broadly abreast of it, in the hope of borrowing insights, maybe, or in the expectation of coming across findings which fit in fruitfully with what has been found in our own science already. If, on the other hand, a science seems too distantly relevant to make the effort of becoming acquainted worthwhile, we consign it to a mental outer darkness and allow ourselves to forget that it exists. Every discipline has, as it were, its nicely graded surround of intimates, friends, acquaintances and contacts.

Until the middle of the last century geology, botany and zoology saw one another as intimates—if not indeed closer even than this. A naturalist was anyone who subscribed to the study of the variety and processes of the earth: to be fully deserving of the title, therefore, a person needed to be able to demonstrate familiarity with the subject right across its range. In the eighteenth-century tradition the test of mastery was breadth, not depth, of a philosophy articulated and underpinned over the widest possible span. The aim of learning was roundedness, and the intellectual globe-trotter was still accustomed to travel hopefully. For the purposes of this exploratory essay, I have assumed a degree of homogeneity in natural history and its

[204]

component studies that more detailed work may show to be unfounded. To make fruitful comparisons at the gross level of analysis attempted in this paper, some hazardous generalisation forms an unavoidable preliminary. It has been necessary to disregard, for example, the often doubtless divergent attitudes and behaviour of the small minority of professionals as long as this has been a preponderantly amateur field of study simply because they constitute no more than a small minority, which may accordingly be set aside as exceptional. Similarly, for ease of comparison I have limited my terms of reference to Britain. I am nevertheless conscious that the pattern in other countries will prove in important respects to have been different and that much that is asserted on the strength solely of British experience is going to need substantial qualifying.

'Natural history' is used in this essay in the sense which has prevailed since around 1800, of the scientific study of the surface detail of the earth and of the organisms that inhabit it—in other words, those aspects which are amenable to observation, without requiring recourse to laboratory apparatus. As such, it has been able to remain open to the amateur, indeed in botany and zoology is still predominantly contributed to by amateurs, and so has survived essentially unchanged the general professionalisation which has so profoundly altered the rest of science. For this reason 'natural history' still seems to be both valid and useful as a term.

The conception of natural history as a single entity was greatly aided by the fact that geology's most popular aspect, the collecting of fossils and minerals, was manifestly descended from those very same 'curious' cabinets of the dilettanti as the collecting of specimens of animals and plants. Many fossils were plainly just so many shells, scarcely to be distinguished from those ordinary products of our shores which had once provoked 'la conchyliomanie' and still sustained its attenuated outcome. Others were equally plainly bones—and bones were the province of the zoologist. To a reassuring extent geology thus merged insensibly into these sister facets.

That this undifferentiating outlook bequeathed by the cabinet persisted at least till the very end of the eighteenth century is well shown by the bewildering omnivorousness of the journal kept by Robert Jameson on the occasion of his visit to London in 1793.[1] One moment he is admiring 'a very fine specimen of the Labrador Stone', the next a 'Great crowned Indian Pigeon', then some engravings of plants from Botany Bay, then back again to a stalactite from the famous Grotto of Antiparos'. Amongst George Humphrey's 'natural curiosities' his eye lights on a beautiful group . . . of Rock Chrystal of a vast size valued at £30.0.0.' and—the very next item—'a beautiful specimen of the Pennantian Parrot for which he asks £4.4.' All the time Jameson is dashing hither and thither from one great collection to

---

[1] J. M. Sweet, 'Robert Jameson in London, 1793', Ann. Sci., 1963, xix, 81–116.

another: one evening to Dr Crichton's fossils, another morning the herbarium of Dr Shaw, the next afternoon Sir Ashton Lever's birds. Almost every corner of creation, it seems, is capable of arousing the enthusiasm of this polymathic nineteen-year-old.

It was not merely the outlook of the collector that preserved this indiscriminateness. The very trend in the study of the earth at that period, with its dominant emphasis on the classifying of minerals, kept the subject in a taxonomic groove and thereby allowed it to continue to resemble the rest of natural history. Indeed, it was doubtless this common legacy of the classificatory approach that was in large part responsible for the study tending in that particular direction in the first place. Certainly it is suggestive that it was the French and the Germans, those much more determinedly system-minded peoples, who took the drive to systematise mineralogy farthest and deepest.

To escape from this sisterly overshadowing, it was necessary for some major new development to occur in the study of the earth which could act as a liberating nonconformity. This in due course arrived in the shape of Huttonian theory. So abruptly unfamiliar was such territory for those rooted in the taxonomic tradition that their disinclination to move into it further opened the way to the emergence at last of a true geology. The later dethronement of the mineralogical approach itself, partly consequent upon the abandoning of the Wernerian system,[2] made this autonomy yet more certain.

Even so, despite having wrenched loose, geology remained just alongside for a further extended period. The relationship had been too prolonged and close to admit of an easy severance. As a result there continued for some while yet some traffic between the three, as botanists tried their hand at geology or geologists sampled zoology.

Unlike before, however, geology now had some dangerous advantages— and not a few who thus wandered over ended up by staying. The very distance the study had achieved from the rest of natural history gave it a slight allure of the exotic. More potently, it also carried the appeal of intellectual forbidden fruit; it was here that the reality of organic evolution gave greatest promise of being uncovered. Above all, it accorded best with the then modish Romanticism. At a period when some acquaintance with science had become essential standard equipment for the upwardly striving, this was at once the most obvious area for newcomers to set about cultivating.

Probably there were homelier causes too. Naturalists are particularly given to being obsessional, and those most deeply obsessed can have found only the one pursuit at a time endurable. Buckland, for example, had started out with the customary schoolboy's addiction to hunting for birds' nests

2 R. Porter, *The making of geology*, Cambridge, 1977, pp. 170–6.

[206]

and eggs and might well have continued as a zoologist (as indeed his son later did) had he not chanced upon the more tantalisingly mysterious and (for him) more dashingly eccentric activity of hunting and collecting fossils —and thereupon found it necessary to make a wholesale switch. Jameson's conversion, similarly, was to be a permanent and exclusive one—and regardless of the fact that the chair he occupied was titularly one of a broader Natural History. Lyell, on the other hand, likewise lured across from the botanico-zoological wing, kept a better balance. The son of a well known botanist commemorated in the moss genus *Lyellia*, he had been primarily an entomologist till won over by Buckland's lectures while at Oxford. In his case the earlier loyalties proved to have taken hold too well for the break to become total; for he was to write frequently on zoological topics in after years and, with lasting fruitfulness, biological considerations never ceased to inform his preponderantly geological thinking.

Returning the compliment, leading botanists like Babington and Henslow faithfully remained Fellows of the Geological Society. This mere deed was not of course demanding and to some extent it must be seen as no more than a token of respect for a sister science that had superior standing. With botany in particular, however, geology had a palpable affinity and it was only to be expected that botanists with broader outlooks should look in this direction in particular. Out of around four hundred and twenty members whom it now proves possible to trace of the ill-documented Botanical Society of London, which flourished for twenty years from 1836, as many as twenty-three belonged to the Geological Society as well and at least another ten are known to have had geological interests.[3] Taking into account the not inconsiderable number whom it has not yet proved possible to identify, perhaps as many as one in every nine of these botanists was sufficiently geologically-inclined to take this to the point of forming a collection of fossils or at least being prepared to meet the relatively heavy cost of a specialist society subscription. These, moreover, were by and large the most active and capable field botanists throughout the country: the mere men-about-town who loomed so large in the metropolitan societies mostly opted instead for the grander and more exclusive Linnean. The extent of the overlap between the Botanical and Geological Societies is thus probably as good a measure as any of the two sciences' contemporary interpenetration. Below this level, in the strictly local and regional societies, separate sections for the different sciences were not as yet the rule and so the proportional allegiances are irrecoverable.

Botanists had a special reason to interest themselves in geology at this

---

[3] D. E. Allen, *The botanists: a history of the Botanical Society of the British Isles throughout a hundred and fifty years*, Winchester, 1986, pp. 3–65, 202–21. This appears to be the only metropolitan society of this period which has been the subject of an intensive membership analysis. See also idem, 'Arcana ex multitudine: prosopography as a research technique', *Arch. Nat. Hist.*, 1990, xvii, 349–59.

period because of the then fashionable concern with explaining plant distributions largely in terms of the underlying rocks. Areas of outstanding appeal to the fossil hunter or the geological mapper also had a marked tendency to be good botanical hunting grounds as well. These two sciences thus had the appearance of being particularly natural bedfellows.

Geology and botany were further akin in representing the non-animal side of natural history: entomology automatically grouped itself with ornithology by virtue of the fact that both of these were concerned with living creatures. Both of the latter, moreover, held out the sporting appeal of a chase. The various major segments of natural history thus mentally ranged themselves along a spectrum, with geology at one end of this, conchology next, botany in the middle, entomology beyond that and ornithology at the other far extreme. The membership of the Botanical Society of London roughly reflects these degrees of affinity in its pattern of secondary affiliations.[4]

As knowledge expanded, however, attempting to ride more than one scientific horse began to become increasingly uncomfortable. To achieve success in doing so, indeed, now became a sign of special genius. Strickland is the outstanding example here, making his mark at much the same period as ornithologist and geologist equally. In the space of a mere fifteen years he not only earned the coveted Readership in Geology at Oxford, but also gave a decisive direction to the study of birds in Britain, converting this 'from a "scientia amabilis" into a serious science', partly by showing the systematists important topics to investigate.[5] Historians of ornithology believe his geological experience may have been partly responsible for his originality.

Yet had Strickland only been spared for a full-length career, it is hard to believe that he would not have settled down as either a geologist or an ornithologist unequivocally. Certainly, in perhaps the best known other contemporary instance, that of Edward Forbes, there is the distinct impression of the intellectual splits. Forbes's first love, throughout his life, was marine biology. Botany was a subsidiary enthusiasm of his schooldays, but this had begun to pall by the time he went to university. Yet, when his father went bankrupt and financial straits forced him (like De la Beche and Robert Bakewell) to turn his recreation into his profession, contrary to all his expectations, the best paid work he could find was a combination of the Curatorship of the Geological Society with the even less remunerative Professorship of Botany at King's College, London. The strain of working in

---

[4] In so far as data on this point are now recoverable, at least 34 members of the Botanical Society were also entomologists (as against 43 with geological interests) but only 14 were also ornithologists. Anomalously, no more than 14 are revealed as conchologists, though a further 5 took in marine zoology in some other form.

[5] E. Stresemann, *Ornithology: from Aristotle to the present* (tr. H. J. and C. Epstein, ed. G. W. Cottrell), Cambridge, Mass. and London, 1975, p. 225.

[208]

three fields simultaneously, and even more the intense frustration of not being able to give himself wholly to the one that he greatly preferred and to which he looked for his reputation, no doubt played their part in undermining his health and bringing about his death prematurely.[6]

Within a few years versatility such as this had become fatally suspect. Knowledge had expanded to a point where it was no longer possible to make out that there was just the one single discipline with a series of specialised branches. True, it was just at this very same point that a central principle was revealed which enabled these to be grappled together logically far more tightly than before. Yet the unifying effect of evolutionary theory was to be slight in the face of this much deeper functional disintegration. The practical realities which govern the discrimination and demarcation of disciplines are necessarily more compelling than any merely conceptual counter-influence.

In any case, geologists were slow to react to *The origin of species*. J. Challinor has pointed out:

> The publication of Darwin's book did not at once cause a rush among palaeontologists to find more evidence as to the manner in which new fossil species appeared in the rocks. One might have thought that attempts in evolutionary palaeontology would have been very much to the fore in the eighteen-sixties, but it was not till nearly the end of the century that deliberate studies began to be made in Britain.[7]

Perhaps this is to be seen as just one more indication of the widening estrangement. Geologists had simply become accustomed by then to looking in quite other directions.

As further conclusive evidence of this, geologists and naturalists of other persuasions from around this time cease to exhibit their previous propensity to intermarry. This had been the most concrete testimony of all that the devotees of natural history of whatever variant constituted a single, indivisible community. What is more, as proof that it was their branch of the subject that had now risen to dominance, it had been the up-and-coming men of geology who had lately been winning the hands of the daughters of natural history's Establishment. De la Beche, for example, had married the daughter of Lewis Weston Dillwyn, co-author with Dawson Turner of the pioneer *Botanist's guide* of 1805 as well as a prominent conchologist. Strickland, going one better, had become the son-in-law of Sir William Jardine, the wealthy ornithologist and conceiver-cum-sustainer of the long-running *Naturalist's library* that helped to buttress immediately pre-Victorian zoology. After mid-century no more such alliances are detectable; and the

[6] G. Wilson and A. Geikie, *Memoir of Edward Forbes*, Edinburgh, 1861, *passim*.

[7] J. Challinor, *The history of British geology: a bibliographical study*, Newton Abbot, 1971, pp. 139–40.

inference must be that geologists had dropped right out of a marriage market that had by now been rendered irrelevant.

Given the vast outpouring of more and more specialised knowledge, it was only to be expected that a greater divergence should have begun to occur, that geology should finally have broken away from the main land-mass of natural history and been borne off majestically on its intellectual magma in some other, as yet unpredictable direction. But it was much less clear that this necessarily had to coincide with a severe downward movement in its public following.

Of this decline there can surely be no question. Before mid-century, geologists worked in the full public glare. Even as late as 1858 it was still apparently justifiable to claim: 'There is no branch of Science which attracts so general—it may be said so popular—an interest as Geology.'[8] By the end of the century all but fellow geologists were becoming oblivious of its doings. True, there was a general falling-off in those years of the readiness of the man-in-the-street to try to keep abreast of scientific developments, as discoveries rapidly proliferated and as science as a whole became infinitely more technical and specialised. Yet in geology the waning of interest does seem to have been more than ordinarily widespread and pronounced.

A variety of explanations for this can be adduced. Romanticism had gone off the boil. Terrible monsters had lost their initial shock. Limitless age no longer seemed so impressive. From the 1860s the thrust for origins became man-centred—and that meant a shift to anthropology and in due course to archaeology as well. The turnpikes and the canals had long since been built and by now the majority of the railways too, so there was a decline in conspicuous excavation, with its proneness to generate fossil hunters. The eventual unveiling of evolution had deprived the study of its appealing subversiveness. The big and simple finds had all been made: everything after that was bound to seem undramatic by comparison and as drama attracts performers so the age of great performers was consequently dead. Most simply of all, geology had been the fashion and, as with all things that fall prey to fashion's spell, the pace had become too hot to last: quite literally the interest had exhausted itself.

Tendencies within the science itself must also have contributed. Its very maturing intellectually ushered in a general cooling, relieving it of its famed disputatiousness—and thereby ridding it of those hangers-on who had merely come (as Lockhart said of himself) 'to see the fellows fight'. With the healing of those rifts there grew up a greater disciplinary solidarity, with the emphasis on communal endeavour rather than on combat between individual gladiators. The instituting of the Natural Sciences Tripos at Cambridge in 1851 had opened the way to a steadily broadening professionalisa-

[8] *The Geologists' Association, 1858–1958*, ed. G. S. Sweeting, Colchester, 1958, p. 2.

tion; and young men dependent on their salaries and looking to their careers could not afford the luxury of hitting out regardless in the manner of the gentlemen-scholars. In any case they had far less cause to, for on more and more of the essentials of the study there had now developed a broad consensus.[9] Polemics belonged with the heroics of that now-past age of geology.

In the eyes of the rest of science, too, the subject was experiencing a downgrading. Once it had been the undisputed leader: after mid-century it was doubtfully even the first among equals. For evidence of this, as Kennard has shown,[10] we need look no further than the annual choices for President of the British Association: from 1831 to 1894, eighteen geologists received that honour; from 1894 to 1931 (even allowing for the much shorter period), it was thought worthy of only five. In part this can be explained simply by the greater number of disciplines expecting a share of an unalterably-sized cake, but in part it seems likely to reflect a loss, relative or absolute, in standing. Yet this does not necessarily imply that the subject was in any way deficient at this period intellectually. What it was deficient in, more fatally, was glamour. It was old-established; it was not an experimental study; it was not pursued by members of the new, white-coated priesthood.

The introduction of geology into the curricula of higher and further education only served to widen the severance from botany and zoology. A high proportion of the students who took it were bound for mining or engineering or other bleakly industrial destinations; the world of technology with which they identified was emphatically not the world of natural history. Geology had to fight for its place in the academic sun, and to begin with could thrive only as an ingredient in more general elementary courses.[11] To escape from this treadmill existence, senior teachers inevitably pressed for, and took for themselves, higher-level courses which gave greater opportunities for specialisation. As a result their diet of geology became purer and purer and, often too, more and more esoteric, taking them out of touch with the wider base of their discipline and, more particularly, with the work of their colleagues in the sciences that abutted on it. The splitting of the chair of Natural History at Edinburgh in 1871 (followed, soon after, by a separate laboratory for the zoologists) was symbolic of an alienation occurring more generally.[12] Compounding this, the scholarly action—as with the flare-up of interest in petrology after 1870—was increasingly in just those areas of the subject that had escaped the attentions of the earlier

[9] R. Porter, 'Geology in the Cambridge Natural Sciences Tripos, 1851–1914', unpublished paper, p. 8.

[10] A. S. Kennard, 'Fifty and one years of the Geologists' Association', *Proc. Geol. Ass.*, 1948, lviii, 271–93.

[11] R. Porter, 'The development of the teaching of geology in Britain 1660–1914', unpublished paper, p. 10.

[12] J. B. Morrell, 'The patronage of mid-Victorian science in the University of Edinburgh', *Sci. Stud.*, 1973, iii, 353–88.

workers precisely because of their remoteness from, and incongruence with, their essentially field concerns. To this extent there was a parallel with the contemporary opening-up of novel, necessarily laboratory sub-sciences by the burrowers of the New Biology.

Inevitably, too, a growing professionalisation threw up its daunting ring-fence of technical terms and insiders' jargon. Even had the self-taught and non-specialists not been deterred already, this alone was enough to repel them in discomforting numbers. 'Original articles are . . . often too technical to be understood', one of its Presidents was complaining to the Geologists' Association by 1894;[13] 'the advances are made chiefly by specialists many of whom write in cipher, whose ways are dark, and whose language is by no means plain.' It was in the nature of all too much of the subject, moreover, to evolve into a scarcely manageable complexity. By 1886 the total number of fossil species known from Britain alone was estimated at upward of 19,000.[14] No ordinary collector could expect to cope with such overwhelming diversity—and yet if his specimens remained nameless, much of its meaning went out of his pursuit.

Nor did it help that the systematic primary survey of the country, which in all other fields was to present the amateur with a vast and almost inexhaustible challenge, had become in geology the responsibility of a special corps of professionals, who were prosecuting the work with unmatchable expertise and thoroughness. The big expansion of the Geological Survey that occurred in the 'sixties merely served to heighten the impression of a take-over and intensified the mandarin apartness.

It says much for the stolidness of the amateurs who clung on that they were able to make such a success—eventually—of the extra-national body which had been called into being in 1858 specially in response to their needs.[15] So hauntingly similar to the then just-extinct Botanical Society of London as to seem almost its reincarnation, the Geologists' Association, like that predecessor, saw itself from the first as a mutual-aid association for beginners. More deeply, it embodied a current of defiant primitivism: the products of the Working Men's College in Great Ormond Street who banded together to form it, felt themselves closer to the ground, truer guardians of the field tradition than the essentially indoor, comparatively pompous Geological Society—which was seen as the home, rather, of 'the illustrious Professors and Masters in the Science' (in the words of the Association's original prospectus).[16]

It was an exact repeat of the split that had taken place in metropolitan

[13] H. B. Woodward, 'Geology in the field and in the study', *Proc. Geol. Ass.*, 1894, xiii, 247–73.

[14] F. W. Rudler, 'Fifty years' progress in British geology', *Proc. Geol. Ass.*, 1887, x, 234–72.

[15] T. R. Jones, 'The Geologists' Association: its origin and progress', *Proc. Geol. Ass.*, 1883, vii, 1–57.   [16] See note (8).

botany twenty-two years earlier. And that it had not occurred till now in geology bespeaks a greater cohesiveness, perhaps attributable to the early lead given by the Geological Society in fostering cooperative work on a nation-wide basis[17]—in marked contrast to the long lethargic Linnean—as well as to the absence of any dispute in geology carried to lengths as bitter as that prolonged ostracism of J. E. Gray by the Linnaeans,[18] and so to the absence of any alternative nucleus of distinction around which a new body could cohere. Contrariwise, the appearance at this point of the very same pattern in geology bespeaks a similarly unbridgeable rift, the arrival at that crux where the discordancy of aims had grown too acute to be contained within a single corporate framework any longer. The out-and-out amateurs accordingly went one way, the out-and-out professionals another—even though, luckily, these were never to become more than polarities: a common allegiance to the field served to bridge the two groups and prevented any more than a partial cleavage.

Indeed, as O'Connor and Meadows have recently reminded us,[19] the development of a separate professional world was uniquely protracted in geology, largely thanks to the vigorous survival of this reverence for investigation out of doors. Geologists, virtually to a man, continued to believe that they were field men or they were nothing. It never occurred to them to copy the new wave of botanists and zoologists and seek to accentuate their newness by dismissing all such work as the stigma of a discredited past.

It is almost impossible for geologists, with their serene inheritance of the field tradition, to conceive of the hostility, even downright virulence, with which this was assailed and rejected by the upholders of the new laboratory creeds of the botany and zoology of the late Victorian period.[20] Admittedly, the teaching of the rudiments of systematics had descended to a peculiar nadir of aridity at the hands of their professorial predecessors. Admittedly, old-style scholars like Babington at Cambridge did cling to their chairs and the coveted departmental funds with an exasperating stubbornness. Yet it is hard to accept that these frustrations warranted such a prolonged display of iconoclastic fury. And it was iconoclasm in very truth: much that was wilfully stamped upon was in its way of great value and for all too many years had no hope of being replaced.

[17] M. J. S. Rudwick, 'The foundation of the Geological Society of London: its scheme for cooperative research and its struggle for independence', *Brit. J. Hist. Sci.*, 1963, i, 324–55.

[18] A. E. Gunther, *A century of zoology at the British Museum through the lives of two keepers, 1815–1914*, London, 1975, p. 44; J. E. Gray, 'Sowerby's *English botany*', *J. Botany*, 1872, i, 374–5.

[19] J. G. O'Connor and A. J. Meadows, 'Specialization and professionalization in British geology', *Soc. Stud. Sci.*, 1976, vi, 77–89.

[20] F. O. Bower, *Sixty years of botany in Britain (1875–1935): impressions of an eye-witness*, London, 1938, provides the best insight into this. The subject is treated at greater length in chapter IX of my *The naturalist in Britain: a social history*, London, 1976, pp. 180–4.

Starved of professional inspiration, cut off from the flow of potentially invigorating new knowledge, field botany and zoology consequently stagnated and remained almost wholly amateur studies. As a result, the image of mustiness which their detractors hastened to fasten on them came for a time all too uncomfortably close to the reality. Sapped, moreover, by sentimentalism, which the scholarly element had become too enfeebled to keep suppressed, they acquired a reputation that was doubly unfortunate.

All of this geology escaped. And the very fact that it did escape it, is conclusive testimony in itself that the break with the rest of natural history had by then become more or less complete.

Ever since, geologists on the one hand and botanists and zoologists on the other have stared at one another across a chasm. The Geologists' Association and the Botanical Society of the British Isles, two of the largest bodies in their respective fields, have evolved along quite remarkably similar lines into structurally almost identical organizations—yet have only ever been in contact once, and then quite informally. Of the many general natural history societies that today exist in this country scarcely any even attempt to embrace geology, let alone boast of a section specially devoted to it. Even in the avidly proselytising world of conservation there is doubt whether the bounds of natural history can now credibly be pushed out as far as this. 'Some Trusts', runs a statement in a recent newsletter of the Society for the Promotion of Nature Conservation,[21] 'might even feel that geology is not within their brief.' However, it goes on, 'this would be unfortunate'. Only in the inherently antique world of museums, most of them local ones, has the old unity been granted preservation—and mummification might be a truer, if unkinder word for this.

Yet, viewed from a different angle, the separation appears unreal, a mere artefact of just one conceptual scheme in particular. The landscape which has been depicted in this paper is a purely cognitive one: the positioning of the disciplines is their positioning merely from the standpoint of scientific knowledge. If, instead, they are viewed from the standpoint of social function, we are confronted with a very different picture. Class geology as a field study, group it with the now-reinvigorated field aspects of zoology and botany—with ecology and ethology, with population genetics and experimental taxonomy—and what do we have but a contemporary cluster of ways of directly investigating the environment which is no more and no less than an updated natural history? In this sense of a series of intrinsically cognate activities the old unity remains unchanged. Despite their divergence intellectually, the three disciplines still share a core of attitudes and functions, which has the effect of keeping them together. From the sensing of

[214]

this truth, even though it eludes rational articulation, spring those continuing, puzzled moves to reassert the threeness of natural history.

It has been traditional up to now for historians of science to subscribe exclusively to the cognitive scheme of things. But as the viewpoint of the social historian impinges, a shift to alternative forms of categorisation can be expected. To define disciplines in terms of how they are organised and of the modes in which those who belong to them carry out their work, instead of in terms of their particular siting within the landscape of knowledge, may even be more helpful for those who have to take the decisions for their institutional nurture and support. Sciences may march together in the pattern of their activities while standing far removed in the paradigms that bound them intellectually. To regard geology, therefore, as an integral part of a wider 'field science', over and above its existence as a discipline in itself, would seem to be as defensible as it may prove to be conceptually beneficial. For by looking at it as part of this other, wider whole, we may hope to arrive at a deeper understanding of it—no less than of natural history too.

ADDITIONAL BIBLIOGRAPHY

D. E. Allen, 'The early professionals in British natural history', in A. Wheeler and J. H. Price (eds.), *From Linnaeus to Darwin: commentaries on the history of biology and geology*, London, 1985, pp. 1–12.

P. S. Doughty, *The state and status of geology in United Kingdom museums*, Special papers in paleontology, 1979, no. 22, pp. 17–26.

S. G. Kohlstedt, 'The geologists' model for national science, 1840–1847', *Proc. Amer. Phil. Soc.*, 1974, cxviii, 179–95.

R. Porter, 'Gentlemen and geology: the emergence of a scientific career, 1660–1920', *Historical J.*, 1978, xxi, 809–36.

J. A. Secord, 'The Geological Survey of Great Britain as a research school, 1839–1855', *Hist. Sci.*, 1986, xxiv, 223–75.

XV

The natural history society in Britain through the years

WHY SOCIETIES?

Let us start by confronting a paradox. How has it come about that a group of studies that have carried with them down the centuries an aura of solitariness—the patient observer in his "hide", the furtive wielder of a net or lone chipper of rocks, Darwin encased with his theory in the *Beagle* or marooned on his sofa at Downe, Parson White endlessly patrolling his isolated country parish—how has it come about that these studies have also given rise to dense thickets of societies, to a mirror existence of crowds and noise? How is it that those so often shy and elusive creatures, naturalists, are so freely lured to their own equivalent of the watering-hole or the bird-table?

The answer, of course, is obvious. Though many of us are solitaries by temperament, many more of us are not; though most of us find it necessary or simplest to go into the field alone, this does not mean that we never want company. Like the devotees of any other cult or enthusiasm, we prefer to share it with fellow converts as often as we can, meeting those we have written to or whose work we have read, exchanging gossip, comparing records or collections, listening to lectures or passing on tips.

Apart from all these there is an extra impulse to socialise that comes from the very nature of our pursuit. Except for the bird-watchers, in these days when binoculars are commonplace, students of natural history seem unavoidably odd, comical or even menacingly suspicious as they engage in their esoteric activities and especially if they brandish their peculiar, typically archaic equipment. In those immortal, well-known words of Kirby and Spence (1826: 525), authors of British entomology's most sacred text: "With all your implements about you you will at first be stared and grinned at by the vulgar." But naturalists, they knew, learn to grow thick skins. The general public, they were happy to reassure the beginner, "will soon become reconciled to you, and regard you no more than your brethren of the angle and the gun. Things which are unusual are too often esteemed ridiculous". Nevertheless there is no escaping the fact that we *are*, all too often, considered ridiculous by those who know no better. Naturalists as a result tend to have a special self-consciousness, a heightened sense of being exposed to embarrassment, which when they are out en masse and enjoying the protection of numbers gives them the feeling of belonging to a company of actors and encourages them to put on a performance for the benefit of the public. Botanists know this feeling well, entomologists even better, but whether it extends to every kind of naturalist is less certain. The useful extra solidarity that it imparts to the world of natural history is not the less important for going unremarked.

XV

THE PIONEERS

It should come as no surprise, therefore, that natural history societies have existed ever since there were naturalists numerous enough to meet together regularly. As one would expect, in the earliest cases the arrangements were informal, the groups tiny and the meeting-places normally one another's homes. For this reason there were probably many of which no knowledge has come down to us, for as they published no accounts of their proceedings we are dependent on casual mentions of them in letters or in print. Moreover, as they rarely rose to anything so elaborate as minute-books or other tangible evidence of an institutional reality, it is often difficult to decide whether they were really more than just a loose coterie of friends. This is the problem with the *socii itinerantes*, the words employed with a seemingly not unintended consistency to refer to the group of London apothecaries who were riding out with Thomas Johnson on his pioneer plant-hunting trips, or "simpling voyages", by 1629 and during the ten years following, if not later (Kew & Powell, 1932; Gilmour, 1972). The word *socii* is temptingly suggestive of "society"[1] and some have been led to draw the obvious conclusion; but there may be no more to it than the literal translation implies, that they were simply Johnson's "travelling companions". Moreover, Johnson states quite explicitly, in the two printed accounts of his trips that he has left to us, that at least the earlier ones were made under the auspices of their livery company, the Society of Apothecaries. Would they have ventured, or seen any need, to identify themselves as a society within a society?

Well, perhaps they might, if the Temple Coffee House Botanic Club—the first undoubted society that we know of—is anything to go by. For that arose, in or around 1689, at the start of the reign of William and Mary, as an offshoot of the august and by then well-established Royal Society, from whose ranks it drew at least the majority of its 40 or so members (Pasti, 1950; Stearns, 1952). Sir Hans Sloane is believed to have taken the initiative in fostering it out of frustration at one of the phases of inertia through which the early Royal Society all too regularly passed (Mulligan & Mulligan, 1981); but a subsidiary reason was probably that from 1667 the Society, in conformance with the London 'season', went into recess for the whole of the summer, leaving the field botanists uncatered for (Hunter, 1976: 19). As its
* title indicates, the Temple Coffee House Club had its regular venue and the meetings are known to have been on Friday evenings. There was also a programme of excursions. But in that century and the succeeding one people tended to mean by 'botany' what we nowadays distinguish as horticulture, and it could well be that this and other "botanic clubs" that cropped up in the provinces not long after, mainly concerned themselves with matters outside the strict domain of natural history. In the absence of any written record of what they studied or discussed we cannot be sure.

Luckily, we can be sure, though, about another small London society which flourished for a few years in the early 1720s, for of that there is a surviving minute-book in the Botany Library of the British Museum (Natural History), which amply testifies to field interests among its members. That body, too, like Johnson's group of friends, effectively owed its existence to the Society of Apothecaries and the long-lasting focus that provided for the continuing handful of Londoners who were attracted to searching for and identifying more than just the standard medicinal herbs. Even so, cramming students for their medical exams seems to have been one of its primary functions and when its founder and driving-force, John Martyn, was presently invited up to Cambridge to help cram the medical students there, it unfortunately petered out (Allen, 1967).

Pure and unadulterated natural history in a corporate guise thus begins, to the best of our knowledge, with the Aurelian Society, the first of a series of bodies to bear that name, all of which—for a change—specialised in entomology. This one was in being by 1740 and might well have persisted for many years, had not all of its possessions, and very nearly its members' lives too, been lost in one of the fires that plagued London in that era.[2]

THE LEGACY OF LINNAEUS

Once natural history began to become fashionable, from the 1760s onwards, under the impulse of the new Linnaean ideas and the burgeoning of Romanticism, societies proliferated. They sprang up particularly numerously round Manchester and in the neighbouring parts of Lancashire, where their membership consisted in the main of working men, and their meetings, necessarily, were on Sundays at some favourite local inn. Sunday meetings, by contrast, seem to have been far less popular further south—or at any rate in the metropolis, where one society is on record as having broken up when a move to these was insisted on (Drewitt, 1928: 103). The founder of that short-lived body, a Chelsea entomologist by the name of William Jones, was so bruised by the experience that when a friend of his subsequently talked of starting a new natural history society in London he advised instead "a breakfast to our select friends once a quarter" (Smith, 1832: 175). It was well that that advice was disregarded, for the friend was J E Smith and the step that he had in mind was the establishing of what was to become in 1788, after two years of temporising, the Linnean Society of London.

Contrary to what is generally stated and supposed, the Linnean is not the oldest surviving natural history society in Britain. That honour belongs to the Royal Physical Society of Edinburgh, an honour well concealed behind its highly misleading name.[3] Nor was it the first substantial society in London to encompass more than just botany or entomology, for in that it had a predecessor, and indeed a rejected parent, in the Society for Promoting Natural History.[4] Had not the latter declined into a talking-shop, in which, as Marmaduke Tunstall complained to Banks, "grog takes precedence over botany" (Dawson, 1958: 833), it might have been the one that continued to this day.

On the other hand more probably not. For the crucial element of novelty which the Linnean Society embodied was a much greater ambitiousness: it was the first natural history society which consciously aimed at being grand and international. It was the first to see it as essential to own a library and collections, the first to go to the formidable expense (for printing was still a luxury good at that period) of publishing a journal. The launching of the Linnean *Transactions* in 1791 was indeed a historic event, which far outweighed in importance all the trappings and ceremonial in which Smith and his cronies so busily swathed themselves. For, as it came to be realised subsequently, the ability to place on printed record the fruit of their members' work was the main inducement societies had to be scientifically productive—and it

XV

was entirely feasible to be a publishing society in default of, or alternatively by positively choosing to forgo, the other conventional insignia of status.

Yet while the Linnean Society served as a stimulus to the subject by demonstrating that a body devoted exclusively to natural history could be accepted as a member of the topmost tier of metropolitan learning, it was a decided disappointment in most other respects. Once its initial impetus was spent, it ceased to exercise a formative influence on botany and zoology that was in any way comparable with that which the Geological Society had on their sister discipline. The reasons for this are fairly well-known: an over-attachment to the obsolescent Artificial System, a ban on all discussion at meetings (for fear of controversy), and the pledging of its resources to purchase from Smith's executors the Linnaean collections. It was not to be till the 1850s that it would be woken out of a protracted torpor (Gage, 1938).

METROPOLIS AND PROVINCE

By that time the metropolitan scene had been irremediably transformed. Following the advent of the Geological Society in 1807 (with in turn its own journal, from 1811) there had been a general fragmentation. In 1826 the Zoological Society arrived, in 1833 the Entomological Society and in 1836 the ill-fated Botanical Society of London. The first two of these were substantially the fruits of the despair in the zoological world at the Linnean Society's inertia and the consequent departure of the one element in its membership which, thanks to heated debates over the quinarian theory, had temporarily injected it with some liveliness. The Botanical Society, however, though it started off on much the same footing as its counterpart in entomology, had the ill-luck to be overshadowed by a weightier Edinburgh namesake founded almost simultaneously. As a result botany in Britain, unlike the other main branches of the natural history tree, failed to develop a single dominant centre. At the same time this structural weakness in the one discipline on which the Linnean Society was now left preponderantly dependent probably saved that body from withering away completely.

While this drastic rearrangement was taking place in the Capital, to which the rest of Britain tended on the whole to look for its lead, natural history was making equally striking advances in its corporate expression in the provinces. At the end of the eighteenth century the main provincial cities had begun to acquire one by one a type of learned body which aspired to be a kind of national academy in miniature. This was the literary and philosophical society. As the name suggests, it was intended to be all-embracing in its intellectual scope; and the loftiness of its brow was felt to need the accompaniment of both a loftiness of social tone and a loftiness of subscription. As such it would have been of only marginal benefit to natural history. But fortunately, to match their aspirations, the "lit and phils" decided that they must build themselves suitably imposing edifices, variously-titled "institutes", in which it was judged appropriate that there should be not only a lecture-hall and a library, but also a collection of natural "curiosities" and antiquities, more particularly illustrative of the neighbourhood—the one-time "cabinet" of every lady and gentleman of cultivation which was now given the more dignified name of "museum". Before long every town with pretensions to some standing had seen fit to found such an establishment. Its collections, however, obviously required attentive and informed curation, and the practice grew up of appointing local experts for this task in an honorary capacity. Among these, necessarily, were naturalists. In this way provincial natural history came to be provided with a chain of working collections for reference before it had acquired a chain of societies special to itself. Indeed so central to its needs was the formation of a museum considered to be that in one or two places, for example Torquay and Newcastle, it was the building that materialised first and the natural history society that accreted around it subsequently.

By the 1830s, when this was beginning to happen, the "literary and philosophical" ambience was either dying or already dead. Writing of its local representative of this, around that date, the *Leeds Monthly Magazine* could find nothing but "empty verbosity . . . the perfect uselessness of all its proceedings . . . the plagiarised papers which are weekly read before it, and the pure unadulterated nonsense which floats through the atmosphere of its hall from the mouth of its dilettante members" (quoted by North, 1956).The class which had ruled over cultural life in the provinces up till then had largely fled the cities and industrial towns, repelled by smoke and squalor, and those who had risen to take their place had tastes that were much more down-to-earth. As Samuel Sidney ([1851]: 79), that acute contemporary commentator, remarked, of Birmingham—though he could equally have done so of any other substantial place—"instead of meeting to discuss points of art, science, and litera-ture," the newly-rich and newly-leisured "read The *Times* and *Punch*, and consult the *Penny Cyclopaedia*". Not for them the high-flown speculation and opinion-airing of their predecessors: what *they* were interested in was facts, the demonstrable hard and fast; and the institutions they had inherited they speedily remoulded to meet their sharply different requirements. The old unity of learning had in any case by then broken down and even within the domain of science the time had come for societies to reflect a more specialised approach. Even so the new stratum that now emerged devoted to natural history exclusively was basically flawed: for it was anchored and urban, stuck with buildings which were a crippling strain financially and set in ways which were increasingly not the ways of those they needed to recruit if ever they were to flourish.

THE FIELD CLUB REVOLUTION

The imprisonment in a harmfully irrelevant magnificence was decisively brought to a stop by the invention of the field club. This took place in Berwickshire, in that Border Country renowned for its natural democracy, as early as 1831, but it was not until the 1840s and 1850s that its impact began to be felt. The germ of the idea had been caught by some local doctors while they were medical students at Edinburgh (Elliot, 1871); that University in turn had owed its development of field teaching to the example of the Society of Apothecaries, after the Apothecaries Act 1815 had had the unintended result of requiring all would-be practitioners of medicine in England and Wales (which included most of the Scottish students) to take a "practical" in the recognition of wild-growing herbs. It was thus a recrudescence of the centuries-old tradition personified by such as Johnson and his *socii itinerantes*.

XV

The essence of the field club was that it dispensed with the ownership of property. Its resulting very low subscription enabled it to recruit extensively among the less well-off, who were additionally attracted by its refreshing informality. Almost from the start there were some indeed who valued it as a social unifier only hardly less than as a vehicle for the advancement of knowledge, the Tyneside Club, the second to appear, even being founded with the aim explicitly, in the words of its president, of "forming a new bond of union between all classes" (Burdon, 1855: 50). In so far as it had need of money for more than the bare administrative essentials it needed it for publication. For its central purpose, as its name implied, was to undertake fieldwork[5]—and fieldwork generated records, on which there was a duty to bestow the preservative of print. Untethered to a headquarters, it could hold its meetings wherever it wished, spreading them around the local area so as to fit in with the convenience of different groups of members in turn. It was thus peculiarly well-suited to the more rural counties, which the pre-existing generations of societies had largely missed. These it now proceeded to colonise with a dazzling rapidity, thanks to the missionary zeal of individual Berwickshire Club members. At least three clubs, on Tyneside, in Ayrshire and in the Cotswolds, were fathered directly by these; several others were their less direct progeny. A fascinating family tree could be constructed by someone who felt so inclined.

So popular had this new model become by around 1860 that it began to penetrate even the cities, despite their distance from the countryside and the apparent difficulty on that account of providing a field programme. At least some of the cities solved this by taking advantage of the very much larger populations they had to draw upon and using their weight of numbers to lever from the railway companies very attractive special rates. Liverpool Naturalists' Field Club, for one, regularly had attendances on its excursions of 200 or more in consequence. Admittedly, a high proportion of these had scarcely any claim to be considered naturalists: they came in response to advertisements in the local press and were welcomed for the difference they made to the outing's economics (Higgins, 1866). Many of them were welcomed for quite another reason as well. As the Liverpool Club, in its first annual report, candidly acknowledged, it was because of "the opportunity it affords of pursuing a pleasing study in company with that sex whose presence doubles the enjoyment both of rural rambles and of scientific investigation." Not for nothing did its Manchester opposite number come to be parodied as the 'Field and Flirtation Society' (Kargon, 1977: 84).

It was indeed the field clubs, and more particularly this later urban wave of them, which taught natural history not to exaggerate the problems of those two great social bugbears of the age: the mixing of the classes and, of even greater delicacy, the mingling of the sexes.

The first of these was seen to pose a problem when the time came for the clubs to take by storm those ultimate fastnesses, the county towns. In those, the social strata and fissures were so exceptionally numerous and durable that even excursions by rail were a source of potentially serious embarrassment: the poorer members expected to have to travel third class while the affluent lorded it in first. At Chester, though, that was neatly sidestepped by invariably insisting that the entire party sit together in second (Dallman, 1947). Charles Kingsley, the author of this cunning little bit of social engineering, was one of several who saw their local societies as major contributors to moderating, or even breaking down, the petty segregation that had for so long held such communities in thrall.

How best to accommodate the women proved more problematic. One frequent device was to restrict them to election as honorary members (or, as the Botanical Society of Edinburgh preferred, after 1846, "extraordinary members"). Some societies were happy to enrol them from the very first on the same terms as men. Surprisingly, these included even metropolitan ones like the Zoological, Ornithological and Botanical Societies of London. The last-named even made a special play for them and encouraged them to contribute papers, albeit the response proved disappointing (Allen, 1981a). The Liverpool Naturalists' Field Club and its Manchester counterpart were particularly noteworthy for the high proportion of women among their members—in the case of the Liverpool one no less than 29 per cent in 1862. "Their field arrangements," remarked one disapproving contemporary, "seem to be considerably adapted to the convenience of the fair sex, as regards length of walks, etc", most of their excursions being limited just to afternoons (Brady, 1867). Women, in short, were widely regarded as a drag. For that reason the Cotteswold Club, with a distinctly lower tolerance threshold, confined their field attendances to a special Ladies' Meeting once a summer—on the pattern of masonic dinners. It was not to accept them to membership till 1920 (Fletcher, 1946: 9). Other societies, however, while admitting women, did so on terms that can best be described as ostentatiously grudging. In the 1860s Saffron Walden Literary and Scientific Institution permitted its female members to enter its library only between the hours of twelve and two and only through the special entrance provided for them (Collar, 1933: 139). Even as late as 1887 the Linnean Society was prepared to modify its male exclusiveness only to the extent of allowing in women to meetings at which papers were to be read of which they were the sole or joint authors (Gage, 1938: 87).[6] Chauvinism of such an extreme was perhaps no more than to be expected of bodies like these, respectively a relic of the literary and philosophical tradition and an adjunct of London's "Clubland". Yet it was to be a field club, the Woolhope Club of Hereford, that held out against admitting women members by far the longest of all, surrendering to the inevitable only as very recently as 1954, just over a century after its founding.[7] And that is the odd thing: there is no discernible pattern to how societies behaved on this point. It was one that was stuffy enough for its members invariably to wear morning dress at indoor meetings, the Ashmolean Society of Oxfordshire, that was one of the first two to elect a woman president (Bellamy, 1908: 71). Neither geography nor history nor scientific subject matter nor general social atmosphere seem sufficiently to explain the pattern of embraces and rejections. Which serves to remind us that for all their outward appearance of uniformity the similarities between one natural history society and another are only skin-deep.

By contrast, children were absorbed virtually without comment. Admittedly it was not until the very end of the century that this began to happen—when, for example, the Newcastle Society introduced the special category of Associate Member, with a considerably reduced subscription, for those under 21 (Goddard, 1929: 102)—and by that time such a move was no more than in keeping with the general social climate. Before that it had no doubt been thought undignified to have junior members, at any rate officially; afterwards it must have seemed absurd and self-defeating that they had not been encouraged to join all along.[8]

XV

CENTRE VERSUS PERIPHERY

Till well past the half-century mark natural history in Britain continued to be arrayed in two largely separate tiers, the one local and the other metropolitan. Travel up to the capital—even if that meant Edinburgh or Dublin rather than London—tended to be very much more laborious and expensive for naturalists in the provinces than it was later to become and well-nigh prohibitive for the isolated country vicars and hard-up working men who by then constituted so high a proportion of their number. While many of them subscribed to metropolitan societies in order to receive their journals, the hard facts of geography decreed that they could not hope to be active in the affairs of such bodies and must direct their energies locally instead.

There were two ways in which that gap between centre and periphery was bridged. The first and more obvious was through the annual meetings of the British Association for the Advancement of Science. From its founding in 1831, on a model that had proved its worth in Germany, this was enormously influential in keeping the provinces in touch with what was happening in the scientific front line. By directing its mammoth visitations to different regional centres in turn, it acted like a bellows on local activity while at the same time introducing the leading national figures to the research potential of the areas visited. The benefits, which were marked and enduring, were unquestionably reciprocal as far as natural history was concerned.

The other bridging mechanism was the co-operative collecting of data. Pioneered in the first decade of the century by the Geological Society of London (Rudwick, 1963), this was taken to ambitious new lengths in the 1830s and 1840s by the Botanical Societies of London and, to a lesser extent, Edinburgh through the machinery they developed for regular, nationwide exchanges of specimens for herbaria (Lousley, 1957; Allen, 1986). So productive and smooth-running did this become at the hands of the untiring and ruthless H C Watson, as a means of working out the distribution of Great Britain's vascular plants, that he was led eventually to conclude that it had rendered redundant the type of organization to which natural history had by then grown accustomed. "The objects for which scientific societies used to be instituted," he confidently asserted, "are now better effected by periodical literature, by travelling, by correspondence, and by exchanges" (Watson, 1849: 488). His personal disposition, however, was a notably austere and unsociable one, deeply antipathetic to the notion that naturalists have need of one another for purposes over and above extending their knowledge or operating with maximum efficiency. At the same time, in so far as he was hinting that the national societies could usefully follow the lead of the field clubs in shedding their encumbrance of premises and collections, it was an insight that was surely well-founded.

Various forms of co-operative research were to continue for the rest of the century and beyond, with ornithologists gradually overtaking the botanists and soon leaving them far behind in their mastery of the techniques appropriate to that; but it was not to be until the 1920s that these essentially non-local—if not necessarily "central"—initiatives began to claim the allegiance of societies and not just of teams of individual enthusiasts. The networks which they had given rise to represented indeed an altogether novel kind of organization: national groupings which were both non-metropolitan and like the field clubs in being devoid of property. Their focus, moreover, was not a discipline or a geographical area but a particular method of investigation which was brought to bear on particular gaps in knowledge. For long they were loose, temporary syndicates, operating without subscriptions, and were only to acquire for the first time any permanent substance when the British Trust for Ornithology was established in 1932.

After the demise of the Botanical Society of London, just after mid-century, none of the national data-collecting schemes could be claimed as essentially metropolitan. The London societies had by then largely turned their backs on the provinces as a field for investigation and looked instead to the wider world overseas. Only the British Association continued to give encouragement to work at the local level and then only fitfully. In effect, the periphery was left to its own devices.

Fortunately it was anything but lacking in confidence. More and more local societies were continuing to come into being, and the number which rose to a publication, the hallmark of a certain standing and stability, after increasing sharply in the 1860s maintained that increase right on through into the 1880s.[9] By then, according to a recent count (Lowe, 1978), there were no fewer than 158 local scientific societies with journals, with a combined membership of some 35,000. But that of course was merely the cream: there were certainly many more without the wherewithal or pretensions to reveal their presence in print. If they were included, the total strength was at least 50,000, one contemporary estimated (Abbott, 1896).

Perhaps indeed there were *too* many, as people were beginning to complain. On the one hand it could be held to be beneficial for every town or district in the country to have its organized assemblage of naturalists; on the other hand if that assemblage was too slight or too passive to produce a periodical in which to put on record what its members discovered, then there hardly seemed much point in their bothering to carry out fieldwork at all—unless it was for the purely private pleasure of extending their personal collections. Even if a periodical was published, it was commonly so transient or obscure that its contents were liable to remain unknown to the outside world. Even the diligent Boulger (1896) was "tempted to wish there had never been a field club at Stubbleton or Blankham, when a complete set of their *Transactions . . .* is neither to be found in the local library nor in that of the British Museum." A further criticism made (Meldola, 1896) was that local natural history societies were stultifyingly parochial, failing to make themselves aware of what was being done even in adjoining districts, with the result that there was much wasteful duplication of effort. There were even some critics who went so far as to query whether many of them even deserved to exist. In the words of one of the more acidulous: "Everywhere we find narrow scientific cliques, so-called 'Societies', apparently formed merely for the sake of having social gatherings and by means of a local periodical facilitating the cheap publication of the papers of such as contribute" ("SGP", 1874). It was a gibe that in too many cases was uncomfortably close to the truth.

THE MOVE TO FEDERATE

The obvious answer seemed to be regional federations. A first move in that direction had taken place back in 1861, when four small societies in Yorkshire formed a co-operative, under the title of West Riding Consolidated Naturalists' Society, and

XV

thereby put together sufficient funds between them to float a mutual journal. This was such a compelling idea that gradually more and more societies joined, until in 1877 the name had to be changed to the Yorkshire Naturalists' Union to reflect the fact that by then it was county-wide. Six years after that there were 38 societies affiliated, the journal was monthly and there was an annual *Transactions* as well. It was too conspicuous a success to go uncopied; and very soon a Midland Union followed, with a substantial journal in its turn. After that a string of similar bodies came into being one by one — in the East of Scotland, in Ireland, in South-east England, in other of the larger counties such as Lancashire and Lincolnshire — until a large part of the British Isles had been covered, very much as the naturalists' trusts were to carpet Great Britain after World War II.

The conscious model for these federal enterprises was the British Association. Like that, they were distinctive in being peripatetic, holding their meetings in different towns in turn; like that, too, they formed specialist sections and research committees (Lowe, 1976). The model, however, was so faithful a one, and their popularity so striking and fast-spreading, that the British Association quickly realised that it had serious competition. Its response was to insert into the programme of its annual meeetings, from 1884 onwards, a grandly-titled Conference of Delegates of Corresponding Societies. Within twelve years this was 66 strong and representative of an estimated 24,000 members (far from all of whom, though, were naturalists); but as it was only a once-a-year event and drew on no particular territorial loyalty, it was a flabby alternative to its regional rivals. Moreover, as the British Association meetings had become by that period showgrounds for the science professionals, an appendage of this kind, put on for the benefit in the main of small-town amateurs, could not help but have a somewhat patronising air to it. Perhaps not surprisingly, therefore, when these developments predictably led to talk of some kind of national federation of local societies under the aegis of the Association (Abbott, 1896), there proved to be little support.

SPECIALISATION'S INROADS

One reason for the British Association's rather desperate fishing was its awareness of the alienation of amateurs from the new world of professional science which had emerged since the 'sixties, a world which made no secret of the fact that it despised the field and regarded the laboratory alone as capable of yielding discoveries of value. Another reason was the growth of specialisation, among amateurs no less than among professionals, which was causing the local worker to feel more and more isolated.

Of the second of these trends there had been ominous signs shortly after the mid-century. The British Ornithologists' Union and the Geologists' Association, founded within a month of one another in 1858, formed the vanguard of what was proving to be a further row of central bodies, occupying niches not adequately filled by the pre-existing metopolitan layer. For specialists were now appearing in such rapidly growing numbers that it was steadily more feasible to float societies, and — even commercially — journals too, tailored to their more particular interests. It was one step further on in the seemingly inexorable process of breaking up the once-grand unity of natural history into ever finer and finer segments, each a self-contained little world more or less oblivious of what went on next door and in any case kept by language barriers from communicating with its neighbours.

The formation of the BOU and the GA, however, augured more than just that. The BOU represented the spearhead of what was soon to reveal itself as an enormous thrust into overtowering prominence of what till then had been merely one component of an undifferentiated zoology. Strangely slow to discover its superior appeal, ornithology was now to pursue an increasingly separate course while so outgrowing the rest of natural history as to inflict on it a damaging lopsidedness. So extreme would that lopsidedness become by the middle of the century following that the ultimate absurdity was reached of the hatching out by Canterbury and District Birdwatchers' Association of a section devoted to botany. Certainly, its sister disciplines owe ornithology a very great debt for sustaining natural history's prestige when the high tide of Victorianism went out and for largely making possible the renewed surge of popularity of recent years; but at the local level its behaviour has not always been sufficiently supportive of the wider cause and in some cases has even been harmfully divisive.

The Geologists' Association was similarly the first embodiment of what, along a quite separate axis, would also emerge as a source of divisiveness. This was the organising of field meetings all around the country by national, specialist bodies (Himus, 1954). From one point of view this could only be seen as a healthy development : these national societies were merely extending and deepening the tonic infusions of the British Association. But from another point of view they were subtly undermining their local counterparts, splitting the loyalties of the more scientifically sophisticated among their members and luring these further into atomising special-isms. Collaboration between the two parties, in the form of joint meetings, would have been the enlightened course to take; but this happened all too rarely, partly through the national societies lacking the necessary contacts at the local level and partly through a combined failure of imagination. A further twist of the screw resulted when national but non-specialist bodies materialised as well, like the British Empire Naturalists' Association (to give it its original, suitably imperialistic title), which saw it as their mission to reproduce themselves in numerous local branches. The duplication at local level which that produced in some places lives with us yet.

IMPACT OF THE CONSERVATION MOVEMENT

The competition, already intense from these causes by the 1890s, was intensified even further by the solidifying in corporate form of the new ground-swell of protectionist concern. This occurred both at the national level, most notably in the formation in 1889 of the Society for the Protection of Birds, and at the local level, in the founding of a county bird protection society in Essex in 1896. True, there had earlier been a short-lived Yorkshire Association for the Protection of Sea Birds and in 1888 the Breydon Wild Birds Protection Society had distinguished itself by securing the Norfolk Broad of that name, but those had been more specialised initiatives. It was only in the 'nineties that what we now recognise as the primitive opening phase of the nature conservation movement took shape at the centre and spilled out marginally into the provinces. The next milestone on that particular road was to be the establishment in 1926 of Norfolk Naturalists' Trust, the first of the county landholding

XV

bodies to manage an enduring existence. Twenty years later in two other counties, Yorkshire and Lincolnshire, significantly the seats of strong federations, it was local societies which were to be responsible for the birth of the two next trusts (Sheail, 1976 : 227); but after that the newly-arrived Nature Conservancy, impatient for a national network with which it could fruitfully interact, would ignite the brushwood and touch off a wildfire spread. The outcome has proved happy for nature conservation in Britain, but less happy for the sensible ordering of main-line natural history. Despite their different objectives the two have become competitors in places, instead of complementing one another. In one large and populous county today, which shall be left anonymous in its disgrace, the naturalists' trust has attracted to itself so much of the field activity that the long-established field club now boasts geology as its sole remaining natural history, the ornithologists — as so sadly often — have hived off into a separate society of their own, and there is no longer any local medium for the systematic publishing of botanical or other zoological records; to add to the confusion, it is under the auspices of the trust, hardly appropriately, that a new county Flora is in course of preparation. This may be an exceptional state of affairs, but it does show what can happen when the engine of conservation takes too much of the local fuel.

MOTORISATION

A final factor which brought to an end the clear-cut dichotomy of national and local was the advent of motor transport. The regional federations of the late-Victorian period could hardly have come about had it not been for the ever-denser crisscrossing of the railway system. But that was not enough to induce a radical alteration in the way in which the societies behaved. Nor was the addition of pneumatic tyres to "bone-shakers" : that merely encouraged the more enterprising to include in their annual programmes occasional colourful cycle runs. The internal combustion engine, however, was destined to be more shattering. In June 1906 a motor car first finds mention among the transport used on the field meetings of Worcestershire Naturalists' Club. In July 1910 the members of that club travelled all together for the first time by what were described as motor wagonettes ("the exhilarating runs . . . were much appreciated", the report in their *Transactions* reads). By 1915 they were hiring motor coaches regularly (Jones, 1980 : 163, 169). The Worcestershire Naturalists, though not in the lead, were probably not untypical.[10] The effect of this new form of propulsion was greatly to extend a local society's horizons and drastically alter its idea of what constituted its "district". A territory that was no longer strictly bounded began to lose its magic hold as the standard by which the value of records had traditionally been assessed. Freed of the constraints of time-tables or the limitations of their legs, owners of cars could even cease to be locals altogether and spend their time touring the national attractions instead.

Yet if motorisation at the local level was ambivalent and even destructive in its impact, it was surely all gain at the centre. Without the use of cars the historic Census of Heronries of 1928, the first major test of large-scale, short-term "network research", would not have been nearly such a success as it was. Nor could the various national mapping schemes which have followed in recent years have achieved anything like the coverage they have, had it not been possible to bring attention to bear by this means on to the remoter, underworked squares.

GROPINGS FOR UNIFICATION

Today both centre and periphery are flourishing. Yet fifty years ago few would have predicted that matters would turn out as they have. Many believed that the local societies had finally had their day, that they no longer had any useful place in twentieth-century natural history. The ecologist Charles Elton even went so far as to pen their obituary : "Like the bamboo," he concluded, they had "burst into flower, produced enormous masses of seed and then died with the effort" (Elton, 1927: 2). Similar lamentations persisted into the post-war years. Local societies were in decline throughout the country, pronounced another figure at that period : the reason, he supposed, was partly that there is less semi-skilled collecting to do, partly due to the complexity of the techniques by which the subject is being overtaken (Darling, 1943: 36). These prophets of doom reckoned, of course, without television, without the great expansion in higher education, without the lengthening of leisure. But even had they known of these, they might still have refused to accept that they would succeed in revitalising the subject at the local level. And indeed that this has happened on the scale it has is perhaps something of a surprise. For it has happened despite soaring printing costs, which have largely annihilated the old-style Proceedings or Transactions, replacing them with usually more ephemeral newsletters, and despite a general shift to passiveness as the earnest instruction of days gone by has tended to give way to visual entertainment. It has happened despite a greater reluctance to abandon the sitting-room of an evening and despite a growing mercenary trend on the part of invited speakers. It has happened, too, despite no slackening in the competition from the centre.

The explanation may be that for the centre to remain vigorous there has to be vigour on the periphery as well, that the two are interdependent, that some pushing and pulling between them constitutes a necessary creative tension. This need not mean that an overall co-ordinating body, a "national union of naturalists" as someone has put it (Cooper, 1948), is for that reason misconceived. Pistons, after all, do not function the less efficiently for being given some protective casing. Shortly after the last war there was indeed more than one leading figure who saw such a step as highly desirable. By bringing the regional federations that existed already under a single, overarching umbrella, they suggested, "something more comprehensive and carrying a greater weight of opinion behind it" would be produced. "A frequently-published organ to bind them together" (Cooper, 1948) and the subsidising by such a body of publications for those local societies unable to afford these (Gilmour, 1948) were extensions of this idea. The Council for British Archaeology, which has been such an asset to that cognate field, was an obvious and enviable model here. And indeed the Council for Nature which did eventually emerge at the end of the 1950s gave promise in its title of being an operation analogous to that. Alas, though, it was a title that gave rise to unrealistic hopes: the Council for British Archaeology owed its success to having been founded back in days when archaeology had but a feebly-developed centre; whereas by the time the Council for Nature was brought into being natural history had a thick crust already of long-established central bodies, which were loath to yield precedence to an upstart for whose creation they could see no compelling necessity. The result was that Britain's natural history societies, unlike its archaeological ones, proved unwilling to entertain the sizeable regular subscriptions which alone could have assured such a body of a permanent

XV

staff and a continuing existence. In default of that support only short-term funding could be obtained and that only at the price of an overwhelming emphasis on conservation. Altogether, it was a disillusioning experience.

But maybe it was an error to have aimed that high. Maybe it would have been better to have pitched the attempt one level lower down, to have sought a federation of the national societies alone. Unfortunately, the one precedent for that suggests that the prospects there are even worse. In 1858, with an imaginative reformer at last in its presidential chair, in the person of Thomas Bell, the Linnean Society sought to repair the damaging fragmentation that had befallen zoology in the metropolis with the first of a series of proposals to its offspring societies for closer collaboration. The initial one was no more bold than that the Linnean journals should be thrown open to such contributions as might be suitable from the other societies' fellows (Gage, 1938: 59). No more was heard of that. Eight years later the suggestion of a joint winter programme was taken up to the extent that the Zoological Society deigned to hold its scientific meetings in the Linnean Society's rooms — but they were given on different evenings and still under its independent auspices (Scherren, 1905: 144; Gage, 1938: 60). The experiment proved very short-lived. Eight years after that it was the turn of the Entomological Society. From that body came the proposal that its members be affiliated to the Linnean, with a specially reduced subscription. After protracted discussion nothing at all came of that either (Gage, 1938: 72). Ever since the three societies have gone their separate ways completely.

But perhaps we are expecting too much. Perhaps the natural history world is the dupe of a unitary fallacy. Made aesthetically uncomfortable by the lack of a neat, well-ordered pattern, perhaps we try to render too tidy a scene that is better left in all its sprawl and clutter. Instead of seeking to top out the structure with a shaky, even superfluous capstone, perhaps we should concentrate on strengthening the joints that hold it fast nearer to the middle: that precious handful of bodies which straddle all of the disciplines that comprise the subject and which serve to counterbalance its eternally disruptive leaning out of true.

THE PATTERN IN OTHER COUNTRIES

This has been a survey of how the natural history society has developed in Britain. In other countries we must expect matters to have turned out in many ways differently, though in all probability the broad trends have been much the same. But too little has been published yet to enable us to be sure.[11] Let us hope it will not be very long now before these gaps begin to be filled.

NOTES

[1] A contemporary Southampton apothecary actually refers to it as a society (T D Whittet, pers comm).

[2] If the small group of friends who met regularly at William Arderon's house in Norwich (Whalley, 1971: 31) gave itself a title, it would run the Aurelian Society close in its date of founding (1746). It would also rank as the earliest society devoted to natural history as a whole. Unfortunately, though, it cannot be established from Arderon's papers that it enjoyed so formal a status (Whalley, pers comm).

[3] The Royal Physical Society was founded in 1771, twelve years before the Royal Society of Edinburgh. In 1812 it absorbed the Natural History Society of Edinburgh, a University student society originally started by J E Smith and four or five friends in 1782 (Allen, 1978).

[4] In 1755 Taylor White, a leading barrister and a major patron of the subject, made an unsuccessful attempt to float a general natural history society in London (Allen, 1981b). This was 27 years before the founding of the Society for Promoting Natural History.

[5] The Berwickshire Club even dispensed with a winter indoor programme entirely. But that was an untypical extreme.

[6] Ironically, its exact contemporary, the Linnean Society of Paris, admitted *dames associées-libres* from the first years of the nineteenth century (Aymonin, 1974).

[7] The Herefordshire Botanical Society owed its founding in 1951 to the refusal of the Woolhope Club to admit women members.

[8] Much earlier, in 1835, there had been a society, the Swaffham Prior NHS, that was founded and run by children alone. It held fortnightly meetings for the reading of papers, organised collecting expeditions and even rose to the keeping of minute-books (Cooper, Perkins & Tottenham, 1928: 270). In addition, there had long been school natural history societies. That of Bootham School, founded in 1834, is the oldest of these still existing today.

[9] It should be stressed that this finding (by Lowe, 1978) relates only to the increase in the number of publishing *societies*. It does not necessarily follow that their *membership* growth displayed the same trend. In the case of the national societies, the latter measure shows a pronounced peak in the 1860s in the biological sciences and a weaker one in geology (Cohen, Hansel & May, 1954). It was of course easier to go on adding to the number of societies than to expand those in existence already. Indeed analysis of the Geological Society's membership figures from 1810 through to 1950 reveals that these grew at such a steady rate that a Gompertz curve shows a reasonably close fit (Cohen *et al.*, 1954). The peak in the 1860s at the national level is thus likely to have been due to the founding of additional societies coinciding with, and no doubt reflecting, the academicisation of biology. Evidently that innovatory wave spent itself a full two decades before the field club impetus similarly began to fade at the local level.

[10] The Folkestone NHS is known to have organised an excursion by motor coach as early as 1908. Other local societies did not become motorised till after World War I.

[11] Laissus (1976) has provided a historical survey of scientific societies in France, but to the best of my knowledge those concerned just with natural history have been the subject of a general overview only in Canada — albeit rather briefly, in one chapter of a wider-ranging work (Berger, 1982). I am indebted to Mr S R Clayden for bringing the latter to my attention. Bowler (1976), in an even briefer account of the Canadian experience, includes natural history societies in a discussion of scientific societies more generally. Natural history features even less centrally, on the whole, in the papers on the scientific and learned societies of the early American Republic in the pioneer volume edited by Oleson & Brown (1976).

REFERENCES

ABBOTT, G, 1896 The organisation of local science. *Natural Science* 9:266–269.

ALLEN, D E, 1967 John Martyn's botanical society: a biographical analysis of the membership. *Proceedings of the Botanical Society of the British Isles* 6: 305-324.

ALLEN, D E, 1978 James Edward Smith and the Natural History Society of Edinburgh. *Journal of the Society for the Bibliography of Natural History* 8: 483–493.

ALLEN, D E, 1981a The women members of the Botanical Society of London, 1836-1856. *British Journal for the History of Science* 13: 240-254.

ALLEN, D E, 1981b A stillborn society of the 1750's. *Society for the Bibliography of Natural History: Newsletter* 10: 5-6.

ALLEN, D E, 1986. *The botanists. A history of the Botanical Society of the British Isles through 150 years*. Winchester.

ANON, 1870 Natural history societies, II. *Nature* 3: 141-142.

AYMONIN, G G, 1974 *Adansonia*, fêtes champêtres et linnéens français. *Taxon* 23: 155-162.

BELLAMY, F A, 1908 *A historical account of the Ashmolean Natural History Society of Oxfordshire, 1880-1905*. Oxford.

BERGER, C, 1982 *Science, God, and nature in Victorian Canada*. Toronto.

BOULGER, G S, 1896 What shall we do with our local societies? *Natural Science* 9: 168-171.

XV

BOWLER, P J, 1976 The early development of scientific societies in Canada. *In* OLESON, A & BROWN, S C (eds.) *The pursuit of knowledge in the early American Republic*, 326–339. Baltimore and London.

BRADY, G S, 1867 Naturalists' field clubs; their objects and organization. *Natural History Transactions of Northumberland & Durham* 1: 107–114.

BURDON, R, 1855 Address to the members of the Tyneside Naturalists' Field Club. *Transactions of the Tyneside Naturalists' Field Club* 3: 48–56.

COHEN, J, HANSEL, C E M & MAY, E F, 1954 Natural history of learned and scientific societies. *Nature* 173: 328–333.

COLLAR, H, 1933 The Saffron Walden Literary and Scientific Institution. *Essex Review* 42: 81–89, 139–141.

COOPER, J O, PERKINS, M G L & TOTTENHAM, C E, 1928 The Coleoptera of Wicken Fen. *In* GARDINER, J S (ed.) *The natural history of Wicken Fen*, 267–297. Cambridge.

DALLMAN, A A, 1947 A Kingsley note and reminiscence. *North Western Naturalist* 22: 163–164.

DAWSON, W (ed), 1948 *The Banks letters*. London.

DREWITT, F D, 1928 *The romance of the Apothecaries' Garden at Chelsea* (3 ed). Cambridge.

ELLIOT, SIR W, 1871 Opening address. *Transactions of the Botanical Society of Edinburgh* 11: 1–41, 193–255.

ELTON, C, 1927 *Animal ecology*. London.

FLETCHER, T B, 1946 *The Cotteswold Naturalists' Field Club 1846–1946*. Gloucester.

GAGE, A T, 1938 *A history of the Linnean Society of London*. London.

GILMOUR, J S L, 1948 A directory of natural history societies. *In* FISHER, J. (ed) *The new naturalist*, 186–187. London.

GILMOUR, J S L (ed), 1972 [Introduction to facsimile reprint of] *Thomas Johnson: botanical journeys in Kent and Hampstead*. Pittsburgh.

GODDARD, T R, 1929 *History of the Natural History Society of Northumberland, Durham and Newcastle upon Tyne, 1829–1929*. Newcastle upon Tyne.

HIGGINS, H H, 1866 On the field clubs of the United Kingdom. *Report of Liverpool Naturalists' Field Club* for 1865–6: 9–20.

HIMUS, G W, 1954 The Geologists' Association and its field meetings. *Proceedings of the Geologists' Association* 65: 1–10.

HUNTER, M, 1976 The social basis and changing fortunes of an early scientific institution: an analysis of the membership of the Royal Society, 1660–85. *Notes & Records of the Royal Society* 31: 9–114.

JONES, M M, 1980 *The lookers-out of Worcestershire*. Worcester.

KARGON, R H, 1977 *Science in Victorian Manchester*. Manchester.

KEW, H W & POWELL, H E, 1932 *Thomas Johnson, botanist and royalist*. London.

KIRBY, W & SPENCE, W, 1826 *An introduction to entomology*, Vol 4. London.

LAISSUS, Y, 1976 Les sociétés savantes et l'avancement des sciences naturelles. Les musées d'histoire naturelle. *Actes du 100ᵉ Congrès National des Sociétés Savantes*: 42–67.

LOUSLEY, J E, 1957 The contribution of exchange clubs to knowledge of the British flora. *In* LOUSLEY, J E (ed) *Progress in the study of the British flora*, 19–29. London.

LOWE, P D, 1976 Amateurs and professionals: the institutional emergence of British plant ecology. *Journal of the Society for the Bibliography of Natural History* 7: 517–535.

LOWE, P D, 1978 *Locals and cosmopolitans: a model for the social organisation of provincial science in the nineteenth century*. University of Sussex M Phil thesis.

MELDOLA, R, 1896 The work of local societies. *Nature* 54: 114–116.

MULLIGAN, L & MULLIGAN, G, 1981 Reconstructing Restoration science: styles of leadership and social composition of the early Royal Society. *Social Studies of Science* 11: 327–364.

NORTH, F J, 1956 The local society in the community of today. *Advancement of Science* 13: 163–174.

OLESON, A & BROWN, S C (eds), 1976 *The pursuit of knowledge in the early American Republic*. Baltimore and London.

PASTI, G, *Jr* 1950 *Consul Sherard: amateur botanist and patron of learning, 1659–1728.* University of Illinois PhD thesis.

RUDWICK, M J S, 1963 The foundation of the Geological Society of London: its scheme for co-operative research and it struggle for independence. *British Journal for the History of Science* 1: 324–355.

"S G P", 1874 An appeal to our provincial scientific societies. *Nature* 9: 162.

SCHERREN, H, 1905 *The Zoological Society of London.* London.

SHEAIL, J, 1976 *Nature in trust: the history of nature conservation in Britain.* Glasgow and London.

SIDNEY, S, [1851] *Rides on railways leading to the lake and mountain districts of Cumberland, North Wales, and the Dales of Derbyshire.* London.

SMITH, LADY [P] (ed), 1832 *Memoir and correspondence of the late Sir James Edward Smith, M D* 2 vols. London.

STEARNS, R P, 1952 James Petiver, promoter of natural science, c 1663–1718. *Proceedings of the American Antiquarian Society* N S 62: 243–365.

WATSON, H C, 1949 Notes on certain British plants for distribution by the Botanical Society of London. *Phytologist* 3: 478–488.

WHALLEY, P E S, 1971 William Arderon, F R S, of Norwich, an 18th century diarist and letter-writer. *Journal of the Society for the Bibliography of Natural History* 6: 30–49.

XVI

Naturalists in Britain: some tasks for the historian

Dr John Ramsbottom, the President of this Society for many years and in whose memory this biennial lecture has been instituted, won international renown for his work in mycology. Yet, like many another naturalist (and this is a label I do not think he would have disdained), the narrowness of the front on which his scientific attention was focused was more than made up for by a breadth of interest in other directions. Among these, as a bibliophile pure and simple, with a marked fondness for the more esoteric byways of natural history literature, he was typical of probably the majority of the members of this Society throughout its history. As a professional taxonomist, too, he was aware of the practical necessity of delving into the lives and work of naturalists of the past and fixing precisely the dates of their writings. And on one occasion at least his long-sustained sympathy with amateurs led him into becoming, if only temporarily, an unalloyed historian. That, at any rate, seems the justifiable description of the author of the survey of the origins, development and current problems of natural history societies in this country which formed the subject of his presidential address to the first post-war Conference of Delegates of Corresponding Societies at the meeting of the British Association in 1947.[1]

Our late President, it thus seems fair to claim, represented in his person in at least some degree each of those three distinct scholarly streams that achieve their confluence in this Society. Others of its members have surely done so too. For in these head-waters of the subject the strength of the interflow is such that the separate, contributory identities become largely lost. We who journey to natural history's sources are inevitably merged into generalists.

Even so it is helpful, I think, to recognise that these three streams do exist, for their currents carry those who are brought by one rather than by another in significantly different directions. Where they meet, as in this Society, there must therefore occur a certain eddy. Eddies can be dangerous beyond a reasonable size; but the very fact that they exist betokens a continuing dynamism. From the rival pulls comes something far more powerful than the constituent flows produce in their separate running.

This dynamism fails if ever one stream preponderates overmuch at the expense of the others. In this Society, therefore, it seems of fundamental importance that there should be a full and strong flow of each. All are vital to its well-being; all are equally worthwhile and reputable; all are manifestly productive of scholarship of a very high order. I distinguish them merely in order to clarify, not to advocate one in preference to the others. For, as I have said, it is in preserving a balanced admixture that I see the greatest value.

The first of the streams – and first only because least needs to be said about it – is that of bibliography. I use this in the sense of that whole range of critical analysis and documentation of anything that has appeared in print: the parade-ground of expertise of all those for whom a book or periodical is more than just a collection of pages waiting to be read. Here the book collector, the printing historian and the librarian meet and intermingle, exercising what seems best described as a rigorous connoisseurship. The depth of knowledge and the keenness of scrutiny that they bring to bear are analogous to those of experts on painting or music – indeed, for some of them it is not so much a corner of natural history as an extension of the art world. Like so much of art scholarship, too, it tends to exist in and of itself: it is not – or at least not as yet – grounded in any articulated body of ideas; it cannot be claimed as a distinct intellectual discipline. It advances only in terms of a progressive enrichment of knowledge and a steadily more intensive probing. It is not a science; yet its standards fully bear comparison with those of other studies with pretensions to being scientific.

The second stream is what I propose to term 'taxonomic archaeology'. In this I group all that remarkably varied delving into the past that has developed as an outgrowth of taxonomy and museum work: the identification of collectors, the reconstruction of the routes of pioneer explorers, the pinpointing of type localities, the more precise annotation of specimens, the inside story of how particular institutions have come by what they have. At one extreme this grades off into work that is full-bloodedly biographical; at the other extreme, particularly in the matter of establishing priority of publication for nomenclatural purposes, it becomes inseparable from bibliography. What it is not, however, is history – in the strict meaning of that term. Its *raison d'être* is the clarification of matters that are essentially scientific: it does not set out to illuminate the past for its own sake. The framework of ideas in which its efforts find intellectual bearings and significance is that of biological systematics, not that of human ideas, human behaviour and human values.

The truly historical stream, which is my third one, is by comparison still hardly more than a trickle. Until very recently, in so far as it had emerged at all, it was made up of the bare chronicling of scientific progress, the stringing together of bundles of biographies, and celebratory accounts of institutions of a stifling parochialism. There was a general lack of incisiveness, a dearth of criticism, an almost total absence of enlivening speculation.

Yet so little of the preliminary groundwork had been done that it is scarcely surprising that these authors were unable to do better. For much of their material they necessarily relied on the unrelated burrowings of a mainly print-oriented 'taxonomic archaeology', largely oblivious of the far fuller and often very different story to be obtained from the examining of manuscripts. As early as 1866, in his lengthy, anonymous appendix to Trimen and Dyer's *Flora of Middlesex,* the Rev. W. W. Newbould had revealed the massive potential riches of the Sloane manuscripts in the British Museum, but no one else could match his single-minded dedication in braving those dusty and pathless wastes. In any case few if any of those who tried their hand at resurrecting their naturalist antecedents had had more than a schoolboy's previous acquaintance with the craft of the historian. It simply did not occur to most of them that there was another, far vaster, subterranean world of records waiting to be exploited in addition to what confronted them in print.[2] Their contributions, moreover, were invariably *ad hoc*: they did not see themselves as specialists ploughing a particular long-term scholarly furrow: there was seldom any broader prospect before them as they wrote. It was sufficient for them to have pieced together some portion of natural history's past, however small or disconnected, to have satisfied their own curiosity and to have deepened the delight in the subject of at any rate a handful of their fellow naturalist friends.

It was in the 1940s that the raising of the standard at last occurred — and with a jolting suddenness. This was the work of just one book: Canon Raven's matchless study of John Ray.[3] This was more than just a biography — and certainly very much more than what naturalists had become accustomed to understand by this term up till then. It depicted Ray in his full historical setting, and it did not flinch from penetrating character sketches of even comparatively minor figures. Written in an enviably muscular prose, it radiated massive confidence in its grasp and in its judgments. To those who had had no inkling before of the subject's possibilities at the hands of practised professional scholars this book must surely have come as a revelation.

Very soon afterwards the first ripples of the history of science as an academic discipline began to break upon our shores. Although their numbers were tiny, and at first they were almost all American, research students started to appear with a voracious interest in this country's manuscript resources. No less novel than their thoroughness was this daunting anxiety to 'get their hands dirty'. This very novelty of their approach, indeed, caused many to work in a greater isolation than need have been the case — or was conducive to the infecting of a wider circle by their example. That George Pasti's uncovering of the existence of the Temple Coffee House Botanic Club,[4] our earliest undoubted natural history society,   ∗ became known in Britain only at second hand,[5] and very belatedly even then, is all too typical of the deplorably slight traffic in knowledge that resulted. It also reflects badly on the failure of those of us in this country who shared an interest in the subject to develop till only the last year or two an institutionalised setting in which this traffic could be encouraged. For the fact that the historians of science have tended to publish exclusively in specialist journals of their own and have remained neglectful, or even unaware, of those which historically-inclined naturalists have tended to prefer has meant that communication through the printed word has been abnormally inefficient.

At the same time one must be careful not to exaggerate the impact of the historians of science, actual or potential. Except in geology their overlap with the world of natural history has to date been disappointingly slight. Except for the history of medicine the emphasis has been heavily and persistently on the mathematical and physical sciences. The preoccupation with the history of ideas has on the whole made natural history forbidden territory — outside the stockade of Darwin and evolution, where the ground has been dug and re-dug now almost to the point of sterility. As matters stand with them at present, the greater portion of our subject's past they seem unlikely ever to touch.

So we must fend for ourselves. We must emulate their standards and take from them all we can, but we must be prepared to undertake the task largely without their help. And this, I think, is no bad thing. For to 'get inside' our subject historically, it is almost essential to be — or at least to have been at some time — a naturalist oneself. Only someone with first-hand experience of the tenuous subtleties of the natural history world in action can really expect to comprehend these and capture them on paper. Too much, and especially on the key working mechanisms, has never been set down in words; the main flesh does not show up in either the published literature or the unpublished records. Much of natural history is intensely ritualised, a network of practices and observances that have developed over a very long period of years and have been passed on by one generation watching and copying another. It is a subject that is soaked up: it is rarely something that is expressly and explicitly taught.

Because of this, because natural history is more a set of activities than a cluster of theories and concepts, the standard approach of the historian of science is inappropriate in any case. It cannot properly come to grips with something so elusive and slippery. An ampler kind of history is called for, which for want of a more inclusive term can best be called 'social'. This has been my theme on one occasion before already and I do not think I need to inflict it on you further.

Social history, by its very nature, is best studied in terms of one society in particular. And because acquiring the necessarily deep and intimate knowledge of an alien society is very uphill work, the obvious and sensible course is to begin at home: to concentrate in the first instance on natural history within the British Isles. This has the advantage as well that it is the aspect that has the primary appeal for the vast majority of the naturalists of this land — and if there is value for naturalists in knowing and understanding their past, as I fervently believe there is, then the opportunity of interpreting the subject to far and away the largest likely audience is not one to be lightly passed up.

A further advantage of the social history approach is that it forces one to wander crisscross through the whole entire field in the hunt for patterns and relationships. One of the great drawbacks to most of the historical work that has been done in our subject to date is that it has been so closely hemmed in. It is not merely that studies have tended to be restricted just to botany or zoology or geology exclusively, but that no more than a fragment of a portion of each of these has customarily come in for scrutiny. The result has been an impoverishing loss of vision. Unable to place what they discovered within a wider setting, historians have forfeited the stimulus of generalising. Thereby they have deprived themselves of the chance of making out those parallels and regularities that constitute the subject's basic architecture. And thereby, in turn, they have defaulted on their primary duty of revealing natural history in its wholeness. For until and unless naturalists themselves can be brought to see their subject as a single, overall entity and so learn to understand and value it to the very full, it will continue to be only bittily perceived, and hence too cursorily discounted, by the layman in the street and through this feeble impression fail to achieve its rightful place within our wider culture.

Let me now give some examples of what I mean by 'crisscross wandering', by this talk of 'parallels' and 'regularities'. And in the process let me try to demonstrate that this approach is not only capable of producing new insights, but in its sudden perceptions of affinities and patterns is fully as exhilarating as, and indeed remarkably similar to, the practice of taxonomy. For this very reason naturalists should take to it instinctively and can be expected to outshine most others as its exponents.

In offering these examples, I want at the same time to use them to draw attention to what seem to be major gaps in our present knowledge and understanding. While the main struts of the subject have now been disclosed and it is probably fair to say that we can see in general terms how the different parts relate to one another and go to make up the wider whole, there are still numerous areas which remain to be investigated in detail — or for that matter at all. I suggest that it is in these areas that our historical efforts ought to be concentrated from now on. While there is undoubtedly scope for much useful infilling in those areas already tolerably well known, as long as there are so few of us to undertake the work there seems everything to be said for some strategic positioning of our communal labours. Here, accordingly, are some topics which seem to me could usefully be among these priorities for investigation.

First, and most obviously, we need to try to reconstruct the social networks. By this I mean all those loose, essentially informal groupings in which certain sets of naturalists have become linked together by reason of a common disposition, interest or purpose. These can take many forms. At one extreme are the correspondence networks — or 'colliterations', as I have suggested we might more happily term them[6] — that served as the main binding mechanism before the rise of societies and which spring forth so vividly from the pages of Nichols' many-volumed *Illustrations of the literary history of the eighteenth century*.[7] Some day someone is going to tell us precisely who was writing to whom at any one period and provide us with an analysis of the strength of the links on the basis of the number of the surviving letters. A computer might well be of help here — as one has been called in aid already in the closely comparable case of book subscription lists.[8] From such an analysis we may hope to learn not merely how extensive these networks were and how long they held together, but also how quickly knowledge travelled and which particular forms of it travelled fastest and travelled best. Certain naturalists, no doubt, were particularly to the fore in activating the newslines; but these need not have been the ones who were closest to the actual discoveries. There were probably always some who specialised, rather, in passing information on: the less original, perhaps, who had more time on their hands and who found in this role some compensating importance.

At the other extreme come the quasi-political alliances, like that convoluted 'Cambridge Network' that Walter F. Cannon[9] has so shrewdly laid bare for us. Mid-Victorian natural history certainly had its team of similar like-minded entrepreneurs, who tried out their brainwaves on one another and tended to act on them in concert. Names like George Johnston, J. E. Bowerbank, J. E. Gray, H. E. Strickland, H. T. Stainton and William Yarrell turn up with noticeable frequency wherever some promising new initiative is afoot. These were men of established reputation in their fields, often — and significantly — moving with ease in more than one branch of natural history, and with a proven record of running things efficiently. They could be relied on to know what was best for the subject, what was particularly needed and what was most likely to be fruitful. Some, like Gray and Stainton and Yarrell, regularly rubbed shoulders in the London societies; but others, like Johnston, were geographically peripheral and operated largely by letter — and would have stood little hope of being listened to had they not risen to national prominence first.

Personality was all-important here. The men who got things done were not necessarily the leaders scientifically (even though, by definition, they were at least near the van): it was more essential that they were open-minded, moderate and flexible. Above all, they had to be men of drive. N. B. Ward moved in the same circles, was fully as respected and was host at just as regular and popular soirées as Stainton; but he was just not a 'doer' and had conspicuously failed to exploit his own successive inventions of the Wardian case and the aquarium. Nor was it sufficient to be a good and prolific writer or the proprietor of a journal: these were valuable and influential roles as well, but they were different ones, demanding different qualities and liable in any case to be too all-consuming of leisure and energies for anything else to be taken on. It is striking how Edward Newman, so otherwise ubiquitous, seldom features in initiatives that are not purely publishing ones.

Cantankerous people, like H. C. Watson, were clearly unfitted for this nimble-footed, tactful little world. Watson had plenty of original and sensible ideas and ample determination to see them through; but he was too pugnacious, too unpredictable and touchy, to glide in and out of alliances in this way. He was not a starter just for the sake of starting things — as the purest type of the intellectual entrepreneur tends to be. He hung on like a snarling bulldog to his own particular bone and was quite prepared to nudge everyone out of the way if they came between him and his intentions. To secure an effective organised exchange of plants on the lines he himself had been responsible for devising, he had no compunction at all in taking on the task within the democratic harness of the Botanical Society of London and thereafter conducting it on his own autocratic terms entirely.

Ray Lankester, 'the stormy petrel of the zoological world' (as he has been called),[10] was very much Watson's counterpart, if of a rather later generation. Intensely self-righteous, tactlessly forthright and utterly fearless as a critic, he was apt to provoke antagonisms in just the same way. In just the same way, too, he identified himself wholeheartedly, to the extent that only ferocious egotists can, with particular causes that happened to coincide with his personal ambitions and fought for these persistently and mightily. The Marine Biological Association was turned into his personal tool no less ruthlessly than Watson manipulated the Botanical Society — or, for that matter, Smith the Linnean Society or Druce the Botanical Exchange Club.

Domineering people like these were capable at best of only fleeting alliances — and then typically with men just like themselves (as P. L. Sclater teamed up with Richard Owen). Autocrats tend to respect only one another: accustomed to subordinates, they see only indignity in working with anyone else on level terms. Their temperamental aversion to compromise and their very intolerance additionally prevent them from functioning as network men.

The same goes, too, for the incurable manoeuvrers: those who, in their over-readiness to trim and their continual twists and turns, have all the suspect sleekness of the professional politician. These men go too far, they are too unreliable, they are too blatantly self-servers. But at least a studied charm can make them companionable, to the extent that they can be tolerated, if warily, as short-run allies — which is more than can be said for that other group of unacceptables: the impossibly unpleasant. Of these, mercifully, natural history has always had extremely few. Indeed the only major figure who immediately springs to mind is the abominable Owen (can the Prince Consort *really* have liked him, as we are so blithely given to assume?).

The relationship between these network and non-network people is an intriguing topic in itself. What form in fact did it take? Did the spiky outsiders have a useful role in the inside world nonetheless? Could it be that they served the function of battering-rams, brought into play, albeit reluctantly, when a particularly intractable situation was encountered? Were they, perhaps, the weapons of last resort, released on the foe after every milder stratagem had been exhausted? Or were they regarded as altogether too incorrigible and permanently cold-shouldered?

In so small a world every naturalist who rose to prominence must surely sooner or later have been 'typed' from this standpoint of political reputability. Yet a man's reputation in the politics of natural history need not, and doubtless did not, reflect in any way on his scientific or his social reputation. Richard Owen was universally recognised and esteemed for his brilliance, but few if any could stomach him as an associate. No one was more popular than Ward, but he had to be propelled by others into the battle-line of causes.

On the other hand a social reputation, and even more an elevated social position, could be turned to good use in the political service of natural history by those who had the inclination. Murchison and Lubbock, salon hosts in the grand tradition stemming from Banks, were outstanding examples of this. Indeed, like Banks and together with others like De la Beche, they operated on a social circuit that was one level up from the essentially middle-class one that we have just been examining.

At this loftier level there are not merely *horizontal* networks, of fellow entrepreneurs, to be considered, but also *pyramidal* networks, centred on individual patrons. The whole subject of patronage in relation to natural history is an immense one in itself, well deserving of special study. The key role in the development of the subject played by Sloane and Banks and the Duchess of Portland is far too well-known to need stressing; but apart from this bald fact we still know remarkably little. No one has yet traced in detail the full reach of their respective tentacles and we appear to be entirely ignorant of what their activities amounted to in actual money terms. Although much of the patronage dispensed by Sloane and Banks took the form of placemanship and so was monetary only indirectly, that of the Duchess (as of other, lesser collectors) was purely monetary in character, inasmuch as her activities did not extend beyond employing people herself or making payments for specimens. In theory, therefore, the pattern of her patronage should be precisely measurable.

Patronage in this last sense of just a rather deeper-than-normal customer-client relationship has continued down to the present – though it is now the government or firms that play the role of patron. But patronage in the sense of barefaced placemanship we tend to think of as something that belongs to a now very distant past. It comes as quite a shock, therefore, to learn that as late as 1864 Arthur O'Shaughnessy, best known today as a minor *fin-de-siècle* poet, owed his appointment to a post in the British Museum zoology department to the fact that he was a nephew of the mistress of one of the Trustees.[11] Though qualified on paper, it is said he "did not know a butterfly from a moth or a beetle from a bug"[12] and fully justified the low opinion entertained of him by his scientific colleagues from the outset.

A very exceptional outburst of placemanship about which we could usefully know much more is that which occurred in the early 1760s consequent upon the accession of George III. The new king, though twenty-two, was still strikingly immature emotionally, and he hero-worshipped his tutor, the Earl of Bute, to an extent that was embarrassing. As soon as he was on the throne he would have this man and no other as his principal minister – and, because of these special circumstances, thereby made him the effective ruler of the country. As luck would have it, Bute had an enthusiasm for botany dating back many years and this enthusiasm was shared, what is more, by the king's mother, the Dowager Princess of Wales.[13] It was thus predictable that one result of this freak windfall of power would be some lush appointments for the friends he had made in natural history.

The prime beneficiary proved to be John Hill, who was awarded the Master Gardenership at Kensington Palace. This was a more substantial prize than it sounds; for, if the poet Thomas Gray[14] is to be believed, the emolument that went with the post was close on two thousand pounds – a gigantic sum in eighteenth-century terms. Gray also reports[14] that another naturalist friend, Benjamin Stillingfleet, seized the opportunity to try to enlist Bute's backing for a favourite scheme of his: to send some qualified persons to reside in Attica with a view to studying its natural history, in order the better to understand the writings of Classical authors like Aristotle and Theophrastus. There must surely have been several more such approaches, of which mention may yet be found in the correspondence of the period.

Blatant jobbery of this kind has given the word 'patronage' a permanently ugly ring. Yet the system also had its good side: just as there was 'white' magic as well as black magic, so there was 'white' patronage. The dark side could be justified by reference to the benefits it brought when wearing this other countenance. Though employers had their whims and could doubtless be imperious, it is wrong to think that those who accepted their patronage were necessarily required to be servile. The relationship was governed by conventions and could only have been workable given a good deal of tact and restraint on either side. Moreover, patronage was brought to bear by no means only on people: private wealth could also be used to sustain an institution or a journal. The *Magazine of Zoology and Botany,* the short-lived forbear of the *Annals and Magazine of Natural History,* was kept alive solely on Sir William Jardine's money, which also provided the crucial floating-off for the long series of volumes constituting the 'Naturalist's Library' that bears his name. To the patrician generosity of the Rothschilds we similarly owe Tring, the Society for the Promotion of Nature Conservation and Woodwalton Fen.

Private funds have always had the advantage over public ones of greater flexibility. Just as the private foundations today are often one step ahead of their government equivalents in support for novel fields and new kinds of initiatives, so wealthy individuals have repeatedly given a helping shove where governments have been hesitant to tread. The private patron has the eternal asset of not having to pay heed to the current public consensus.

There are some innovations, moreover, that are clearly less suited to the public domain by their very character. One of these is the recruitment of foreign nationals. From an early period the dearth of trained taxonomists in Britain forced wealthy naturalists with collections they were anxious to have worked on to look abroad for the necessary talent – and in particular to Germany, with its unrivalled reputation for painstaking thoroughness and with a long-continuing oversupply of dedicated scholars. It was from Giessen in 1721 that Johann Jakob Dillen, otherwise Dillenius, was brought over by William Sherard and launched on the whirlwind career that gave us almost at once a new and much-needed British Flora and then, ten years later, an even more needed revival of botany in Oxford. It was from Göttingen in 1800 that Carl Dietrich Eberhard König was invited to arrange the collections of Queen Charlotte at Kew, subsequently passed into the employ of Banks as his assistant librarian and eventually, in 1806, created the precedent of joining the staff of the British Museum. It was from Tübingen, albeit indirectly, that the Museum was later, in 1857, to acquire another of its natural history keepers, Albert Günther. And it was from Berlin, after Breslau and Königsberg, that Ernst Hartert was plucked by the youthful Walter Rothschild in 1892. By that time our national institutions had grown so desperate that they had been forced into a conscious policy of positively seeking foreigners, culminating in a special 'head-hunting' expedition to the Continent by the new Director of Kew, Thiselton Dyer. As a result of this policy Kew acquired the Austrian, Otto Stapf,[15] and the British Museum the Belgian, George Albert Boulenger. In recent years, after the end of the Second World War, the Museum temporarily had to revert to the practice, securing for the European herbarium a Latvian exile in Sweden, Alexandrs Melderis – the first successful raid on Sweden, it would appear, since Peter Collinson and John Ellis prevailed upon Linnaeus to send them Daniel Solander.

This tradition of importing expertise has profoundly enriched natural history in this country. It has meant that foremost international specialists have been placed in positions from which their work could have a maximum influence domestically. It has provided a very necessary corrective to our ingrained native parochialism and hastened the introduction of British naturalists to foreign literature and their acquiescence in foreign ideas. It was Hartert, by no accident, who effected the naturalisation here of zoological trinomials. It was Günther who opened the eyes of the Science Commission in 1872 to how much better the staffing of museums was organised in Germany. It was only a professional outsider like Günther, too, who had the unfettered boldness to write, in answer to one of Francis Galton's questionnaires: 'In English scientific society there is too much regard paid to rank and personal influence at the expense of real acquirement and merit.'[12] It is the duty of the alien to bring home to us unpleasant truths such as this – and none can bring them home to us more tellingly than he who has lived among us, and gained our respect, over a lengthy period of years. Compared with the opinions of a resident, the impressions of a visitor, like Kalm or von Uffenbach or Fabricius or Haller, however acute can always be brushed aside as mere tourist snapshots taken out of focus.

Another kind of social network which often had some undertones of patronage was that based on kinship. It is a familiar fact that large segments of the natural history world in Britain, particularly in the Victorian period, have been closely interrelated. So extensive are the ramifications of cousinship, indeed, that it is doubtful if we shall ever succeed in running them down in full. And beyond a certain point this is probably in any case wasted effort; for it is hard to believe that at more than one or two removes the ties of kinship had any practical social or political effect. Yet even within the comparatively restricted limits of more or less immediate family circles the size of the concatenations that come to light is such that they cannot fail to have exerted a powerful influence – if only in converting to the subject those who grew up in them or came into them through marriage. As actual job-securing agencies, however, they are easily overrated, and those conspicuous cases where posts passed down as if they had become the monopoly of one family – the Hookers, the Grays, the Sowerbys; or the Martyns and the Sibthorps with their father-to-son transmission of the chairs of botany at Cambridge and Oxford respectively – were probably the rule-proving exceptions.

Indeed, it may be not by unravelling the relationships within individual families so much as by comparing one family with another and looking for suggestive patterns that we have most of value to discover here. Has anyone spotted, for instance, how disproportionately frequently leading naturalists have had naturalist uncles – and, more particularly, naturalist mother's brothers? Thomas Gray had just such an uncle in Robert Antrobus, John Phillips in William Smith, Philip Henry Gosse in Thomas Bell, Professor F. O. Bower (though he soon forsook the field for the laboratory) in the Rev. F. O. Morris, J. H. Gurney in Sir John Lubbock, and – in our own day – James Fisher in A. W. Boyd. None of these, I feel quite sure, would ever have suspected that their relationship was of a kind to excite the interest of a social anthropologist. Yet the link between a boy and his mother's brother comes in for especial emphasis in numerous primitive societies, and why this should be so has been the cause of a good deal of arguing among anthropologists over the years. This argument is still unresolved, and no useful purpose would be served by rehearsing the various rival theses here. However, if the frequency with which this relationship shows up in natural history is more than just coincidence – as I suspect it is – then it is axiomatic that it reflects some rather special behavioural situation; and even though the cause of this may be peculiar to the

XVI

subject itself, it could well be instructive, and of more than parochial interest, to try to identify what this is. My own guess is that the explanation is really very simple: that mothers who have sons are the more likely to foster in them a liking for such a pursuit if they have already had the experience of growing up with brothers who delighted in just this enthusiasm. Fathers, by contrast, are much less liable to encourage their sons in a pursuit if the model for this has to be some other adult male than themselves.

Seemingly no less frequent, but more difficult to suggest an explanation for, are the marriages of naturalists to other naturalists' nieces. George Montagu was a nephew by marriage of the Earl of Bute; George Graves of William Curtis; the Rev. Andrew Bloxam, a leading pioneer of the study of brambles and roses, of Thomas Purton, the author of the *Midland Flora;* the Rev. Leonard Jenyns, the founder of the Bath Field Club, of Charles Daubeny, Professor of Botany and Geology at Oxford; Edward Forbes of the Rev. George Rooke, a president of the Berwickshire Naturalists' Club; F. H. Waterhouse, the librarian of the Zoological Society, of J. E. Gray; P. M. C. Kermode, the most prominent of the Isle of Man naturalists, of Robert Garner, the central figure in Staffordshire natural history — and no doubt quite a number of further cases could be found if one were to search really thoroughly. It is almost as if young naturalist suitors translated into their own special terms the time-honoured maxim: 'Don't marry money, but marry where money is' — substituting for 'money' 'natural history'. Could the explanation be that, while all those mothers were rearing naturalist sons on the model of their brothers, their husbands were no less busily infecting their sisters' daughters? Or was it, more simply, that a taste for the subject had a tendency to spill out right across an extended family and the very concentration of its occurrence as a result proved exceptionally alluring to the free-flying naturalist?

It is salutary, at any rate, to be reminded that, in being handed down, natural history is just as likely to travel diagonally as vertically. Sometimes, too, it may skip a generation: Dr George Fordyce — for example — that influential figure of the 1760s (of whom we badly need a good biographical study), turns out to have been the grandfather of the great botanical systematist, George Bentham. In cases like these it almost looks as if a bent for natural history builds up, as it were, in the blood, eventually surging forth all the more emphatically for the long postponement.

It is not just family backgrounds that we need to inspect closely, in order to uncover the web of motivation and influence. There are also certain wider backgrounds, whole miniature cultural traditions, which have been especially prone to produce naturalists over very lengthy periods.

The most striking of these, without question, were certain of the larger communities of weavers — most notably those in Spitalfields, in Norwich and in the environs of Manchester. From the first of these came Joseph Dandridge along with (one suspects) many of his fellow members of the first Aurelian Society, which he seems to have been primarily responsible for founding.[16] Afterwards, for a century and more, entomology remained endemic in that area; and it was from an obscure little bunch of these enthusiasts in Haggerston, in 1858, that there hatched out the elder parent of what is now the largest local grouping of naturalists probably anywhere in the world, the London Natural History Society. From the second, Norwich, came a strong ground-layer in which the outstanding contributions of that city to our subject were substantially rooted.[17] Quite a number of naturalists who made their name elsewhere will probably prove to have had their origins in this. Suggestively, for example, the cousins H. B. and B. B. Woodward — 'Humble Bee' and 'Bumble Bee' respectively (matching their characters) to their British Museum colleagues[18] — had a Norwich weaver as one of their great-grandfathers. From the third, Manchester, came oft-recurring outbreaks of numerous tiny societies from the 1760s onwards, which similarly did much to nourish a wider regional natural history. An inn bearing the name "The Naturalist" still stands in Prestwich in fitting commemoration of their one-time local prominence.

Trevelyan in his *English Social History* assures us that 'the love of gardening and of flowers that . . . became so characteristic of the English, was in part taught them by Huguenot refugees from the Low Countries, settled in Norwich and in London.'[19] It was the Huguenot weavers in Spitalfields, he points out, who started the first gardening societies in this country. But if it was to that wave of outstandingly enterprising immigrants that we owe this impressive and enduring substratum of interest, what was so special about them that they should have continued to take such a delight in collecting beautiful insects and searching out and studying flowers? Could it be that as the heirs to generations of designers and finishers of fine fabrics, representatives of a great craft tradition far more deep-seated and highly-developed than any English counterpart, they had acquired — or, possibly, even, had bred in them selectively — an ultra-sensitivity to the brilliant colourings and intricacies of form exhibited by nature? Certainly, it seems suggestive that in these same weaving communities there was also displayed a marked, and no less unexpected, fondness for geometry[20] Mathematical societies, as well as gardening and natural history ones, underwent a diaspora from Spitalfields.[21] It has been argued that weavers with a mathematical turn of mind would naturally tend to favour geometry — at the expense, for example, of algebra — as the loom ruled out the use of the hands and developed instead the power of visualising the 'constituent parts of figures which have never been exhibited to the eye.'[21] But it might equally be that with their family flair for pattern-making they also obtained a more than ordinary pleasure from the mere envisioning of shapes.

Clearly, we need to know much, much more about this particular strain in British natural history's heritage. If possible, it should be traced back across the Channel and studied there as well. For it could be that the Huguenot influence went far wider and it merely happens to have been its conspicuousness in such highly localised communities as the weavers that has caused it to be exclusively identified with these. Not all the refugees from France and Flanders were artisans: quite a number were professional people from what was then the most cultivated of any national middle class. In the early eighteenth century Huguenots were particularly favoured by the wealthier English as tutors for their sons, on account of their French, their famed industriousness and their uncompromising principles. Were there any naturalists among these, one wonders — bearing in mind that a taste for such a pursuit would have doubly recommended them to parents who shared this too, rather as that keen lepidopterist, the Duchess of Beaufort, used the pretext of a tutorship to have the help and company of William Sherard?

Just as with the Apothecaries Act of 1815, so with the Revocation of the Edict of Nantes in 1685:[22] there is something rather humiliating in the fact that it has been only as an entirely accidental by-product of greater happenings elsewhere that natural history in this country seems to have been the recipient of two of its most massive and far-reaching infusions. What course would the subject have taken in Britain without the irruption of the Huguenots or without compulsory examinations for all students of medicine in the recognising of herbs? There is interesting scope here for that so-called 'counter-factual' history that has lately become popular in some academic circles. Without the powerful aesthetic impulse that the Huguenots are presumed to have contributed, would the conversion of the subject

into something so much broader and more appealing than the mundane occupation of
herbalists and fowlers have been far longer retarded? Had they not awakened when they did
that fondness for flowers in us, might we have missed inventing that indispensable bridge to
Romanticism, the *jardin anglais?* Or do we underrate the lyrical ingredient in the 'herbarising' excursions of Thomas Johnson and his *Socii Itinerantes?* Is it just that we cannot sense
sufficiently in the writings of the sixteenth and seventeenth-century English pioneers — so
fragmentary though these are as well — that quiet undertone of delight that was to surface
so unmistakably in *The natural history and antiquities of Selborne?* In their hurry to collect
and list did our earliest naturalist forbears simply omit to communicate the feelings that
accompanied their searching for specimens? Even had their letters and journals come down
to us in greater quantity, would we for that matter recognise this always elusive element
in such deeply different modes of expression? Had they left us drawings or paintings instead
of simply having written, our conception of them might indeed be otherwise. Significantly,
the drawings of John White, the artist member of the first Virginia colony (and Governor of
the second), reveal that at least one Elizabethan Englishman took a delight in wildlife that
was unambiguously aesthetic.[23]

We forget too easily how extremely little we know of the natural history of this earliest
period. If William Turner and his compatriot John Falconer both learned the art of forming
a herbarium from Luca Ghini at Padua — as they seem likely to have done, for both were
pupils of his and all three are known to have been among the first to build up reference
collections[24] [25] — then it may well be that formal instruction in the field goes back at least
to the 1540s, almost a century before the earliest known 'herbarising' of the Society of
Apothecaries. A field class implies a modicum of social cement. It is by no means impossible, therefore, that the history of our subject as a social pursuit stems right from its
Turnerian dawn — even though the line of descent may not have been wholly within this
country.

It is too much to hope that there is evidence still lying undiscovered that will enable us to
establish the facts of so long distant a past. But there is almost certainly much more than
we suspect in our own and other countries' archives that could greatly illuminate more recent
periods. Mesmerised by print, we have tended to assume far too prematurely that nothing
more is now likely to be known. Till only the last few years no one seems to have supposed
that there was anything more that could be learnt about that 'Lady' Glanville after whom
the Glanville Fritillary is named and of whom Moses Harris had written in so highly tantalising a fashion. Even Canon Raven[3] could apparently make no progress down that minor
alley. Yet Dr Wilkinson[26] and — more particularly — Dr Bristowe,[27] [28] in turn, have
speedily reconstructed from a most impressive array of records the life-story of the woman
in a quite astonishing detail and fullness, revealing in the process that it was also one of a
moving poignancy. Never again after this can we safely wash our hands of even the mistiest
early figure. Somewhere in those formidable mounds of paper that now fill our libraries and
record offices almost to overflowing we can be reasonably sure that at least some further
evidence is lurking — and probably a good deal of it at that.

If two recent experiences are anything to go by, many a key missing item may yet turn
up — and in the least expected place. In 1956 the late J. E. Lousley[29] appealed for any
further information that might throw light on the intriguingly mysterious circumstances
surrounding the demise of the Botanical Society of London almost exactly a century earlier.
Six years later he was able to report the discovery of what was a clearly crucial document in
this connection: a letter from H. C. Watson to the Society's subsequent salvager,

J. G. Baker.[30] Ironically, this had lain all the time between the pages of a book that he had in his own library.

Then again, only the other day, Dr Wilkinson found documentary proof that it was, after all, the Northumberland squire P. J. Selby who gave the Doubleday brothers the idea of painting trees with a sugar mixture as a means of attracting moths — something that those of us who had looked into this matter had suspected but had despaired of ever clinching. The proof was in a letter written by Edward Doubleday in 1841 to a correspondent in America: and there it was, reposing among the latter's papers, in the Science Museum in Boston.[31]

Perhaps, then, there is still hope of finding a letter to or from James Sutherland confirming that Edinburgh was indeed copying Chelsea in laying on 'herbarisings' for its apprentices shortly after 1695. Or evidence that William Curtis actually put to use for natural history purposes that fishermen's oyster-dredge which he so carefully studied in 1786.[32] Or the telltale written chat that will finally confirm the still only circumstantial evidence that Hooker and Graham and Henslow *did* act in concert in the early 1820s in instituting their field classes at Glasgow, Edinburgh and Cambridge respectively — and in modelling these directly on the time-honoured 'herbarisings' of the London Apothecaries.

Nevertheless there is no escaping the sad truth that a great deal of this much-needed documentary material has already been lost irreparably. The very individuals to whom one is most inclined to look for enlightened action in this direction were often themselves indeed the worst offenders. Of J. E. Gray it has been written:[33] "He had little use for documentation, and seldom preserved his correspondence. Much of what has survived of his letters from foreign naturalists was rescued by Albert Gunther from his waste-paper basket in the last years". It was a general nineteenth-century practice, we find, to treat official correspondence as personal — and thereby has perished, with maddening thoughtlessness, the greater part of the records of the Natural History Department of the British Museum and of many another institution besides.

In this differential survival of the records lie pitfalls for the unwary historian. The most profusely documented people are by no means necessarily the most important, just as the most scantily represented may well be those of the greatest significance.[34] There is an ever-present temptation to generalise from what may be in reality the only very particular.

There are pitfalls, too, in other directions than this. With less than the full record to go on, it is all too easy to arrive at serious misjudgments of both people and institutions. Reputations can vary over time very considerably. Some people have bad spells in their careers, especially through ill-health. Before the days of pensions professional men tended to toil on in jobs for far longer they were really capable. Both Jameson and Gray have been unreasonably belayed in print by those who knew them only in their unhappy closing years, when they were clinging on to outmoded ideas almost as if this was a means of clinging on to life itself. Unfortunately, history is written by those who follow afterwards — and it is those much younger than themselves that tired and ill old men are most liable to infuriate. There is little doubt that many a reputation has suffered utterly unduly through this simple inability to live on to counteract traducers. Nor has it helped that we have all been far too ready to accept the verdicts of the survivors merely because these have been set down in the seeming authority of print. The systematic blackening of characters was a favourite pastime of the eighteenth century in particular: Richard Bradley[35] and John Hill[36] are two who have almost certainly been discounted quite unjustly in the eyes of an over-credulous posterity through this.

Terminology can change over time as well, and no less deceptively. Was the so-called 'botany' of eighteenth-century fashion anything more than a synonym for horticulture for the greater part of that era? How far indeed can we be sure that even the 'natural history' of those years, so glibly hailed as selling "the best of any books in England" (Collinson in a letter to Linnaeus in 1746) and as "the favourite study of the time" (the *Critical Review* in 1763), was what we recognise as this to-day — and not in large degree that mere fancying of animals and flowers to which the subject extends only on the shelves of all too many book-shops?

Such laxity of definition presents historians of our subject with a very special problem. If we cannot be sure what commentators mean by the popularity they are ever almost too anxious to see and report, how are we to obtain some tolerably accurate measure of the undoubted ups and downs which form so crucial a basis for understanding the effectiveness of naturalists at different periods? In particular, how are we to obtain this for periods when societies were more or less non-existent and we do not even have the crude yardsticks of the number of these being founded and their membership figures?

The answer, I am inclined to think, must lie in devising indices from counts of certain key types of published material: for example, the number of natural history books reviewed in general periodicals, the output of new titles at different levels of the market, the number of specialist journals launched. In studying the Victorian fern craze,[37] I was much struck by the helpfulness for this purpose of the lists of the successive editions of numerous popular works that N. Douglas Simpson so laboriously compiled for his monumental *Bibliographical index.*[38] Although this is confined to British botany, and just to items containing localised plant records at that, it offers a unique means of charting the rise and fall of publishing flurries in satisfyingly quantitative terms. In order to do this, of course, one first needs to have a reasonable idea of the relevant range of titles to look for — and not all topics have the comfortable discreteness of the naming and collecting of ferns. Yet the task can scarcely be regarded as impossible even in those branches of natural history which are not compar-ably served. Here surely, then, is an ideal opportunity for bibliographers to join together with historians in injecting into the subject this extra element of precision.

In proposing such a task, I am naturally assuming that some definite relationship exists between trends in publication and trends in the size of the following for all or any aspects of natural history. It is hard to believe that this is not so. Yet the relationship is probably very far from straightforward; and just to learn more exactly what forms it takes, and whether these themselves exhibit regularities, could be reward enough for all the work entailed. For there can be few other subjects so long, so profusely and so intimately bound up with its specialist literature and for this reason it is a field of peculiar potential for important general insights about the interdependence of publishing and learning.

At present we cannot provide an answer to so simple yet basic a question as: Do pub-lishers lead, or follow, the shifts of interest among naturalists? Probably they do both, at different times; but we lack solid evidence that this is so, as we lack in turn the necessary detailed case-histories that could lay bare the mechanisms. And even when we have these, we shall need to be rather cautious when we set about interpreting them. For books that set trends may do so wholly unexpectedly, taking by surprise both the author and the publishers. In such cases is it other than unhelpful to describe this as *leading* the market —

with its implication of a public taste intelligently anticipated? All it may really mean is that some publishers on some occasions are confident (or innocent) enough to wander from the commercial straight and narrow and expand their lists into hitherto unfamiliar territory. This is no more and no less than the hit-and-miss approach that is the standard mode of innovation of the small-scale producer: there is no reason why such a publisher should be praised, when he chances to be successful, for the shrewdness of his marketing. Indeed, natural history has always been too specialised a field for the general run of publishers to want to operate within it innovatively. Those who have settled down with it — and they have never been that many — have typically stayed unadventurous, churning out a dull, repetitive diet of hints for the beginner and collections of paintings dressed up as works of identification. In so far as they have been willing to experiment, this has customarily taken the form of merely reissuing a once-popular book and hoping to trade on the magic ingredients that are blithely assumed to have accounted for its success. It has only been when naturalists themselves have been able to exert the initiative that this uninspiring norm, with its chronically depressing effect on the general health of the subject, ever seems to have been departed from. Where bold new directions have been taken almost invariably there has been someone with a keen personal interest in the subject forcefully at the helm. For this reason it is of prime importance that we know more of the action and influence behind the scenes of leading publisher-naturalists — like John Van Voorst, Lovell Reeve, Robert Hardwicke and Harry Forbes Witherby. How much do we owe, in fact, to their surreptitious private generosity? Was it only because he was his brother-in-law, and because he was guaranteed against loss, that W. H. Lizars persisted so heroically with Sir William Jardine's long-unprofitable works? What benefit, if any, was there when a firm had a naturalist on its staff even in a humble capacity, like George Samouelle at Longman's? Questions like these call for the printing historians, in turn, to make some energetic sallies into our subject.

It is not only by studying trends in titles that we can expect to learn much about naturalists themselves at different periods: even the physical shape in which books were brought out may have something to tell us of significance.[39] Huge, sumptuous folios packed with magnificent plates are clearly never intended for the worker in the field: as Thomas Knowlton was moved to exclaim in disgust at that eighteenth-century torrent of these, they are "made for pompe, to fill a library, and more for outward show than real use, . . . having very little within".[40] To produce and sell them can only be feasible when natural history is high fashion and when there is also a sufficiency of affluent book-collectors of a sort who find admiring a preferable activity to reading. More valuably informative, by contrast, are volumes of an exceptional minuteness. Apart from the ones aimed specially at small children, there have been two separate and noteworthy waves of these: the first in the 1840s, when Babington's new *Manual of British botany* was evidently designed to slip into a saddle-bag or shooting-jacket pocket, and Moore's *Handbook of British ferns* was nicely characterised as "small enough to be carried in a lady's reticule"; and the second in the early years of this century, when Hayward's *Botanist's pocket book* accompanied the wider move to the brief synopses of field-characters rendered necessary for bird-watchers who now had binoculars to wield in place of guns. Only those with first-hand knowledge of the practical requirements of the field could have wrung out of publishers such tailor-made productions as these. And only if they were numerous enough, and sufficiently vocal about their needs, are they likely to have been able to prevail against the trade and its customary rigidities.

It is a truism that books are the lifeblood of a subject such as ours. And this is so not merely because we need them to identify what we see, to extend our knowledge or to have

XVI

an outlet for our data: it is also because they serve, and perhaps always have served, as the most effective means of attracting recruits. Out of a sample of teenage naturalists questioned recently about how they came to acquire their interest in the pursuit, three in every four gave the cause as books.[41]

So although I have laid much emphasis in this lecture on the need for historians to beware of the beguiling accessibility of print and to dig well down beneath its ever-treacherous surface, I return now, paradoxically, to nominate the scrutiny of the published literature as the candidate of the richest promise of all for deepening our understanding of how natural history really, basically works. For it is books and periodicals that constitute the most critical sinews of the subject, that in the end bind it together overall just as they also give it much of its marvellous elasticity. Natural history without publications would quickly become atomised, listless and banal. Without the spur of perpetuation in print most of this huge modern industry of record-making and observing would gradually run down and come to a halt. There would simply be too little inducement to warrant so much care and effort. And for the tiny, dedicated core who would still remain, those constant few in every generation who absolutely *have* to be naturalists, the subject would revert to its pre-Linnaean embryonic state: a matter of private journals, unco-ordinated investigations and unknown trips.

NOTES AND REFERENCES

[1] Ramsbottom, J., 1948. The natural history society. *Adv. Sci.* **5**: 57–64.

[2] A notable exception was the prominent Essex naturalist, R. Miller Christy (1861–1928). Well-versed in the use of records through a parallel interest in local history and genealogy, he was the author of a series of biographical papers based on research of a quite unprecedented depth and rigour.

[3] Raven, C. E., 1950. *John Ray, naturalist.* Cambridge. R. T. Gunther's *Early British botanists and their gardens* (Oxford, 1922) bears comparison with Raven's book in scholarly panache, but it is much more limited in scope and, being privately published, far less well-known. Its impact, consequently, has been negligible. The same is true of Gunther's lengthy series of volumes on *Early science in Oxford,* another pioneer production of exceptionally high standard.

[4] Pasti, G., *Jr.,* 1950. *Consul Sherard: amateur botanist and patron of learning, 1659–1728.* Unpublished doctoral thesis, Univ. of Illinois Library.

[5] Stearns, R. P., 1953. James Petiver, promoter of natural science, c. 1663–1718. *Proc. Amer. Antiq. Soc.* n.s. **62**: 243–365.

[6] Allen, D. E., 1976. *The naturalist in Britain: a social history* Allen Lane, London, p.20.

[7] Nichols, J., 1817–31. *Illustrations of the literary history of the eighteenth century.* Six vols. London.

[8] Wallis, F. J., 1974. Book subscription lists. *The Library* **29**: 255–286.

[9] Cannon, W. F., 1964. The role of the Cambridge Movement in early 19th century science, in *Proc. Tenth Internat. Congr. Hist. Sci.* (1962) 317–320 (Hermann, Paris); Scientists and broad churchmen: an Early Victorian intellectual network, *J. Brit. Studies* **4**: 65–88.

[10] Gunther, A. E., 1975. *A century of zoology at the British Museum through the lives of two keepers, 1815–1914* Dawsons of Pall Mall, London, p.440.

[11] Paden, W. D., 1964. Arthur O'Shaughnessy in the British Museum; or the case of the misplaced fuses and the reluctant zoologist. *Vict. Stud. Indiana Univ.* **8**: 7–30.

[12] Gunther, A. E., op. cit., p. 367.

[13] The Royal Botanic Gardens, Kew are the chief legacy of this accidental shared enthusiasm.

[14] Gray in litt. to Thomas Wharton, 31 Jan. 1761: Letter 331 in *Correspondence of Thomas Gray,* ed. P. Toynbee and L. Whibley, Clarendon Press, Oxford, **2**: 725.

[15] Recruited for Kew in 1891 while working under Kerner. Subsequently Keeper of the Herbarium and Library, 1908–22.

[16] Allen, D. E., 1966. Joseph Dandridge and the first Aurelian Society *Ent. Rec. & J. Var.* **78**: 89–94.

[17] Smith, J. E., 1804. Biographical memoirs of several Norwich botanists. *Trans. Linn. Soc. Lond.* **7**: 295–301.

[18] Gunther, A. E., op. cit., p. 370 note.

[19] Trevelyan, G. M., 1944. *English social history* Longmans, Green & Co., London, p. 247.

[20] "Pen-and-Ink", 1850. Cultivation of geometry in Lancashire. *Notes & Queries* Ser.1, **2**: 8. T. T. Wilkinson, 1850. On the origin and progress of the study of geometry in Lancashire. *ibid:* 57–60.

[21] "Pen-and-Ink", 1850. On the cultivation of geometry in Lancashire. *ibid.*: 436–438.

[22] Though, strictly speaking, it is misleading to identify the Huguenot immigration just with that particular year and event. In part, too, the weaving communities were made up of the descendants of earlier waves of immigrants from Flanders, who may also have had pronounced natural history leanings. It may well be significant that Mathias de l'Obel (1538–1616), one of the chief formative influences on early English botany, came here as a refugee from civil war in Flanders. James Cole, too, his botanist son-in-law, was engaged in the silk trade and evidently maintained intimate relations with the Low Countries up until his death (R. T. Gunther, *Early British botanists. . . .*, p. 247).

[23] Hutton, Paul & Quinn, D. B., 1964. *The American drawings of John White 1577–1590.* 2 vols. British Museum, London & Chapel Hill.

[24] Randall, J. H., *Jr.,* 1961. *The school of Padua and the emergence of modern science.* Padua.

[25] Saint-Lager, J. B., 1885. Histoire des herbiers. *Ann. Soc. bot. Lyon* **13**: 1–120.

[26] Wilkinson, R. S., 1966. Elizabeth Glanville, an early English entomologist. *Ent. Gaz.* **17**: 149–160.

[27] Bristowe, W. S., 1967. The life of a distinguished woman naturalist, Eleanor Glanville (circa 1654–1709). *Ent. Gaz.* **18**: 202–211.

[28] Bristowe, W. S., 1975. More about Eleanor Glanville (1654–1708). *Ent. Gaz.* **26**: 107–117.

[29] Lousley, J. E., 1956. The Botanical Society of London. *Proc. Bot. Soc. Brit. Is.* **2**: 102.

[30] Lousley, J. E., 1962. Some new facts about the early history of the Society. *ibid.* **4**: 410–412.

[31] Wilkinson, R. W., 1976. Prideaux J. Selby, the Doubledays and the modern method of 'sugaring'. *Ent. Rec. & J. Var.* **88**: 23–25.

[32] Curtis, W. H., 1941. *William Curtis, 1746–1799, botanist and entomologist* Warren & Sons, Winchester, p. 68.

[33] Gunther, A. E., op. cit., p. 165.

[34] Joseph Dandridge is perhaps the best illustration of this: as he left no known written works, not even in a popular periodical, he has been almost completely overlooked. Yet he appears to have been the driving-force in English entomology throughout most of the first half of the eighteenth centry. See in particular W. S. Bristowe, 1967. The life and works of a great English naturalist, Joseph Dandridge (1664–1746). *Ent. Gaz.* **18**: 73–89.

[35] For a counter to the traditional 'Martyn' view of Bradley see H. Hamshaw Thomas, 1937. The rise of natural science in Cambridge. *Cambr. Rev.,* 434–436. It was the discovery at Cambridge of Bradley's lecture notes that led to this first step in the gradual restoring of his reputation.

[36] Professor George S. Rousseau of the University of California is engaged on a major study of Hill which promises a similar reinstatement.

[37] Allen, D. E., 1969. *The Victorian fern craze: a history of pteridomania.* Hutchinson, London.

[38] Simpson, N. Douglas, 1960. *A bibliographical index of the British flora.* Bournemouth.

[39] Bertrand H. Bronson, in his *Printing as an index of taste in eighteenth century England,* New York Public Library, 1963, p. 11, has pointed out that, as the reading public swelled to take in lower social levels, the size of books in general tended to decrease, resulting in far fewer folios and quartos and many more octavos and duodecimos at the end of the eighteenth century as compared with the beginning.

[40] Knowlton in litt. to Dr. Richard Richardson, 31 Oct. 1736; printed in *Extracts from the literary and scientific correspondence of Richard Richardson, M.D., F.R.S. . . . . . .,* ed. Dawson Turner, Yarmouth, 1835. p. 350.

[41] Jones, B., 1976. Natural history books in schools. *Nat. Hist. Book Reviews* **1**: 6–8.

XVII

J. F. M. DOVASTON,
AN OVERLOOKED PIONEER OF FIELD ORNITHOLOGY

JOHN FREEMAN MILWARD DOVASTON (1782–1854) features in the *Dictionary of National Biography* mainly on the strength of his reputation as a minor Romantic poet. It could be argued that he has a far worthier claim to inclusion for his contributions to early nineteenth-century ornithology. Like so many early workers, his importance has been overlooked due to the fact that he published no books.[1] Even the few papers of his that appeared in print were all written in a popular vein, some of them even under a pseudonym. The discovery that hidden in these are accounts, all too tantalisingly brief, of practices and experiments in ornithology that up till now have been generally assumed to be far more recent in origin underlines the importance for historians of science of not only exploring the relatively less learned early journals, but taking care to scan the frankly popular and apparently quite ephemeral matter so often contained in them.

The journal in this instance is Loudon's *Magazine of Natural History*, which began in May 1828, appearing at first bimonthly, price 3s. 6d. It was aimed originally at young people, but soon began to attract such a large following among naturalists of all ages and became so generally read that by 1835 it had turned into a medium for quite substantial scientific papers of wide general interest. In its pages in that year, for example, were published the important speculations of Edward Blyth, recently claimed as a crucial yet unacknowledged source of Darwin's main evolutionary hypotheses.[2] Previous to this more learned period, however, there were many contributions of a light-hearted or more or less trivial nature; and one of the more frequent suppliers of these was Dovaston, either under his own name or under an anagram of it, " Von Osdat ". On the occasion of his first piece, dated May 1829, he explained that he had written it " principally to gratify the urgent entreaties of some students of nature in these parts; particularly those of my amiable friend Mr. Richard Tudor, surgeon, who, I may almost say, can neither eat, drink, nor even sleep without your Magazine ".[3]

" In these parts " refers to the Shrewsbury district and the nearby parts of North Wales. Dovaston[4] was the owner of a small estate, known as " The Nursery ", in the village of West Felton, midway between Shrewsbury and Oswestry. The estate was the creation of his father, John Dovaston (1740–1808), an equally accomplished man of wide culture, who after becoming interested in botany on a visit to the West Indies built up his ancestral seat as a highly prosperous tree-nursery, catering for the fashion for planting then prevalent among the landed aristocracy and gentry. His son progressively improved and extended it, and though never wealthy by the standards of the time[5] he latterly lived the amply comfortable life of a bachelor country gentleman. In his way of life, his unexpectedly radical views and his mild, if rumbustious, eccentricities he strongly recalls Charles Waterton, his Yorkshire contemporary, with whom he shared a passion for birds and a highly untypical insistence on their never being shot at or molested within the bounds of his estate.[6] The two appear to have exchanged letters only once or twice,[7] however, and Dovaston was certainly no traveller: he seems indeed to have left home only very seldom and reluctantly, proclaiming as late as 1838 that he had never yet been on a railway train and had no great desire in fact to go on one.[8]   On the other hand, he was no recluse.   He seems to have led an active social life, was much in demand at amateur theatricals and sat for some years on Shrewsbury Town Council.   In 1814, when still only thirty-two, he was presented with the Freedom of the Borough of Oswestry—then a place of only some 3,500 souls— presumably on the strength of his personal popularity and the national reputation he had won with his first volume of poems.

Like his father he combined wide literary and musical interests with manual skill and a highly intelligent approach to natural history.   He was a dilettante, certainly, but none the less one with a keenly enquiring mind.   His education had included both Oswestry Grammar School and Shrewsbury School (then at a low ebb), followed by Oxford, to which he went on an exhibition—and where he acquired the nickname, on his own claim,[9] of " Crazy Jack of Christ Church ". He then entered the Inner Temple and was called to the Bar in 1807, the same year in which he took his M.A.   Finding he hated practice, however, he abandoned it not long after, having meanwhile succeeded to the family estate.   Unlike that of the average country gentleman of the time, therefore, his mind was a well-trained one and, perhaps even more unusually, he did not let it rust, favouring intellectual pursuits in place of field sports.   To these twin facts we owe the singular originality of his work.

By the age of forty his knowledge of birds had clearly become very considerable.   About this time he had rounded off a tour of the Lake District with a special journey to Newcastle to do homage to Thomas Bewick, famous by then for his wood-cuts and his enormously popular *History of British Birds*.   A friendship had at once sprung up and over the next year Dovaston sent " large heaps " of additions and corrections to the fifth edition.   He also procured many orders for Bewick's works among his friends, passed on specimens and notes to him from his naturalist neighbours and even went so far as to draft the preface for the sixth edition,[10] which came out in 1826.

It was in the same letter with which he enclosed this preface that he first described what he termed his " Ornithotrophe " (an ingenious pun on " trough " and the Greek word for a trophy, meaning a conspicuous display).   This was the name he had coined for a wooden trencher, " with a rim, and perforated slightly to let out the rain ", which was suspended by three harpsichord wires from an iron hook or ring designed to move along a cord stretched between two trees outside his study window.   " This I trim with food, and with a wand from within, can slide it to and fro along the line. . . .   I have also perches about and near it, and fasten half-picked bones and flaps of mutton to the trees."   In this way he had found a means of " alluring even the shyer birds close to my residence, particularly in the winter months ".   On one snowy day, he reported, he had counted as many as twenty-three species at it.[11]   This is the earliest-known instance of a feeding-device for wild birds.   By the following December some of his neighbours were copying his example[12] and, thanks to the publicity Bewick had given it in his book, " many gentle-minded people " erected similar devices in the course of the next nine years.[13]   It is not clear whether this interest persisted.   Waterton, certainly, disapproved of feeding wild birds.   Bewick was different: " I have, all my life, busied myself with

J. DOVASTON—A PIONEER OF FIELD ORNITHOLOGY   279

feeding Birds ", he told Dovaston, " but I had not (like you) the same kind of apparatus nor convenience of doing all this so well as I wished—to obtain all the information in my power, respecting Birds, in younger Days."[12] Loudon, some years later, played around with the idea desultorily[14]; in 1877 the Rev. F. O. Morris wrote a letter to *The Times* to try to arouse public interest; but it was not, it seems, until the long frost of the winter of 1890–91 that the practice became, for the first time, very widespread.   All the leading newspapers that winter joined in advocating it, and as a measure of their success one dealer in bird-seed reported that he had never before sold so much in small quantities, which he presumed was being bought for feeding to wild species.[15]   Bird-tables duly became common in the 'nineties.   It is not clear how far they had been in use before this—one writer in 1894 refers to having used one " for a great number of years "[16]—and it is clearly unsafe to assume any connection between these and Dovaston's device.   Even so, the conception of enticing birds by artificial means so that they can be carefully observed for scientific purposes from close at hand (which represents one of the most fundamental steps forward taken by man in his behaviour towards wild creatures) may have passed down in a direct line from its origin at West Felton.

Closely associated with the idea of attracting birds to the house with food is the practice of encouraging them to nest round about by the provision of artificial nesting-holes and -boxes.   Dovaston was also using these.   " The *foraminous* birds ", he wrote to Bewick in 1825,[11] " I accommodate with artificial building-places in the woods; and others after their kind."   In a later note he makes it clear that this extended to putting up pots and boxes on walls and trees, in which birds came and nested freely.[17]   In this practice, however, he undoubtedly had predecessors; it is quite possible, indeed, that the idea had merely been borrowed.   The method had been utilised in various parts of Europe since the late Middle Ages as a means of ensuring a more ready supply of wild birds' eggs for food.[18,19]   In the United States, rather similarly, small boxes on the tops of poles had long been erected in gardens for wrens to nest in,[18] because of the large number of injurious insects they were known to destroy[20]; and this practice seems to have extended to encouraging other kinds of birds to nest in gardens, perhaps for more purely aesthetic reasons.   (Bartram, for example, had a box for martins in his garden.)   Charles Waterton, there seems little doubt, was the first person to put up artificial nesting-places in Britain, at least for non-utilitarian reasons.   This was in 1813, on his return from a trip to Guiana, " having suffered myself and learned mercy ".[21]   He began with barn-owls and went on to extend the idea to making nesting-holes for starlings. Precisely when he moved on to boxes is not clear; but, certainly, there were numbers of these hidden in the trees on his estate in later years.[22]   He, too, may possibly have borrowed the idea.   They were being used in Germany for scientific observation by 1836[23] and may well have been quite widespread on the Continent even before that date.   Like feeding the birds, however, they did not apparently catch on, and it was not until the 'nineties, again, with the main upsurge of protectionist enthusiasm, that their value was rediscovered.[24]   Most of the models even then were at first imported from Germany.

A third outcome of Dovaston's wish to study birds closely without resorting to the usual device of shooting them was that he customarily made use of a field-glass.   This, which he jocularly termed his " Ornithoscope ", was also described to Bewick sometime in the second half of 1825.   It was " a small spy-glass, which he can instantly and silently draw out to three distinct foci. . . . By this he has acquired numerous points hitherto unknown."[25]   Again, however, like nest-boxes, this was not an altogether original device for bird-watching, even though Dovaston may have hit upon the idea quite independently. John Denson, who acted in effect as editor of the *Magazine of Natural History* for Loudon, revealed that he had been using one since about 1823.[26]   A third observer, writing from Epping Forest in 1830,[27] " having long felt an abhorrence at taking away the life of any of the brute creation ", drew the attention of the readers of the same magazine to the value of " a good pocket telescope, magnifying about thirty times ", which he found afforded an excellent view of various shy birds.   It was possibly after reading this that Waterton acquired his " excellent eight and twenty guinea telescope ", a very powerful instrument mounted on a moving table in his study, through which he watched waterfowl on his lake in 1832[28] and to which in later years he became " inestimably indebted, for a wholesome correction of many early conceived and erroneous impressions of the habits of various birds".[29]   Two years later he was carrying "a good telescope " with him while studying sea birds at Flamborough Head."[28]   Others did likewise: Edward Blyth, for example, for scrutinising bill colour in bramblings,[30] and a certain J. S. Brown, apparently a friend of Denson's, who was able to examine a crossbill very minutely because " I had my telescope with me (which, indeed, I always take out on my rambles) . . . I never carry a gun, or I could easily have obtained it."[31] Not everyone, it is clear, shot birds in those days—or even needed to shoot them, to establish identification—as up till now we have always been led to suppose.   That field-glasses (and their concomitant, skilled field observation of the living bird) did not come into general use for so long we can blame on the sheer bloodthirstiness of Victorian ornithologists and the corrupting influence of over-vaunted field sports and of mass-produced cheap guns. Even in the " dark ages " of the middle 1850's one or two, we find, still used them, like Robert Garner, the Staffordshire naturalist, who regularly carried " an opera or pocket-glass " for watching birds on his excursions[32]; or like Thoreau in New England, who exchanged the gun for a telescope in 1854. Even so, it was not until 1880, coinciding with the first appearance of the vanguard of modern field ornithologists with their general acceptance of skilled observation as a substitute for reckless killing, that advice began to appear in books that the observer should " provide himself with a first-class telescope or field-glass, which, like his note-book, should be his inseparable companion ".[33]

Dovaston's innovations did not stop merely at gadgets.   He also carried out numerous experiments on behaviour.   He had tried growing mistletoe " with tolerable success " on twenty-three different sorts of trees[34]; he enclosed a piece of grassland in order to make observations on hares[35]; he attempted to record bird songs by musical notation—only to find the task impossible (only cuckoos and blackbirds, in his experience, sometimes emit recognisable notes).[34] More interestingly, he once caught a pair of swallows and their young in an anglers' landing-net and fastened round their necks rings made of very fine 'cello wire.   When four of them reappeared the following year, this furnished him with the proof he sought that migrants return to, and build in, the very places they have left.   He then followed this up with a more sophisticated experiment: to the neck of one he added a thin piece of copper inscribed in Latin *Quo abis a Salopia*? (" Where hast thou gone to from Shropshire? "), hoping that it would be returned to him in due course.   Unfortunately, it never was; and he lost heart.[34,36]   Once more, though original, this was not the first idea along such lines.   Even if the many early falconers and owners of water-fowl who marked their birds with name-plates or -bands as proof of ownership be excluded, there are other, previous instances of bird-marking in Britain, in America and on the Continent (starting with Ludolf of Sudheim, who antici-pated Dovaston's basic experiment, banding swallows' legs, around the year 1350).   Many other marking experiments, mainly out of scientific curiosity, took place more or less haphazardly during the rest of the century.   Modern bird-ringing is regarded as having begun only in 1899 with the work of Hans Mortensen, a Danish schoolmaster, whose aluminium rings were the first to bear an adequate address for recovery as well as a serial number.   Once more, however, the real point of interest is that Dovaston had conceived the idea within a wider conceptual and technical framework of remarkably modern out-look.

Dovaston's ultimate achievement was to stumble, albeit dimly, upon the phenomenon of bird territory.   This seems to have occurred in the winter of 1830–31, when as a result of carefully observing the behaviour of robins at his bird-table he became " confirmed in the opinion advanced by an ingenious friend, that each bird of this species has a regular beat of his own, to which he thinks himself justly entitled, and the pugnacity which he exerts is to expel some daring intruder's raid on his own personal property "[37].   Two years later he expanded on this:

> " I am certain all birds have their particular beats, or haunts; and very rarely intrude on those of others; when the invaded never omit repelling the forcible entry, by taking the law into their own hands.   Robins have their own beats, even on the different sides of a small cottage: there are four dis-tinct pairs of robins around this house; and one is attached exclusively to my brewhouse.   In the wide and wild woods, too, I am certain they keep to the same beats; as I noticed for months by the singularly loud, and unusual sort of, song in one belonging to the great cedar of Lebanon near my south entrance: and another, while I was working in a wood, lit on the handle of my spade . . . ; this I chanced to catch, and, marking him with a scissors by a black cross on his breast, I found he continually kept to the same spot."[36]

Later still, he was pronouncing quite confidently that a bird " will never leave his beat. . . .   Of this I have made repeated trials.   I keep suspended trenchers on which I feed birds; and sometimes I mark them; and have even noticed that birds visiting that at the east window of my book-room will not visit that by the south window of my dining-room, nor the contrary."[34]   These birds were caught for marking at the trenchers in a special trap cage.   The feeding-device thus served a doubly useful scientific purpose.

Unknown to him, several earlier writers, beginning with the Italian G. P. Olina in 1622, had already noted that robins have special territories from which rivals are excluded.[38]   Dovaston, however, it will be noticed, went further than this: he did some preliminary mapping of territories and secured proof by means of marking experiments.   Probably no one before him, either, had established quite how sharply the boundaries of such territories can be demarcated.   His remarks, nevertheless, fell on deaf ears and it was not till the elaborate marking experiments of J. P. Burkitt in the early 1920's that the study of territory in robins was carried any further forward.

Had there been more people like Dovaston, and had there only existed some central organising person or body to seize on what was important and ensure for it the necessary currency, field ornithology in Britain might have achieved its technical " take-off " some sixty years earlier than it did.   In many ways at that period the thinking was already astonishingly modern.   In 1834, for example, one writer even went so far as to propose the noting of passage movements of sea-birds " by the cooperative Agency of Naturalists residing near Headlands on the Coasts "[39]—in other words, what today we know as " network research ", the central achievement of modern field natural history.   The picture we are left with, after reading the words of these progressives, is a very different one from the traditional picture, with its canvas entirely populated with gunmen.   It must heighten interest, too, in the sixth edition of Bewick to know that so much of the additional information it enshrines was obtained by methods that were so remarkably advanced for their time.   Most of all, it calls in question at least one authoritative view, that " the value of the *History of British Birds* rests on its wood-cuts alone ".[40]

[1] His main scientific publication was a list of local birds in W. A. Leighton's *Guide to Shrewsbury* (Shrewsbury, 1850).

[2] Loren C. Eiseley, " Charles Darwin and Edward Blyth ", *Proc. Amer. Phil. Soc.*, Vol. 103 (1959), pp. 94–158.

[3] *Mag. Nat. Hist.*, Vol. 1 (1829), p. 219.

[4] Apart from his published writings and the brief account in the *Dictionary of National Biography*, there are various allusions to him scattered through local books, magazines and newspapers.   In addition there are two valuable collections of letters: twenty-six written to him by Thomas Bewick in 1824–28, now in the British Museum (Egerton MSS. 3147), and some twenty-seven written by him to the Rev. Thomas Archer, a friend from Oxford days, between 1805 and 1844, now in Shropshire Record Office (MS. 1422).   The latter, hitherto unknown, make excellent reading.   They are written in a somewhat florid style, with much gusto and humour, and are often highly self-revealing.   He is also known to have kept a journal of copious notes (*cf. Mag. Nat. Hist.*, Vol. 5 (1832), p. 425) and with his friend J. E. Bowman wrote a journal of their tour in Scotland in 1825, intended to be kept as a family heirloom (Bowman to Dovaston [among Bewick letters], 18 Jan. 1827; Bewick to Dovaston, 2 July 1827).   The latter of these is now among the Bowman family papers in the possession of Sir John Bowman, of Newbury (K. B. Thomas, *Medical Hist.*, Vol. 10 (1966), p. 245).   His library of 3,250 volumes was sold by auction at Shrewsbury in February, 1910.

[5] Ten years before his death he described his income as rather more than £1000 per annum (Dovaston to Maria Archer, Mar. 1844).

[6] Bewick to Dovaston, 15 Aug. 1827.

[7] Cf. *Mag. Nat. Hist.*, Vol. 6 (1833), p. 6.

[8] Dovaston to Archer, June 1838.

[9] Dovaston to Archer, July 1830.

[10] Bewick to Dovaston, 26 Nov. 1825: " My friends must admire and approve of " the preface " which we all ardently wish to see in print."   Dovaston had a far readier pen and doubtless volunteered this task in order to speed up work on the new edition.

[11] Quoted by Bewick, *A History of British Birds*, Ed. 6 (Newcastle & London, 1826), Vol. 1, pp. iv–v footnote.

[12] Bewick to Dovaston, 21 Dec. 1826.

[13] *Mag. Nat. Hist.*, Vol. 6 (1833), p. 3.   There is a remarkable parallel to this in the almost contemporaneous discovery by entomologists of the value of strong-smelling sugar as a means of attracting hitherto scarcely-seen types of moths.   In 1832 the Doubleday brothers caught no fewer than sixty-nine species in this way.   The fashion was slow to catch on, but eventually caused a revolution in collecting.   At least one early user saw the possibilities of the method as a means of studying the duration of various species and the varying ratios between the sexes, but entomologists of that period were not as enlightened as ornithologists and this scientific avenue seems to have been left by them unexplored.   For a full account

see D. E. Allen, " The origin of sugaring ", *Entomologist's Record*, Vol. 77 (1965), pp. 117–121.

¹⁴ See, for example, a letter of his to Waterton in 1839 reproduced in the latter's *Essays on Natural History*, Second Series (London, 1844), p. 11.

¹⁵ *Nature Notes*, Vol. 2 (1891), p. 33.

¹⁶ G. T. Rope, *Nature Notes*, Vol. 5 (1894), p. 4.

¹⁷ *Mag. Nat. Hist.*, Vol. 5 (1832), p. 502.

¹⁸ J. Rennie, *The Architecture of Birds*, Ed. 2 (London, 1844), p. 339 *et seq.*

¹⁹ B. Campbell, " Nestbox ", in *A New Dictionary of Birds*, ed. Sir A. Landsborough Thomson (London, 1964), p. 526.

²⁰ Anon., *Time's Telescope*, Vol. 2 (1815), p. 143.

²¹ *Mag. Nat. Hist.*, Vol. 5 (1832), pp. 9–15.

²² R. Hobson, *Charles Waterton: His Home, Habits, and Handiwork*, Ed. 2 (London, 1867), p. 33.

²³ Cf. *Mag. Nat. Hist.*, N.S., Vol. 2 (1838), pp. 399–406.

²⁴ *Nature Notes*, Vol. 8 (1897), p. 77; J. R. B. Masefield, *Wild Bird Protection and Nesting Boxes* (Leeds, 1897).

²⁵ Bewick, *op. cit.*, p. iv footnote.

²⁶ *Mag. Nat. Hist.*, Vol. 4 (1831), pp. 450, 464.

²⁷ A.B., " A new mode of examining birds, etc.", *Mag. Nat. Hist.*, Vol. 4 (1831), p. 145. The initials may well have been those of the Rev. Andrew Bloxam, later to become a well-known botanist, whose father several times visited Dovaston about this time (*cf.* Dovaston to Archer, Jan. 1831 and May 1832).

²⁸ *Mag. Nat. Hist.*, Vol. 8 (1835), pp. 162–165, 166–169, 361–364.

²⁹ Hobson, *op. cit.*, p. 312.

³⁰ *Mag. Nat. Hist.*, N.S., Vol. 1 (1837), p. 132.

³¹ *Ibid.*, Vol. 9 (1836), p. 202.

³² [R. Garner], *Holiday Excursions of a Naturalist* (London, 1867), pp. 95, 124.

³³ C. Dixon, *Rural Bird Life* (London, 1880), p. 354.

³⁴ Dovaston, *Three Popular Lectures; One on Natural History, and Two on National Melody* (Shrewsbury, 1839), pp. 5–29. These lectures were delivered three times in all in the winter of 1837–38, one audience being Shropshire & North Wales Natural History & Antiquarian Society, founded in 1835.

³⁵ H. E. Forrest, " Two old Shropshire naturalists ", *Trans. Caradoc & Severn Valley Field Club* for 1910, Vol. 5 (1911), pp. 125–135. I have not been able to locate the source of Forrest's statement.

³⁶ Dovaston, " Chit-chat. No. II ", *Mag. Nat. Hist.*, Vol. 6 (1833), pp. 1–11.

³⁷ ' Von Osdat ' [Dovaston], " The Robin ", *ibid.*, Vol. 4 (1831), pp. 410–412.

³⁸ Details of the various precursors of H. Eliot Howard, the true founder of territory theory, are given in D. Lack's *The Life of the Robin*, Ed. 4 (London, 1965). Dr Lack has confirmed (*in litt.*, June 1966) that Dovaston's work has till now remained quite unknown to him.

³⁹ J. D. Salmon, *Mag. Nat. Hist.*, Vol. 7 (1834), p. 573.

⁴⁰ W. H. Mullens, " Some early British ornithologists and their works. VIII. Thomas Bewick (1753–1828) and George Montagu (1751–1815) ", *British Birds*, Vol. 2 (1909) pp,. 351–361.

XVIII

The plagiarisms of Thomas Henry Cooper

Passing off someone else's observations as one's own is a form of plagiarism to which natural history is particularly exposed.[1] Less gross than the manufacturing of records or the attribution of false provenances to specimens, too often it goes unnoticed. For as with putting one's name to someone else's written work, it grades off into mere carelessness in the matter of acknowledgement and on this more charitable assumption its perpetrators tend to evade reproof. Yet the damage it can do to the cause of learning is surely more profound than plagiarism of the usual literary type, inasmuch as records form the very raw material of natural history and laborious edifices of error may be constructed out of them should they be incorrect in the first place. Through plagiarism ill-founded or dubious records may acquire an undeserved reputability and so become embedded in the literature. Equally, quite valid and useful ones may be placed under needless suspicion and so be lost to knowledge irretrievably.

Where the matter misattributed is at all extensive, there is the likelihood of serious historical distortion too. In certain cases the crediting to a wrong author of just a single work may be enough to alter a whole perspective while at the same time conferring a spurious eminence on the individual in question.

Thomas Henry Cooper is a striking example of one who has benefited from this. On the strength of his responsibility for *The botany of the county of Sussex* (1834)[2] Victorian compilers came to class him among their "Authors of County Floras" and on the strength of this in turn he qualified for inclusion in the *Dictionary of national biography*.[3] Yet, in reality, his botanical attainments were of the slightest and his obscurity among his contemporaries was such that (quite exceptionally in that work for so recent a figure) there is obvious uncertainty in the *DNB* entry about even his very identity.[4]

In order to try to understand his plagiarising it is first necessary to establish who he was. Here his Sussex list provides a helpful starting-point: for it is evident from this that he was a man of some scholarly education, which suggests at once membership either of the cultivated landed gentry or of one of the learned professions. Of the latter, medicine stands out as the likeliest candidate, in view of the marked tendency at that period for doctors to acquire an interest in botany through encountering it as part of their training. And, sure enough, in two of the standard medical reference works [5,6] someone of this name does indeed appear whom it has proved possible to identify as the botanist with the additional help of the Society of Apothecaries' Licentiate records.[7] An obituary notice [8] of the Sussex antiquary, William Durrant Cooper, which mentions a 'Dr T. H. Cooper' as a surviving brother, gives independent confirmation.

From these and further sources it emerges that Cooper was born in 1813[9], the second of four sons of Thomas Cooper and Lucy Elizabeth Durrant. His father, a solicitor in Lewes, came of a line of Sussex squires long settled at Icklesham. The eldest son was sent to Lewes

Grammar School, which at that time enjoyed a high reputation, and probably the other brothers went there too.

At fifteen the eldest left school to be articled in his father's firm and was soon combining a keen interest in political reform with a passion for antiquarian pursuits. These found joint reflection in a study of the county's Parliamentary history which he contributed to a two-volume work by a local Unitarian minister, T. W. Horsfield, *The history, antiquities, and topography of the county of Sussex.* In the preface to this, which bears the date September 1834, Horsfield makes clear that William Durrant Cooper's help was in fact very extensive more generally, the accounts of several of the parishes being his work alone. As he was at that time only twenty-one and most of the knowledge he drew upon was presumably acquired over a considerable period previously, he was patently of outstanding precociousness in his scholarly ability. The section on the botany of the county, which his brother was prevailed upon to provide for the Appendix, would have needed to be brilliant indeed if it was not to suffer by comparison. It is possible therefore to see William Durrant as the archetypal over-shadowing elder child, provoking in the other a compulsive emulation which might account for the pattern of behaviour in his subsequent life.

By that time Thomas Henry, similarly apprenticed at fifteen (to a surgeon in Marylebone),[7] was a medical student at the recently-founded University of London, taking botany as one of his subsidiary subjects, with John Lindley as his professor.[9] This explains how he had come by the 'several very judicious observations' for which Lindley is thanked in the introduction to his Sussex list. It also explains how he was able to secure election to the Linnean Society in May 1834 at so early an age and before having published anything: it was Lindley, his Fellowship certificate reveals, who put him up and who doubtless obtained the impressive list of seconders headed by George Bentham. Apart from an ordinary teacher's pride in his pupil, Lindley may have seen this as a way of enhancing the prestige of the new "outsiders' " university.

The botany of the county of Sussex, a mere seventeen pages in length, must have been published later in that year, for 'F.L.S.' appears after his name on the title-page. It had not in fact been intended to appear till 1835, when it was to be just one contribution among many tucked away in Horsfield's massive book. But this was altogether too subdued for this par-ticular author's taste — as well as perhaps too long to wait — and he accordingly had a few copies offprinted and bound up for private distribution in advance.[10] The Linnean Society and W. J. Hooker (then still at Glasgow) were two of the select recipients. Separately pagi-nated and bearing a different date, these must be counted as a distinct, earlier publication.

The work itself is notable for the novel device of presenting the information in three dif-ferent ways in succession: first by habitats, then topographically, finally in accordance with the Natural System. The ecological emphasis is interesting and, for the time, unusual, albeit not taken very far. The general impression, indeed, is one of a superficial modishness, just the kind of clever student's play with fashionable concepts that so often passes for a properly deep knowledge of a subject. True, a long list of localities for the rarer species in the county follows, but except in just one or two cases no authorities for these are cited, though we are assured that they have been 'in many instances confirmed by personal observation'. Thanks are extended 'particularly' to William Borrer, of Henfield, 'for his communications in refer-ence to this list'.

Sixteen years later Borrer himself was to paint a very different picture. The list, he declared, had been 'taken almost entirely, as to the names and stations of the plants, from a catalogue which I had supplied'.[11] One of the foremost field botanists of his generation,[12] characterised by H. C. Watson, that severest of judges, as 'an exact and cautious observer, a truthful describer and faithful recorder of what he saw',[13] a country gentleman and magistrate of ample means, Borrer was hardly a person to make such an allegation idly. Rather, he would appear to have been if anything a man of uncommon restraint. What is more, at the time he wrote those words — words which could have been actionable — Cooper was still a fellow member of his in the Linnean Society and for all he knew continued to see the specialist literature. It must therefore have been a particularly intense exasperation that drove him to write as he did.

Nevertheless this indictment of Borrer's, seen in isolation, might well not be taken by a reader all that seriously. Cooper, after all, was a mere twenty-one-year-old at the time he wrote and his solecism could be pardonably put down to the casualness of youth. Alternatively, that enduring failure to publish for which Borrer was all too well-known could be ascribed to a sub-aristocratic fastidiousness which might have led him to seek through a surrogate the vulgar publicity of print.

Unfortunately for these arguments, apparently unbeknown to Borrer Cooper had repeated his behaviour the very next year, after moving up to Nottinghamshire.[14] The victim on this occasion was Borrer's local counterpart, Dr Godfrey Howitt (brother-in-law of the writer Mary Howitt), who had worked hard on the flora of that county for a considerable period. This time the plagiarism went further, for Cooper allowed H. C. Watson to suppose (and, more brazenly, to go on supposing for the rest of his days)[15] that he was solely responsible not only for the marked catalogue submitted to him for use in his forthcoming *New Botanist's Guide*[16] but for the large number of voucher specimens sent in as well (which are now in Watson's herbarium at Kew). In reality, these had been entrusted to Cooper by Howitt for passing on to Watson. As Professor Carr was to observe many years later, Cooper 'was almost a stranger in the county, and had enjoyed few opportunities of botanizing there',[17] so that his usurping of the role of leading authority on the Nottinghamshire flora was even more outrageous than in the case of his native Sussex. This time, moreover, it is impossible to give him the benefit of the doubt, even supposing that Howitt had also been of a social rank that ordained the total shunning of publicity; for in his eventual Nottinghamshire flora[18] there is pointedly no mention of Cooper whatsoever.

The few details that can be established of Cooper's subsequent career are similarly suggestive of a thrusting opportunism. To be able to lay claim to some more broadly scientific accomplishments, especially in a field so fashionably elegant as botany, still had clear professional advantages then for an aspiring medical practitioner. Surgeons (such as Cooper became) did not enjoy the assured social standing of physicians and thus had all the more inducement to make some show of cultivation. It is perhaps not without significance therefore that putting up for election to the Linnean Society (at that period moribund scientifically but still prestigious socially) should have been his first action when on the point of qualifying.

His next step, out into the provinces, proved a mere short-lived, sideways manoeuvre. For within three years he had procured a return to London and was established in practice at a good address off Fitzroy Square. Membership of the Royal College of Surgeons followed, in 1843, with in due course a move to Camden Town and appointment as Surgeon to the St Pancras Infirmary. Perhaps now able to relax a little (or perhaps just needing some supplementary income) he also about this time gave lessons on botany (with the title of Professor) at an agricultural school at Hoddesdon, in Hertfordshire,[5] and maybe with a view to building up a herbarium for this forsook the Linnean Society for the less glamorous (but more practically beneficial) Botanical Society of London in 1846.[19]

But all this evidently led nowhere. For around 1850 he opted afresh for the provinces, and this time for the depths of the country, turning up as District Medical Officer of the Barnstaple Union.[5] A fruit of this change was a guide to Lynton and its neighbourhood in North Devon:[20] once again, a suspiciously confident undertaking for so recent a newcomer.

Once again, too, Devon turned out to have been but an interlude. After just a year or two the frantic zigzag was resumed, taking him now overseas, to the grand-sounding post of Medical Inspector of the West India Islands.[6] Yet even with this there was apparently something wrong, for by 1857 he was back, this time as Physician to the Great Western and Metropolitan Railways and with a life divided between Paddington Station and Slough.[5,6] At this point, image-conscious to the last, he chose to suppress all details of his foregoing career from the annual *London and provincial medical directory* with the solitary exception of his MRCS. This exception is explained by his elevation to FRCS in the very next year.

Yet this belated clambering up on to the platform of professional respect seemingly did him little good; for when he died, over twenty years later, on Christmas Day 1881, he left the comparatively paltry sum of £865.[21] His will, made eighteen years before, was brief and to the point. Everything went to his widow except for his two silver snuff-boxes and a pair of cases of stuffed birds. These last each of his daughters was to have, 'whichever she may select'. For the rest, it was his wish that 'my funeral be as quiet and inexpensive as possible without expending thereon one single penny more than is absolutely necessary and if practicable to be a walking funeral'. A melancholy ending for one who had begun with such a partiality for show.

NOTES AND REFERENCES

[1] In the eighteenth century it was especially rampant. A. M. LYSAGHT, 1970. *J. Soc. Biblphy nat. Hist.* 4:330, instances no less a figure than Thomas Pennant as one of its more glaring exponents at that period.

[2] COOPER, T. H., 1834. *The botany of the county of Sussex.* Sussex Press, Lewes. Republished as pp. 5–22 of the Appendix to Vol. 2 of T. W. HORSFIELD, 1835. *The history, antiquities, and topography of the county of Sussex.* Sussex Press, Lewes.

[3] JACKSON, B. D., 1887. Thomas Henry Cooper, *in* STEPHEN, L. (ed.), *Dictionary of national biography.* 12: 152–3. Smith, Elder & Co., London.

[4] As shown by the wildly wrong dates proposed for him: 1759?–1840? It is odd that so experienced a scholar as Jackson, the Linnean Society's Botanical Secretary for some years by then, should have omitted to consult the Society's own records – which would at once have shown that Cooper (whom he had correctly identified as a one-time Fellow) was meeting his subscriptions as late as 1846. Nevertheless the *DNB* entry is sufficiently informative in other respects to allow no excuse for the misidentification with a Captain Thomas Henry Cooper, of North Walsham, author of three works on infantry tactics, perpetrated by the British Museum *Catalogue of printed books.*

[5] *The London and provincial medical directory*, 1846. John Churchill, London.

[6] POWER, SIR D'ARCY, 1930. *Plarr's lives of the Fellows of the Royal College of Surgeons of England*, John Wright & Sons, Bristol. Vol. 1, p. 274.

[7] Court of Examiners' entry books of qualifications of candidates for the licence of the Society of Apothecaries, 1815–88, Ms. 8241, Guildhall Library, London.

[8] CAMPKIN, H., 1877. The late William Durrant Cooper, F.S.A. . . . , *Sussex Arch. Collections*, 27: 117–151. A shorter account of this brother is also in the *Dictionary of national biography.* 12: 154–5.

XVIII

THE PLAGIARISMS OF T. H. COOPER   279

[9] Student records, University College London. Also, index to death certificates, General Register Office, London.

[10] T. H. Cooper to W. J. Hooker, 25 November 1834: Hooker Letters, Kew Archives, Vol. 4, Letter 41. In this letter, the only one of Cooper's I have been able to locate, he claims to have 'spared no means' in making the list 'as complete as possible'.

[11] BORRER, W., 1851. Botanical memoranda. *Bot. Gazette,* **3**: 98. This passing reference to Cooper seems to have been generally overlooked. Note the words 'almost entirely'. Later accounts (by Jackson, *loc. cit.,* and by F. H. ARNOLD, 1887. *Flora of Sussex.* Hamilton Adams, London. p. xx) water this down to 'much of the information', and imply that the Rev. G. E. Smith, another able Sussex botanist of the period, was also a substantial, equally unacknowledged contributor. I prefer to read Borrer literally. If some records did indeed come from Smith as well, then Cooper's contribution must have been more negligible still.

[12] For a recent account of his life and work see SMAIL, H. C. P., 1974. William Borrer of Henfield, botanist and horticulturalist, 1781–1862. *Watsonia,* **10**: 55–60.

[13] WATSON, H. C., 1872. *Supplement to the Compendium of Cybele Britannica.* Printed for the Author, Thames Ditton. p. 115.

[14] Probably from this period date his (presumptive) visits to North Wales, Co. Durham and various parts of Scotland attested by records standing to his name in FRANCIS, G. W., 1837. *An analysis of the British ferns and their allies.* First edition. Simpkin Marshall, London. Most of the records cited by Francis were passed on to him by Watson, with whom Cooper was in correspondence around 1835.

[15] A supremely punctilious person, Watson would surely have deleted Cooper's name against the records and specimens attributed to him had he ever been made aware of the deception.

[16] WATSON, H. C., 1835. *The new Botanist's Guide to the localities of the rarer plants of Britain. Vol. 1. England and Wales.* Longman, London. pp. 265–271.

[17] CARR, J. W., 1906. Botany *in* PAGE, W. (ed.), *The Victoria county history of the county of Nottingham,* Vol. 1. James Street, London. p.43.

[18] HOWITT, G., 1839. *The Nottinghamshire flora.* Hamilton Adams, London.

[19] Botanical Society of London minute-book for November 1844–November 1851, now in the keeping of the Linnean Society. Cooper's departure from the Linnean Society does not seem to have been made under pressure: he simply left off paying his subscription and, as was quite usual in those days, was struck off the membership list only after reminders repeated over as long as eight years. I am indebted to Mr T. O'Grady for assistance in consulting the records concerned.

[20] COOPER, T. H., 1853. *A guide, containing a short historical sketch of Lynton and places adjacent in North Devon, including Ilfracombe.* John Russell Smith, London.

[21] Calendar of wills, Principal Probate Registry, London.

XIX

The botanical family of Samuel Butler

Two lists of herbaria of British plants compiled and published in recent years have left unidentified a 'Canon T. Butler, fl. 1882', whose collection is known to have once been in the possession of Ludlow Natural History Society,[1] and a 'Rev. T. Butler, fl. 1880', who was responsible for specimens from Somerset, Nottinghamshire, Derbyshire, and Merioneth.[2]

Neither of these compilers felt able to depart from their primary tasks into further investigating such minor collectors. Had they done so, however, the fact that they were concerned with a Church of England cleric would surely have taken them straight to Venn's *Alumni Cantabrigienses* [3] — and there it would have at once become apparent that this obscure Victorian botanist is none other than the father of the novelist Samuel Butler and thus the model for the appalling Theobald Pontifex in that masterpiece of autobiographical fiction, *The way of all flesh.*

Had there been botanists among the students of literature who have looked into the background of that classic, they too might have come to this discovery from the opposite direction. For not only is Theobald Pontifex depicted as the owner of a *hortus siccus,* but the various accounts of Samuel Butler's family which have been published make it clear that botany was one of his father's more especial interests. One of them[4] indeed even quotes tributes to his work in this direction, making his botanical identity quite explicit.

Thomas Butler (1806—1886) was in his turn the son of the hardly less famous Dr Samuel Butler, the great headmaster of Shrewsbury — where, inevitably, he was sent to school. From there he went up to St John's College, Cambridge, as a Classical scholar, graduating in 1829. He wished to go into the Navy, but at his father's insistence he entered the Church. On ordination he at once returned to his old school for five years as an assistant master, combining that post with the Curacy of Meole Brace, a village just outside Shrewsbury. In 1834 he was appointed Rector of Langar-cum-Barnston, a small village in the Vale of Belvoir some twelve miles south-east of Nottingham and close to the Leicestershire border; and there he was to remain for forty-two years. Preferment came in 1855 in the form of the Rural Deanery of Bingham (held till 1872), followed by his being appointed a Canon of Lincoln in 1868. In 1876 he retired and returned to make his home in Shrewsbury, where he occupied his final years in overhauling and extending the botanical collections of the museum. As a person he is described as quiet and retiring, 'as open and simple-hearted as a child', little resembling — except in his hot temper — the monster so graphically portrayed by his son.

His introduction to botany was due to none other than Charles Darwin. The two had been schoolboy contemporaries at Shrewsbury, but two or three years' difference in age had

meant that they had then known one another only slightly.[5] In the summer of 1828, however, they found themselves both members of an undergraduate reading-party at Barmouth,
and in the course of occasional long mountain rambles Darwin 'inoculated me with a taste
for botany which has stuck by me all my life'.[5]

He next surfaces as a keen collector of British plants. A specimen of his in H. C. Watson's
herbarium at Kew is labelled as having been distributed through the Botanical Society of
London in 1841. That Society's sole surviving minute-book [6] includes his name in the long
list of members who subscribed to the cost of portraits of Watson and the president,
J. E. Gray, in November 1846; and he was still participating in its exchange activities when
the last published report on these appeared in 1852. However, apart from a brief note in the
Phytologist in 1842, reporting his discovery of a rare sedge on Brean Down, he does not
appear to have ventured into print. Even so 'much useful work' by him in the Belvoir
district is acknowledged in two of the successive floras of Leicestershire.[7]

In all probability it was his marriage, in 1831, that was the making of him botanically.
For his wife was one of the four sisters of Miss Anna Worsley (1807–1876), the most
accomplished woman field botanist of the day and subsequently, under her married name,
well-known for the over seven hundred drawings of British fungi which are now in the
Department of Botany, British Museum (Natural History). Their father, Philip John
Worsley (1769–1811), was a sugar refiner in Bristol, where the family, staunch Unitarians,
were among the leaders of the city's intellectual life.

Anna Worsley began by being devoted to entomology and only moved over to botany
after some years. It was a list of the flowering plants of the Bristol area which she contributed, indirectly, to Watson's *New Botanist's Guide* (Vol. I, 1835) that first won her the
notice, and then increasingly the respect, of that ferociously discriminating man.[9] Two
years later she was largely responsible for a catalogue of the plants of the Newbury area,
drawn up at the request of Dr Joseph Bunny (1798–1885), one of her relations.[10] By that
time she had begun also studying cryptogams.[11]

For a long time after the two families became connected they remained unusually close,
'the Worsleys staying with the Butlers at Langar and the Butlers visiting the Worsleys in
London'.[12] One or two of the specimens contributed by Anna Worsley to the exchanges of
the Botanical Society of London (which she appears to have joined about the same time as
her brother-in-law and which she continued with for at least as long) were collected by her
at Langar. Another fruit of one of her visits was a note in the *Zoologist* on the behaviour of
a bat, which she had observed while sitting sketching by the rectory.[13]

In 1844, at the age of thirty-seven, she became the wife of Frederick Russell, of
Brislington, near Bristol [14] (where they lived for some years before moving to Kenilworth).
This brought another brother-in-law [15] of distinction in the person of Dr James Russell
(1818–1885), Professor of Medicine at Queen's College, Birmingham, and the eminent
Physician to the General Hospital there. Little appears to be known of her husband, but
evidently it was through a shared fondness for botany that the two came together, for she
contributed specimens of his collecting to the Botanical Society's distributions at least three
years before they wed.[16] He was the author of a letter to the *Annals & Magazine of Natural
History* in November 1840, in which he refers to his having received a report on a certain
botanical rarity 'some years since'.[14]

With two such powerful sources of infection it would have been surprising indeed if none
of the next generation had succumbed botanically as well. In fact three at least of them did.

Tom, the Canon's younger son, was proudly acclaimed by his aunt in print as the discoverer of a great rarity, *Sonchus palustris,* in the Norfolk Fens in 1856.[17] He was then a Cambridge undergraduate and, according to her account, had showed the plant to Professor Babington. Four years earlier a family letter [18] describes him hunting for plovers' nests, and it may be that his interest in natural history was never more than a very general one. Subsequently he was to become alienated from the rest of the family, desert his wife and children and die in Corsica before attaining fifty. The younger of his sisters, May, on the other hand displayed very definite signs of strictly botanical knowledge in her letters.[19] And their cousin Alice Worsley, daughter of Anna's elder brother Philip,[20] was botanist enough in later years to be capable of supplying a catalogue of the plants around St Fillans in Perthshire for Watson's *Topographical botany,* at the special instance of her aunt.[21]

Samuel Butler, however, appears to have been immune — and that despite the fact that his godmother was Anna Worsley[22] (the model, perhaps, at least in part, of Alethea Pontifex). It is true that in his early student days he gave evidence of a zeal for cultivating ferns, but that was doubtless no more than a following of that violent craze of the mid-1850s. One useful legacy of it, even so, was a lasting familiarity with the names and characters of the hardy genera and species, which enabled him to recognise them in the wild and collect them as occasional presents for his father in later years.[23] To that extent botany provided one frail and slender bridge over the chasm of their relationship.

In other respects Samuel Butler's writings betray little sympathy with botany — or at any rate with botanists. In his notebooks he queries by what right they give themselves airs 'over the draper's assistant' and, in disclosing a plan to scatter the seeds of attractive exotics in Epping Forest and round about London, he recognises that 'this would puzzle botanists' but objects that 'there is no reason why botanists should not be puzzled'.[25] Botanists, in other words, were arid, pompous people in need of being humbled — people just like his own parents and relations. So too, perhaps, were scientists more generally. Maybe from this came that profound ambivalence towards science observed in his writings: that failed god which fell victim in its turn to his reflex of iconoclasm.

NOTES AND REFERENCES

[1] Kent, D. H., 1958. *British herbaria: an index to the location of herbaria of British vascular plants with biographical references to their collectors.* Bot. Soc. Brit. Is., London, p. 47.

[2] CLOKIE, H. N., 1964. *An account of the herbaria of the Department of Botany in the University of Oxford.* University Press, Oxford, p.142.

[3] VENN, J. A., 1940. *Alumni Cantabrigienses. Part II: From 1752 to 1900.* University Press, Cambridge, Vol. 1, p.478.

[4] GARNETT, Mrs R. S., 1926. *Samuel Butler and his family relations.* J. M. Dent & Sons, London & Toronto, especially pp.41–43.

[5] Thomas Butler to Francis Darwin, 13 Sept. 1882, Darwin Papers, Cambridge University Library, DAR 112. I am indebted to Miss Nancy Mautner for bringing this letter to my notice.

[6] Now in the possession of the Linnean Society of London.

[7] KIRBY, M., 1850. *A flora of Leicestershire,* Hamilton, Adams & Co., London, p.x. HORWOOD, A. R. & NOEL, C. W. F., 1933. *The flora of Leicestershire and Rutland.* University Press, Oxford, p. ccxiii.

[8] GARNETT, *op.cit.,* p. 150.

[9] Cf. the glowing terms in which he speaks of her in *Topographical botany,* Ed.2 (Bernard Quaritch, London, 1883), p. 562.

[10] [GRAY, E. W.], 1839. *The history and antiquities of Newbury and its environs: also a catalogue of plants found in the neighbourhood.* pp. 310–340. See her note on the background to this publication in the *Phytologist*, 1849, 3: 716.

[11] Reports of the meetings of the Botanical Society of London in September and December 1841 mention donations by her of British mosses.

[12] GARNETT, *op.cit.*, p. 175. Some of the Worsleys later moved from Bristol to London.

[13] WORSLEY, A., 1843. Anecdotes of bats flying by day-light. *Zoologist* 1: 212.

[14] RUSSELL, F., 1841. *Saxifraga umbrosa. Ann. Mag. nat. Hist.*, (1) 6: 314.

[15] BAGNALL, J. E., 1891. *The flora of Warwickshire.* Gurney & Jackson, London & Cornish Brothers, Birmingham, p. 505. Their father, James Russell (1786–1851), a prominent Birmingham surgeon, sanitary reformer and geologist, features in the *Dictionary of national biography.* He in turn was the son of a once-prosperous merchant ruined by the American War of Independence and the nephew of a man whose house was burnt down in the "Priestley Riots" of 1791. James Russell's eldest son was another botanist, Thomas Hawkes Russell (1851–1913), of Edgbaston, a Birmingham solicitor, F.L.S. and author in 1908 of a book on mosses and liverworts. The Russells, like the Worsleys, were Unitarians.

[16] For example, *Coeloglossum viride* from Houndstreet, Somerset, a specimen of which is now in Watson's herbarium at Kew.

[17] RUSSELL, A., 1857. *Sonchus palustris. Phytologist*, (2) 2: 279.

[18] GARNETT, *op.cit.,* letter reproduced between pp. 174 and 175.

[19] GARNETT, *op.cit.,* pp. 98, 108, 115.

[20] Through the wife of this brother the Worsleys were connected with another leading Unitarian family, the Taylors of Norwich. Her father was John Taylor (1779–1863), a London mining engineer who served as Honorary Treasurer of the Geological Society for twenty-eight years, while Richard Taylor (1781–1858), F.L.S., F.S.A., of the printing firm of Taylor and Francis, was one of her uncles.

[21] *Topographical botany,* Ed. 2, pp. 555, 562.

[22] *The family letters of Samuel Butler 1841–1886,* ed. Arnold Silver. Jonathan Cape, London, 1962, p. 115.

[23] *ibid.,* p. 142.

[24] *Samuel Butler's notebooks,* selections ed. Geoffrey Keynes & Brian Hill. Jonathan Cape, London, 1951, p. 264.

[25] *ibid.,* p. 145.

XX

C.C. Babington, Cambridge botany
and the taxonomy of British flowering plants

A modified version of a lecture given at a conference of
the Society for the History of Natural History at Cambridge on 9 May 1998

Introduction

Through most of the 19th century two botanists towered over their contemporaries, one in carrying further forward the discriminating of the taxa of flowering plants and ferns to be found in the British Isles and the other in mapping their distributions. These were Charles Cardale Babington and Hewett Cottrell Watson.

The two men could hardly have been less alike in character. Where Babington was gentle and pious, Watson was pugnacious and agnostic. Babington would go out of his way to avoid hurting feelings, whereas Watson enjoyed nothing so much as the parry and thrust of an argument. After conversion to a dogged belief in the truths of that odd study, phrenology, Watson delighted in diagnosing people's failings with all the provocative cold-bloodedness of a 20th-century Freudian, but he was impossibly touchy if anyone wrote or said the slightest thing that might be interpreted as a criticism of *him*. As Babington was once moved to remark to a friend, "He seems to think he may *say* and *print* whatever he likes of others and that they must not ever hint at anything on the other side."[1] Scientifically, too, their interests sharply diverged. Babington was essentially a taxonomist, Watson a plant geographer of the Humboldtian school; that is, his aim in laboriously working out the distributions of the individual species was to demonstrate the various environmental factors operating to bring these about – a kind of ecology without any concept of vegetational succession (at least in Watson's case) or of plant communities.

The two clearly respected each other but wisely kept their distance. Watson

XX

could hardly have resisted baiting Babington, who would surely only have been hurt if he had attempted to respond. They consequently danced an extraordinary *pas de deux* through the British botany of that era: Babington, though a Cambridge man, threw in his lot with the Botanical Society of Edinburgh, a respectable, gentlemanly crowd, while Watson, an Edinburgh graduate, masterminded the struggling, distinctly ungentlemanly Botanical Society of London. Initially, both these bodies had the large-scale exchange of herbarium specimens as central activities, and, in return for the invaluable assistance Watson and Babington gave in ensuring that the specimens sent out were correctly named, each was granted the special privilege of helping himself to the large stock of duplicates his particular society held, to the great enrichment of his own personal collection.[2] Watson's society, however, was the only one that made a success of its exchange scheme, so much so that it was carefully preserved and continued after the society itself was forced into bankruptcy and became defunct after a 20-year existence (Allen, 1986, pp. 11–65). Yet, despite the potential usefulness for his own researches the specimens circulated would have had, Babington pointedly stood aloof from the successor body which carried on the scheme, the Botanical Exchange Club – and, even more pointedly, joined it at long last only and immediately on Watson's death (Allen, 1986, p. 78).

When Babington's Edinburgh connections led to his being invited to join the editorial team of the most respected of the contemporary specialist journals, *Annals and Magazine of Natural History*, this promptly aroused the suspicion of the always slightly paranoid Watson, who persuaded himself that a menacing Northern network was coming into being which might well exercise a near-monopoly control over what appeared in print on British botany.[3] Baseless though that was, Watson's image of Babington as a privileged 'insider' never ceased to rankle; and Babington further irked him, unwittingly, by the many new names that his taxonomic researches kept on introducing into the British list.[4] As a compiler of a series of massive compendia on the distribution of the individual British species, Watson had a vested interest in names remaining unchanged. For that reason he was vociferously hostile to the splitting-up of familiar entities and the supplanting of long-customary names which the finer discrimination pre-eminently identified with Babington repeatedly showed to be necessary. "There are species, there are subspecies, and there are Bab-ies," he once quipped to a friend with his customary biting wit.[5]

The two men were alike in one curious respect, though: both limited their travelling to the British Isles almost exclusively, each venturing overseas on a single occasion only – Babington to Iceland, Watson to the Azores. This was the more remarkable in Babington's case, for he could well have afforded to range much further afield and had developed numerous Continental contacts, which were indeed of key importance to his work. Perhaps it was a natural timidity that caused him to shun alien cultures, for, as his diary reveals (Babington, 1897), he was by no means averse to roughing it when he explored the wilder parts of Scotland and Ireland.

Watson's stridency and his sharply-etched character have combined to ensure that the imprint he has left on British botanical history is very distinct and enduring. Babington, by comparison, is remembered rather hazily.

3

Where Watson is loudly black-and-white, Babington is a muted grey. Symptomatically, the literature is graced today with a *Watsonia*, but not with a *Babingtonia*. The particular furrow that Babington ploughed did not stand out sufficiently from the general run: there have been too many others, before and since, whose contribution to knowledge has been broadly similar, even if not so significant historically. It is high time that the man and his work were brought into clearer focus.

Early years

One of the keys to comprehending the man is his family background and upbringing. For the Babingtons were one of the pillars in that imposing Evangelical edifice known as the Clapham Sect. Another pillar was constituted by the Macaulays: Lord Macaulay, the great historian, was one of his many cousins. Samuel Wilberforce, the most famous member of all, * was one of his father's friends. That deeply earnest religious culture which Babington imbibed effectively from the cradle left a lifelong mark. If he had not had the good fortune to become a scholar of independent means, he would surely have followed his father's example in taking holy orders and perhaps even become a missionary.

At the time of his birth, in November 1808 (the year after the passing of the act abolishing the slave trade, for which the Clapham Sect had striven so hard), his father was a physician in the country market town of Ludlow, in the far south of Shropshire. It would have been a perfect place for the boy to have grown up (it is a famously attractive town to this day), but unfortunately his father soon afterwards decided to change careers, became ordained and was forced to subject the family to frequent moves, initially round the Midlands and later in Wessex, moves reflected for the son in frequent changes of school. That must have been very unsettling, but far worse was to come, for his parents stupidly sent him away at the age of 12 to board at The Charterhouse, that school which the novelist Thackeray had found so unbearable as to dub it "the Slaughterhouse". As at all the big boarding schools at that period, bullying was rife and, all too predictably, the young Babington, who one can infer was a sensitive child, must soon have been deeply unhappy there. In a brief autobiographical sketch that he left (Babington, 1897) he makes out that it was because he was "not getting on well with my learning" that his parents removed him after a year or two at his own request; but it is more likely that he was simply unfitted for the ferocious rough-and-tumble of the place. Instead, he became a day-boy at a school in Bath, where his parents had recently finally settled, his father having been forced to abandon his clerical career through losing the use of his legs. In this different, much calmer environment Babington apparently blossomed. His father had meanwhile passed on to him his own fondness for botany and fed it by introducing him to some of the handbooks then in vogue, and he began to spend much of his time in those teenage years scouring the local countryside for plants. This was to culminate eventually in a slender volume, written only after he had graduated from university and published later still, presumably at his own expense (Babington, 1834).

At that same period a parallel keenness for entomology developed into a passion for collecting Coleoptera. These were to be the subject of more

4

XX

than half of his earliest published papers and so dominated his leisure hours at university as to earn him the nickname "Beetles" (Boulger, 1909). After building up a collection of some 4000 specimens, however, he gradually shed that rival enthusiasm, and after 1840 botany increasingly monopolised his scientific attention (though he was to be hardly less devoted to antiquarian studies too for the rest of his life).

Arrival at Cambridge

Fortuitously, the year before Babington went up to Cambridge in 1826, John Stevens Henslow had been appointed Professor of Botany, as the somewhat belated response by the University to the Apothecaries' Act of 1815, which had had the result of requiring all medical students intending to enter general practice in England and Wales to qualify for the licence of the London livery company, the Society of Apothecaries. The exam for that included as one of its options a test of competence in medical botany, a subject which therefore suddenly had to be taken much more seriously. Henslow had written off to his opposite number at Glasgow, W.J. Hooker, for tips on how best to set about things; and Hooker had strongly recommended copying his example by supplementing lectures with class excursions into the countryside, so that the students could learn to recognise herbs in the living state and in the wild.[6] Henslow's consequent excursions, lectures and evening parties for students were already starting to attract a large and enthusiastic following around the time that Babington came up. What is more, Henslow's college, St John's, was the one to which Babington had chosen to come, in the footsteps of his father and three of his father's brothers.

While it was predictable that the two would become firm friends, it was less predictable that Babington would later become Henslow's *de facto* teaching assistant and eventually deputy during the Professor's absences after 1839 for much of each year tending his Suffolk parish. Absentee professors were something to which the University had long become inured, but it is clear from his letters (Babington, 1897, p. 297) that Babington secretly resented the degree to which he was thus put upon by Henslow. The situation was made worse by the knowledge that, however hard he worked and however much his own botanical reputation grew, there was no prospect of a second teaching post in the subject being created in the foreseeable future and he could therefore expect no advancement in his status until such time as Henslow deigned to step down from the Chair. That he hankered after this is shown by his nearly applying for the analogous position at King's College London in 1841 (Babington, 1897, p. 110).

Fortunately for Babington, he could afford to wait and had no *need* to move elsewhere in order to earn a living, for both his parents had meanwhile died, leaving him financially independent. So, after graduating, he kept on his rooms in College and settled into a comfortable bachelor existence there. Not elected a Fellow till very much later (in 1874), presumably on account of his preference for not becoming involved in College affairs, his consequent lack of ties and duties enabled him to give almost all his time and energy to his personal research. When a further change in the medical regulations caused a drastic collapse in the student demand for botany in the early 1840s (Becher, 1986, p. 24), such teaching as he had been doing became more or less

5

informal, confined to sharpening the taxonomic acumen of undergraduates whose interest in the subject was firmly non-vocational. Many of those who came under his beneficial influence later produced county Floras or otherwise rose to prominence as field botanists, and he was tirelessly patient in answering their queries or determining the specimens they sent him in subsequent years. In effect, during his many years as Professor-in-waiting, he built up his own 'shadow' research school, though one at a distance for the most part and made up entirely of amateurs.

Travel and research

Babington's influence on undergraduates was exerted especially through the Ray Club, of which he served as Honorary Secretary for the remarkable span of 55 years, its weekly meetings coming to fill the role previously played by Henslow's parties. His more particular protégés, whom he came to know primarily through that means, sometimes became his companions on the tours of exploration he made each year, all summer long, to virtually every part of these islands. That last word is used with reason, for it was his fieldwork in the Channel Islands, in 1837 and 1838, that first brought him deserved renown. David McClintock (1975, p. 27), who was to follow in his footsteps over a century later, has marvelled at "how much he managed to see and record and describe and collect . . . in the seven main islands of the Archipelago . . . in a total of only 18 weeks". Moreover, the book which resulted (Babington, 1839), the second of the three British local Floras he was to write, was produced "remarkably quickly. He left the Islands on 8 August 1838, and was immediately actively botanising as far north as Northumberland, and writing his *Manual of Botany* at the same time"; yet his *Primitiae Florae Sarnicae* (as he unappetisingly chose to call it) appeared as early as the following June. Before his visits the Channel Islands had been little known to mainland botanists and his work at last opened eyes to their rich floristic potential.

Much as one suspects that he would have preferred to repeat that exhilarating experience and investigate other promising areas with comparable intensiveness, Babington evidently felt under an obligation to make his focus broadly national, leaving the compilation of local Floras to those who were more anchored, many of them his own disciples. To that rule he was to make just one, very special exception – his *Flora of Cambridgeshire* (Babington, 1860), the summation of his work over many years in the county he had come to make very much his own. Pleasingly timed to coincide with the bicentenary of Ray's *Cambridge Catalogue* (Ray, 1660), this small octavo volume followed the practice, which Babington himself had been responsible for making fashionable, of dividing the county into a series of botanical districts and grouping the localised records under them. A more novel feature, in which he anticipated *Flora of Hampshire*, by one of his ablest pupils, Frederick Townsend (1884), was the inclusion of an appendix of notes on some of the more difficult groups. The work as a whole greatly gained from the wide attention he had paid to these as well as from his extensive knowledge of the European flora more generally. Another appendix provided "a complete list of the [130] plants which have been recently found growing in Wicken Fen", which it is instructive to compare with a modern list.

The taxonomy of the higher plants of the British Isles had lapsed into a shameful insularity by the time Babington appeared on the scene. This was largely the result of their prolonged cultural isolation from the rest of Europe during the Napoleonic Wars. Partly through the difficulty, if not impossibility, for so many years of crossing the Channel and studying Continental plants at first hand, partly through the interruption to the inflow of Continental specimens and books, and partly owing to the conservative influence of J.E. Smith, British botany had failed to keep abreast of many of the advances in European taxonomy. Numbers of our supposedly endemic species had never had their identities checked against similar entities described from neighbouring countries; equally, Continental botanists had been busily describing new taxa which might or might not have been the same as their seeming counterparts over here. There was a great deal of catching-up to be done, and Babington alone had the taxonomic ability, the willingness and, not least, the freedom from other commitments to lead the way in carrying out that overdue undertaking; this was to be much the most important of his contributions to contemporary knowledge.

At the same time there was a pressing need for a new, concise, scholarly handbook which incorporated the results of this continuing task of bringing British usage into line with that in France, Scandinavia and, above all, Germany. Babington's *Manual of British Botany* (Babington, 1843), nine years in preparation, not only had all these assets but was also convenient for field use by being made small enough to slip into a pocket. Regularly revised in successive editions, of which eight appeared in Babington's lifetime and two more after his death, it is credibly held to have revolutionised British field botany. Such was the intense excitement with which his great friend W.W. Newbould received his copy of one of those earlier editions that he sat down there and then and studied it from cover to cover till four o'clock in the morning (Anon., 1886). While that response was no doubt an extreme one, it well illustrates what a key part Babington's *Manual* played among the *cognoscenti* of British field botany almost throughout the Victorian era.

Brambles

Sooner or later Babington had to decide whether to tackle what were then seen as the two chief problem groups among British flowering plants – the brambles and the hawkweeds. These were turning out to be so exceptionally diverse that to attempt to capture that diversity with the standard classificatory categories required the description of more and more species and varieties (and, in later years, further categories as well). The majority of botanists jibbed at that, refusing to accept that what seemed to their eyes scarcely distinguishable variants deserved to be ranked on a par with the Common Daisy, say, or Chickweed. Opposition was especially fierce from those wrestling with the almost overwhelming diversity of tropical floras, who feared the collapse of taxonomy as a serviceable tool if more entities were given scientific recognition than could be encompassed by the human brain. The battle between the so-called 'splitters' and 'lumpers' was to rage for the best part of a century and always inconclusively, for neither side had the necessary understanding of the unusual breeding systems which cause certain groups to consist of a multitude of distinguishable minor entities, an understanding that would come only from advances in other branches of botanical science.

Babington began collecting *both* hawkweeds *and* brambles, as his correspondence reveals (Babington, 1897, pp. 113–116), but he soon decided to concentrate on the latter. More people had had a go at them already, so they presented a more obvious challenge to someone who relished the role of grand tidier-up. Two British botanists in particular appeared to be making some headway with the group and had begun describing new entities which Babington would need to take account of in preparing his *Manual*. One of these was Andrew Bloxam, a Leicestershire vicar, and the other Edwin Lees, a printer-turned-journalist in Worcester who was combing the nearby Malvern Hills. Unlike the Cambridge region, those are both areas in which brambles exist in considerable diversity and the two botanists had found it possible to discriminate the more widespread of their local entities, greatly aided by the fact that they lived among them and so could become fully familiar with them by seeing them regularly on their walks. Unlike them, Babington had the ill luck to inhabit an area where the soil is mostly clay or chalk, which most kinds of brambles cannot tolerate. Although he did try to make up for that disadvantage by growing many of the entities in the University Botanic Garden (Babington, 1897, p. 319), that was not enough. Apart from the fact that they would not have exhibited there the range of variation to be encountered in the wild, he was normally away from Cambridge during their flowering period.

That was not the only serious handicap that Babington laboured under. He also became convinced that the different kinds of brambles vary too much in their floral characters for these to serve as a reliable basis for classification. That was convenient for him, as those characters are lost in dried material and he therefore felt justified in working largely with herbarium material. We now know that that was a fatal mistake. In disregarding the flowers, which are the equivalent in a bramble of the features which make up a person's face, enabling anyone once familiar with any one kind to recognise it at a glance, Babington was left with no alternative but to depend mainly on the characters presented by the stem and the leaves. There are plenty enough of these, but to go on them alone is to be in the position of a forensic pathologist asked to identify a series of headless corpses.

Worst of all, in common with all of his contemporaries, Babington was not mentally disposed to accept that a group of clearly closely related plants (or animals for that matter) could consist of more than a strictly limited number of classifiable entities. That generation began studying brambles, we have to remember, during the era when virtually everyone still subscribed to the idea that species were the handiwork of the Divine Artificer and fixed for all time. People believed also that hybrids rarely occurred in nature and that, when they did, they betrayed themselves by their inevitable sterility. If that generation had realised quite how many different kinds of brambles there really are in Europe – several thousand, on any reckoning – it would have had to accept that the Creator had apparently had a brainstorm and temporarily lost control. As that was beyond conception, it had to be assumed that the number of kinds involved was not as great "as all that" and that it could only be intellectual failing on the part of classifiers if that presumed strict limit on the size of the group was not being accurately reflected in the quantity of taxa described. Babington, as we have seen, was particularly devout: unlike Watson, one of nature's rebels and an early and ardent convert to Darwin's theory of evolution, it was not in his character to question received beliefs. As late as 1887, near the end of his life, we find him confessing to a fellow field botanist, F.J. Hanbury, a Quaker: "I have but little belief in evolution or hybridization, but time will shew." (Babington, 1897, p. 414).

Not surprisingly, therefore, Babington imprisoned himself within far too restrictive a classificatory framework. In the words of a later expert on the group, the Revd Augustine Ley, the study of British brambles during the period in which Babington dominated it "resembled the attempt to force 150 apples into a basket designed to contain 40: as fast as one was forced in another jumped out." (Ley, 1904). The number of entities given taxonomic recognition, even including those admitted in the subordinate category of varieties, was impossibly too small to be reconciled with the actual situation in nature. Only when that straitjacket was loosened shortly after Babington's death, chiefly thanks to the work of the Revd William Moyle Rogers as far as Britain was concerned, was the study of the group at last placed on the broader foundations on which it has since been much more successfully built.

Babington's first book-length monograph on the brambles appeared when he was on the threshold of 40 (Babington, 1846), his second just after he had turned 60 (Babington, 1869), and he had largely written a third at the time of his death in 1895. In all he spent half a century grappling with their complexity, devoting to them much of his intellectual energy during most of his working life. Fortunately, the work he had accomplished in other directions had made his reputation and the buffers he had run into with *Rubus* did not detract from it. In 1851 he had been elected to Fellowship of the Royal Society, in 1853 and again in 1861 to the Presidency of the relevant section of the British Association, and in 1861 also, at long, long last, to the Cambridge Chair. He rounded things off with a late marriage, five years after that, to a lady who shared his lasting commitment to Evangelical mission work.

Final years

Babington's final years were, alas, to be sad ones. By the time he had attained the Chair, the ground was shifting beneath him: academic botany had swung right away from its once total preoccupation with description and had turned to new aspects of the subject with which he felt no affinity intellectually. His departmental colleagues (for there *were* some by then) despised him as contemptibly 'old hat' and resented the space and resources devoted to the herbarium and its library instead of to a badly-wanted laboratory (Bower, 1938, p. 102). Failing health then intervened and forced him to start reducing his activities. Then his wife fell down the stairs and could barely walk for five years afterwards. Finally, he himself had an acute attack of pneumonia succeeded by a rheumatic condition which confined him permanently to a wheelchair. That ended his research and visits to his beloved herbarium. A deputy, in the person of Francis Darwin, had to be appointed, to whom Babington made over half of his professorial stipend; but in accordance with the custom of the day his tenure of the Chair terminated only with his death.

That occurred four years later, in July 1895, by which time he was just three years short of 90. By then he had been for some time the University's oldest resident member, and it was to the University that he left, as everyone must surely have long expected, his extensive library of books relating to systematic botany, his voluminous botanical correspondence and, of course, the multitudinous specimens collected by him over the years or acquired from many others. The prize core of these last, for that small handful of us who follow today in those more especial footsteps of his, are the sheets upon sheets of brambles, so darkened with age by now as to put one in mind of the pages of 'penny blacks' treasured by philatelists. Numerous taxa with "Bab." following their names stand in addition as a greener memorial; but, if he were with us today, nothing surely would please him more than to know that his batological descendants regularly murmur to one another "*Rubus babingtonii*" and, more rarely, "*Rubus babingtonianus*" – two names which have magically survived successive purges and continue legitimately in currency.

Acknowledgement
I am indebted to Miss Jean Lamont for searching the J.H. Balfour Letters at the Royal Botanic Garden, Edinburgh, at my request for Watson's words quoted at the end of the fourth paragraph of this article.

Notes
1 C.C. Babington to J.H. Balfour, 23 January 1846, in Balfour Letters, Royal Botanic Garden, Edinburgh.
2 H.C. Watson to C.C. Babington, 14 August 1847, in Babington Letters, Department of Plant Sciences, Cambridge; C.C. Babington to J.F. Duthie, 13 August 1874, in Duthie Letters, Royal Botanic Gardens, Kew.
3 H.C. Watson to Sir William Hooker, 3 May 1844, in Hooker Letters, Royal Botanic Gardens, Kew (English Letters 22/348).
4 H.C. Watson to J.H. Balfour, 30 December 1844, in Balfour Letters, Royal Botanic Garden, Edinburgh: ". . . his ridiculous monomania for species-making and name-changing".
5 H.C. Watson to J.H. Balfour, 26 November 1846, in Balfour Letters, Royal Botanic Garden, Edinburgh (Vol. 12, Letter W. 34). He continued: "Small by degrees – we can say of a Linnean species that it is divisible into so many Babingtonian babies."
6 W.J. Hooker to J.S. Henslow, 14 April 1827, in Henslow Letters, Cambridge University Library.

References
Allen, D.E. (1986). *The botanists. A history of the Botanical Society of the British Isles through a hundred and fifty years*. St Paul's Bibliographies, Winchester.

Anon. (1886). [Obituary of W.W. Newbould]. *Proceedings of the Linnean Society of London*, **1885–6**: 145–146.

B[abington], A.M., ed. (1897). *Memorials, journal and botanical correspondence of Charles Cardale Babington*. Macmillan & Bowes, Cambridge.

Babington, C.C. (1834). *Flora Bathoniensis*. Collings, Bath.

Babington, C.C. (1839). *Primitiae Florae Sarnicae*. Longmans, London.

Babington, C.C. (1843). *Manual of British Botany*. J. van Voorst, London.

Babington, C.C. (1846). *A Synopsis of the British Rubi*. J. van Voorst, London.

Babington, C.C. (1860). *Flora of Cambridgeshire*. J. van Voorst, London.

Babington, C.C. (1869). *The British Rubi*. J. van Voorst, London.

Becher, H.V. (1986). Voluntary science in nineteenth century Cambridge University to the 1850's. *British Journal for the History of Science*, **19**: 57–87.

Boulger, G.S. (1909). Babington, Charles Cardale. In: *The Dictionary of National Biography*, ed. by S. Lee, **22**: 90–92.

Bower, F.O. (1938). *Sixty years of botany in Britain (1875–1935): impressions of an eye-witness*. Macmillan, London.

Ley, A. (1904). The late W.H. Purchas. *Journal of Botany*, **42**: 80–82.

McClintock, D. (1975). *The Wild Flowers of Guernsey*. Collins, London.

[Ray, J.] (1660). *Catalogus plantarum circa Cantabrigiam nascentium*. Cambridge and London.

Townsend, F. [1884: "1883"]. *Flora of Hampshire, including the Isle of Wight*. Reeve, London.

THE DISCOVERIES OF DRUCE

"'Have you seen all the British plants?' I asked, and
he replied that he had, though the last ten had given
him a hard struggle. 'Are you the only botanist who
has seen them all?' I went on, but he merely smiled.
When I inquired about an orchid so very rare that it
has been seen only a few times, he modestly said that
two of the times he had seen it himself".

The words are those of Canon Andrew Young, self-styled
'botanophil' and respected poet, recalling a once-only,
awestruck encounter with the veteran and by that time almost
legendary George Claridge Druce (Young 1985: 73). Unwittingly,
they capture Druce at what is surely his most quintessential:
the competitive hunter, the man with a longer 'life list' than
anyone else, the one who in tireless pursuit of that end, in
the words of McClintock (1966: 97), "covered Britain as perhaps
no one has done before or since".

Character and Botanical Position

Druce had six special assets which enabled him to become
the outstanding field botanist of his generation - the
generation which spanned the fourth quarter of the last century
and the first quarter of this. He had a superabundance of
energy combined with a robust physique. For most of his life he
was without domestic ties and was self-employed, which gave him
the freedom to take time off at will. Latterly, at any rate, he
had the means to travel as often and as far as he wished. He
had a ready charm (or, as his detractors saw it, an ability to
ingratiate) which brought him a country-wide network of eager
informants. He was located in a leading academic centre, with
ready access to first-class libraries and collections. Above
all, however, he had an inner demon which gave him a relentless
urge to be 'top of the class' and to be seen to be so.

Note: The majority of Druce's plant descriptions were
published in the Reports of the Botanical Society and Exchange
Club. In the text the date of description is given as the date
of the title of the Report in which each description appeared;
the date of publication, however, was the year following.

XXI

176

There were some among his contemporaries - E.S. Marshall, for instance, or Frederick Townsend, or the Linton brothers - who were by no means his inferiors intellectually or in taxonomic acumen. True, they had enjoyed educational advantages that had been denied to him; but they had the handicaps, which Druce had not, of professional ties, or rural isolation, or straitened economic circumstances. There were others, like Charles Bailey and F.J. Hanbury, with far greater wealth than he (at any rate in his younger days) and able to use this wealth to build, far more speedily, extensive private herbaria; but they were obliged to keep much more tightly within the shafts of their businesses, and so did not have the leisure, nor maybe the inclination, to roam so wide geographically or socially. There were still others, like Arthur Bennett and F. Arnold Lees, who were no less assiduous in compiling records and in determining specimens sent to them by correspondents; but they were irredeemably anchored, unable or unwilling to move around and meet their fellow botanists in the flesh and see the species occurring outside their home areas growing in their natural habitats.

Druce was lucky, furthermore, in the period in which he happened to live. The two giants of the first half of the Victorian era, Watson and Babington, had both had their day by the time he was appearing on the scene, and there were no equally commanding figures to take their place. Syme, who alone had the standing and the disposition to do so, was marooned on a run-down estate in Fife and was by then a sadly spent force. Baker, who had been Watson's great hope, was weighed down by his official work at Kew, and in any case was too self-effacing ever to have taken on the role of national leader. Newbould, incomparably knowledgeable but virtually a recluse, was an even less likely proposition. Quite fortuitously, the centre of the stage was invitingly bare.

There was an organisational hiatus too. There was no true national botanical society, certainly not one specialising in the flora of the British Isles, and without it no journal free of the dictatorial sway and the personal whims and prejudices of its editor. The Botanical Exchange Club, a tiny body, could continue to function only by being kept tiny, and could only afford reports which were comparatively brief and published no more than annually (and sometimes not even as frequently as that). There was exceptional scope, accordingly, for anyone with driving ambition enough to want to push themselves to the forefront.

Although he certainly had in full measure the ordinary field botanists's delight in working unknown ground, in turning

up a novelty or at least a rarity, and in the very beauty of
the plants themselves, it is obvious that Druce's labours all
along owed much to a powerful need to win applause. That is not
to say that most of us do not also have a strain of this in our
botanical make-up; in Druce's case, however, the need was on a
scale with the immensity of the efforts he put into satisfying
it with practical accomplishments. It was the type of
compulsion of which heroes are made, and for lack of which
lesser mortals are ever destined to be, by comparison, midgets.

Early Life and Botanical Conversion

This compulsion had its origin in his illegitimate birth,
and consequent guilt-ridden upbringing, in a village in the
depths of rural Northamptonshire. It was a background from
which he was proud, and with justice, to have risen, but he was
to spend the rest of his life burying its emotional effects.

That life, and the botanical career which formed its
central thread, was to have a certain poetic symmetry, in that
the county to which he owed his botanical awakening was to be
the county which formed the subject of both the first and the
last of his many publications on local floras. It was somehow
fitting, too, that one who was to spend so much of his life
working England, with unexampled thoroughness, should have had
his origin at almost its centre.

Druce himself has left on record a precise recollection of
his birth as a serious botanist (Druce 1930: ix):

"One night in the autumn of 1872, as in a feverish cold
I lay awake waiting for sleep that would not come, I
determined that in the following year I would begin a
Herbarium, and commence a Flora of my native county".

Surprisingly, he was twenty-two when this sudden
conversion took place: an exceptionally late age by field
botany standards. However, he soon more than made up for the
time he had lost. Before his twenties were out he had
substantially realised the second of his two aims and was in a
position to bring out something not far short of a Flora of
Northamptonshire - although admittedly this was published only
in parts, in the journal of his local natural history society.
After an eye-opening trip to the Thames Valley (made in order
to see the Military Orchid) in the summer of 1878, he left
Northamptonshire in the following year to set up in business as
a chemist in the High Street in Oxford. The next sixteen years
were spent working successively on Floras of the two counties
(Oxfordshire and Berkshire) which that city so conveniently
straddles. These were both first-class productions, especially

the second to appear, that of Berkshire (1897). This is on an enviably spacious scale, two of Druce's subsidiary obsessions, nomenclature and the history of early British botany, receiving especially lavish treatment - for by this time he was well-to-do and could at last afford to spread himself.

Indeed, only eight years later he was affluent enough to be able to retire and devote himself full-time to his leisure interests. From then on his horizons widened and the South Midlands received less and less of his attention and energies. It was consequently not until late in life, in 1926, that Buckinghamshire also fell to his pen, and not until 1930, in his eightieth year, that he finally dignified the flora of his native county with the book which he had dreamed of in his youth and which for far too long it had lacked. Meanwhile he had further extended his empire eastwards by editing the section on botany for the Victoria County History of Bedfordshire (Hamson and Druce 1904), and by contributing the analogous account for the volume on Huntingdonshire (Druce 1926a).

Midland Botanist

Druce was thus, first and foremost, a Midland botanist and it was the flora of its southern belt that he knew best of all and in which he did his most productive work. It was accordingly there that he was to be the first to discriminate several of the species and lesser taxa that have best stood the test of the years. For there he was much less the roving hunter, eternally in a hurry, more the patient accumulator of observations, tethered to just one stretch of countryside for season after season.

The best of these discoveries, which might be termed Druce's 'home' ones, was his very first one of all. In July 1888 he came across an odd-looking Brome-grass dominating a fallow-field on the Berkshire chalk. Finding nothing like it in published works or herbaria, he sent it to the leading European agrostologist, Professor Hackel. Hackel had likewise never encountered anything similar, decided that it was best placed as a variety of what we know today as *Bromus hordeaceus*, and coined for it the epithet *interruptus*. Seven years later, in 1895, strengthened in his belief in its distinctiveness, Druce promoted it to a full species. That he was entirely right to do so has been borne out by recent biosystematic work. It is in fact - or rather was, as it now seems to be extinct in the wild - one of our few 'good' endemics (if one discounts its presence in the Netherlands, whither it is supposed to have been introduced from Britain). It has since come to light that it had been collected almost forty years earlier, in Bedfordshire (Perring 1962, Donald 1980), but to Druce remains the credit for having been its original distinguisher.

Of his next novelties two were Brambles - despite the fact that he is not usually thought of as a specialist in critical groups. *Rubus* was in fact the only major apomictic genus in which Druce was reasonably well-versed, for, unlike the others, not only was it strongly represented in his home region, but there were also experts around to guide him in the field and to help him with determinations. The account of the genus in the first edition of his *Flora of Oxfordshire* (1886) was substantially his own work. In later life he was never disposed to give to any critical group the necessary degree of undivided attention to allow him to become proficient in it. His determinations of Hieracia, in particular, were "far below the standard" of all the more reputable specialists and "on the whole unreliable", in the opinion of Sell and West (1968: 75). In this and other genera the furrow he ploughed was essentially the shallow one of the compiler, and it was as a supplier of a rich mass of raw material that he made his principal contribution.

In 1889, the year after his *Bromus* find, he noticed a conspicuous Bramble on Boar's Hill, near Oxford. This was the first British record of what we now know to be *Rubus egregius*, which had already been described on the Continent by Focke. It has since been found in several of the neighbouring counties as well. Eight years after that, in the *Flora of Berkshire* (1897), he provisionally suggested the varietal name of *bercheriensis* for "a handsome bramble with elegant leaves and striking armature" which "is locally so abundant" in that county (Druce 1897: 181). Later described properly by Rogers, who eventually raised it to the rank of a species, it has proved to be widely distributed in south-east England, although Berkshire is certainly its headquarters.

Meanwhile, in 1893, Druce had discovered a very distinct and beautiful Pondweed growing in abundance along a three-mile stretch of the River Loddon. It retained its characters under cultivation and, despite the special appeal of its flowering spikes to swans, sufficient fruits were procured to enable his friend Alfred Fryer to conclude that it was a species new to science, and to christen it *Potamogeton drucei* in its finder's honour (Druce 1905a). But Fryer, it turned out, had not mastered that difficult genus adequately; for when Dandy and Taylor came to overhaul it afresh in the 1930s, they realised that the plant was none other than a well-known Continental species, *Potamogeton nodosus*.

By contrast, Druce's *Orchis fuchsii* happily remains with us still (even though now placed in the genus *Dactylorhiza*). He had been aware for many years that the Spotted-orchids of the Midland woods and quarries were different from those of heaths, but it was not until 1914 that he felt sufficiently sure of his ground to describe the former as a new species. Two other Orchids he described, however, have since been demoted to subspecies: the mainly Irish *Orchis okellyi*, now placed under *Dactylorhiza fuchsii*, and the widespread Marsh-orchid of southern Britain, *O. praetermissa*, now placed under *D. majalis*. The second of these two he had first collected in Northamptonshire in 1878 but did not describe until 1913.

In the same way it was not until 1911 that Druce got around to naming an Elm with a curious, straggling, swept-topped crown, which grew by the roadsides of Northamptonshire and certain districts to the north. Supposing it to be the tree discriminated by Robert Plot in his *Natural History of Oxfordshire* (1677), he named it, with a nice historical touch, *Ulmus plotii*. This, alas, has proved to be another wrong shot: according to the latest opinion (Richens 1983) it is neither the tree of Plot nor a good species - but merely a local variety (var. *lockii*) of the bewilderingly variable *U. minor* (*U. carpinifolia*). An analogous fate has overtaken *Rosa rothschildii*, another supposed Midland novelty, which Druce described in 1912 and which is now included in *R. obtusifolia*.

Apart from these taxonomic forays, local patriotism combined with his intimate knowledge of the habitats and plant communities of the South Midlands led him to champion the claims of two Berkshire novelties to be considered native and not, as orthodox opinion held, introduced. These were *Festuca heterophylla*, a prize of 1907, and *Ajuga genevensis*, discovered in 1917 - this latter being the first correct record for Britain. Both claims have been discounted, but it could be that there is more to them than those without Druce's depth of local knowledge have preferred to believe.

Extended Range

For any other Midland botanist this would have been haul enough to last a lifetime. But for someone of Druce's gnawing ambition that region on its own offered much too little scope. Increasingly, it was the British Isles as a whole which he saw as his arena and adding to the total number of vascular plants on that much grander board of honour, the 'British list', which came to seem a worthier and more appetising challenge.

There were three areas in particular which seemed to hold

**POTAMOGETON DRUCEI IN THE RIVER STOUR,
CHILD OKEFORD. DORSET, 1931.**

Plate 1

G.C. Druce examining *Potamogeton drucei* (*P. nodosus*)

From the Christmas Card sent to members
of the Botanical Exchange Club in 1932.

out promise of as yet undiscovered native species, and it was on these three that he noticeably concentrated his efforts. They were the Channel Isles, the Scottish Highlands, and Orkney and Shetland. Ireland might have been a fourth, had he not been effectively pre-empted there by Praeger.

As far as the Channel Isles were concerned, much of the apparent success he had was to prove a mirage. *Koeleria albescens* and *Salvia marquandii*, the latter of his describing, are now submerged in the synonomy of *K. macrantha* and *S. verbenaca* respectively. What he was encouraged to believe was a variety of the hitherto non-British *Orobanche ritro* was subsequently deemed to be merely a form of the common *O. minor* after all, as originally supposed. *Agrostis semiverticillata* (*Polypogon semiverticillatus*), while certainly a genuine addition, is not now regarded as the native species he wished it to be. He had no luck, despite searches on five occasions, in locating *Milium scabrum*, which someone had previously collected in Guernsey but could not recollect exactly where (Druce 1920: 794). It fell to a very young rival, A.J. Wilmott, to detect *Myosotis sicula* in that much-visited Jersey locality, St. Brelade's Bay, in 1923. Only *Spergularia bocconii*, which Druce came back with in 1906, remains as a really solid memorial to his long-persisting efforts.

Scotland

At the opposite end of the British Isles his luck was no better. *Plantago edmondstonii*, described by him in 1920 as a new species of Unst and Orkney, is no longer regarded as distinct from *P. maritima*. There were some 'good' local variants, like *Senecio aquaticus* var. *ornatus*, on which he was able to be the first, and usefully, to bestow a Latin label but there were none of those juicy sub-arctic novelties for which he must have yearned.

The Highlands, too, were a continuous source of disappointment. Here the many mysteries perpetrated long before by George Don were one obvious starting-point, and Druce was to try, time and time again, to turn up the more likely-sounding of those species, of which he never quite abandoned hope. He it should have been, if anyone, who had *Homogyne alpina* as his reward. Instead of a Don rediscovery, all Druce was able to come up with was *Aquilegia pyrenaica*, found on rocks at the head of Caenlochan Glen, in Angus, in company with R.H. Corstorphine in 1916 - and even Druce was forced to admit that this might well have been sown, a suspicion which has hardened ever since. In any case the find was not the new one which he supposed, for Ewing (1897) had reported it from the same

locality earlier, although under the name of *A. alpina*. Time
has been no less cruel to his frustratingly scanty finds of
supposed arctic-alpine novelties. His *Plantago hudsoniana* has
gone the way of his *P. edmondstonii* - and disappeared back into
the variable *P. maritima;* his *Sagina scotica*, which Robert
Brown had collected on Ben Lawers in 1794 without recognising
its distinctiveness, is now considered to be a hybrid between
S. procumbens and *S. saginoides;* his putative endemic variant
of the Continental *Rumex arifolius* has turned out to be merely
R. acetosa. Alone of the major Scottish taxa of his creation
there survives ssp. *septentrionalis* of *Gentianella amarella*,
described by him in 1921.

How furious he would have been had he known of the
treasures he missed: *Koenigia islandica*, *Artemisia norvegica*
and *Diapensia lapponica*. His fault probably lay in
concentrating too exclusively on the areas known to be best for
rarities. Even so, it was at a site very close to much-visited
Ben Lawers that *Carex microglochin* was discovered in 1923. In
this find Druce had the humiliation of being beaten by two of
his acolytes, Lady Davy and Miss Gertrude Bacon (later Mrs
Foggitt).

Scotland was Druce's botanical second home. He had first
visited it as a youth of eighteen, even before taking up botany
seriously, when, on a walking tour paid for by his employer, he
had (*inter alia*) climbed Ben Nevis. Evidently that had whetted
his appetite, for nine years later, in 1877, while still a
Northamptonshire 'unknown', he volunteered to help H.C. Watson
by paying special visits to two still-virgin vice-counties,
West Ross and Wigtownshire, and providing him with lists from
them. These visits took place in 1880 and 1882 respectively,
and Druce returned with several hundred records from each.
Great was his indignation, therefore, when he found all this
hard work either largely ignored or, far worse, credited to
someone else. Why this occurred has an explanation too
complicated to go into here (Druce 1905b, 1932: xix-xx) but
suffice it to say that Druce was clearly grievously wronged.
The incident is noteworthy, however, for the forthright snub
which was administered to him on that occasion by the editor of
the *Journal of Botany,* James Britten. Pooh-poohing Druce's
protest about his mistreatment, Britten wrote: "We cannot but
feel that the anxiety for 'credit' in connection with first
records, and still more in the making of new combinations in
nomenclature, is becoming greatly overdone; a botanist's
reputation does not depend upon trivialities of this kind".
Trivialities or no, unfortunately these were what Druce most
relished - as the rest of the botanical world was well aware.
Already he was in ill odour with not a few of his

contemporaries for what they saw as blatant name-mongering. This apparent evidence of record-grubbing as well was seen to be all of a piece with that. By that time, however, Druce was incurable: new taxa, often petty in the extreme, continued to flow from his pen, and his combing of the country for additions to the British list never slackened in its fervour.

Some Interesting Varieties

Although his passion for the discovery and naming of varieties had much of a stamp-collector's addiction, it must at the same time be said that it had the effect of bringing to notice quite a number of entities of definite geographical or ecological interest, which in the absence of taxonomic recognition would have continued to pass unrecorded. Examples are his var. *nana* of *Stachys officinalis*, the dwarf cliff ecotype of south-west England and elsewhere, which has since been brought into cultivation as an attractive rockery plant; the deep golden-yellow form of *Melampyrum pratense* which he named var. *hians* and which (although he ascribed to it other characters which are now known to be invalid) has turned out to be neatly restricted to the regions overlying the oldest rocks (Smith 1963); his var. *grandifolia* of *Arabis* (*Cardaminopsis*) *petraea*, a larger- and earlier-flowered plant of Ben Laoigh and Ben More in Argyll and Glen Nevis in Westerness, which he proved in cultivation in Oxford to be hardier than the type and intriguingly, unlike that, neglected by slugs (Druce 1893); and his var. *dentata* of *Peplis* (*Lythrum*) *portula*, which has since revealed itself as the middle range of an east-west topocline in the length of the outer calyx teeth (Allen 1954).

In the same way, Druce's tireless, if undiscriminating, practice of sending off material to Continental specialists, with the aim of extending the British list and notching up a 'first', did result in bringing some significant but overlooked species into recognition in Britain. One of these was *Veronica catenata*, a 'split' from *V. anagallis-aquatica* for which Herr Gluck was responsible (although he knew it by the confusing name of *V. aquatica*).

Errors and Disappointments

Too often, though, Druce took such names blindly on trust, succumbing to the bad old British habit of bowing to Continental expertise regardless. As a result, his initiatives in this direction probably did more harm than good, by introducing into our literature many worthless entities or outright misidentifications, which were subsequently only dislodged after a good deal of effort which could have been better spent. Glück, for example, foisted on him the supposed *Utricularia bremii*, Murr the equally dubious *Senecio erraticus*, and Buser's over-confident pupil Jaquet no end of misdetermined microspecies of *Alchemilla*. Druce similarly took too seriously O.E. Schulz's many new taxa in *Erophila*, Almquist's in *Capsella*, and Ronniger's in *Thymus*. This was a trap he also laid for himself at the hands of our own native specialists: the multiplication of names by Drabble, for example, in *Viola*, and Britton in *Centaurea* and *Melampyrum*, were accepted apparently without question or demur.

One unworthy, if all-too-human reason why he positively encouraged this torrent of new 'splits' was surely because so often the new species were named after *him*. What a remarkable number of these there were - yet how remarkably few of them have survived! *Capsella drucei*, *Rosa drucei*, *Saxifraga drucei*, *Centaurea drucei* - all now are gone. Druce himself was sufficiently shamefaced about *Sedum drucei* to consign it eventually to the synonymy of *S. acre*. Even *Thymus drucei*, carefully salvaged from the bonfire of Ronniger's many microspecies, is now known by another name (*T. praecox* ssp. *arcticus*). *Gentianella amarella* ssp. *druceana* is now known to be the aestival form of *G. amarella* ssp. *septentrionalis* (N.M. Pritchard pers. comm.) and so not worthy of taxonomic recognition. The only species to bear his name still is a Dandelion - *Taraxacum drucei*.

This sorry catalogue of misadventure could go on, for little has been said yet of that still further number of additions to the British list mistakenly reported by him from parts of these islands which were lower in his exploration priorities. In 1923, for example, he believed he had found the grass *Agropyron campestre* at Chichester. It is now considered to have been just another form of the hybrid between *Elymus pycnanthus* and *E. repens*. In 1927 he announced the discovery at Byfleet of another Continental grass in the shape of *Festuca sulcata* (*F. rupicola*), allowing, though, that it was "possibly introduced". It has since been decided that this was merely a form of the common *F. ovina*. Yet another false alarm was his determination, in 1894, of a specimen from R.F. Towndrow from Malvern as *Sagina reuteri*, the first of quite a number of records for that species. The British plants, however, are now thought to be only a form of the common *S. apetala* ssp. *apetala* (otherwise *S. ciliata*).

Successes

But enough of woe. Let us switch instead to the more cheerful subject of Druce's successes - for naturally such

XXI

186

diligent scouring of these islands by someone so well-prepared,
ever on the look-out for likely spill-overs of species known in
neighbouring parts of the Continent, did meet with its just
reward on at least a few occasions. One or two of these have
been mentioned already in the context of his special regional
searches; but there were excellent, indisputably gilt-edged
discoveries in other parts of the British Isles as well.

One of these was *Orobanche reticulata*, a parasite of
thistles. Druce was the first to recognise it in Britain, in
north-east Craven, in 1908, since when it has been reported
from several further localities in Yorkshire. Three years later
he came across an unfamiliar Fescue growing "in great quantity"
on the sands at Skegness and soon afterwards established that
it was another wanted addition, *Festuca juncifolia*. Another
seven years after that there was more rejoicing when a specimen
of *Centaurium scilloides*, a 'Lusitanian' species, arrived in
the post for him from the Pembrokeshire sea-cliffs.

Supreme Discovery of Career

None of these finds could compare in drama and in sheer
stylishness with his great *coup* of 1904, however, undoubtedly
the supreme one of his whole botanical career. What made this
so exceptional, and so peculiarly gratifying, was that it arose
directly out of his deep special interest in the work of his
early botanical forebears; more specifically, out of the
Herculean labour he had been undertaking in cleansing his local
Augean stables - to wit, the Oxford Botany School and its
dirt-encrusted strata of long-neglected, antique herbaria. One
of these was the collection left by Dillenius, the German
brought over to England by the Sherards early in the eighteenth
century and later the first holder of Oxford's Sherardian
Chair. While going through this one day, Druce came across some
unlabelled specimens which Dillenius had specially kept apart,
evidently with the intention of publishing an account of them
in some never-achieved supplement to his 1724 edition of Ray's
Synopsis. They included three specimens of a grass of the genus
Koeleria, which on examination proved to be not the usual
British species, but apparently *K. vallesiana* - the European
range of which extends no closer to England than the valley of
the Loire. Some ingenious detective work established that it
must be the 'Spartium montanum, radice bulbosa, fungosa' of
which there was a lengthy and detailed description in
Dillenius' hand on a loose label which had been separated from
the specimen and inserted inside the cover of a grass species
belonging to quite another genus (and of which, subsequently,
an accompanying engraving was found in the Botany Department at
the British Museum among the Dillenian papers acquired with the

herbarium of Sir Joseph Banks). Dillenius' note recorded that
the plant in question had been found *"satis copiose"* - i.e., in
fair abundance - on rocks at a place called Uphill, on the
Somerset side of Bristol. Luckily there survives a diary kept
by him of his journey into Wales in 1726 and this showed that
he collected the specimens there on July 16th of that year.

At this point Druce's own graphic account can best take
over:

"The specimen which I sent to Prof. Hackel was pronounced
by him to be *Koeleria valesiaca* [sic]. My identification was
not made until October last year; but late as it was in the
season, I went down on Oct. 16 to the Uphill habitat, and
within a quarter of an hour I succeeded in finding some
flowerless specimens growing in the turf to the south of the
church, and eventually saw it in plenty on the steep
limestone terraces near the great quarry which faces the sea;
in this place the dead spikes were still attached to the
plant, and put its identification beyond dispute" (Druce
1905c).

Druce then proceeded to trace it on to another series of
limestone ledges to the south, and found that it was abundant
over at least a mile of Brean Down. The following summer
Bristol botanists located it in several further places to the
north, and on another hill seven miles to the south-west.
Ironically, it turned out that there had long been a specimen
from Brean Down sitting in the British Museum unrecognised,
which had been collected by the younger Hooker in 1837. Domin,
the Austrian specialist in the genus, had then only recently
examined it and pronounced it to be *K. vallesiana*, but the
importance of his determination had failed to register.

To round off his triumph, Druce was further able to
satisfy himself (although not, it has turned out, posterity as
well) that there was an earlier valid epithet for the species.
As a result, he was to have the added delight of announcing the
new addition to the British flora under the altogether more
impressive name of *Koeleria splendens*. What is more, in keeping
with the nomenclatural practice then current, the author to be
cited after that name was none other than Druce himself.

It is a pleasing story, not least because it shows Druce
at his most typical as well as at his very best. His knowledge
of the distribution of the vascular plants of the British Isles
was not only uniquely extensive, but it had an unparalleled
historical depth as well. No one else has ever acquired a
greater familiarity with what was found where by botanists of
earlier generations. With that historical sense of his, Druce

was conscious wherever he went in these islands of walking in the footsteps of Turner and Johnson, of Ray and Dillenius, of Lightfoot and Smith. It imparted to his botanizing an extra dimension that too few others have ever succeeded in gaining.

Conservationist

Moreover, hunter though he was at heart, dedicated collector though he remained to the end of his days, it is clear from his writings that the countryside was very much more to him than a kind of giant bran-tub in which to dip for specimens. The tide of destruction that he saw being visited on many of the choicest localities affected him deeply, and in his later years he was to lend his energies unstintingly to the Society for the Promotion of Nature Reserves in its task of identifying the sites which seemed to be the prime candidates for conservation. The fact that he made that Society one of the two residuary legatees of his extremely large estate (Sheail 1976: 66) is testimony that this was no mere attempt at image-enhancement by a guilt-ridden collector.

Indeed, lest there be any doubt at all about his sincerity on that score, let a passage be quoted from his very last work, written when he knew his days in the field were finally over (Druce 1932: vi):

"Many journeys will, I trust, the book make with you, through long tramps up mountain glens, when Bracken gives place to Heather and the Pines disappear, by trickling rivulets on whose sides are *Saxifraga Aizoides* and *stellaris* and *Epilobium alsinifolium*, leading up to the rocky cliffs on which grow *Saxifraga rivularis*, *Poa alpina*, *Cerastium Cerastoides*, *nigrescens* and *alpinum* and their hybrids, *Polystichum Lonchitis*, *Sagina scotica*, besides countless Hieracia. Or it may be your visit is to a village by the sea, above which towers a shapeless hill whose slopes are aglow with *Ulex Gallii*, amid which is the crimson-flowered *Boretta cantabrica*, and where *Erica mediterranea* gladdens the eye. Below one are trembling bogs in which lurk *Utricularia*, and then sea-wards there is a strip of emerald green turf and yellow sands, offering *Arabis Brownii*, *Spiranthes spiralis* and deep crimson-flowered *Orchis pyramidalis*. Then there is the zone of the tawny orange fucus-covered rocks and the opalescent sea".

These words make a fitting close to this paper - and indeed to this conference as a whole.

[Note: *Boretta cantabrica* = *Daboecia cantabrica*; and *Orchis pyramidalis* = *Anacamptis pyramidalis*].

References

ALLEN, D.E. (1954). Variation in *Peplis portula* L. *Watsonia,* 3: 85-91.

DONALD, D. (1980). *Bromus interruptus* (Hack.) Druce - dodo or phoenix? *Nature in Cambs.,* 23: 48-50.

DRUCE, G.C. (1886). *The Flora of Oxfordshire.* 1st edition. Oxford.

DRUCE, G.C. (1893). *Arabis petraea,* Lamk., var. *grandifolia,* Druce. *Rep. Botanical Exch. Club Brit. Isles,* 1: 353-354.

DRUCE, G.C. (1897). *The Flora of Berkshire.* Oxford.

DRUCE, G.C. (1905a). Additions to the Berkshire flora. *J. Botany [London],* 43: 14-25.

DRUCE, G.C. (1905b). The "Supplement to 'Topographical Botany'". *J. Botany [London],* 43: 217-219.

DRUCE, G.C. (1905c). *Koeleria splendens* as a British plant. *J. Botany [London],* 43: 313-317.

DRUCE, C.G. (1920). The extinct and dubious plants of Britain. *Rep. Botanical Exch. Club Brit. Isles,* 5: 731-799.

DRUCE, G.C. (1926a). Botany. In *The Victoria History of the County of Huntingdon.* (Ed. W. Page and G. Proby). Vol. 1, pp. 29-80. London.

DRUCE, G.C. (1926b). *The Flora of Buckinghamshire.* Arbroath.

DRUCE, G.C. (1930). *The Flora of Northamptonshire.* Arbroath.

DRUCE, G.C. (1932). *The Comital Flora of the British Isles.* Arbroath.

EWING, P. (1897). Report of meeting held on 28th April 1896. *Proc. Trans. Nat. Hist. Soc. Glasg.,* 4(NS): 383-384.

HAMSON, J. and DRUCE, G.C. (1904). Botany. In *The Victoria History of the Counties of England. Bedfordshire.* (Ed. H.A. Doubleday and W. Page). Vol. 1, pp. 37-67. Westminster.

McCLINTOCK, D. (1966). *Companion to Flowers.* London.

PERRING, F.H. (1962). *Bromus interruptus* (Hack.) Druce - a botanical dodo? *Nature in Cambs.,* 5: 28-30.

PLOT, R. (1677). *The Natural History of Oxfordshire, being an essay towards the Natural History of England.* Oxford.

RICHENS, R.H. (1983). *Elm.* Cambridge.

SELL, P.D. and WEST, C. (1968). *Hieracium* L. In *Critical Supplement to the Atlas of the British Flora.* (Ed. F.H. Perring and P.D. Sell). London.

SHEAIL, J. (1976). *Nature in Trust.* London.

SMITH, A.J.E. (1963). Variation in *Melampyrum pratense* L. *Watsonia,* 5: 336-367.

YOUNG, A. (1985). *A Prospect of Flowers.* 2nd edition. Harmondsworth.

ADDENDA ET CORRIGENDA

VII – Bricks without straw: reconstructing the Botanical Society of London, 1836–1856

A similar account but set in a wider context (as well as describing certain sources that have been subsequently relocated) has appeared in print as '*Arcana ex multitudine*: prosopography as a research technique', *Archives of Natural History*, 17 (1990), pp. 349–59.

VIII – The women members of the Botanical Society of London, 1836–1856

p. 242 & p. 251: Anna Atkins (b. 1799, not 1797) was not a novelist, as I originally stated in this article: she is confused in the *Dictionary of National Biography* with an author of the same name.

p. 247: A further body admitting women as ordinary members at this period was the Entomological Society of London. In striking contrast to London's Linnean Society, its Parisian namesake admitted 'dames associées-libres' from the first years of the nineteenth century.

p. 252: The subsequent discovery of letters has enabled Charlotte Wilkins to be identified with certainty. Her birth year was 1804.

IX – The struggle for specialist journals: natural history in the British periodicals market in the first half of the nineteenth century

p. 119: Stainton did not edit the *Entomologist's Monthly Magazine* till 1866, having been preceded for two years by its founder, Thomas Blackburn.

p. 123: The *Entomologist* has since been revived afresh.

XV – The natural history society in Britain through the years

p. 244 (& XVI, p. 93): L. Jessop in 'The club at the Temple Coffee House – facts and supposition', *Archives of Natural History*, 16 (1989), pp. 263–74, has since shown that the original source of statements about that body, a 1950 doctoral thesis, contains unwarranted assumptions. All that can be safely asserted, it seems, on the evidence traced is that a group calling itself 'ye club' and concerned at least in part with examining plants met at a coffee house with that name in 1698, and that Sloane and Petiver were two out of four identifiably connected with it in some way. Whether it had any formal existence, how long it lasted and how far its activities extended all remain unknown.

p. 258: The reference for Darling (1943) was accidentally omitted. It should have been: Darling, F.F., *Wild Life of Britain*. London.

XX – C.C. Babington, Cambridge botany and the taxonomy of British flowering plants

p. 4, para. 2, line 5: For 'Samuel Wilberforce' read 'William Wilberforce'.

INDEX

Rousseau, Jean-Jacques: II 343
Royal Geographical Society: VII 9
Royal Institution: VII 10
Royal Physical Society of Edinburgh: III 491
Royal Society: III 488; IX 108, 115; XI 25,
  34; XV 244; XX 9
Royal Society of Edinburgh: VII 4
Rudbeck, Johannes: I 341
Ruskin, John: V 404; VI 16
Russell, Anna: see Worsley, Anna
Russell, Frederick: XIX 134
Russell, James: XIX 134

Sadler, John: I 360
Saffron Walden Literary and Scientific
  Institution: XV 249
Salisbury, E.J.: XIII 210
Salisbury, Richard Anthony: see Markham
Salisbury, William: I 345–6
salons: II 340; V 394; XVI 97
Salter, J.H.: I 359
Samouelle, George: XVI 105
School of Mines, Natural History Department
  of: XI 365; XII 23
Schulz, O.E.: XXI 185
Science Commission (1872): XVI 99
Sclater, P.L.: XVI 96
Scott, Robert: I 351
Scottish Rights of Way Society: I 354
seaweeds: IV 5; V 397–400
Seba, Albertus: V 395–6
Sedgwick, Adam: I 356; II 339; X 7
Seemann, Berthold: IX 119
Selborne, The Natural History and Antiqui-
  ties of: II 335, 344; XVI 102
Selborne Society: XIII 208–9
Selby, P.J.: IX 114; XVI 103
Sharpe, R. Bowdler: XII 32
Shaw, George: X 5
Shepherd, John and Henry: VI 11
Sherard, William: II 336; X 4; XVI 98, 101
Shoolbred, W.A.: XIII 209
Sibbald, Robert: I 341–2
Sibthorp, Humphrey: II 338; XVI 99
Sibthorp, John: XVI 99
Sierra Leone: VII 9
Sims, John: III 485; IX 110
Skrimshire, Fenwick: III 490
Sloane, Hans: V 395; X 5; XV 244; XVI 92,
  96
Smith, Annie Lorrain: VIII 250
Smith, James Edward: II 344; III 483–91;
  VIII 245; IX 110; XV 245; XVI 96; XX
  7; XXI 188
Smith, William: XVI 99

Smithsonian Institution: I 356
Society for Preventing Wanton Cruelty to
  Brute Animals: XIII 204
Society for Promoting Natural History: III
  485–6, 488
Society for the Promotion of Nature Reserves
  (later, of Nature Conservation): XIII
  209; XIV 213; XVI 98; XXI 188
Society for the Protection of Birds (later,
  Royal): XI 369; XIII 209, 211; XV 253
Society for the Protection of Wild Flowers
  and Plants: XIII 210
Society of Antiquaries of Edinburgh: III 485
Society of Apothecaries: I 342–6, 350, 358–
  60; II 338; VII 10–11; XV 244, 247,
  XVI 102–3; XX 5; see also Chelsea
  Physic Garden
socii itinerantes: I 361; XV 244, 247; XVI
  102
Solander, Daniel: II 338; X5; XIII 204; XVI
  98
South London Natural History Society: XII
  36
Southey, Robert: VII 12
Sowerby, James: II 344
Sowerby family: IV 6; XVI 99
Stackhouse, John: V 399
Stainton, H.T.: IX 118–19; XII 29; XVI 95
Stansfield, F.W.: VI 14
Stapf, Otto: XVI 98
Stazione Zoologica, Naples: V 406
Stillingfleet, Benjamin: II 341, 343; XVI 97
Stockar, Jean: III 485
Stokes, Jonathan: III 485
Strickland, Hugh Edwin: XIX 207–8; XVI 95
Stukeley, William: I 350
Surgeons, College of (Edinburgh): I 343, 349
Surgeons, Royal College of (London): I 349;
  XVIII 277
Sutherland, James: I 349; XVI 103
Swainson, William: X 9; XII 26
Syme, J.T.: IX 119; XXI 176

Tansley, A.G.: XIII 210
Taylor & Francis, publishers: IX 118
Taylor, G.: XXI 179
Taylor, Richard: IX 115, 118
Temple Coffee House Botanic Club: II 335;
  XV 244; XVI 93
territory in birds: XVII 281
Theophrastus: XVI 98
Thiselton-Dyer (formerly Dyer), W.T.: XIII
  208; XVI 92, 98
Thomson, John: III 491
Thomson, William: III 485, 488